W0035932

SAGE was founded in 1965 by Sara Miller McCune to support the dissemination of usable knowledge by publishing innovative and high-quality research and teaching content. Today, we publish over 900 journals, including those of more than 400 learned societies, more than 800 new books per year, and a growing range of library products including archives, data, case studies, reports, and video. SAGE remains majority-owned by our founder, and after Sara's lifetime will become owned by a charitable trust that secures our continued independence.

Los Angeles | London | New Delhi | Singapore | Washington DC | Melbourne

Advance Praise

An excellent study of the causes and effects of the Global Financial Crisis. The author judgement is good and his writing is clear and lucid. It is a fine contribution to the literature in this field, and those who wish to learn about the GFC will benefit by reading it.

—Charles A. E. Goodhart,
Professor, The London School of Economics and
Political Science, UK

I have seen the chapter outlines, and I am deeply impressed by the coverage. It includes a good literature survey and has raised almost all critical issues that surfaced after the crisis. It is indeed a comprehensive book and has the added merit of a view from a seasoned central banker of a developing country. This book should be useful not only to policymakers but also to the regulators and practical bankers.

—C. Rangarajan, Former Chairman, Economic Advisory
Council to the Prime Minister; Former Governor, RBI;
Chairman, Madras School of Economics, Chennai, India

Dr Mishra should be complimented for writing an eminently readable book on a complex subject of great contemporary interest. The impact and implications of Global Financial Crisis on the theory and practice of financial sector are brought out very clearly. It has the imprint of deep insights, long experience and clarity in articulation. The book should be of interest to academics as well as practitioners, since it explores public policy, keeping in view the lessons from Global Financial Crisis.

—Y. V. Reddy,
Former Governor, Reserve Bank of India, India

The Global Financial Crisis, the deepest and the most ferocious since the Great Depression of the 1930s, triggered an enormous amount of analysis aimed at understanding its causes and consequences. A lot has already been written about the lessons learnt from the crisis, the reforms instituted drawing from those lessons, and importantly, whether the corrective action is insurance enough against another crisis. Even in such a crowded intellectual field, this book stands out for its comprehensive coverage, cogent argumentation and real-world perspectives. It is a testimonial to Mishra's passion for scholarship and commitment to analytical rigour.

—D. Subbarao,
Former Governor, Reserve Bank of India, India

Many lessons have been learned from the Global Financial Crisis leading to several reforms which have been elucidated excellently and comprehensively in the book. As the title indicates, macroprudential regulation is evolving but the book could not have come at a more propitious time since we face the danger of forgetting the causes and consequences of the crisis leading to calls for a dilution of the regulatory framework. The book raises relevant questions and also provides solutions. It is a great work, which I strongly recommend for general and for teaching purposes.

—Shyamala Gopinath,
Chairperson, HDFC Bank, and Former Deputy Governor,
Reserve Bank of India, India

Macroprudential policy represents a paradigm change in the regulation of the financial system in the aftermath of the Global Financial Crisis. It is a new area and there is considerable amount of research going on. Dr Rabi Mishra's book covers vast ground in this area. It is a comprehensive book capturing the nuances of one of the biggest crises that the financial world ever saw. Dr Mishra has indeed taken pains to put together the full wherewithal of the Global Financial Crisis and the evolution of the financial world thereafter. The book covers almost all important issues in the design and implementation of macroprudential policy and would be of immense benefit to researchers, central bankers, regulators, policymakers and students.

—Anand Sinha,
Former Deputy Governor, Reserve Bank of India, India

Ten years after the financial crisis, lessons are still being drawn and debated about the causal factors and appropriate responses to them. One area of broad consensus is that portfolio decisions of large financial institutions could have macroeconomic consequences. The paradigm of macroprudential regulation is based on this premise. Dr Mishra was an early participant in this process by virtue of his association with the RBI's Financial Stability Unit. He combines his analytical skills with his practical exposure and experience in this book, bringing a very important emerging market perspective to this critical issue. It will be a major contribution to a growing literature.

—Subir Gokarn,
India's Executive Director at IMF and
Former Deputy Governor, Reserve Bank of India, India

It is a delightful guide, full of important information for those of us who want to know everything about the Global Financial Crisis (GFC)—its origin, its impact and its consequences. The biggest learning from the GFC was the fact that the silo-based approach from the regulator is not going to work anymore and the extant macro view needs to be diligently strengthened across the world. Dr Mishra was one of the key minds behind the development of the macroprudential framework at the RBI and the way he has dealt with the subject reciprocates his in-depth grasp on the subject.

—H. R. Khan,
Former Deputy Governor, Reserve Bank of India, India

Since the Global Financial Crisis of 2007–2008, the economics profession, the central banks, financial regulators and the international financial institutions (IFIs) have been searching their souls to understand what went wrong and how to prevent such a disaster from happening again. Much of the blame for the GFC has been placed on the central banks, financial regulators and supervisors in each country, as well as on the international financial regulatory institutions for failing to foresee the problems in the financial system and for not doing their jobs, that is, of being asleep at the switch.

In his timely and very important book, Rabi N. Mishra, an official at the Reserve Bank of India and a specialist in financial regulation, has written a highly useful survey of the issues and the solutions to financial instability proposed by the financial authorities in the key advanced countries and in the IFIs, especially the BIS and FSB. The chapters in the book explain in useful detail the state-of-the-art new tools of macroprudential regulation being developed, especially capital and liquidity ratios, and other techniques such as stress tests and international standards and policy cooperation. This book will be of enormous value to regulators, financial practitioners and students of the international financial system.

—Michael D. Bordo,
Distinguished Professor of Economics, Rutgers University,
Distinguished Visiting Fellow at the Hoover Institution,
Stanford University, USA

This book is a tour de force! Dr Mishra has a sure grasp of the micro-economics of finance which allows him to explain in simple terms those key areas which need effective regulation—asymmetric information, principal–agent problems, the tragedy of the commons and many others. He understands the close link monetary policy has with systemic risk. He has been a consummate insider in the international regulatory reform process for years. But he does not hesitate to identify the intellectual blind spots and wishful thinking of some of those in the regulatory community.

—Philip Turner,
PhD (Harvard), former member of the senior management of
the Bank for International Settlements, and
Deputy Head of Bank for International Settlements's Monetary
and Economic Department, Switzerland

The Great Recession and Global Financial Crisis were, one would hope, teachable moments. In the aftermath of these roiling economic events, we have the potential to learn not only how to supervise and regulate our financial systems better but also how to 'think' about our economic systems better. The assumptions that markets are self-righting, that agents are rational and that asset prices convey the information necessary for efficient market clearing (to name a few) have all been profoundly challenged by the events of the recession and crisis. If we recognize that markets can sometimes be self-destructive, irrational and inefficient in transmitting information, we will do better in designing our financial systems to withstand the sorts of disruptions that arise from such behaviour. Dr Mishra's book recognizes these shortcomings in our understanding of financial systems and explores in detail the multiple margins on which countries have made advances in making their systems more robust to the inevitable financial disruptions. In doing so, he provides a valuable compendium of views on the causes of the crisis, the consequences and the proposed solution. I can think of no one who is in a better position to do so than Dr Mishra, from his perch at the Reserve Bank of India.

—Jeffrey C. Fuhrer,
Executive Vice President and Senior Policy Advisor, Federal
Reserve Bank of Boston, MA, USA

The financial sector is truly global today with significant linkages between nations. The Global Financial Crisis beginning in the USA in 2008 spread fast and seriously disrupted many economies. Many a common man suffered and the anger lingers as people still believe that those responsible have not been held to account. Dr Mishra's experience and perspective give him a unique perch. He provides a detailed analysis of the crisis, examines the technical, regulatory and ethical aspects, and suggests ways to work towards a more stable system. This is a valuable addition to the literature.

—Professor C. Gopinath,
Suffolk University, Boston, MA, USA

Dr Rabi Mishra was the first Chief General Manager of the Financial Stability Unit of the RBI that was set up in the aftermath of the 2007 Great Financial Crisis. His vision and enthusiasm helped to drive the agenda of getting data and models to help regulators to look at the risks in the Indian financial system in a more holistic way as befits macroprudential policy. Supported by the then Deputy Governor, Shyamala Gopinath, Dr Mishra was instrumental in mandating who-to-whom bilateral balance sheet data from major banks (including foreign banks in India) and non-bank financial institutions such as insurance companies and mutual funds. This was a first of its kind. I was brought in as senior consultant (2011–2014) to set up a digital financial network map and model the banking and financial market balance sheet interconnectedness for India. My brief was to give granular data visualization and provide a systemic risk metric that reflected the perils of leverage in the network of financial liabilities, and thereby avoid the pitfalls of paradoxical market price-based risk measures that underestimate risk when leverage is growing. I was impressed by the pragmatism and good sense of the RBI senior management who were refreshingly free of the dogma that blindsided their counterparts in the West. Having actively used countercyclical risk weights long before it became the mantra in the West and also through measures such as banning exotic options, the RBI regulators, in the run-up to the crisis and during it, had a better track record than many other central banks. I expect Dr Mishra's book to reflect such sound principles of stewardship and openness to new holistic approaches for risk management.

—Sheri Markose,
Professor of Economics and Founder Director (2002–2009),
Centre for Computational Finance and Economic Agents
(CCFEA), University of Essex, UK

The book is an excellent overview of the changing landscape for financial sector analysis and policies in the post-crisis world. Rabi Mishra discusses in-depth reasons why we now need to reorient financial sector surveillance towards monitoring the accumulation of systemic risk and how do the recent regulatory reforms including Basel III and the introduction of macroprudential policy help maintain financial stability. In the analytical area, attention is given to early warning systems and stress-testing—two key tools that were with us before the Global Financial Crisis but experienced substantial improvements recently to serve as useful guidance for implementing and calibrating macroprudential policy tools. Rabi Mishra does not stop here though; he opens additional topics on which there is no clear consensus yet, such as global coordination of monetary and financial sector policies and emergence of new risks that are under-researched as to their possible impact on future financial stability.

—Adam Gersl,
Lead Economist at the Joint Vienna Institute, an IMF Austria
Regional Training Center

The Global Financial crisis had varied reasons and many ramifications. The world economic order has been reset, and it is important to capture full dimension and consequences of the crisis to learn the lessons and emerge as a stronger and more resilient nation. This book evidently exhibits the significant macroprudential policies laid down by the regulators with an intent to counter the forces of crisis. I believe that this book is a guide for the policymakers, researchers and academicians. The insights of Dr Rabi Mishra are incisive and perceptive. He has the fabulous ability to synthesize a complex topic into truthful simplicity.

—Sunil Mehta, Chairman, Indian Bank's Association,
MD and CEO, Punjab National Bank, India

This book has aptly described the evolution of macroprudential policy, taking examples of various causes of the Global Financial Crisis 2008 and the lessons learnt from it. Wearing a regulator's hat, the author dwelt on post-crisis regulatory reforms to mitigate various risk elements and finally narrated a crisis management framework and stress-testing mechanism. The book is an interesting read for the students of economics as well as the practising bankers to gain a holistic idea about the subject.

—J. N. Misra,
CEO, Indian Institute of Banking & Finance, India

Ten years since the GFC is a good time to evaluate the responses to it: their effectiveness determines whether we can prevent its recurrence. Dr Rabi Mishra has the knowledge and experience to undertake this task and the result is a compelling read for all concerned with the subject, that is, all of us.

—Sanjay Kallapur,
Professor, Indian School of Business, India

This is a useful and important contribution to the debate about the forces that contributed to the global financial crisis. The book also provides a practitioner's insights about what is needed to fix in financial systems so that they are less vulnerable to systemic crashes and also how to deal with such crashes if they do occur.

—Eswar Prasad
Tolani Senior Professor of Trade Policy at Cornell University,
Senior Fellow at the Brookings Institution, and New Century Chair
in International Economics at Brookings

Much has been written about the Global Financial Crisis—a defining event not just for the global economy but also for the economics discipline. Dr Mishra has written a wide-ranging book that is a worthy contribution to the debate.

—Claudio Borio
Head of Monetary and Economic Department, Bank for
International Settlements, Basel, Switzerland

In the ten years since the Global Financial Crisis, we have made great strides in understanding its causes and consequences, and perhaps most importantly, what might be done to avoid a similar catastrophe. Rabi Mishra's book provides a thorough treatment of these lessons, and a fresh perspective, from someone who spent the time period sufficiently involved to develop a deep understanding, but sufficiently distant to avoid many potential biases.

—Shawn Cole
John G. McLean Professor of Business Administration,
Harvard Business School

SYSTEMIC RISK AND MACROPRUDENTIAL REGULATIONS

SYSTEMIC RISK AND MACROPRUDENTIAL REGULATIONS

Global Financial Crisis and Thereafter

RABI N. MISHRA

Los Angeles | London | New Delhi
Singapore | Washington DC | Melbourne

First published in 2019 by

SAGE Publications India Pvt Ltd
B1/I-1 Mohan Cooperative Industrial Area
Mathura Road, New Delhi 110 044, India
www.sagepub.in

SAGE Publications Inc
2455 Teller Road
Thousand Oaks, California 91320, USA

SAGE Publications Ltd
1 Oliver's Yard, 55 City Road
London EC1Y 1SP, United Kingdom

SAGE Publications Asia-Pacific Pte Ltd
18 Cross Street #10-10/11/12
China Square Central
Singapore 048423

Published by Vivek Mehra for SAGE Publications India Pvt Ltd. Typeset in 10.5/13 pt Adobe Caslon Pro by Zaza Eunice, Hosur, Tamil Nadu, India.

Library of Congress Cataloging-in-Publication Data

Names: Mishra, Rabi N., author.
Title: Systemic risk and macroprudential regulations: global financial
   crisis and thereafter/Rabi N. Mishra.
Description: Thousand Oaks : SAGE Publications India Pvt Ltd, [2019] |
   Includes index.
Identifiers: LCCN 2019015017| ISBN 9789353285425 (print(hb)) | ISBN
   9789353285432 (e-pub 2.0) | ISBN 9789353285449 (e-book)
Subjects: LCSH: Global Financial Crisis, 2008-2009. | Monetary policy. |
   Economic policy.
Classification: LCC HB3717 2008-2009 .M57 2019 | DDC 339.5–dc23 LC record available at https://
lccn.loc.gov/2019015017

ISBN: 978-93-532-8542-5 (HB)

SAGE Team: Rajesh Dey, Vandana Gupta, Madhurima Thapa and Kanika Mathur

Disclaimer: The views expressed in the book are the personal views of the author, not of the Reserve Bank of India.

Dedicated to

My small family who unknowingly made all the sacrifices for this cause.

Kamala (Mami)—My wife

Manojita (Moon)—My daughter

Namit—My son-in-law

Tara—My two-year-old granddaughter

Let she be inspired to be an author in her 20s only!

Thank you for choosing a SAGE product!
If you have any comment, observation or feedback,
I would like to personally hear from you.

Please write to me at **contactceo@sagepub.in**

Vivek Mehra, Managing Director and CEO, SAGE India.

Bulk Sales

SAGE India offers special discounts
for purchase of books in bulk.
We also make available special imprints
and excerpts from our books on demand.

For orders and enquiries, write to us at

Marketing Department
SAGE Publications India Pvt Ltd
B1/I-1, Mohan Cooperative Industrial Area
Mathura Road, Post Bag 7
New Delhi 110044, India

E-mail us at **marketing@sagepub.in**

Subscribe to our mailing list
Write to **marketing@sagepub.in**

This book is also available as an e-book.

Contents

List of Abbreviations

ABCP	asset-backed commercial paper
ABF	Asian Bond Fund
ABIF	ASEAN Banking Integration Framework
ACMF	ASEAN Capital Markets Forum
ACMI	ASEAN Capital Markets Infrastructure
ACU	Asian Currency Unit
AE	advanced economy
AEC	ASEAN Economic Community
AFS	available for sale
AFTA	ASEAN free trade area
AI	artificial intelligence
AIG	American International Group
A-IRB	advanced IRB
ALA	alternative liquidity arrangement
ALM	assets liabilities management
ALPM	advanced ledger posting machine
ALRB	additional leverage ratio buffer
AMA	advanced measurement approach
AMC	Asset Management Company
AMF	Asian Monetary Fund
AMRO	ASEAN+3 Macroeconomic Research Office
APCERT	Asia Pacific Computer Emergency Response Team
ARM	adjustable-rate mortgage
ASEAN	Association of Southeast Asian Nations
AT1	Additional Tier 1
ATIGA	ASEAN Trade in Goods Agreement
BCBS	Basel Committee on Banking Supervision
BCP	Basel Core Principle
BFSN	bilateral financial safety net
BHC	bank holding company

BIS	Bank for International Settlements
BRRD	Bank Recovery and Resolution Directive
BSFI	banking sector fragility index
CBDC	Central Bank Issued Digital Currency
CBS	core banking solution
CCAR	comprehensive capital analysis and review
CCB	capital conservation buffer
CCCB	countercyclical capital buffer
CCG	Contingency Contact Group
CCIL	Clearing Corporation of India Limited
CCLB	countercyclical leverage ratio buffer
CCP	central counterparty
CD	certificate of deposit
CDO	collateralized debt obligation
CDS	credit default swap
CEBS	Committee of European Banking Supervisors
CEG	Compensation Experts Group
CEN-SAD	Community of Sahel-Saharan States
CERT	Computer Emergency Response Team
CET1	Common Equity Tier 1
CFPB	Consumer Financial Protection Bureau
CFR	Council on Foreign Relations
CFTC	Commodity Futures Trading Commission
CGFS	Committee on the Global Financial System
CLAR	Comprehensive Liquidity Analysis and Review
CLF	committed liquidity facility
CLO	collateralized loan obligation
CM	common market
CMCG	Compensation Monitoring Contact Group
CMF	crisis management framework
CMG	Crisis Management Group
CMI	Chiang Mai Initiative
CMIM	Chiang Mai Initiative Multilateralization
CMM	crisis management mechanism
COAG	cross-border cooperation agreement
CoCoS	Contingent Convertibles
COMESA	Common Market for Eastern and Southern Africa

CORF	corporate operational risk framework
CoSP	conditional shortfall probability
CoVaR	conditional value at risk
CP	commercial paper
CPSS	Committee on Payment and Settlement Systems
CRA	credit rating agency
CRAR	capital to RWA ratio
CRD	Capital Requirements Directive
CRR	Capital Requirements Regulation
CSIRT	Computer Security Incident Response Team
CU	Customs Union
DFA	Dodd–Frank Act
DICGC	Deposit Insurance and Credit Guarantee Corporation
DIP	debtor in possession
DOMF	debt-oriented mutual fund
DSGE	Dynamic Stochastic General Equilibrium
DSIB	domestic systemically important bank
DTCC	Depository Trust & Clearing Corporation
DTI	debt-to-income
EAC	East African Community
EAD	exposure at default
EBA	European Banking Authority
ECB	European Central Bank
ECCAS	Economic Community of Central African States
ECL	expected credit loss
ECOWAS	Economic Community of West African States
EEA	European economic area
EEC	European Economic Community
EF	economic function
EFSD	Eurasian Fund for Stabilization and Development
ELA	emergency liquidity adjustment
EMDE	emerging market and developing economy
EMS	European Monetary System
EMU	Economic and Monetary Union
ENISA	European Union Agency for Network and Information Security

ERM	exchange rate mechanism
ESMA	European Securities and Markets Authority
ESRB	European Systemic Risk Board
ESS	European Statistical System
EU	European Union
EUN	Economic Union
EWI	early warning indicator
EWM	early warning mechanism
EWS	early warning system
FASB	Financial Accounting Standards Board
FC	financial conglomerate
FCSE	Financial Crisis Simulation Exercise
FDIC	Federal Deposit Insurance Corporation
FED	Federal Reserve
FIRST	Forum of Incident Response and Security Teams
FLAR	Latin American Reserve Fund
FMI	financial market infrastructure
FOMC	Federal Open Market Committee
FPC	Financial Policy Committee
FRB	Federal Reserve Board
FRDI	Financial Resolution and Deposit Insurance
FSA	Financial Services Authority
FSAP	Financial Sector Assessment Program
FSB	Financial Stability Board
FSD	Financial Stability Department
FSDC	Financial Stability and Development Council
FSF	Financial Stability Forum
FSI	Financial Stability Institute
FSN	financial safety net
FSOC	Financial Stability Oversight Council
FSU	Financial Stability Unit
FTA	free trade area
FVOCI	fair value through other comprehensive income
FVTPL	fair value through profit or loss
FX	foreign exchange
GAAP	generally accepted accounting principles
GATT	General Agreement on Tariffs and Trade

GBC	growth in bank credit
GBD	growth in bank deposit
GC	global citizenship
GCC	Gulf Cooperation Council
GCS	Global Civil Society
GEC	global economic crisis
GFC	Global Financial Crisis
GFSN	global financial safety net
GLIEF	Global LEI Foundation
GMFS	Global Monetary and Financial Stability
GNPA	gross NPA
GRC	governance, risk management and compliance
GSCB	global super central bank
G-SIBs	global systemically important banks
G-SII	global systemically important institutions
HFT	high-frequency trading
HQLA	high-quality liquid asset
HTM	held to maturity
IADI	International Association of Deposit Insurers
IAIS	International Association of Insurance Supervisors
IAS	International Accounting Standard
IASB	International Accounting Standards Board
IASC	International Accounting Standards Committee
IBOR	inter-bank offered rate
IBSV	index of banking sector vulnerability
ICAAP	Internal Capital Adequacy Assessment Process
ICT	information and communications technology
IFAC	International Federation of Accountants
IFR	investment fluctuation reserve
IFRS	International Financial Reporting Standards
IGAD	Intergovernmental Authority on Development
IHC	intermediate holding company
IIFSR	International Integrated Financial Services Regulator
ILG	International Liquidity Guidelines
IMF	International Monetary Fund
IMFC	International Monetary and Financial Committee

IMS	International Monetary System
Ind-AS	Indian Accounting Standards
IOSCO	International Organization of Securities Commissions
IoT	Internet of Things
IRB	internal ratings-based
IRF-FC	Inter-Regulatory Forum for monitoring Financial Conglomerates
IR-TG	Inter-Regulatory Technical Group
IS	investment–saving
ISDA	International Swaps and Derivatives Association
IT	information technology
IWST	industry-wide stress test
KA	key attribute
KPM	key performance metrics
KRM	key risk metrics
LCR	liquidity coverage ratio
LEF	large exposure framework
LEI	legal entity identifier
LGD	loss-given-default
LM	liquidity preference–money supply
LOLR	lender of last resort
LOU	local operating unit
LRA	logit regression analysis
LTCM	long-term capital management
LTV	loan-to-value
MAS	Monetary Authority of Singapore
MOF	Ministry of Finance
MOU	memorandum of understanding
MPOE	multiple point of entry
MREL	Minimum Required Eligible Liabilities
MRT	material risk-taker
NBFC	non-bank financial company
NBW	New Bretton Woods
NCCD	non-centrally cleared derivative
NDB	New Development Bank
NOP	net open currency position

NPA	non-performing asset
NPL	non-performing loan
NSFR	net stable funding ratio
OBS	off-balance sheet
OCA	Optimum Currency Area
OCC	Office of the Comptroller of the Currency
OCU	Optimum Currency Union
OFR	Office of Financial Research
OLA	Orderly Liquidation Authority
ORM	operational risk management
ORMF	Operational Risk Management Framework
OTC	over-the-counter
P&S	principles and standards
P2P	peer-to-peer
PAT	Purchase and Assumption Transaction
PCA	prompt corrective action
PD	probabilities of default
PPNR	pre-provision net revenue
PRA	Prudential Regulation Authority
QBO	qualifying banking organization
QE	quantitative easing
RAF	risk appetite framework
RBSC	Reserve Bank Staff College
RC	resolution corporation
RCAP	Regulatory Consistency Assessment Programme
RCEP	Regional Comprehensive Economic Partnership
RCG	regional consultative group
REC	regional economic community
REER	real effective exchange rate
Repos	repurchase agreements
RFA	red flagged accounts
RFR	risk-free rate
RoA	return on asset
ROC	Regulatory Oversight Committee
RRE	residential real estate
RRP	recovery and resolution planning
RSCB	regional super central bank

RTGS	real-time gross settlement
RWA	risk-weighted asset
SADC	Southern African Development Community
SAFE	Systemic Assessment of Financial Environment
SAFTA	South Asian Free Trade Area
SCAP	Supervisory Capital Assessment Program
SCAV	Standing Committee on Assessment of Vulnerabilities
SCB	stress capital buffer
SCCM	Sub-Committee on Crisis Management
SCSI	Standing Committee on Standards Implementation
SDRM	sovereign debt restructuring mechanism
SEA	signal extraction approach
SEC	Securities and Exchange Commission
SELT	Singapore Electronic Legal Tender
SES	systemic expected shortfall
SFT	securities financing transaction
SIB	systemically important bank
SIFI	Systemically Important Financial Institution
SIV	Structured Investment Vehicle
SLR	supplementary leverage ratio
SOP	Standard Operating Procedure
SPOE	single point of entry
SR	slippage ratio
SRA	Systemic Risk Analytics
SRB	Single Resolution Board
SRC	Supervisory and Regulatory Cooperation
SSF	SIFI Stability Fund
STF	Stress-Testing Framework
STS	stress-testing system
SyRB	systemic risk buffer
Systemic CCA	Systemic Contingent Claims Analysis
TARP	Troubled Asset Relief Program
TBTF	too-big-to-fail
TEI	total economic integration
TLAC	total loss absorbing capacity

TMCM	Taylor multi-country model
TPP	Trans-Pacific Partnership
TR	trade repository
UAE	United Arab Emirates
UMA	Arab Maghreb Union
VaR	value at risk
VAR	vector autoregression
VC	virtual currency
WFA	World Financial Authority
WPI	wholesale price index
WTN	world trade network
WTO	World Trade Organization

Foreword*

Modern financial institutions, like many other man-made social constructs, simultaneously offer enormous advantages and yet present major risks. An essential need in virtually any economic system is to enable the families and businesses whose current income exceeds their planned spending to transfer resources to others who face the opposite imbalance. A system that does so effectively not only mobilizes more saving in the aggregate, thereby allowing the society to invest more in its future economic growth and well-being, but also facilitates putting the resources that are transferred to better use. Although many people could find ways to give or lend their intended saving to someone else on an individual basis, specialized financial institutions can accomplish that task more efficiently, just as specialized businesses are more efficient at producing food or cars or computers, and just as specialized institutions in other realms of human activity are better able to cure the sick or educate the young or enforce the laws.

At the same time, the fact that financial institutions are human endeavours inevitably exposes them to the risk of miscalculation or misdoing, and the more specific character of how most financial institutions in the modern world accomplish the mobilization and allocation of saving—particularly through the pooling of interests and uncertainties along a variety of dimensions—magnifies the potential economic damage if the wrong set of circumstances becomes reality. At least since the South Sea Bubble crisis in 1720, and on many occasions since then, financial institutions and financial systems have magnified the impact on non-financial economic activity arising from one misfortune or another, and in some cases have created disruptions that would not otherwise have occurred. The typical results have been

*Parts of this Foreword draw on my earlier work; for further elaboration, see Friedman (2015, forthcoming) and Friedman and Kuttner (2011).

lost jobs and incomes; reduced production, consumption and investment; and associated human suffering. In some cases, the economic
disruption has been great enough to threaten the existing social and
political order (e.g., in both America and France in the 1930s) or even
to overturn it (Germany in the same period).

Ten years ago, a new financial crisis, together with the protracted
economic downturn that it triggered in many countries around the
world, represented one of the most significant economic events since
the Second World War. The collapse of major financial firms, the
decline in asset values and consequent destruction of paper wealth,
the interruption of credit flows, and the loss of confidence in both
firms and credit market instruments were all extraordinary. In many
countries, the real economic costs—in terms of reduced production,
lost jobs, shrunken investment and foregone income and profits—
exceeded that of any post-war decline. Further, in many countries,
the recovery from the downturn proved frustratingly slow. In some,
it is still not complete.

It is hardly surprising that these events have prompted new thinking
about economic and financial policies. Policymakers at the time, in
many countries, responded to the crisis in extraordinary ways, introducing new ways of rescuing troubled financial institutions and new
means of carrying out monetary policy. Some of those innovations
persist even now, that the crisis has passed. Many countries, either
individually or in coordination with others (e.g., through the Basel
process), have overhauled their regulation and supervision of financial
institutions. 'Macroprudential' policy is now on the agenda of virtually
all of the world's economically advanced countries, and many developing economies as well.

At the same time, nearly everyone—policymakers, operators of
financial institutions and economists—now understands that knowledge of the underlying economic behaviour that led to the crisis is
seriously incomplete. The process of rethinking financial economics,
and the role that financial institutions play in influencing (including sometimes disrupting) aggregate economic activity, stands at an
earlier stage than that of redesigning monetary policy or updating

the regulation and supervision of individual institutions. But the two are related in a fundamental way. As has long been true, progress in economic policymaking and policy design depends on progress in fundamental economic thinking.

***

Two factors at work today make both the advantages and the risks associated with the working of financial institutions greater than ever before. First, advances in electronic data processing and communications have made possible kinds of transactions and arrangements that not so long ago were conceivable but in no way practically implementable. It is difficult today to recall that even such basics as third-party credit cards and diversified mutual funds did not exist just a few decades ago. Options to buy or sell securities existed only under specially arranged circumstances. While experts understood that a typical government bond was equivalent to a package consisting of a sequence of interest payments followed by a single further payment at maturity, and a typical home mortgage consisted of a sequence of interest payments and an associated sequence of principal payments, in neither case could anyone readily buy or sell the individual constituent elements. Nor, apart from one-at-a-time arrangements, could a bank or other credit institution have money on loan to a business firm while some other institution bore the risk of the borrower's failing to meet its obligations. Today, each of those transactions, and many more besides, is not just possible but routine.

Second, again prompted not only by the developments in electronic communications but also by improvements in transportation as well as the prevailing geopolitical climate, since the Second World War, the world economy has entered a new stage of globalization. In some respects—most obviously, cross-border movements of people— globalization today lags behind conditions that prevailed in the late 19th century and the first decade of the 20th century, at what proved to be the end of the last great period of economic globalization. In other dimensions of economic activity, such as trade in goods and flows of net investment funds, the scale of today's globalization (relative to the size of the participating national economies) is about what it was then. But in the financial arena broadly defined, where gross purchases and sales of financial assets and liabilities across borders now dwarf the corresponding net flows of funds, today's globalization stands out from historical experience. And, following the temporary interruption caused by the 2007–2009 financial crisis, it is progressively and rapidly advancing further.

The challenge of harnessing the power of financial systems—making the greatest advantage of what financial institutions, either individually or collectively, have to contribute to the functioning of the overall economic system while at the same time exposing the economy to the least possible risk of disruption on that account—has traditionally fallen, as in so many other areas as well, to governments. Most governments, as a matter of public policy, license the right to engage in a wide array of financial businesses (just as they license the right to produce and sell drugs, or practice law, or even drive a car on the public roads). Banks, insurance companies, mutual funds and many other kinds of institutions require a government-issued charter, or some other form of authorization, to do business. Governments, also as a matter of public policy, likewise restrict the kinds of transactions in which the institutions that they have authorized can engage and further subject these institutions' ongoing activities to prudential supervision and regulation.

No one believes that this restriction of who can do what, or the corresponding compliance with the imposed regulation is costless. It is, rather, the price society pays to avoid the even greater cost associated with the risk that financial institutions inherently create. Restrictions of this kind applied to financial institutions—and on precisely these grounds—have been familiar since the days of Adam Smith, who advocated a ceiling (5%) on the interest that banks could charge on loans along with limits on banks' ability to fund their lending via deposits. The benefit of these regulations is the resulting reduction of the attendant risks to which financial institutions expose the economy and the society. The cost is not just the direct cost to the public sector of maintaining the relevant authorities, and to the financial institutions themselves of compliance, but also the unobservable economic loss associated with transactions that do not occur and initiatives that do not go forward. Getting right the balance between these benefits and costs is a challenge of front-ranking importance in any modern economy. It is even more obviously so in the wake of what happened 10 years ago.

Most of the world's advanced industrialized (and post-industrialized) economies have made significant progress on just this front in recent decades, and since the 2007–2009 crisis many have intensified their efforts. At the most basic level, the first-order institutional lacunae that allowed the depression of the 1930s to develop into a worldwide economic disaster no longer exist, and the 2007–2009 crisis did not do that. (It is also difficult to imagine the world's central banks repeating the monetary policy mistakes of the 1930s, and indeed they did not.) Even before the recent crisis, just in the USA alone, events such as the failure of virtually all of the major banks in Texas when world oil prices declined in 1986; the stock market crash on 19 October 1987; the progressive collapse of the nation's savings and loan industry, and parts of the banking industry, in the later years of the 1980s; the spillover from the Asian financial crisis of the late 1990s; the collapse of Long-Term Capital Management (importantly, a firm operating outside the reach of the ordinary prudential regulation) in 1998; and the terrorist attacks of 11 September 2001 were all noteworthy events within the financial markets. But none resulted in any significant disruption of non-financial economic activity.

Many developing countries have done less well either in putting in place ongoing supervision and regulation (in some countries, even basic accounting and disclosure standards) or in equipping their public authorities to undertake prompt and effective intervention of the sort that normally emerges in response to such situations in the industrialized world. The 1997–1999 Asian financial crisis demonstrated the risks of commonplace private sector practices, and the weakness of public sector safeguards, across a swath of countries not limited to Asia. Many developing economies also fell victim, in greater or lesser degrees, to forces emanating from the financial sectors of the more advanced economies during and following the 2007–2009 crisis. Some of those countries have subsequently moved forward to address the problems that these events dramatically revealed, and among those who have done so, some have made more progress than others. Yet, others have done little in this regard at all. But the need is no less great.

Many countries in the developing world also have very high saving rates, compared to the higher income economies, and so at first thought one might suspect that the need for effective financial markets to mobilize and allocate saving there is less severe. The opposite is true. One reason low-income economies are what they are is that they have inadequate stocks of productive capital and lack the technology to which they could gain access only by having that capital. But having the right kind of capital, in the right place, and operated by those who can make proper use of it, is just as important as considerations of sheer quantity. What differentiates financial systems in many developing countries from what the higher income countries have is also a matter of how well the relevant decision-makers allocate the capital that is created. That too is subject to influence—for better or worse—by public policy.

***

Individual countries acting on their own can do only so much, however. To repeat, today's financial system is increasingly global in scale and in operation; the actual and potential advantages it provides are global; and the attendant risks are global. One basic implication is simply that countries need to coordinate their individual financial policies to avoid the familiar 'race to the bottom', in which institutions that can operate from anywhere, as a practical matter, opt to domicile themselves in whichever country offers the laxest regulation, or the lowest tax rates, or the blindest and most corrupt enforcement. But at a more complex level, the transnational nature of much of today's financial activity requires more than just the coordination of policies set by individual countries. Regulation and supervision, if they are to be effective, need to take into account the international setting in which many markets and institutions now operate.

For just this reason, economists and others in recent years have increasingly turned their attention to the design of the 'international financial architecture'. Everyone understands that private sector actors, in the financial arena surely no less than elsewhere, respond to the incentives and constraints created not just by specific rules and regulations, but also by the overall environment in which they operate. What is sometimes lost in the discussion is that these reactions can, and often do, act in ways that may initially be counter-intuitive from the perspective of what is shaping the environment in the first place. For example, in the absence of any secondary response, restrictions on what transactions financial institutions can undertake, or regulatory burdens on how they undertake them and what aspects of their transactions they must disclose publicly, would clearly reduce the amount of market activity, and thereby presumably lessen the role of the financial system in mobilizing and allocating saving. But, if market participants (both actual and potential) then see their participation in the marketplace as less exposed to the risk of institutional failure, or less subject to potential loss arising from corruption and self-dealing, the volume of transactions may increase rather than fall, and the financial system's ability to contribute to the functioning of the non-financial economy may be enhanced. Such matters are clearly more complex, and more subtle, in a global context.

And global financial architecture is also more complicated simply because it involves more than one country. The eminent sociologist Daniel Bell famously remarked that many of the world's problems are too small in scale to be addressed by nation states, and the rest are too large. Whether or not this is true, the increasing globalization of economic activity, in general, and of financial markets and institutions, in particular, is surely a source of strain on the nation state system. The response to date includes informal cooperation among countries (e.g., swap agreements among many central banks), formal treaty commitments (like those produced by the successive rounds of trade negotiations under the GATT and now the WTO), the role played by international financial institutions (most prominently, the World Bank and the IMF), and even the abdication of national sovereignty in specifically designated areas (e.g., the creation of a common currency, and therefore the imposition of a common monetary policy, under the direction of the European Central Bank). The world of banking and securities markets has also progressed in this regard, for example, the common capital standards established under the aegis of the Bank for International Settlements. But the world's political structure remains, at its fundamental core, one of nation states, and so the challenge is to devise elements of a broader system that resolves, as best as possible, the tension between preserving the advantages of decentralized private sector financial systems and minimizing the associated risks and, further, that can develop and operate within the nation state system as well.

***

The challenge to be addressed, either in any single country or in the global context, is not merely political but intellectual as well. How to strike the right balance between potential gains and attendant risks is central to what economics as a discipline is all about. So is analysing the likely change in behaviour, by institutions as well as market participants more generally, to new modes of regulation and supervision, or even whole new market structures. And so is inferring what new overall outcome will ensue when both the market environment and the behaviour of the various actors within it change. Positive economic analysis of financial institutions and the financial system as a whole to gain an understanding of the underlying behaviour and normative analysis of the consequently appropriate public policies are important, indeed crucial, requisites for making progress in this area. The issues at stake are central to the well-being of modern societies, and economic thinking of both forms has much to contribute.

Like the worldwide depression of the 1930s, and the pervasively high and persistent inflation of the 1970s and 1980s, the 2007–2009 financial crisis was in part a consequence of happenstance and idiosyncratic events. Also, like those two formative episodes, however, the crisis was the product of incomplete understanding, and consequently flawed thinking, solidly within the sphere of economics as an intellectual discipline. It is never possible to replay with confidence, under one counterfactual assumption or another, the historical development of any given line of thought, much less the real-world consequences that follow from it. But it seems likely that if economic thinking, in the decades leading up to the financial crisis, had provided a fuller understanding of the relevant financial behaviour and the risks attendant with it, the mindset behind the crisis, among both economists and policymakers, would have been different. Hayek wrote, 'Human affairs are guided by intellectual forces', and Keynes famously argued that the ideas of economists in particular 'are more powerful than is commonly understood'. With different economic thinking, at least some of the important underpinnings of the crisis probably would not have been present, and many of the responses to the crisis would have been different too.

Several elements of economic thinking—thinking before the crisis to be sure, but to a great extent continuing today as well—seem especially important in this regard. One is the pervasive disregard of credit markets and, in parallel, the lack of attention to the differences among various credit market assets. Although that subject was central to the theorizing of an earlier era, markets for debt instruments issued by an economy's private agents sit uncomfortably within the methodology of modern macroeconomics in particular. If two firms or two households are identical, there is no reason one would borrow from, or lend to, the other. The representative–agent construct, a device of convenience that now enables much of formal macroeconomic theorizing, therefore excludes markets for private assets and liabilities except in the abstract sense that a market can exist, and an 'implicit' price or return may be determined, with no volume of trading—in this context meaning no actual borrowing or lending. Familiar ways of relaxing this restriction include distinguishing young households from old ones, as in overlapping generations models, and distinguishing risk-tolerant households from risk-averse ones. But these highly stylized departures fail to capture most of what happens in actual credit markets.

One reason this absence of credit markets from so much of modern economic theorizing has attracted so little concern is the lingering conceptual legacy, from the 'monetarism of a half-century ago, of treating all non-money assets as perfect substitutes. Milton Friedman's monetarism normally omitted assets other than money, and therefore omitted private sector liabilities altogether. Proponents of this line of thought understood that households and firms do own assets and issue liabilities. But the assumption, supposedly grounded in empirical inference, was that the quantity of assets held by the public 'other than money' did not matter for aggregative economic outcomes, nor did differences among those non-money assets, nor did either the quantity or the character of liabilities issued by the public; in short, all non-money assets are perfect substitutes for this purpose.

In combination, the lack of attention to private credit markets in general and the assumption that if such instruments exist, they are all perfect substitutes, rendered much of modern economic thinking unequipped either to anticipate or to address, once they had arisen, many of the phenomena at the root of the 2007–2009 financial crisis. For example, in the years leading up to the crisis, many economists understood that the USA was building too many new houses (more than 2 million per year during much of 2004, 2005 and 2006). However, only few paid attention to the credit market conditions that enabled this extraordinary surge of home construction: increasingly lax underwriting standards, hence the sale of many of those houses to owners with fragile prospects of servicing the debt they took on in order to finance their purchase. In parallel, significant exposure of the lenders, some of them highly leveraged, to risk in the event of delinquency or default by the borrowers and the further compounding of these problems by the proliferation of derivative instruments magnified the exposure and attracted yet additional classes of investors to assume it. It is no accident that these phenomena, as they built up, attracted attention primarily among finance specialists and practitioners, not economists.

***

A second contributor to economists' failure to anticipate the 2007–2009 crisis was the application of overly rigorous notions of optimization by individual households and firms, including in particular, the assumption that these actors assessed their economic environment according to so-called 'rational' expectations. The idea that individuals and firms act to further their self-interest dates to the very beginnings of modern economics. Unlike the mercantilists who preceded him, Adam Smith assumed that people mostly understand what is in their self-interest when they act as producers of goods and services. (Interestingly, Smith never applied this assumption to people's behaviour as consumers; on the contrary, he was dismissive, often contemptuous, in his scorn for the foolishness and childishness of many consumers' misguided choices.) Given this prior assumption, he then proceeded on the assumption that people act accordingly. The subsequent introduction of utilitarianism, in the 19th century, ultimately facilitated the extension of the pursuit of self-interest to optimization, according to which people not only act to further their self-interest but also do so to the maximum extent possible.

Along the way, everyone, of course, recognized that expectations of future economic conditions and events matter for many economically relevant choices. In the early 20th century, Keynes emphasized the role of expectations, but he had little to say about how they are formed. Following the work of Muth and Lucas in the later decades of the century, the standard working hypothesis in many areas of economics became that expectations are 'rational'—meaning that individual agents, on average, form their views of the future as if they know and apply the model corresponding to the process that actually delivers future economic outcomes. In an explicitly dynamic context, standard analysis accompanied this assumption with the further requirement that individual agents, on average, do not make the mistake of acting as if any process that cannot go on forever (again, under the model corresponding to the process that determines actual outcomes) will do so.

Taken on their own terms, this set of assumptions is not necessarily a bad way to discipline economic analysis. In the absence of either optimization or some well-specified alternative to it, a very broad range of representations of economic behaviour are potentially consistent with pursuit of self-interest. Similarly, in the absence of either model-consistent expectations or some well-specified alternative to them, any representation of beliefs about the future is potentially admissible. Given the practical limitations on empirical identification and inference, such undisciplined thinking risks absorbing degrees of freedom well beyond what most economic analysis can bear.

But assumptions can unhelpfully restrict thinking as well, and the recent crisis stands as a case in point. The question here is how rigorously to apply the presumption that people always act optimally, or that on average they form their beliefs about the future 'rationally'. Surely, no one interprets the optimization assumption to mean that nobody ever does anything foolish. But to what extent can foolish behaviour 'predominate' in one market sector or another? Similarly, no one interprets 'rational' expectations to imply that no price, in any market, is ever at an incorrect level—meaning, again, a level other than the appropriately conditioned equilibrium implied by the solution of the model corresponding to the process that determines outcomes. But what kinds of departures are admissible?

Most economists accept that the market can mis-price the shares of any one company, or any one borrower's bonds. Can the market mis-price the equity of an entire class of companies?

Or the debt of an entire category of borrowers? Can the stock market as a whole establish a 'wrong' price? Can the bond market? Even if they did not take these familiar assumptions to their logical extreme, most economists during the build-up to the 2007–2009 financial crisis were unwilling to give serious thought to the prospect that the price being paid for the extraordinary supply of new houses being built in the USA (and in the secondary market as well) was too high, or that the interest rate being charged on a wide class of mortgage debt was systematically too low, or that the price of the securities backed by these instruments was therefore too high, or that large numbers of institutions that invested in these securities were bearing risk well outside their safe range of tolerance.

A further lacuna in thinking that compounded this excessive reliance on the assumption of optimizing behaviour and 'rational' expectations was the failure to take account of principal–agent relationships. Many of the individuals buying these mis-priced securities did so using not their own funds but those of institutions by whom they were employed, and whose interests were at best loosely aligned with their own. In the end, the key figures whose actions led to the failure, or near-failure, or failure-but-for-government-intervention, of many of these institutions mostly came out very well personally. The shareholders of the institutions that employed them did not.

The mindset shaped by these interrelated assumptions largely blocked serious consideration of what would have been corrective policies. In line with the overbuilding of houses in the USA, the epicentre of the 2007–2009 financial crisis was the US market for residential mortgage lending. Beginning well in advance of the crisis, not only some private individuals but various agencies within the US government urged a tightening of mortgage lending standards, or restrictions on institutions' freedom to invest in mortgage-backed security products, or both. These warnings were systematically ignored, and the proposed initiatives blocked or rejected, largely on the ground that government regulation of credit markets populated by rational investors was unnecessary. The prevailing thinking was that investors would 'rationally' judge the value of the instruments that they bought. Similarly, depositors holding bank liabilities in amounts exceeding the limits covered by deposit insurance would presumably monitor the balance sheets of the banks to which they lent and would thereby exercise a non-government (and therefore, presumably more effective) regulatory function by not lending to those banks that took on excess risk. This form of privately imposed safety-and-soundness regulation would apply even more so to 'shadow banks', whose liabilities were entirely uninsured and which did not have access to central bank lending in the event of any difficulty. In the end, these beliefs were dramatically falsified.

***

Finally, in the same way that relying on private market participants to impose discipline on lending institutions led both economists and policymakers astray, many economists' commitment to the belief that markets clear, always and everywhere, clouded their assessment of potential corrective actions after the crisis had developed. Central banks' lender-of-last-resort policy provides an apt illustration. Once the reality of an out-and-out financial crisis became apparent, many long-time students of monetary economics urged central banks to follow Walter Bagehot's famous dictum of lending freely to solvent institutions, at a penalty rate, on good collateral. The Bagehot principle has much to recommend it—if it is clear which institutions are solvent and what collateral is good. Under conditions of dysfunctionality like those prevailing in markets like the US residential mortgage market and the corresponding market for mortgage-based derivative instruments, however, neither judgement is straightforward.

The problem in applying the Bagehot rule in such circumstances is conceptually different from merely needing to evaluate some credit market instrument, or some investing institution's portfolio, under disorderly market conditions. During the crisis, markets were sufficiently broken that whether some credit was worth 80 or 40, or perhaps nothing at all, depended crucially on what action the central bank itself would take. Would the central bank intervene? If so, what instruments would it buy? And how much? What instruments constituted 'good collateral', and which institutions were solvent, were in both instances endogenous with respect to the central bank's own actions. Under such conditions, the Bagehot rule becomes operationally meaningless, not just as a matter of technicalities of implementation, but also in its fundamental logic. The task now facing economists and policymakers is not merely to rethink the economics underlying the behaviour that can lead to a crisis situation but also to design new policies and procedures governing who should do what once such an episode is under way.

It is impossible to know what would have happened differently if the ideas and methods with which economists approached the 2007–2009 financial crisis and then assessed potential reactions to it—not just the concrete models they had in their toolkit, but also the underlying insights that shaped their intuition—had been different in any of these respects. But as both Keynes and Hayek agreed, fundamental thinking matters, and thinking about economics matters for many aspects of life that are important to families and firms individually as well as to the societies that they comprise. Today's effort to develop a new, and better, economic thinking about these issues is an endeavour well worth undertaking.

***

I am honoured to contribute a foreword to this volume by Dr Rabi N. Mishra.

Some years ago, Dr Mishra spent a year, on leave from his responsibilities at the Reserve Bank of India, as a Visiting Fellow in the Department of Economics at Harvard University. During that time, he not only took an active part in the intellectual life of the department, participating in classes and seminars as well as countless informal interactions with faculty colleagues, but also exerted a significant influence on many Harvard students. He also pursued an energetic and systematic investigation into the question of financial risk and how to manage it, and the consequent challenges for public policy, which he addressed here. I hope that what he has written will prove to be of practical value in India and elsewhere. It was a privilege to learn from his research. It was my pleasure to enjoy his friendship.

—Benjamin M. Friedman
William Joseph Maier Professor of Political Economy,
Harvard University
December 2018

References

Friedman, Benjamin M. 2015, June. 'Has the Financial Crisis Permanently Changed the Practice of Monetary Policy? Has It Changed the Theory of Monetary Policy?' *The Manchester School* 83: 5–19.

———. Forthcoming. 'Intellectual Origins of the Financial Crisis'. *Karl Brunner and Monetarism*. Cambridge, MA: MIT Press.

Friedman, Benjamin M., and Kenneth N. Kuttner. 2011. 'Implementation of Monetary Policy: How Do Central Banks Set Interest Rates?' In *Handbook of Monetary Economics*, Vol. 3, edited by B. M. Friedman and M. Woodford. Amsterdam: North-Holland.

Preface

It was a typical 'dare to dream' story—a schoolboy of rural India dreaming to author a book one day.

The seeds for this grand dream were sown when I landed in the city of New York for the first time in the late 1990s and hopped across the cities of Washington, London, Frankfurt, Paris, Rome, Basel and Bern, looking for an understanding of the rising star products of the financial space then, securitization and credit derivatives. I interacted with commercial/investment bankers, financial insurers–reinsurers, credit rating agencies, regulators, supervisors, experts in the IMF, the World Bank and the BIS and reputed freelancing financial sector specialists. The financial sector was exploding with these products being perceived as its nucleus. I was told about the ingenuity of the young financial wizards who were able to create money out of money.

Few years into the millennial, I proudly landed at the economics department of the Harvard University to do a postdoctoral research programme under the supervision of Professor Benjamin Friedman. There were 'whispers' in the library on the havoc, securitization and credit derivatives are going to play. Even the fundamentals of these products had changed for the negative by then. What were defined to be backed by 'homogenous pools of assets with clearly discernible cash flows' were now increasingly seen to be the fruits of falsehood backed by 'nothing'. Financial castles were constructed out of such 'nothing' (CDO^2, CDO^3 and so on) and finally (as a logical conclusion) collapsed like a pack of cards. Global inter-connectedness spread the gloom arising from those 'nothings' all over the world, and a global recession could be smelt in the air. While my 'hero' of the late 1990s—overall risk diversifier—was turning into the 'villain'—systemic risk creator—of mid-20s, I was running out of sensible topics to do research on. The fear was sensible as the 'transitoriness' of macrofinancial situations was getting revealed.

An idea struck into my mind. In fact, Professor Friedman suggested me to toy with such an abstract idea. Why not think of a globe that agrees to be governed like a village to pursue the cause of economic prosperity! Sounded utopian then! But since the human mind has no boundary, I persuaded myself to work on that.

I thank Professor Benjamin Friedman for this intellectual persuasion and for remembering me all these years and finally writing the foreword for this book after over a decade.

I returned to India.

In the next two years, Lehman Brothers collapsed.

The global gloom spread far and wide in the form of a financial crisis without precedent.

When the Global Financial Crisis (GFC) unleashed itself in its deadliest form by 2009–2010, policy makers moved with alacrity. The Financial Stability Forum (FSF) transformed into the Financial Stability Board (FSB) and spearheaded lots of reforms that are continuing till this day. I got an opportunity to head the newly created financial stability unit (FSU) in India for three years and later to advise the Central Bank of Oman to set up its FSU for another three years. And I also became RBI's nominee to the FSB's Analytical Group of Vulnerabilities (AGV)—a Committee meant for the quarterly assessment of vulnerabilities in the G20 economies. Every quarter, we were holding assessment meetings in one of the G20 economies. Country experiences gained in these meetings instilled in me the confidence to take the stand that macroprudential policy governance is better done on a global level, reflecting policy spillover effects that were evidently quite prominent by then. These also sparked my interest to understand how fallen financial firms could be resurrected to their original healthy forms. This area was new and interesting. Being in the financial sector, we were deep in the know of the other story—their cradle to the grave one. I got the zeal to take on this 'yet-to-be-born' story. I thank the then authorities in the RBI who gave me not one but two almost consecutive chances to deal with the study of financial instability/distress/crises management.

This new-found work area continues to enthral me and I decided to share the knowledge/expertise/experiences gathered among the new generation of students/researchers/workers in financial economics.

The idea really started taking shape in 2015–2016 while I was working on various facets of macroprudential policymaking at the Central Bank of Oman. Mr Rubhen Jeya helped me in developing my thoughts and in preparing the skeleton of the project. He is a Sri Lankan working in Australia. I was sitting in Muscat. What an example of global intellectual coordination! I profusely thank him for showing interest in the project.

Back from my deputation, I was posted as the Principal of Reserve Bank Staff College (RBSC) at Chennai, India. 'Fleshing out the skeleton' started there with a group of very talented faculty members joining in to help. I have no words to thank Jayakumar, Sundar Murthi, Ayyappan Nair, Sreeramulu, Satish Rath, Sirin Kumar and Shubhashree for their contribution to this cause. Since I was also teaching macroprudential policy, I could imagine what needs to be explained to what measure in sync with the learners' expectations. By March 2018, the preliminary draft was ready. By then, I was back in Mumbai as the Head of Risk Monitoring Department of RBI. The first draft of the book was happily accepted by Rajosik Banerjee for thorough quality editing. My sincere thanks is due to him.

The help of Santosh Pandey, Ashish Gupta and Saket Kumar in effecting editorial improvements and giving it the shape of a book to solicit interests of the publisher was immense. I thank these brilliant young minds while wishing them good luck in their lives. And finally, my profuse thanks is due to Dr Jay Surti of IMF who extended the last finishing editorial touch to the final draft.

I will fail in my duty if I do not place on record the 'blessings' showered on me by the prominent personalities with 'endorsement messages' for the book. I genuflect before them for their kindness and generosity.

And finally, I thank SAGE, especially Rajesh Dey and Vandana Gupta, for guiding me on the manuscript for its final publication.

Introduction

What we know about the Global Financial Crisis is that we don't
know very much.

—Paul Samuelson

The GFC, dubbed the 'The Great Recession', was undoubtedly the
most severe financial crisis the world had witnessed since 'The Great
Depression' of 1929. The crisis has been dissected and analysed by a
number of experts offering their own distinct perspectives, narratives
and counter-narratives. Notwithstanding the variety of opinions and
arguments, everyone agrees that we cannot let a crisis of this magnitude, estimated at an output loss of $1.25 trillion, to go to waste
and should take adequate measures to create a much more resilient
financial system. This book is an attempt to combine together at one
place the different ideas and thoughts propounded as the cause of
the crisis, the consequences and the response. From a public policy
perspective, the crisis brought to the fore many gaps in the existing
frameworks. The structural weakness in regulation and supervision
was a principal cause of the crisis. This book looks at the regulatory
reforms that have come about as a response to the crisis and what more
can be added to the policy toolbox to build a safer financial system that
supports the real sector rather than pose a threat to it.

The Genesis

Financial crises have a venerated history and also a familiar ring to
them. They all have a humble beginning aided by enthusiasm among
the public and driven by cheap and easy credit. Over time, as more and
more people join, buoyed by optimism and overconfidence, it results
in speculative excesses or manias. This generally continues for a sufficiently long period, so-called booms. Eventually it dawns on investors
that most of the excesses are driven by irrational exuberance and not

based on fundamentals and the boom gives way to distress and panic. Ultimately, the market crashes as investors resort to fire sale of their assets, banks stop credit and a crisis ensues. As Walter Bagehot said, the large blind capital (stupid people having large amount of stupid money) leads to even more craving for it, leading to further speculation eventually resulting in someone taking this blind capital away which culminates into a panic. This process has played out many times since the 17th century and eloquently written by Charles Kindleberger in his seminal book, *Manias, Panics, and Crashes: A History of Financial Crises*. The only difference is the intensity of the crisis and its impact on the real economy, which in turn decides the actions of the public policy authorities and the government. Going by historical standards, 'The Great Recession' like 'The Great Depression' is a once-in-a-lifetime event that altered the financial landscape and explored policymaking in uncharted territory. Indeed, as Olivier Blanchard and Larry Summers (2017) showed in their paper, the output per working age in the USA would likely have grown less over the 12 years since the crisis started as compared to the 12 years since the start of the Great Depression. It is important, therefore, to clearly understand the real causes of the crisis in order to formulate appropriate policies.

A crisis of this severity cannot be pigeonholed into 'I told you so' narratives. As Ben Bernanke explained in detail, in both his book *The Courage to Act* and a series of lectures, the GFC was the result of vulnerabilities that were building up since the start of the new millennium. Moreover, like previous financial crises, this one too had a familiar ring to it in as much as it reflected a pattern of easy liquidity, high leverage and 'madness of crowds', all contributing to a bubble, and finally, a run on the financial system. The exception this time, as Gary Gorton rightly said, was that the run happened on the shadow banks—entities such as money market funds, securitization vehicles, investment banks, etc.—that perform credit intermediation outside the regulatory perimeter.

Prior to the financial crisis, central banks exclusively and may be excessively focused on price stability with little or no importance given to the linkage between the financial system and the real economy. Financial stability was not thought to be inalienable adjunct to price stability and was everyone's responsibility, which translates into no one's responsibility. The prevailing economic theory did not consider the role of the financial system and its interlinkages with the economy and missed these in its models. This was largely due to the fact that the existing models—which are abstracts of reality, rather perceived reality—were working well, the economies were growing and the inflation was under control. Notwithstanding the many fissures building up in the financial system, policymakers were so presumptuous in their belief that 'all is well' with the economy that they failed to recognize these vulnerabilities and also did not give credence to any dissenting voice. The criticism of Lawrence Summers, the former treasury secretary of the USA, of Raghuram Rajan's views that modern finance has made the real economy susceptible as 'slightly Luddite' and Bernanke's response on the danger posed to the economy by the housing bubble that 'I guess I don't buy your premise. It's a pretty unlikely possibility. We've never had a decline in house prices on a nationwide basis' are cases in point. These examples highlight the dominant ethos prior to the crisis. The human psyche is such that the first reaction to any problem is denial. The eventual acceptance goes through a process of blame where one tries to rationalize the problem as if it has nothing to do with him or her. Take, for instance, Bernanke's above-mentioned response on questions relating to housing bubble when asked in 2005 on the danger posed to the economy by the housing bubble. When the crisis actually erupted in 2008, he reassured the world that it would be 'contained', and Hank Paulson, Treasury Secretary at the time, promised 'the worst is likely to be behind us'. Although one may argue that Bernanke and Paulson were responding to questions based on available information at the time, their words have more power than they imagine and public confidence can easily erode very fast if they turn out to be inaccurate. It will not be farfetched to quote Henry Ford, who said, 'It is well enough that people of the nation do not understand our banking and monetary system, for if they did, I believe there would be a revolution before tomorrow morning.'

Vulnerabilities in the financial system which led to the crisis were not restricted to private sector participants alone. Public sector was equally responsible for not building safeguards and letting the financial system self-regulate. The growth in shadow banking was an outcome of deficiencies in public sector policies as much as the private sector players' effort at regulatory arbitrage and search for yield. In fact, the regulation of shadow banks or the lack of it, a theme I will return to later in the book, continues to be a concern as most of the crisis responses have been to regulate an already over-regulated banking system.

So what were these vulnerabilities? First, dependence on short-term and unstable wholesale funding. Since credit intermediation was largely done by shadow banks (largely NBFCs in context of India), which did not have access to retail deposits, the reliance on different types of wholesale funding such as the repos, securities lending transactions, margin funding, etc., to fund the balance sheet grew at an exponential rate before the crisis. The low interest rates and excess liquidity encouraged participants to borrow heavily and purchase assets, many of them liquid only on paper, thereby leveraging the balance sheet 30, 40 or 50 times. The risk with such a strategy is the rollover risk—the risk that when you try to roll over the deposit, the lender either may ask a higher interest rate or does not roll over at all. Moreover, unlike retail deposits which have some deposit insurance, these short-term funding were uninsured and susceptible to runs. And everyone knows how human psyche works when they sense danger. A run on one entity can easily snowball into a run on the entire system as fears become self-fulfilling. It can also blur the distinction between a solvent and insolvent entity, forcing the authorities to bail out all of them, resulting in moral hazard issues.

Second, the easy availability of short-term funding coexisted with a proclivity for acquiring any assets linked to real estate, underlying or derivatives. Traditional banks, shadow banks and even financial institutions that are not in the credit intermediation business—AIG, for example—wanted a piece of the real estate pie and were willing to lap up any exposure that had some linkage to the real estate. Mortgage-backed securities, asset-backed securities and other alphabet soup consisting of collateralized debt obligations (CDOs), collateralized loan obligations (CLOs), etc., were the main assets held by majority of banks and shadow banks. To make matters worse, the risk management systems were inadequate. Poor credit underwriting standards—loans were supposedly given to people with no income, no jobs and no assets, popularly known as NINJA—coupled with undue reliance on external ratings for structured instruments provided by rating agencies were some of the anomalies in the risk management and oversight system. The shift from 'originate-to-hold' model where the lender thoroughly screens the borrower to 'originate-to-distribute' model where there is little or no incentive to do credit appraisal amplified these deficiencies. Thus, reliance on short-term funding to purchase financially engineered assets without sound risk management system produced the perfect recipe for a financial disaster. Just like in any natural disaster such as earthquake or hurricane, the buildings with the weakest foundation are the first to succumb to the nature's fury, and sometimes these buildings' debris ensure damage to nearby strong buildings, when financial tsunami hits, the institutions with weak balance sheets first experience losses and because of the interconnectedness between the entities in the financial system, even the ones with strong balance sheets can come under serious pressure.

Financial innovation has always been touted as a good thing. It is supposed to make the allocation of capital even more efficient, thereby contributing to the growth of the 'real' economy. New products such as securitization and credit default swaps (CDSs) are good inasmuch as they enlarge the pool of capital, create liquidity as well as transfer risk among those who have the capacity to bear. The trouble is that if they are seen as a quick way to make money, it only results in transfer of wealth from one entity to another without any socially useful outcome or 'real output'.

Take, for example, securitization. The original concept was to convert illiquid loans into liquid securities, thereby freeing up the existing capital for more productive investment. It also reduced the borrowing cost as one could borrow against these securities. For the investors, it added another product to their menu of available investment options. Win-win for both buyers and sellers! Maybe not. The allure of securitization prompted everyone to jump into the bandwagon and securitize any asset that fits the profile. Thus, not only traditional assets with fixed terms such as mortgages and car loans, but also other assets with more variability such as lease receivables and home equity were added to the mix. One of the fundamental issues in financial markets is market failure associated with asymmetric information. Sellers always have more and better information than buyers and in the absence of financial intermediaries to reduce this asymmetry of information, it can lead to market failures. However, securitization sharply reduced the incentive on originators to screen the borrowers and assess their creditworthiness, as even if the original loan goes bad, the loss will be borne by someone else. The securitized products also received the blessings of the credit rating agencies, who without verifying the underlying assets gave most of the products the highest rating, that is, AAA. To make matters worse, the securitized products were repackaged to create exotic securities such as CDOs. With each repackaging, the complexity increased—'tranches' were created to pool securities of varying degrees of risk—and the investor also relied only on the credit rating to judge the soundness of the product. In many instances, the investor was unaware of the risks he/she was taking as the pooling of securities mixed the good assets with the bad ones. Since these were derivatives whose value was strictly dependent on the performance of underlying assets, as soon as there was crisis in underlying market they also fell like a pack of cards.

A similar innovation, CDS is an instrument that offers insurance against corporate default. Like many other derivatives, the primary purpose of CDS is also to hedge risks. Imagine you bought an AAA-rated corporate bond. You expect to receive steady stream of cash flows from the issuer of the bond. However, there is a small chance that the issuer might go bankrupt or default for any other reason. To protect against the possible loss, you can buy a CDS that acts like an insurance policy. You pay a premium for the insurance bought and in the event the corporate defaults, the seller of the CDS reimburses your principal. All good! Well, not quite. Historically, AAA-rated companies neither default nor go bankrupt. If so, why buy the bond and earn a small interest. A better way is to sell the CDS on the corporate and receive the premium with no upfront payment required. This lured many entities and they saw CDS as a tool for speculation. The problem was exacerbated as these entities took so-called naked CDS exposures, that is, no exposure to the underlying asset on mortgage-backed securities and CDOs. As the bonds started defaulting, the sellers could no longer enjoy the 'free lunch' and had to pay up. The most notable among these entities was American International Group (AIG), the largest insurance company in the world prior to the crisis. Unlike other entities who also bought CDS to protect the downside, AIG went a step further and sold only CDS. AIG sold as much as US $440 billion of CDS, a product which it had no business in the first place to trade. As losses mounted, the Federal Reserve had to rescue AIG. Again, a product designed to lead to socially useful purpose of transferring risk and freeing up of capital was misused and put the system at risk.

I have belaboured on this aspect relating to financial innovation to sensitize everyone that notwithstanding the social usefulness of some of these innovations, they can be misused for short-term benefits, thus rendering the original idea immoral and ineffective. It is the responsibility of the regulators to strictly monitor the excesses of the private sector lest financial crisis of this magnitude result in serious damage to the real sector in terms of large unemployment and output loss.

The rise in securitization, CDOs, CDS and other alphabet soup of financial innovations coincided with the rise in repo. To fund purchase of these assets, the shadow banks relied on repo and placed these assets as collateral. Anecdotal evidence shows that the size of the repo market just before the crisis was around $10 billion, equal to the total assets of the regulated banking system (Gorton 2009). Moreover, entities also used these assets to raise resources in the asset-backed commercial paper (ABCP) market. The rise in the repo market and the ABCP market provided cheap and short-term funds to finance the complex and illiquid assets. Thus, both the asset and liability sides of the balance sheets in a sense were intertwined and depended on the performance of the underlying loan. With the rising housing prices, the value of the assets also rose and counterparties did not demand any haircut for these assets. However, as soon as the first sign of the crisis became evident, the counterparties demanded higher haircuts as they became concerned that the collateral may be illiquid. From virtually zero haircut, the average haircut rose to nearly 50 bps in early 2009. The increase in haircuts was tantamount to withdrawal of funds by depositors from a traditional bank. Each action is on account of concerns about the solvency of the financial institution and its ability to service the debt without any loss of value. Repos, like demand deposits, were considered as value-certain contracts by the shadow banking entities. Thus, concerns about erosion in value of collaterals resulted in a panic with attendant dwindling liquidity in both the repo and the ABCP markets.

The crisis also brought to light the ethical deficit and trust deficit that pervaded the system. According to Steve Eisman, the famous investor known for shorting CDOs and one of the principal characters in Michael Lewis's book, *The Big Short: Inside the Doomsday Machine*, in finance industry, 'incentives always trump ethics'. Multiple studies and polls have also shown that the public trust of bankers was at a nadir during the crisis. Even as many lost their jobs, the CEOs and top management officials of many banks who engaged in this financial alchemy walked away with millions as they were protected by their employment contracts. As a recent *Financial Times* series on the 10th anniversary of the financial crisis showed, banks have been fined more than $150 billion by the regulators after the crisis erupted. Whether it is the manipulation of the LIBOR, the Wells Fargo fake account scandal or the London Whale incident at JP Morgan, all indicate that human greed remains insatiable. The proclamation of the lead character, Michael Douglas as Gordon Gekko, in the 1987 movie *Wall Street* that 'greed is good' is still resonating in the financial industry. Ten years since the onset of the crisis, the lost trust has still not been regained. It may be worthwhile to pay heed to Napoleon Bonaparte who said, 'Money has no motherland; financiers are without patriotism and without decency; their sole object is gain.'

While one can understand the private sector's urge to innovate and arbitrage any regulatory loopholes, it is difficult to fathom the actions of the authorities who were given the responsibility to safeguard the financial system. However, they also fell prey to the benefits of financial innovation. To quote Alan Greenspan:

> Recent regulatory reform coupled with innovative technologies has spawned rapidly growing markets for, among other products, asset-backed securities, collateral loan obligations, and credit derivative default swaps. These increasingly complex financial instruments have contributed, especially over the recent stressful period, to the development of a far more flexible, efficient, and hence resilient financial system than existed just a quarter-century ago.

As the ensuing crisis showed, Greenspan's belief that these innovations will lead to the development of a more flexible, efficient and resilient system was misplaced. This was largely due to the free market ideology that was in vogue at the time as regulators pinned their hopes on the private sector's ability to self-regulate. Recognizing the error made by him, in a testimony to the US Congress, Greenspan, after the beginning of the crisis, said, 'The crisis had shaken his very understanding of how markets work, and agreed that certain financial derivatives should be regulated—an idea he had long resisted.' Both the examples mentioned before, that is, securitization and CDS, are in a sense good innovations. However, every now and then private players can engage in socially undesirable activities leading to market failures. Therefore, while I would not subscribe to the extreme view of Paul Volcker, the former Fed Chairman, who said the only socially useful financial innovation in the past 50 years was the invention of ATMs, there is a strong case to be made against the kind of financial innovation prevalent prior to the crisis that was not yielding any socially desirable outcomes.

Third, private sector vulnerability relates to the issue of 'leverage'. Even if entities take risk with their balance sheet as detailed earlier, the negative impact can be cushioned to the extent of availability of loss-absorbing capital. What made the GFC even worse was the extent of leverage that existed in the system. Leverage is good, until it is not (Solow 2010). It is a double-edged sword resulting in oversized profits and losses. Many of the shadow banking entities were not subject to strict capital regulation, which encouraged them to excessively rely on debt to fund their balance sheet. Moreover, as the good times rolled on with each entity declaring large profits and as a corollary significant dividend, the desire to take on even more leverage was rampant. Banks, on the other hand, were required to maintain loss-absorbing capital under Basel norms. However, the increasing competition from the shadow banking entities led them to engage in regulatory arbitrage and employ instruments that qualified as capital but did not stand the test of loss absorption when the crisis hit home. So even though they were technically not overleveraged, in reality given the doubtful quality of the so-called hybrid instruments, they were also highly leveraged. An overleveraged financial system could not cope with the weight of losses and the resultant deleveraging not only crippled the financial system but also had a devastating impact on the real sector. The financial system became dysfunctional and could no longer perform its essential function of efficient allocation of resources. The oft-quoted Jefferson's statement that 'banking establishments are more danger-ous than standing armies' virtually came true at the depth of the crisis within the world economy poised on a cliff edge.

Vulnerabilities in existing regulation and supervision were a key cause of the financial crisis. As Ben Bernanke in his testimony to the US Congress outlined, there were many serious gaps. Lack of regu-lation of shadow banking entities complicated regulatory structure, which helped entities to engage in regulatory arbitrage, for example, AIG's insurance operations were regulated and supervised by insurance regulators, whereas the oversight of AIG's financial products, the same department which led the firm to the precipice, was mostly lacking (the responsibility rested with the Office of Thrift Supervision)—and inadequate information about their activities was one of the deficien-cies. More broadly, the regulatory and supervisory framework was built on the 'Fallacy of Composition', the error of assuming what is true for an individual applies for the system as a whole. Therefore, there was no macroprudential overlay to the microprudential structure in place, which meant that systemic risk was not addressed properly.

The gaps in regulation and supervision were not the only deficien-cies. Even where the authorities had the ability to act, there was no willingness to act as they believed in the ability of private sector to self-regulate and in case of deficiencies, market discipline imposed by counterparties to take care of the rest. Alas, the crisis showed that unfettered private sector allowed to self-regulate is a disaster waiting to happen and it did. The long period of stability before the crisis led to a false sense of security as well as complacency among policymakers, and they did not pay any attention to the build-up of risks. There was no assessment of how sound the risk management systems in banks were; given the nature of exposure they were taking, no effort was made to address market abuses, little attention was given to liquidity risk, which in a crisis could easily transform into solvency risk, and no proper examination was undertaken to find inadequacies in capital standards, the quality of capital in particular. All of the above could and should have been taken cognizance of to build a more resilient financial system.

The problems were compounded due to lack of crisis management tools and the public perception and objection to helping troubled firms. The only legitimate mechanism available to deal with losses to consumers was deposit insurance. However, this was not applicable to shadow banks, broker–dealers, etc., and there was no mechanism to resolve the failure of these institutions. Remember that the epicentre of the crisis was shadow banking. While filing for bankruptcy is the normal course of action for a firm which has become insolvent, it only addresses the issue of creditor rights. To address the larger issue of financial stability, there was a need for a resolution regime and there was none. The inadequacies in resolution frameworks were evident on both sides of the Atlantic. This is the view expressed by Sir Jon Cunliffe, Deputy Governor, Bank of England (Cunliffe 2017): 'The failure of Northern Rock in 2007 and later, of RBS and Lloyds exposed brutally that the UK lacked the tools needed to manage the failure of a bank.' As regards the objection to helping troubled entities, Tim Geithner in his book *Stress Test* puts forward the two types of objections. The first he calls the 'Old Testament View', which is the moral argument about punishing the corrupt or giving justice. The second is the economic argument about incentives, that is, the 'moral hazard' issue relating to bailing out risk-takers and in turn giving them incentives to take on more risks. While both are valid objections and sensible in normal state of affairs, during a stress period taking the high moral ground or worrying about ex-post moral hazard and letting firms fail will only aggravate the stress. As I see it, this is like treating an alcoholic admitted in the ICU. The immediate task is to resuscitate the patient and ensure that there is no relapse. Once the patient is on the path of recovery, take appropriate measures to ensure a healthy lifestyle. Similarly, when it comes to bailing out troubled firms, one should also have a sense of the counterfactual. What would and could happen if these firms are allowed to fail? The unintended and undesirable consequence could be even more harmful for the economy and the very people whom we are trying to protect. It will give a signal to the creditors that their firm may be next in line and encourage them to run with their money as 'in the fog of a panic, nobody looks like a good credit risk' (Geithner 2014). There will not be any differentiation between the strong and weak institutions and rational decisions of individuals collectively become irrational and a stampede breaks out, and as everyone knows stampedes in a crowded place do not end well. In such a situation, 'the truly moral thing to do during a raging financial inferno is to put it out. The goal should be to protect the innocent, even if some of the arsonists escape their full measure of justice.'

Risk is as much scientific as it is psychological. While one can develop models to measure risk, one can never be sure how human beings react to adverse events. As Keynes said, 'The markets can remain irrational longer than you can remain solvent.' Prior to the crisis, there was widespread optimism about the economy, which in turn fanned excessive risk-taking by financial institutions. Chuck Prince, the then Citibank Chairman, echoed this sentiment when he said, 'When the music stops, in terms of liquidity, things will be complicated. But as long as the music is playing, you've got to get up and dance. We're still dancing.' While the private sector was in a partying mood and did not see any emerging risks on the horizon, the policymakers were also asleep at the wheel. As William McChesney Martin, former Fed Chairman, famously said that the mandate of the Federal Reserve is 'to take the punch bowl away just as the party gets going'. Not only the Federal Reserve and other regulators did not take the punch bowl away, but they also unwittingly let the party continue till it became messy. Therefore, when the crisis started, the market, which was so intoxicated with easy liquidity, was not in a position to deal with the sudden stop in liquidity. As the late MIT Professor Rudi Dornbusch rightly said, 'In financial markets things always take longer to happen than you expect but once they happen, events unfold much more quickly than you expect.' Herbert Stein's law, which he expressed as 'If something cannot go on forever, it will stop,' is a fitting illustration of the events preceding the crisis. The crisis thus was a consequence of infirmities, both in the private sector and in the public sector. A crisis this deep and protracted cannot be the result of subprime mortgage lending alone.

A Bubble Waiting for a Pin

Politicians usually undertake populist measures to satisfy their constituencies, and enabling households to acquire their own houses was the most popular initiative of the US government. The long-standing incentive of tax deductibility on interest paid on mortgages, weak underwriting standards, 'teaser' rates on loans, expectation of rising house prices, etc., led to rapid rise in US home ownership over the period 1997–2005. As a corollary, housing prices rose in a spectacular fashion encouraging borrowers to take on more risk and lever up their debt. During the same period, home prices nearly doubled. Lenders too boosted the home buyers' confidence by relaxing their usual standards of carefully assessing the borrowers, say, for example, applying a strict loan-to-value ratio, and provided loans even without documentation. In addition, adjustable-rate mortgages (ARMs), which were indexed to market rates, were promoted on the premise that the interest rates will remain lower for a continued period.

One of the defining characteristics of the US financial system has been that 'it creates large numbers of tradable securities, that is, stores of value that can easily be acquired and sold by investors trying to adapt to the lack of synchronicity between cash receipts and cash needs' (Tirole, Rochet and Dewatripont 2010). Banks and government-sponsored entities such as Fannie Mae and Freddie Mac (these entities were created to promote housing in the USA) saw the opportunity to convert traditional loans into marketable securities. Thus, the mortgages were converted into mortgage-backed securities and, as mentioned previously, were sliced and diced into even more iterations. The abundant liquidity and the search for yield attracted investors from all over the world as they saw this as an attractive investment option. Many emerging countries, such as China, and sovereign wealth funds from Arab countries had huge foreign exchange reserves and invested in these securities. This inflow of investments further accelerated the demand for these securities, which in turn encouraged the originators to accelerate securitization process even more to meet the demand. However, this could be achieved either through loans to new borrowers—one requires an underlying loan in order to securitize it—or through financial engineering. Since most of the prime borrowers had already availed loans, the lenders extended loans to sub-prime borrowers or packaged securities of different quality to create another 'tranche' of 'AAA'-rated securities which resulted in the rate of securitization of housing loans to grow from 30 per cent in 1995 to 80 per cent in 2006. The securitized proportion also went from 46 per cent in 2001 to 81 per cent in 2006 for the sub-prime loans.

The credit-rating agencies were a major contributor to the housing sector boom. The sloppiness of rating agencies is highlighted in their decision to offer preliminary ratings, which in turn allowed issuers to indulge in 'ratings shopping', the fee being as per the value of the issue (better rating leads to better commission), and educating the issuers how to structure the 'tranches' to get the desired rating. Moreover, the rating business was concentrated with the three biggies, namely Moody's, Standard & Poor's and Fitch. This not only enabled them to monopolize the market but also made it easier for them to address the issue of dual rating,[1] whenever required, easily. The fact that many of the AAA-rated securities prior to the crisis had to be downgraded directly to 'default' category after the onset of the crisis rendered the ratings process questionable and counterproductive. It also meant that the rating downgrade was 'sudden' and 'abrupt' which raised eyebrows.

The extensive use of external ratings led to an over-reliance and led the market participants to use them as a risk management tool rather than creating their own assessment capacity. This mechanistic use of external ratings was one of the main causes for the extent and manifestation of the GFC. As the crisis extended, market participants all reacted in a synchronized manner leading to downgrades, thus setting up a pro-cyclical chain.

The low interest rates were also an enabler in fuelling the housing euphoria. The low interest rates coupled with cheap credit from financial institutions provided fodder for excessive risk-taking. Critics have made the argument that since the stated objective of the central banks is to manage inflation and growth, as long as the asset price boom does

---

[1] Issuer requires multiple ratings to meet investor or regulator criteria for issue.

not materialize into generalized inflation, the interest rates should not be altered. The post-crisis discussion indicates that there is a case for including financial stability objectives in monetary policy framework. As the accommodative monetary policy may entail adverse financial market outcomes and a dysfunctional financial system can jeopardize effective transmission of monetary policy as well as cause significant pain to the real sector, the conventional wisdom merits a relook.

As Tamim Bayoumi, in his well-written polemic 'Unfinished Business: The Unexplored Causes of the Financial Crisis and the Lessons Yet to be Learned', says, understanding the less-well-known European half of the story in fuelling the housing price bubble is equally important. Although it was the thinly capitalized investment banks that sold mortgage assets, it was the equally lightly capitalized universal banks in the core Euro Area that provided the cheap funding. According to him, 'A series of intellectual blinkers both allowed these bubbles to develop and increased the costs of the eventual crisis.' The regulatory changes that encouraged creation of 'Too-Big-To-Fail' (TBTF) universal banks and the increasing use of internal models, which allowed these banks to show higher capital levels despite increase in risk, embracing 'light touch' regulation in the UK and Europe, etc., contributed and amplified the housing price bubble.

The housing price bubble, thus, was a result of number of factors: the government's push towards affordable housing, weak underwriting standards, which enabled anyone and everyone to purchase homes, the resultant increase in house prices and construction activity, excessive reliance on credit ratings, the innovations in the mortgage market— securitization, CDOs, etc.—that increased the earnings of major financial institutions, etc. (Dudley 2017). The housing price bubble had all the characteristics of a financial bubble that I mentioned previously and to make matters worse the scale of the bubble spread across geographies. As Michael Lewis wrote in his book *Boomerang*, 'The real estate boom had the flavour of a family lie: it was sustainable so long as it went unquestioned and it went unquestioned so long as it appeared sustainable.'

There is a growing debate about whether the authorities should prick the bubble or deal with the mess after it has burst. Identifying a bubble is hard and misjudgement can cause instability, where there is none. In addition, such actions, given the distributional nature of consequences to the many sectors in the real economy, have to be taken by the government who is accountable to the public and not by a technocratic institution like the central bank. As one can gauge, this is a very tricky proposition as the elected officials may have little incentive to burst the bubble, especially if they know that the next election cycle is around the corner. Therefore, though one would ideally like to prevent a bubble from forming, the difficulties alluded to before suggesting that the only plausible solution to this dilemma, it appears, is to make the system more resilient to deal with the eventual fallout with as little damage to the real sector as possible.

From the history's most famous bubble—the Tulip mania of the 17th century—to the housing boom of the 21st century, the provisions of cheap credit, easy liquidity and irrational exuberance have contributed in many speculative bubbles. Just like all previous bubbles, the housing bubble also burst. The thing about bubbles is that when they burst, there is no soft landing. The following quote from the book *Ubiquity: Why Catastrophes Happen* aptly summarizes the bubble burst process:

> Even the greatest of events have no special or exceptional causes. After all, every avalanche large or small starts out the same way, when a single grain falls and makes the pile just slightly too steep at one point. What makes one avalanche much larger than another has nothing to do with its original cause, and nothing to do with some special situation in the pile just before it starts. Rather, it has to do with the perpetually unstable organization of the critical state, which makes it always possible for the next grain to trigger an avalanche of any size.

Missing the Woods for the Trees

Weaknesses in the regulation and supervision have been the most prominent public policy failure that both propagated the crisis and amplified it. 'The catch me if you can' game between regulators and regulated entities is an old one and its evolution since the first Basel accord in 1988 is well recognized. From regulatory arbitrage under Basel I to regulatory capture under Basel II, the private sector appears to have been perennially one step ahead of the regulators. However, prior to the GFC, prudential regulations were mostly aimed at maintaining and managing the health of the individual institutions, that is, it was microprudential in nature. The systemic stability was to be achieved by making and keeping the individual institutions healthy and safe. The crisis conclusively demonstrated that it was insufficient to regulate individual institutions and that, in addition, it is also necessary to have macroprudential regulations to deal with procyclicality in systemic risk due to build-up of leverage and interconnectedness through common exposures. Therefore, both systemic and specific risks need to be seen and addressed in tandem. Supervision was mainly a compliance-based tickbox approach prior to GFC. Supervising the ever-changing interconnected financial sector requires supervisors to predict the risks and have the ability and willingness to act on them. Supervisors need to adapt to the new emerging risks. The crisis also highlighted that supervisors cannot ignore risks faced by other jurisdictions as they will be caught off guard when risks of others become risks of their own.

The purpose of a financial system is to pool resources and allocate them to the most productive investment so that it leads to socially desirable outcomes. However, when the finance industry tries to exploit the shared resource for its own benefit, it not only results in socially undesirable outcomes but also makes the resource unavailable to the customers who needed them the most. The economic theory calls this the 'Tragedy of the commons', which states that 'individuals acting rationally and independently according to their own self-interest will deplete a shared resource, even if it is contrary to the best interest of the group.'

The GFC can be looked through the prism of the tragedy of the commons as 'credit', a shared resource, was exploited by bankers for their own benefit either through lowering of credit standards or through their ability to package them as securities and distribute it among many uninformed investors. When more and more entities started doing this, the credit, which is 'common' and is a shared resource, was not available for productive investment and instead was used to increase their profits and market share. The regulators on their part, believing in the power of self-regulation, did not treat the misuse of a shared resource as a failure of public policy and stayed on the sideline.

To understand the deficiencies in regulation, it would be useful to know the evolution of Basel accords. Basel regulations were conceptualized to rein in Japanese banks that were growing at a frenetic pace while being undercapitalized. The implicit guarantee of the Japanese government allowed these banks to take more risks vis-à-vis their balance sheet sizes and types. The British and American banks were concerned, primarily due to their inability to compete, and pushed for prudential regulations to improve the resilience and stability of the banking system through higher capital requirements. Basel I was based on a simple formula: capital to risk-weighted assets ratio should be 8 per cent. The only risk that figured under Basel I was credit risk with weights varying from 0 per cent to 100 per cent based on the borrower type. While it led to increase in capitalization of the banking system, there were criticisms too. In particular, the risk weights did not differentiate a risky borrower from a less risky one within the same sector (all corporates were given equal risk weight of 100 per cent irrespective of their business model and creditworthiness). This coupled with incentives to invest in sovereign securities (0% risk weight) resulted in regulatory arbitrage wherein the true risk was not getting captured, thus making the rule not so effective.

Basel II incorporated market risk and operational risk in addition to the credit risk and also permitted banks to use internal models to arrive at appropriate risk weights. It also encouraged banks to use mathematical models and use techniques such as value at risk (VaR) to calculate capital ratios. The use of internal models handed over the key to regulation to banks themselves as they employed PhDs and scientists to develop models that relied on historical data, thereby assuming that the past is a good predictor of the future. The problems with mathematical models in finance and economics unlike those used in physical science are that they generally only explain the qualitative understanding of complex phenomena occurring at the edge and are not robust over the long run mainly due to regime change due to change in economic and regulatory environment and the behaviour of economy stakeholders, which are generally difficult to explain (Tirole et al. 2010). The predicament with reliance on models is best captured by Merton Miller, the co-author of the Modigliani–Miller theorem, who described the debacle of the Long-Term Capital Management, a firm founded by Nobel laureates, as, 'In a strict sense, there wasn't any risk—if the world had behaved as it did in the past.'

The other major drawback with regulations has been that it was procyclical. Both Basel I and Basel II had procyclicality embedded into the rules. Under Basel I, for example, if a bank sustains severe losses in a crisis or at the low end of the financial or business cycle, it would be forced to increase capital or reduce credit. Raising capital, which is scarce and expensive, is an unlikely option and the reduction in credit may be the only possible option available to the bank to meet the required capital ratio. This can have a contractionary effect on the economy if many banks experience similar losses and deleverage their balance sheets. Basel II was equally or more procyclical as the risk weights, which were based on probability of default and loss given default, are likely to increase during a stress period resulting in lower capital ratios. However, banks do maintain more capital than the regulatory minimum in normal times. This is partly due to market discipline. Competition and better rating requirements encourage banks to have higher capital. Therefore, notwithstanding the procyclicality in the regulatory regime, those institutions, which were prudent in the management of capital, fared better during the crisis. This was the expectation of the policymakers as evidenced from the views of Jaime Caruana, former General Manager of BIS: 'When banking systems are adequately capitalized … and risks are correctly assessed within the appropriate time horizon, the financial system becomes more stable, less procyclical, better able to promote sustainable growth, and more resilient during periods of stress.' My sense is that although sensible, this is wishful thinking.

One of the inherent conflicts that policymakers always face is the unintended consequence of their actions. While Basel capital framework and other prudential measures were imposed on the banking system to make it more resilient, many of the credit intermediation activities shifted to entities outside the banking system, the so-called shadow banks. Moreover, banks set up a shadow banking sector of Structured Investment Vehicles (SIVs) and conduits, funded by ABCP, and also provided liquidity and credit enhancements. This allowed banks to shift on-balance sheet items into off-balance sheet contingent liabilities, thereby exploiting the loopholes of the Basel capital requirements. One of the lingering concerns about post-crisis regulatory reforms is that they are still overwhelmingly focused at banking system, with inadequacies in the regulation of the shadow banks still persisting. The Financial Stability Board, which came into existence 'to develop recommendations to strengthen the regulation and oversight of the shadow banking system' (G20 Communique, Seoul, November 2010), frustrated with the lack of consensus, has recently finalized an independent plan to evaluate the post-crisis regulatory framework without the backing of individual regulators.

The inadequacies in anticipating systemic risk and dealing with them were a major shortcoming of the pre-crisis regulatory and supervisory regime. Systemic risks—events having potential to disrupt entire financial system—were not under the radar of the regulators as microprudential regulation focused at the stability of individual institutions and market discipline enforced by creditors and other stakeholders were expected to ensure system stability. Although a banking crisis has been a feature in many countries, the lack of internationalization of such an event on the scale that was witnessed during the GFC may be a reason why policymakers were blindsided when it came to dealing with systemic risk. Basel I and Basel II did not have any macroprudential elements in the regulations. This was surprising since the stated objective of the Basel Committee on Banking Supervision (BCBS) is 'to build a strong and resilient banking system'. The increased focus on macroprudential tools, a major theme of this book which we shall see later, to deal with systemic risk has been a major positive outcome of the crisis.

The amplification of the crisis was largely on account of the size, complexity and interconnectedness of the banking system. Several so-called TBTF firms, firms that had balance sheets larger than the GDP of some of the countries and had close interconnection with the rest of the financial system, were at the centre of this amplification process. Given their complexity and interconnectedness that go along with their size, governments were put in a bind to rescue them as their failure could do significant damage to the financial system and the economy. This creates a serious moral hazard. If creditors know that these institutions will be rescued, there is no incentive for them to enforce market discipline and curtail the risk-taking activities. The management is also encouraged to take on more risk as it expects the authorities to step in if its bets turn ugly.

Bank failures are common in the USA. For instance, the Federal Deposit Insurance Corporation (FDIC) closed 465 failed banks from 2008 to 2012. These were relatively small banks and not expected to cause any systemic risk. Their failures were unnoticed. The failure of Lehman Brothers which was the second smallest among the 'Big Five' stand-alone investment banks at that time woke people up to the systemic nature of problem engulfing the global financial system.[2] The authorities could not risk another failure and were forced to bail out AIG. The lesson from the crisis is clear: any large financial institution that is closely interlinked with other systemically important institutions cannot be allowed to fail. However, it is also clear that the TBTF issue

---

[2] There were other notable failures of large systemically important banks: (i) Wachovia; (ii) WAMU; (iii) Merrill Lynch; and some mortgage finance institutions which had grown quite large, notably, (iv) Country-Wide and Indy Mac (the former of which caused financial damage, to Bank of America, for years. The difference appears to be that in a number of these cases, the failing entities were purchased by other, large entities; e.g., BoA bought ML and JPM bought WAMU, whereas several of Lehman's flagship businesses were wound down. Even Lehman's Asia operations were taken over, largely by Nomura. Among the wider pantheon of SIFIs, there is also the failure of AIG which was engaged in NTNI activities and was very financially inter-connected. The failure of, prior to their government takeover, Fannie-Mae and Freddie-Mac was also striking. Moving beyond the US, there were a number of SIB failures in Europe also. If something distinguishes Lehman, it was the widescale disruption and panic it caused.

must be solved lest these entities undertake activities that 'privatize gains and socialize losses'.

The *Titanic* tragedy and authorities' response may be an apt analogy while discussing the TBTF problem. The ship was thought to be 'too big to sink' and that gave both the passengers and the Captain a false sense of security. The sinking of the *Titanic* gave rise to a 'lifeboats-for-all' solution as it was felt that the lack of lifeboats led to the tragic death of many passengers. The US Congress passed a bill known as the LaFollette Seaman's Act, which mandated lifeboats to the extent of at least 75 per cent of passengers. But there were many design-related issues which did not receive the attention they required and which may have been the principal cause of the disaster in the first place. Another tragedy three years down the lane, when the *Eastland* ship toppled over in Chicago River and killed many passengers, revealed the short-sightedness of the response.

> [The *Eastland*] which had been designed to carry six lifeboats, was carrying 11 lifeboats, 37 life rafts (about 1,100 pounds each) and enough life jackets (about six pounds apiece) for all 2,570 passengers and crew. No tests were conducted to determine how the additional weight affected the boat's stability—even though it already had a troubled history. (Stranahan 2014)

The TBTF problem cannot also be solved through quick-fix solutions.

> Bankers understand the financial safety net—not as something external to their economic balance sheet—but as a politically enforceable implicit contract that they have negotiated with national governments. This contract allows governments to impose capital requirements in exchange for committing themselves to bail out large portions of the financial industry in crisis circumstances. (Kane 2012)

It is paramount to let the private sector know that it cannot be expected to be bailed out with taxpayers' money for its reckless behaviour. This cannot be achieved through moral persuasion alone. First and foremost, these entities should be adequately capitalized. There is a feeling that the post-crisis reforms have resulted in a well-capitalized banking system. Nothing could be farther from the truth. It would be useful to remind ourselves that at the peak of the crisis 'when tangible common equity is measured in a way that is more fit for purpose, the minimum risk–asset ratio requirement was about 1 per cent' (Tucker 2014), and '10 times better than hopelessly lax is not a useful measure' (Vickers 2017). Therefore, we may need three or four times more capital to feel safe. Second, as discussed before, a resolution regime to ensure orderly winding up of these institutions must be in place. Both these measures will ensure that if an entity is systemically important and it is in distress, either it has enough loss-absorbing capital as well as highly liquid assets to tide over the crisis or even if it has to be liquidated, there shall not be destabilizing impact on other financial institutions.

The crisis also revealed fault lines in the supervisory structure. For regulations to succeed, enforcement is a must. The discourse on crisis has been mostly about the inadequacies in the regulations and how to devise better regulations. However, evidence shows that even for countries with similar financial systems and regulations, the impact of the crisis has not been uniform and some countries were less affected. The answer as the IMF study reveals is 'better supervision' (Viñals and Fiechter 2010). Andrew Sheng was right when he said:

> Post-crisis, there is a belief, which I think is mistaken, that the more rules you put in place, the safer is the system. I am more inclined to believe the reverse is the case. Throughout history, enforcement, not regulation, of key red lines—egregious behaviour tackled early—is what prevents or mitigates a crisis.

There is a shift from compliance-based approach to risk-based approach. The crisis revealed serious shortcomings in the governance and risk management practices in regulated institutions. The regulations can only give a broad rule book on the kind of practices expected from the management. Supervisors have to ensure that they not only adhere to these rules in letter but also in spirit. As rule books become more complex with the implementation of Basel III, supervisors have to upgrade their skills to enforce the rules. Without strengthening the supervision, regulatory reforms cannot be implemented.

It is said that the present is pregnant with the future. The financial reforms since the onset of the crisis have made the financial system safe. However, it does not mean that financial crises will not happen in future. I may not stick my neck out and agree with Janet Yellen, when she said in 2017:

> Would I say there will never, ever be another financial crisis? You know, probably that would be going too far, but I do think we're much safer, and I hope that it will not be in our lifetimes, and I don't believe it will be.

But I do believe that the crisis of the magnitude of the financial crisis of 2007–2009 may not happen soon. It is important to distinguish between a crisis and a systemic crisis. For instance, the GFC of 2007–2009 was a systemic crisis, whereas the dotcom bubble of 1994–2000 was not a systemic crisis. It is the systemic crisis that leads to lasting damage and devastation to the real economy.

Having said that the financial system is safe, I venture to add that there are still elements of regulation that are pending and it may not be appropriate to declare victory and take a lap of honour. Basel III implementation is being carried out in a phased manner and it is too soon to judge its lasting impact. There are vulnerabilities in both the advanced and emerging economies, especially relating to debt growth. Many countries have non-financial sector debt-to-GDP ratio far exceeding historical averages. For example, the International Monetary Fund (IMF) in its report of 2016 forecast China's total non-financial sector debt to rise to almost 300 per cent of its GDP by 2022, from 242 per cent in 2015. Countries like India are witnessing asset quality problems in the banking sector that has a significant adverse impact on credit growth. On the other hand, there is strong headwind against tight regulations in the USA with the new administration seeking to undo many aspects of the Dodd–Frank Act. Therefore, while there are green shoots when it comes to regulatory reforms, it may be wise to remind us that achieving financial stability is often an elusive objective and it requires policy coordination at both the national and international levels. This is a key theme I intend to focus in the coming chapters as without coordination among all stakeholders, achieving any long-lasting stability will be difficult. While policymakers are always fighting the last crisis and regulations alone cannot absolutely prevent future crises, it is important to recognize that governments, central banks and other regulators, through better and strong regulations and implementation, can reduce the system's vulnerability to manias, panics and crashes. The goal of financial sector reforms, as Larry Summers says, is to 'make the system safe for failure'. The failure of individual institutions is a given; the objective of the policymakers is to build enough shock absorbers so that the majority of firms withstand the initial shock as well as the aftershock, to borrow an analogy from dealing with earthquakes, thereby limiting the damage to the system. Therefore, we need more capital, less leverage, good-quality liquid assets and stable funding sources. Equally important would be to take stock of past mistakes and analyse them. It would be worthwhile to take a leaf out of the medical profession when designing reforms. Fallible human beings, whether those running the institutions or those supervising, are bound to make mistakes. As Atul Gawande writes in his fascinating book *Complications: A Surgeon's Notes on an Imperfect Science* about the human endeavour in medicine, 'No matter what measures are taken, doctors will sometimes falter, and it isn't reasonable to ask that we achieve perfection. What is reasonable is to ask that we never cease to aim for it.' I'm sure this resonates well with the regulators too. Gawande cites the importance of applying lessons learned from other professions and other ways of thinking. The practice of morbidity and mortality reviews every week to go over the mistakes may be a good lesson for those in finance and economics to practice.

The next financial crisis may not come from the same roots as the present one. It could emanate from some other corner of the world. In an increasingly interconnected global financial system, it is worthwhile to remember that 'We are all connected through the fingers of instability' (Mauldin and Tepper 2014). The lessons from the GFC are also testimony to the saying that 'History doesn't repeat itself but it often rhymes'. Many of the crisis responses had their roots in the wisdom of forgotten economists and policymakers. Bagehot,

Keynes and Minsky are just a few of the dead economists who came to life as policymakers searched for appropriate policy response. In fact, as far back as 1986, Hyman Minsky in his now famous 'Financial Instability Hypothesis' provided evidence that financial system has a natural inclination towards instability. Unfortunately, no one heeded his message as 'it was wholly out of kilter with the then-prevailing zeitgeist' (Dombret 2017).

A robust financial system is essential for economic well-being of people. The crisis exposed many cracks in the financial system and its adverse consequences are being felt even today. The post-crisis regulatory reforms can only succeed if we strengthen prudential oversight and ultimately, behaviour and governance in the private sector. There is already evidence that the crisis is fading into oblivion, at least in some quarters. This book is an attempt to keep the crisis firmly in our memory as we chart a new period of stability.

As mentioned, the book discusses the genesis of the GFC, the developments post-GFC and a forward-looking recommendation about the order of world from now on.

While Chapter 1 deals with the regulatory reforms that took place for strengthening of the capital, liquidity, ring fencing of banks and resolution plans post the financial crisis, Chapter 2 discusses other structural regulatory reforms that were necessitated post the crisis.

Chapter 3 provides an in-depth insight into various sources of systemic risk and provides a framework to manage systemic risk by enhanced macroprudential regulation and its coordination with monetary policy authority. Chapter 4 delves into the importance of early warning mechanism in predicting the crisis, thereby helping in preparedness to prevent the crisis. Chapter 5 provides an insight into the importance of stress-testing at macro level by financial sector supervisors and central banks, thereby helping to identify the weakest link and preparing adequate cushion for an uncertain stressful event. Chapter 6 further provides for various tools for macroprudential regulations that can be adopted by the policymaking institutions. Chapter 7 provides a standard operating procedure/policy toolkit for possible response to a potential financial crisis. Chapters 8–10 deal with coordination in policymaking wherein a case for better coordination among global financial policymaking institutions is envisaged. While Chapter 8 reviews the dynamics of coordination mechanisms in place in between policymaking institutions and the various lessons that can be learnt from such coordination mechanisms, Chapters 9 and 10 list possible challenges to global coordination and various approaches to improve such attempts for coordination. The Epilogue lists down potential risks in the financial sector lurking before the central banks to deal with.

References

Blanchard, Olivier, and Larry Summers. 2017, 8 October. *Rethinking Stabilization Policy: Back to the Future.* Available at https://piie.com/system/files/documents/blanchard-summers20171012paper.pdf (accessed on 18 January 2019).

Cunliffe, Jon. 2017, September. *Ten Years On: Lessons from Northern Rock.* Available at https://www.bis.org/review/r170929d.htm (accessed on 18 January 2019).

Dombret, Andreas. 2017. *Too Little, Too Much, or Just Right? Reforming Banking Regulation after the Financial Crisis.* Available at https://www.bis.org/review/r171206b.htm (accessed on 18 January 2019).

Dudley, William C. 2017. *Lessons from the Financial Crisis.* Available at https://www.bis.org/review/r171107b.htm (accessed on 18 January 2019).

Geithner, Tim. 2014. *Stress Test: Reflections on Financial Crisis.* New York: Broadway Books.

Gorton, Gary. 2009. May. *Slapped in the Face by the Invisible Hand: Banking and the Panic of 2007.* Available at http://citeseerx.ist.psu.edu/viewdoc/download?doi=10.1.1.189.1320&rep=rep1&type=pdf (accessed on 18 January 2019).

Kane, Edward J. 2012, January. *Bankers and Brokers First: Loose Ends in the Theory of Central-Bank Policymaking.* Available at https://www2.bc.edu/edward-kane/Bankers%20and%20Brokers%20First.pdf (accessed on 18 January 2019).

Mauldin, John, and Jonathan Tepper. 2014, January. *Endgame: The End of the Debt Supercycle and How It Changes Everything.* Hoboken, NJ: John Wiley & Sons.

Solow, Robert. 2010, January. 'Hedging America'. *The New Republic.* Available at https://newrepublic.com/article/72405/hedging-america (accessed on 18 January 2019).

Stranahan, Susan Q. 2014. *The Eastland Disaster Killed More Passengers than the Titanic and the Lusitania. Why Has It Been Forgotten?* Available at https://www.smithsonianmag.com/history/eastland-disaster-killed-more-passengers-titanic-and-lusitania-why-has-it-been-forgotten-180953146/ (accessed on 18 January 2019).

Tirole, Jean, Jean-Charles Rochet, and Mathias Dewatripont. *Balancing the Banks: Global Lessons from the Financial Crisis* 2010. Princeton University Press.

Tucker, Paul. 2014. *Capital Regulation in the New World: The Political Economy of Regime Change.* Available at http://paultucker.me/wp-content/uploads/2014/08/Yale-School-of-Managment-Program-on-Financial-Stability.pdf (accessed on 18 January 2019).

Vickers, John. 2017. *Banking Reform Nine Years On.* Available at https://voxeu.org/article/banking-reform-nine-years (accessed on 18 January 2019).

Viñals, Jose, and Jonathan Fiechter. 2010. *The Making of Good Supervision: Learning to Say 'No'.* IMF Staff Position Note. Available at https://www.imf.org/external/pubs/ft/spn/2010/spn1008.pdf (accessed on 18 January 2019).

Yellen, Janet. 2017, 25 August. *Financial Stability a Decade after the Onset of the Crisis.* Available at https://www.federalreserve.gov/newsevents/speech/yellen20170825a.htm (accessed on 18 January 2019).

Part I

Post-Crisis Financial Regulatory Reforms

The financial crisis that began in summer of 2007 was an extraordinarily complex event with multiple causes.

—Ben Bernanke

CHAPTER 1

Strengthening Capital and Liquidity Requirements

The Global Financial Crisis (GFC) of 2007–2008 highlighted the weaknesses in the financial system and brought forward the need for a revamp of the entire financial system to address the evolving risks and vulnerabilities and to ensure that the system can withstand future crises. Ben Bernanke summarized the financial crisis as an extraordinary complex event with multiple causes. The financial system was strengthened by establishment of the Financial Stability Board (FSB) in April 2009 at the initiative of G20. One of the major post-crisis reforms included strengthening of the capital and liquidity standards in financial institutions with a focus on increasing both the quality and quantity of the available capital in them. While these reforms have strengthened the institutions, few areas needed a relook such as assigning risk weights to various assets classes and few lacunae which existed amidst the liquidity regulations. Though significant progress has been made by financial institutions in improving both the quality and quantity of capital and liquidity leading to a safer financial system, there have been talks to reduce the aforesaid additional regulatory burden. The regulatory authorities should not give in to such pressures. The cross-border financial institutions were at the centre of the crisis and considering the gaps in regulating these financial institutions by national supervisors, supervisory colleges may be established for better coordination and regulation of these institutions.

Introduction

The financial crisis of 2007–2008, also known as the GFC, which is considered to be the worst financial crisis since the Great Depression of the 1930s by many economists, brought to the fore gross inadequacies in the regulatory framework and unsatisfactory supervision of financial institutions and financial infrastructure. What started as a sub-prime mortgage lending crisis in the US financial markets accentuated into a catastrophic international banking crisis. This came into prominence with the bankruptcy of Lehman Brothers, a major investment bank. The other investment banks and financial institutions started collapsing one by one, which magnified the financial impact globally. By the end of 2008, the crisis further aggravated leading to high volatility and crash of equity markets around the globe, leading to sinking of consumer confidence. The crisis that played in the form of the global economic downturn was known as the Great Recession. The harm that started in the financial sector spread to the real sector and between November 2008 and April 2009, the US economy lost, on an average, 700,000 jobs per month and with a total loss of around 900,000 jobs, the unemployment rate rose to more than 10 per cent. The home prices, on which the pre-crisis exuberance rode, also declined by about 30 per cent on average nationally. This resulted in nearly 8 million foreclosures, and the homeownership rate declined to levels last seen in the pre-late 1980s. This spurred a massive bailout programme for the financial institutions through various monetary and fiscal measures (Dudley 2017). The crisis was later followed by a crisis in the banking system of the European countries known as the Euro Debt Crisis. Fiscal authorities around the world struggled to rescue giant financial institutions on the verge of collapse as many financial institutions continued to face serious liquidity issues during this period.

Entire revamp of the financial system was the need of the hour then. The financial institutions needed to be strengthened in many ways in order to be able to withstand or overcome any future crises. A menu of dynamic regulatory stipulations was required to constantly address the evolving risks and vulnerabilities in the system. At this juncture, the FSB was established in April 2009 at the initiative of the G20 as the successor to the FSF[1] with a broad mandate to promote financial stability. The FSB has a unique composition among international bodies, as it is an apex body of senior policymakers of finance ministries, central banks, as well as financial supervisory and regulatory authorities from the G20 countries, along with four other key countries—Hong Kong, Singapore, Spain and Switzerland. Additionally, it included international standard-setting bodies along with regional bodies such as the European Central Bank and European Commission, and international financial institutions, such as the BIS, the IMF, the OECD, and the World Bank. The FSB[2] has six regional consultative groups (RCGs), enabling it to reach out to 24 member countries and 73 other representatives and ensuring coordination within a wide diaspora of emerging market and developing economies (EMDEs). Its operation was based on a three-stage process which included systemic risk identification in the financial sector, framing policy actions to address these risks and overseeing responses in terms of implementation of these policy measures. Apart from FSB, the Basel Committee on Banking Supervision (BCBS) is another important body. The BCBS sets the global standards for the prudential regulation and supervision of banks in addition to a regular cooperation forum. It has 45 members that comprise central bankers and supervisors from 28 jurisdictions. The key reforms/standards suggested by

---

[1] FSF was founded in 1999 by the G7 finance ministers and central bank governors for enhancing cooperation among the various national and international supervisory bodies and international financial institutions so as to promote stability in the international financial system.

[2] It has dedicated itself to in a coordinated manner 'identify and address issues that span financial products, intermediaries, and markets; and to avoid the pre-crisis regulatory fragmentation that left financial stability risks unaddressed. The relevance of this platform, to its members and to a changing financial system, is critical to preserving our last 10 years of hard-earned gains'. Quarles, Randal K. (2019), 'The Future of Banking: The Human Factor' Speech at Brussels, Belgium, 2 April.

the FSB and the BCBS that are being implemented currently by 27 member countries include standards on capital and liquidity, and are discussed in this chapter.

Capital and Liquidity Standards

The lessons from the crisis brought to light the inadequate and poor quality of capital held by banks as buffer against losses. The low level of good-quality bank capital necessitated the taxpayers to bail out the banks in distress. The gaps in the risk assessment framework, lacunae in market risk assessment in trading book, excessive reliance on credit rating agencies and/or on internal models, etc., resulted in underestimation of risk and contributed to the precipitation of the crisis. Two major things which came to light during the crisis in respect of trading book exposures were: (a) manifold losses in the trading books as against that computed by the extant value at risk (VaR) models and (b) most losses arose on account of valuation losses due to credit quality deterioration rather than outright defaults. This resulted in the expansion of risk coverage in the new Basel III regulations, especially covering the trading book and those related to counterparties.

Basel III capital adequacy standards with the aim of building more resilient banks and banking systems have not only increased the requirements of quantity of capital but have also laid emphasis on the quality of capital. The focus is on the higher quality capital, namely the Common Equity Tier 1 (CET1) capital in the form of equity and retained earnings. Standards have been put in place to ensure that other types of capital instruments, Additional Tier 1 (AT1) and Tier 2 (AT2), are also truly loss absorbing. They also prescribe higher risk weightages on counterparty exposures, removal of regulatory gaps which helped banks avoid booking losses on their holdings of marketable securities, imposition of capital conservation buffer (CCB) which may be built up during good times and drawn down during stress periods and a framework of countercyclical capital buffer (CCCB) to address procyclicality and to prepare for plausible downturns. The capital framework also prescribes additional capital holding mainly in the form of CET1 capital for banks classified as global systemically important banks (G-SIBs).

Minimum capital requirements remain unchanged at 8 per cent of risk-weighted assets (RWAs) but the stipulation for CET1—the highest quality capital—is 4.5 per cent as compared to only 2 per cent earlier under Basel II. In addition to 8 per cent, banks should keep another 2.5 per cent as CCB in the form of CET1. A CCCB varying from 0 to 2.5 per cent in the nature of CET1 is also required to be built up in the expansionary phase of the financial cycle, if the regulators perceive that the economy is overheating and leading to an unacceptable built-up of systemic risks. Banks designated as too big to fail (TBTF) and systemically important, that is, G-SIBs, are required to maintain a capital surcharge, in the nature of CET1 ranging between 1 per cent and 3.5 per cent. A 1.5 per cent AT1 equity and 2 per cent AT2 (hybrid) forms of capital have also been mandated making the capital requirement to increase to 13 per cent for most banks and to 16.5 per cent for the G-SIBs, if both the capital buffers are accounted for. In addition, the loss absorbency of AT1 and AT2 capital instruments have also been enhanced by inserting a clause that requires them to either be converted to common shares or written down at specified triggers. The implementation of Basel III that started in 2013 is expected to be complete by 2019 across various jurisdictions. BCBS also ensured the implementation of the principle of jurisdictional reciprocity while applying CCCBs. Foreign supervisors are required to apply at least the same additional capital buffers imposed by the host supervisor to their banks' lending to the host country. The objective is to ensure that all banks operate on a level playing field when lending to entities in the host country.

In July 2013, the Federal Reserve, the Office of the Comptroller of the Currency (OCC) and the Federal Deposit Insurance Corporation (FDIC) approved the final rules for implementation of the Basel III capital framework which required the minimum Tier 1 capital ratio to be raised to 6 per cent of RWAs from the existing 4 per cent along with a new minimum CET1 capital ratio of 4.5 per cent. For the G-SIBs, an additional capital surcharge was mandated.

The European Union (EU) has also issued similar Capital Requirements Directive 'CRD 4 package' and the Capital Requirements Regulation (CRR) to implement Basel III stipulations with effect from 1 January 2014 largely based on Basel guidelines. The

UK also proposes to apply a systemic risk buffer of 3 per cent on all the major UK banks, which will ensure that the prescribed minimum CET1 capital ratio is 10 per cent. Further, it also intends to introduce more stringent large exposure limits, sector-specific risk weightages, disclosure requirements, etc., on all or a subset of banks.

But as was first revealed during the Long-Term Capital Management (LTCM) blow-up and again in the Northern Rock episode, focus on adequacy of capital may not eliminate the problem of excessive leverage. Many commercial and investment banks since 2003 saw excessive increase in their leverage even though they continued to be compliant with the capital adequacy requirement. But if they were so heavily leveraged, were they really capital compliant? A closer look at these banks revealed serious deficiencies in their risk measurement methodologies and models.

RWA—The Denominator in the Capital Adequacy Ratio Being Subject to Manipulation?

BCBS observed in its thematic assessments of banks' RWA that banks used the loopholes in the risk-weighted capital adequacy frameworks stipulated under both Basel I and Basel II to manipulate the system. As observed by Stefan Ingves of Riksbank, Sweden (November 2014),

> the banks' risk-weighted assets differ to an extent that goes well beyond what can be explained by business models and historical experiences. If we just take the banking-book results, two banks with exactly the same assets could report capital ratios that differ by as much as 4 percentage points.

The ratio was made to look adequate by lowering the figures of the RWA in the denominator rather than by increasing the quantum of capital in the numerator. The irony was that banks continued to work with the same level of capital even as they accumulated more and more risky assets by devising ways to reduce their risk weights. For example, in Sweden, the risk weights for retail mortgages which stood at 50 per cent during the last 20 years or so was reduced to 35 per cent and further to as low as 6 per cent with the adoption of internal ratings-based (IRB) approach under Basel II which gave the banks the discretion to decide the risk weights of their assets as per the results of their own models.

> In equity terms, this means that instead of SEK 17,000 of their own equity to fund a mortgage of 1 million, banks' models implied that SEK 1,200 was good enough. In retrospect, it is clear that the decrease in risk weights did not reflect actual risks and banks therefore needed more capital. (Ingves 2014)

The practice was rampant in major global banks who redesigned their risk models to underestimate the risk and provide optimistic asset valuations to show lower requirements of capital. The intention was clear: to earn more by expanding assets base without deploying more capital. But this business strategy which compromised prudent behaviour proved dangerous once the financial crisis unravelled.

Thus, RWA far outpaced the level of capital that funded them. For a sample of G-SIBs, while the RWA saw a twelve-fold increase from $2.6 trillion to over $30 trillion from 1993 to 2008, the capital increased by only seven-fold from $125 billion to $890 billion. This showed a trend of decline in the average risk weight from 70 per cent to below 40 per cent even while it was well known to one and all that the risk existed in the system and with the use of complex and opaque products it was only increasing and not reducing. The entire exercise of reporting and maintaining risk-weighted capital ratios including inter-bank comparison was thus becoming increasingly suspect (Ingves 2014).

Though the new Basel III international capital rules have sufficiently enhanced the loss absorbing capacity of banks by stipulating higher quantum of good quality capital, the extant system of risk weights has not been changed and does not adequately distinguish between higher risk and lower risk, thus incentivizing the bank to opt for riskier investments thereby encouraging to leverage their positions in excess of the equity invested (i.e., if a significant proportion of assets are categorized as low-risk weights). Basel III-related proposals are criticized based on the flaws related to low equity levels, system of risk weights adding distortions and availability of poor quality substitutes (Admati 2015).

The GFC brought forth a list of shortcomings related to the IRB models being used by the banks for capital computations such as excessive complexity, lack of comparability and not so robust modelling. To address these shortcomings, the Basel III High level Committee in December 2017 made the following revisions to the IRB approaches: (a) removed the option to use the advanced IRB (A-IRB) approach for certain asset classes; (b) adopted 'input' floors (for metrics such as probabilities of default (PD) and loss-given-default [LGD]) to ensure a minimum level of conservatism in model parameters for asset classes where the IRB approaches remain available; and (c) provided greater specification of parameter estimation practices to reduce RWA variability. The revisions have been carried out with a view to restore RWA calculation credibility and enhance robustness and risk sensitiveness of the models. For example, as per the Basel II standardized approach, exposure to banks had a flat risk weight. However, in Basel III the risk weights are linked to the capital adequacy ratio of the counterparty bank.

Capital Floors—Additional Layer to Uphold Quality of Capital

The BCBS is simultaneously conceptualizing another measure, namely capital floors, to further ensure that the level of capital across the banking system does not fall below a certain level. A risk-weighted capital floor implies that regulatory floors would be stipulated for risk weights of such classes of assets for which the banks are permitted to use IRB approaches to arrive at their internal risk weights. This is presently work-in-progress primarily aimed at addressing issues referred to as 'RWA inconsistency and dispersion', 'low level of models-based RWAs' and 'horizontal inequity in risk-weighted capital requirements', etc. The capital floors are thus expected to enhance the efficacy of risk-weighted capital adequacy framework and make it stronger. The

BCBS has designed a set of floors to limit how low the banks' risk weights can fall by the usage of risk models. In this way, one also limits how low their capital requirements can be (Ingves 2016). Together the two—leverage ratio and capital adequacy framework—would instil confidence in the regulatory capital framework. The BCBS has published the final standard on capital floors, including its calibration and implementation arrangements in December 2017. An output floor designed to minimize the deviation of internally modelled capital from simpler approaches has been set at 72.5 per cent. Banks using internal models will not be allowed to let their estimates for RWAs fall below 72.5 per cent of the level implied by the standardized approach. These output floors will be introduced at an initial level of 50 per cent in 2022 and then gradually rise over the following five years. National supervisors have the discretion to impose the rules earlier if they choose. Using these output floors along with leverage ratio will make the regulatory system robust against manipulations.

Leverage Ratio—The Risk–free Backstop

Excessive on-balance and off-balance sheet (OBS) leverage and severe liquidity mismatches in the banking sector revealed deep vulnerability in the financial system. Financial institutions leveraged themselves to the hilt (as much as 40 dollars of debt to 1 dollar of equity) and had severe mismatches in liquidity (Menon 2017). To address this, the BCBS proposed a leverage ratio for international banks. This ratio is calculated as the amount of capital held by the bank divided by the amount of exposure of the bank. Exposure is the sum of (a) on-balance sheet exposures; (b) derivative exposures; (c) securities financing transaction (SFT) exposures and (d) OBS items, irrespective of the risk-weighting of all these assets. It is essentially a risk-free ratio. The intent is to capture all risks, both on and OBS, for which the bank is liable.

While on one hand, this ratio aims to help contain the build-up of excessive leverage in the banking system, on the other hand, it acts as a disincentive for banks to indulge in dubious ways of RWA reduction and the resultant lower capital requirements. Even if they use such methods, awarding unrealistically low internal risk ratings to riskier assets, shifting risks from banking book to trading book or OBS where capital requirement is relatively lower; the leverage ratio would constrain their growth as it is intended to act as a complimentary backstop to the capital adequacy framework. However, leverage ratio in itself is not a panacea for all evils. A more effective and improvised capital adequacy framework is also required simultaneously. 'Having a leverage ratio as one single rule will offer banks misplaced incentives to take greater risks' (Weidmann 2014). Derivatives trading (particularly credit derivatives) and securities financing business transactions are likely to be most impacted by the new leverage ratio framework, followed by lending commitments on the retail and wholesale side and trade finance. Banks are generally induced to hold a buffer over the minimum requirement on account of uncertainties during good times and deleveraging of the balance sheet during bad times. BCBS, while finalizing the Basel III reforms, prescribes that the leverage ratio G-SIB buffer must be met with Tier 1 capital and is set at 50 per cent of a G-SIB's risk-weighted higher loss absorbency requirements. For example, a G-SIB subject to a 2 per cent risk-weighted higher loss absorbency requirement would be subject to a 1 per cent leverage ratio buffer requirement. This requirement shall come into effect from 1 January 2022.

The USA has, however, proposed a stricter leverage ratio requirement of 5 per cent for bank holding companies (BHCs) with more than US$700 billion in assets or US$10 trillion in assets. Bank subsidiaries of such BHCs would similarly face a well-capitalized leverage ratio threshold of 6 per cent to be applied from 2018.[3] Meanwhile, the EU is still considering possible differentiation of the leverage ratio by business models, size or systemic relevance; though a recent report recommends introduction of a 'LR minimum' to mitigate the risk of excessive leverage. Their stress-testing framework is different in the context of use of CET1 capital in place of total Tier 1 capital as the capital measure for gauging the leverage ratio. Accordingly, in Switzerland, the major banks will be required to meet a minimum

---

[3] The applicable accounting standards in the USA allow for more netting of OBS exposures, and hence these figures are not directly comparable with the 3 per cent Basel III requirements.

leverage ratio of around 4.3 per cent by 2019. The leverage ratio framework in the UK comprises three key elements: the minimum Basel III leverage requirement of 3 per cent and two macroprudential buffers as add-ons additional leverage ratio buffer (ALRB) and countercyclical leverage ratio buffer (CCLB), both of which will apply to the systemically important banks at 35 per cent of a bank's applicable risk-weighted requirements and buffers (Rule 2015). Financial CHOICE Act of 2017, passed by the USA in June 2017, introduces yet another leverage ratio definition (average leverage ratio), which is defined as the 'average of the banking organization's quarterly leverage ratios for each of the most recently completed four calendar quarters'. As brought out by the IMF, this technically resembles a 4-quarter, moving average supplementary leverage ratio (SLR). Further, the denominator of this SLR has also been narrowed down, limiting the definition of leverage exposure by removing cash deposited with central banks, US treasuries and initial margin for derivatives (Chami et al. 2017).

The Federal Reserve has developed a capital stress-testing supervisory programme—known as the Comprehensive Capital Analysis and Review (CCAR) which has become integral for capital level assessments. The CCAR is forward-looking capital assessment and helps protect the safety and soundness of the largest financial institutions and the entire financial system. The CCAR does a quantitative and qualitative evaluation on the capital buffer of financial institution so that it continues to be a viable financial intermediary in stressed market conditions and whether risk management and capital planning processes are well developed and well governed, respectively. Even though the CCAR strengthened the capital levels and improved risk management and capital planning process of the largest financial institutions (Dudley 2017), the US Treasury in June 2017 recommended, among other things, changing the frequency and the severity of the Fed's process of stress-testing the strength of the big banks, scrapping the 'gold plating' of global capital and liquidity standards for the largest US lenders and implementing a looser interpretation of the Volcker rule ban on banks making speculative bets with their own capital, which was criticized by Stanley Fischer, vice-chair of Fed Reserve as 'very dangerous and a terrible mistake' (Fischer 2017).

New Liquidity Adequacy Norms

As the financial crisis unfolded, it also came to the light that the banks were operating with very thin liquidity buffers. In fact, not only were their liquidity buffers inadequate in relation to the maturity mismatch risk which they were carrying on their balance sheet, more and more of their long-term assets had been financed by much shorter term liabilities. The operating assumption that markets would be liquid and be able to finance long-term assets with lesser duration liabilities resulted in repurchase agreements to triple in amount between 2001 and 2007 with particularly high growth in overnight repos which provided a prelude to the impending disaster.

A financial sector funding long-term asset in search of yield with short-term liabilities will suffer serious financial consequences if the long-term assets suffer a significant correction in their market value, which may lead to liquidity issues for short-term markets eventually leading to the solvency issues for weak banks. The initial manifestation of the GFC in mid-2007 was the drying up of liquidity in short-term money markets that resulted in severe funding problems at various banks, the classic example of which was the Northern Rock in the UK which experienced a run on its deposits in September 2007. This was the first major casualty of the GFC which saw the demise of many financial institutions and a first in the UK since 1878. Almost all the central banks of the world used their emergency liquidity adjustment (ELA) facilities to salvage the situations at their end. The extreme liquidity freeze experienced during the crisis and the subsequent use of ELA facilities was an eye-opener of sorts for the central banking community.

It was not as if the central banks didn't know that appropriate collateralized central bank liquidity support is required for solvent banks to contain the perils of bank/liquidity runs, but they had faith in the capabilities of the commercial bankers in maintaining such buffers on their own—a faith which was shattered during the GFC. The GFC revealed that the banks kept the buffer much lesser than what was optimal in favour of its more gainful deployment for increased earnings. When the banks failed in their task, the regulators had to step in. The result was the stipulation of the liquidity ratios—a short-term liquidity coverage ratio (LCR) to withstand a 30-day crisis; and a long-term net stable funding ratio (NSFR) to reduce the inherent maturity mismatch in banks' balance sheets over a one-year horizon under the Basel III regulations. LCR requires banks to hold sufficient high-quality liquid assets (HQLAs)—a kind of self-insurance against liquidity risks that can be easily and quickly converted into cash to cover expected liquidity outflows in a stress scenario over a 30-day period. NSFR is intended to reduce funding risk over a longer time horizon by requiring bank to fund their activities with sufficient stable sources of funding. NSFR became a minimum standard on 1 January 2018.

Stringent Liquidity Standards— Implementation Issues

To achieve their LCR standard, banks are required to hold HQLAs in the form of mainly sovereign security and high-quality corporate papers that are 'traded in large, deep and active repo or cash markets'. However, implementation bottlenecks were felt in jurisdictions such as Australia, South Africa and Norway where government securities were relatively limited in supply and often locked away in long-term invest-ment portfolios. A way out for such jurisdictions was suggested in the form of alternative liquidity arrangements (ALAs) such as committed liquidity facility (CLF) which served as a positive move in creating liquidity provisions during a crisis. For example, on 12 December 2007, the US Federal Reserve announced the establishment of FX swap lines with the ECB and the Swiss National Bank to provide up to $24 billion. Additionally, a Term Auction Facility was established for depository institutions who were considered financially sound by their regulators under the primary credit discount window to borrow against a wide variety of collateral. These measures were taken considering the interruption in the inter-bank markets to ensure that the foreign banks remained dollar liquid which was of paramount importance.

The regulators in US Federal Reserve Board (FRB), FDIC and the OCC in October 2013 proposed to create two sets of liquidity standards—one for all internationally active banking organizations (with \$250 billion or more in total consolidated assets or \$10 billion or more in foreign exposure) and all systemically important non-bank financial institutions and the other for the US banking organizations with \$50 billion or more in consolidated assets. The former obviously was more stringent than the latter. In addition, the Federal Reserve adopted the Comprehensive Liquidity Analysis and Review (CLAR) supervisory programme for evaluating the liquidity of the most systemic banking firms. Liquidity positions within the US banking system have improved substantially since the financial crisis. The US G-SIBs increased their holdings of HQLA from about \$1.5 trillion to about \$2.3 trillion between 2011 and the first quarter of 2017. Corresponding to this increase, these institutions reduced reliance on short-term funding from approximately 35 per cent of assets in 2006 to about 15 per cent of assets as on 2017 (Powell 2017). Both the USA and the EU have stipulated shorter transition periods (as compared to Basel timelines) for achieving the stipulated LCR: the US by 2017 and the EU by 2018, with the LCR directly jumping from 80 per cent in 2017 to 100 per cent in 2018 in the EU. In the UK, Prudential Regulation Authority (PRA) has been asked by the Financial Policy Committee to consider whether there is need for additional liquidity requirements to supplement the LCR on systemic grounds.

Lacunae in the Basel Liquidity Regulation

A few lacunae, however, still remain in the Basel Liquidity Regulation, the most significant being the absence of a regulatory charge stipulation for a bank's use of overnight funding to fund liabilities that mature in less than 30 days. This gives rise to a significant maturity mismatch within the most critical 30-day LCR window itself. This gap has been plugged by the USA by prescribing a regulatory charge on maturity mismatch within the 30-day period. Another major shortcoming of the Basel guidelines on liquidity which calls for an urgent amendment is the calculation of the two ratios, LCR and NSFR, on a fully consolidated basis. There may be a situation where liquidity risk may manifest itself in one part of the organization while the liquidity needed to deal with that stress is trapped in another. US regulators have addressed this shortcoming also by restricting a holding company to include in its consolidated liquidity provisions, only such qualifying assets as held by a subsidiary of the US bank, in excess of the amount of the projected net cash outflows and that can be transferred to the holding company without any contractual, supervisory, regulatory and statutory restrictions.

Another area that needs to be looked into by the BCBS are the impact of LCR and NSFR on account of significant forex transactions being undertaken by certain banks and financial institutions. A research paper by the Swiss Financial Market Supervisory Authority (Pohl 2017) has pointed out certain potential shortcomings in the LCR and NSFR. The LCR's and NSFR's possible shortcomings are the focus on the respective time horizons as disruptions may well be encountered beyond these points.

Assessment and supervision of foreign currency mismatches have been addressed by a number of BCBS publications. The core principles for effective banking supervision supplement it by stating that the supervisor should identify banks that carry out significant foreign currency liquidity transformation. This could be supplemented by undertaking a separate analysis of liquidity and a corresponding strategy. This will lead to the identification of potential currency mismatches, especially so for banks in emerging countries as these country currencies are more volatile and illiquid (generally this is applicable to each market in crisis). Furthermore, for countries with insufficient HQLA in the home currency LCR, the metric also reveals the extent of reliance on foreign currency-based HQLA.

The alternative liquidity arrangements (ALA) have three predefined options for countries with insufficient HQLA in their home currency, namely contractual committed liquidity facilities from the central bank, consideration of foreign currency HQLA and/or consideration of additional Level 2 assets above the usual cap that can be granted to the banks. The extent of banks' reliance on the ALA option may not be established if a separate LCR in home currency is not possible due to the absence of effective monitoring of lack of HQLA in home currency.

Position of Compliance of Basel Standards— Satisfactory and Inspiring Confidence

The Basel III framework includes the following phase-in provisions for capital ratios:

- Regulatory adjustments (i.e., possibly stricter sets of deductions that apply under Basel III) fully phased in by 1 January 2018;
- An additional 2.5 per cent CCB above the regulatory minimum capital ratios, which must be met with CET1 capital, will be phased in by 1 January 2019; and
- The additional loss absorbency requirement for G-SIBs, which ranges from 1.0 per cent to 2.5 per cent, will be fully phased in by 1 January 2019. It will be applied as an extension of the CCB and must be met with CET1.

The assessment of the impact and its monitoring is very important for an effective implementation. BCBS monitors the effects and dynamics of the reforms through a semi-annual monitoring framework based on risk-based capital ratio, the leverage ratio and the liquidity metrics using data of representative samples of national supervisors.

Supplementing its semi-annual monitoring as above, BCBS has also formulated a Regulatory Consistency Assessment Programme (RCAP) through which it periodically monitors the timely and consistent adoption of Basel standards across members. The monitoring, which was initially focused on the Basel III risk-based capital requirements, has since expanded to cover all Basel III standards that will become effective by 2019. The progress in the compliance to these guidelines had about two-thirds of its members being compliant or largely compliant with the Basel standards on risk weights (Ingves 2018). Further, as of end-September 2017, substantial progress was made in compliance of guidelines on LCR and capital conservation.

As of end-September 2018, all 27 BCBS member jurisdictions (Basel Committee on Banking Supervision 2018) have risk-based capital rules, LCR regulations and CCBs in force. Twenty-six-member jurisdictions have also finalized and implemented rules for the CCCBs and domestic systemically important bank (DSIB) requirements. With regard to the G-SIB requirements, all members who are home jurisdictions to G-SIBs have final rules in force. The level of compliance, however, varies across countries. In India also, Basel III risk-based capital regulations as well as the guidelines on LCR and NSFR have been adopted. The phase in of all these except NSFR is expected to complete in 2019. Only 10 of 27 jurisdictions have final rules for NSFR.

Similarly, non-Basel Committee jurisdictions also reported substantial progress in adopting Basel III standards. As per the annual review of progress undertaken by the Financial Stability Institute (FSI)—out of the 109 surveyed jurisdictions, 94 have either implemented Basel II or are in the process of doing so. With respect to Basel III, 89 have implemented the framework or are in the process of doing so.

Insufficient progress recorded in few jurisdictions of NSFR is making some members delay their own processes of implementation. Delayed implementation may put unnecessary pressures on jurisdictions that have implemented or plan to implement the standards based on the agreed timelines, thereby leading to an unfair playing field.

Capital Adequacy and Liquidity: Improving Both in Terms of Quantity and Quality

Since the implementation of the guidelines for strengthening the capital and liquidity, the high-quality capital held by banks has improved steadily. For instance, the eight most systemically important US BHCs have increased by almost $500 billion in 2014, almost double the capital held in 2009 (Yellen 2015). Similarly, the HQLA held by these eight firms have increased by roughly one-third since 2012. Substantial improvement was also observed in common equity capital with more stable funding positions. The health of community banks has improved significantly with about more than 95 per cent of them becoming profitable (Yellen 2016). Similar developments were observed in the UK as well where the capital requirements and buffers had increased at least seven-fold (Rule 2015) in respect of the major banks. Since 2011, the Tier 1 leverage ratio of major internationally active banks has increased by over 65 per cent (from 3.5% to 5.8%), while their CET1 risk-weighted ratio has increased by over 70 per cent (from 7.2% to 12.3%). The bulk of this change was achieved by an increase in banks' CET1 capital resources (from €2.1 trillion to €3.7 trillion). There has also been a corresponding reinforcement of banks' liquidity: holdings of liquid assets have increased by 30 per cent (from €9.2 trillion to €11.6 trillion; Ingves 2018).

Most large internationally active banks now meet the Basel III risk-based capital requirements, including the CCB, even though those rules are not mandatory in full to be met till 2019. But what is more commendable is that the banks have achieved this primarily by accumulating retained earnings (Caruana 2014). In India, due to asset quality levels going down for many of public sector banks, capital levels have depleted during the recent years. Therefore, many of such banks do not meet CCB requirements. However, the regulations in India continue to be more conservative than that of most countries.

Similarly, minimum stipulation for the LCR has been exceeded and the NSFR adherence is on track. All internationally active banks meet the fully phased-in liquidity standards, that is, both the LCR and NSFR, ahead of the 2019 deadline. BCBS in 2018 also started assessing the consistency of implementation of the NSFR and the LEX framework by assessing the implementation in Saudi Arabia and found it compliant with Basel standards. It is planned to complete this review for all member jurisdictions by September 2020.

In the Basel III Monitoring Report of March 2019,[4] published by the BCBS at BIS, which gives position as on end-June 2018 (which is the latest), it was revealed that all Group 1 and Group 2 banks (including all 29 G-SIBs) would meet the CET1 minimum capital requirement of 4.5 per cent and the CET1 target level of 7.0 per cent (i.e. including the capital conservation buffer). Similarly, the average Common Equity Tier 1 (CET1) capital ratio under the fully

---

[4] Data were provided for a total of 189 banks, including 106 large internationally active (Group 1) banks, among them all 29 G-SIBs, and 83 other (Group 2) banks.

phased-in initial Basel III framework worked out to 12.7 per cent for Group 1 banks and 15.5 per cent for Group 2 banks. Group 1 banks' average liquidity coverage ratio and the average net stable funding ratio (NSFR) stood at 135.1 per cent and 116.0 per cent, respectively.

The position of compliance as of March-end 2019 is given in the 16th Pasel 3 monitoring report of May 2019, all the 27 members of jurisdiction had fully complied with the regulations in respect of risk—capital rules, CR, and capital conservation buffer rule. All but one are through in countercyclical capital buffer and D-SIG rules. However, only 11 jurisdictions have the final rules in course.

Could Tougher Regulatory Capital and Liquidity Requirements Slow Down Economic Growth?

The Basel III reforms addressed a number of shortcomings of the previous regulations and laid the foundation for a more resilient banking system making it more immune to future potential vulnerabilities, along with giving a fillip to the real economy (Ingves 2018). The Basel III regulatory framework aimed at improving the quantity of good quality capital and build-up of capital buffers to mitigate procyclicality; supplemented these capital requirements with a risk-agnostic leverage ratio; and strengthened liquidity buffers in banks through its global liquidity standards. The regulations have thus increased the capital and liquidity that all banks are required to keep as compared to the pre-crisis regulatory requirements. This is intended to act as a speed breaker for banks moving in the fast lane of growing their balance sheet.

Impact Analysis of Capital Regulations

A negative corollary of these stringent regulations could be their impact on economic growth, especially if the bank customers do not get the necessary finance to support their business growth.

BCBS performed two studies to assess the impact of regulatory reforms. One study on long-term economic impact (LEI) concluded that net benefits from higher capital requirements remain positive for a broad range of higher capital ratios (Basel Committee on Banking

Supervision 2010a). This report provided an analysis of the LEI of the Basel III requirements related to capital and liquidity reforms. It assessed the costs and benefits of higher capital and liquidity requirements on the GDP growth. The main benefits of a stronger financial system are reduced probability of financial crises and related impact on GDP. Another benefit reflects a reduction in the volatility of fluctuations in output during non-crisis periods, while the costs include the possibility of higher interest rates leading to reduction in the demand for credit and related output losses. It also led to the understanding that there was considerable room to tighten capital and liquidity requirements without impacting the positive benefits.

Another BIS (Basel Committee on Banking Supervision 2010b) report on assessing the macroeconomic impact of transition to tighter capital and liquidity norms in 2010 concluded that the strengthened capital requirements proposed by the Basel Committee were likely to have a marginal impact on growth: GDP may fall by 0.22 per cent below baseline in the 35th quarter since implementation, followed by a recovery of growth towards baseline which implies that annual growth rates will be reduced by 0.03 per cent for 35 quarters, followed by a period during which annual growth will be 0.03 per cent higher. One important result of this study was that when higher capital and liquidity requirements are introduced gradually, the institutions are able to internalize their impact, and therefore the impact of reforms would be minimized on cost and availability of credit while maximizing the benefits associated with reduced probability of financial crises.

In a paper (Ratnovski 2013), it is suggested that 18 per cent common equity to RWAs capital requirement would be needed to fully absorb most asset shocks of magnitudes observed in banking crises in OECD countries over the last 50 years. In comparison, to present common equity capital requirements presented as a part of Basel III, this result appears to be on the higher side. However, it is also mentioned that while higher levels of capital are not prohibitively costly in steady state environment, the costs of raising bank capital strength quickly and during periods of idiosyncratic or systemic crises may be quite substantial.

Another research paper (Fender and Lewrick 2016) assessed the macroeconomic impact of the core Basel III reforms and has concluded that instead of any impact on growth, it would rather lead to a sizeable positive impact on the overall economic growth in a range of 0.4 per cent to 2.0 per cent of GDP each year depending on the impact of the introduction of total loss-absorbing capacity (TLAC) standards on G-SIBs banks' risk-taking discipline and calibration of potential G-SIB leverage ratio surcharge.

There is a current controversy concerning the appropriate size of capital requirements for banks to mitigate systemic losses. In a CIFR research paper (Bui, Scheule and Wu 2016), researchers have attempted to quantify the size of capital buffers required to reduce systemic losses using provisioning data of banks from Australia between 2002 and 2014, and concluded that during bad times, loss rates were negatively related to liquidity, but were positively related to deposit funding and size, whereas during good times, loss rates were positively related to past loss rates and lagged loan growth and negatively related to deposit ratio, bank size and GDP growth.

The Peterson Institute for International Economics (2016) study explores the cost–benefit curves of higher capital requirements for banks in a non-Modigliani–Miller world and arrives at the socially optimal level of capital requirement where the costs and benefits are optimally balanced. As per the study, the optimum level of capital is estimated at about 7 per cent of total assets, with a more cautious alternative (75th percentile) at about 8 per cent, corresponding to about 12 and 14 per cent of RWAs, respectively. These levels are, respectively, about 25 per cent to 50 per cent higher than the stipulated Basel III capital requirements for the large G-SIBs which goes on to prove that the regulations could have been tougher.

Another study carried out by the Bank of Finland (Deli and Hasan 2017) examined the effect of the full set of bank capital regulations (capital stringency) on loan growth and concluded overall capital stringency only has a weak negative effect on loan growth which also offsets in case they hold moderately high level of capital.

Andrew Sheng[5] in an interview with Risk.net has argued that sophisticated models on which the large, advanced banks assessed their risks and calibrated their capital charges were less relevant for emerging market banks, many of which were local lenders, not TBTF and had much less leverage. Hence, to apply very sophisticated Basel III rules was like imposing cancer treatment on patients whose major problems were malaria and public health. Since banks account for 70–80 per cent of national savings and are the major source of funding of long-term projects for infrastructure in emerging markets like India and Indonesia, the rules need to be more flexible.

Do Higher Bank Capital Requirements Really Decrease Systemic Risk?

A study (Bostandzic, Denefa and Weiss 2017) of the European banking sector tried to identify the impact of more stringent capital requirements on systemic risk by using a 'difference-in-differences approach' that exploits the unique setting of the 2011 European Banking Authority (EBA) capital exercise. It was observed that an individual bank's contribution to systemic fragility was decreasing only marginally after the introduction of higher capital requirements and this decrease in systemic risk was only transitory and vanishes two years after the EBA capital exercise. It was also observed that a bank's vulnerability to market shocks increased greatly as the capital strength exercise tends to red flag the banks whose capital buffer is perceived as being too low. Further, as mentioned earlier, LEI study conducted by BCBS concluded that benefit derived from reduction in probability of systemic crisis is quite substantial.

---

[5] Andrew Sheng, who has worked across Asian markets as both a banking and a securities regulator—including the chairmanship of the Securities and Futures Commission of Hong Kong, and senior positions at the Hong Kong Monetary Authority and Bank Negara Malaysia—before serving as president of the Fung Global Institute between 2011 and 2014. Today, Sheng is chief adviser to the China Banking Regulatory Commission and also works with securities regulators in India and Qatar.

There is theoretical belief that capital works as a cushion in absorbing liquidity, information and economic shocks reducing contagious defaults. A World Bank paper on bank capital and systemic stability (Anginer and Demirgüç-Kunt 2016) has examined this issue empirically using a bank level database of 1,200 publicly traded banks in over 45 countries over the period 1998–2012 and concluded that a greater amount of capital provides additional cushion for loss absorption and reduces systemic risk probability. It further concludes that in capital, higher quality capital is to be preferred over lower quality capital. This result is particularly applicable to Indian context, where for banks under RBI's PCA, only CET1 capital appears to be able to absorb losses in a credible manner and other forms of capital actually work as a destabilizing factor.

Evidence on Capital So Far

As pointed out, Basel III has been implemented in most jurisdictions and there has been significant increase in capital levels and banking systems are significantly less leveraged than the situation prevailing during pre-2007 years. During this process of increase in capital levels and decrease in leverage, we have not come across any real evidence which may suggest that higher capital requirements have led to reduction in lending to real sector or in real growth. The evidence is, in fact, quite opposite (Cecchetti and Schoenholtz 2017). It has been observed that strongly capitalized banks lend to healthy borrowers, while weak banks do not. It has also been observed that countries which had better capitalized banking systems in 2006 experienced healthy credit growth during and after the crisis. For these countries, higher capital requirements did not negatively impact the economy. And we have also relevant evidence from Japan and Europe; it was seen in the 1990s, regulatory forbearance delayed necessary deleveraging of Japan's banks for more than a decade leading to phenomenon of lost decade. Undercapitalized banks made loans to ensure insolvent firms do not collapse (Caballero, Hoshi and Kashyap 2007). In the context of ECB's loose monetary policy, it is observed to have provided incentives to weakly capitalized euro area banks for evergreen loans to 'low-quality' firms.

Impact Analysis of Liquidity Regulation

An empirical study (Banerjee and Mio 2014) was attempted to investigate how banks responded to tighter liquidity regulation in the UK. It was observed that the

> banks subject to the International Liquidity Guidelines (ILG) did not adjust the size of their balance sheets to meet tighter liquidity regulation but rather altered the composition of both their assets and liabilities. On the asset side, banks significantly increased the share of High Quality Liquidity Assets (HQLA) to total assets by around 12 percentage points following the introduction of the ILG and the adjustment in the share of HQLA to total assets was entirely offset by an equal and opposite reduction in the share of short-term financial loans, with the share of other assets remaining unaffected. On the liability side, banks subject to ILG increased funding from more stable non-bank and non-financial corporation deposits and decreased their reliance on less stable short-term wholesale and non-UK funding.

In terms of the price impact, there was no strong evidence to suggest that tightening liquidity regulation led to an increase in interest rates on loans to the non-financial sector or that is paid on non-financial deposits in the UK.

Thus, there was no evidence to indicate that the introduction of the International Liquidity Guidelines (ILG) had adversely impacted bank lending to the non-financial sector, in terms of either the quantity or price of lending. However, the results suggested that the reduced size of the inter-bank market as a result of ILG could have implications for the monetary policy transmission mechanism. The simple reason is that liquidity regulation promotes reliance on long-term deposits as compared to short-term money market funding, while money market is the place where monetary authorities have historically intervened to set policy rates. There is thus a chance of an adverse impact on the relation between policy rates' transmission and broader monetary conditions.

It would therefore not be wrong to conclude that tougher capital and liquidity regulations would result in a more resilient banking system with reduced probability of occurrence and severity of crises. Lower funding costs and the blind pursuit of optimum utilization of available funds due to financial innovations and efficient markets at the cost of an undercapitalized banking system had become the norm, which proved to be dangerous in the end. Even though for the likely net positive gains and the difficult-to-quantify opportunity gains of a crises-free system, the trade-off between financial stability and growth may be pronounced in countries with a subdued capital/bond/equity market and from which borrowers could draw funds directly.

Experience in Euro Area

The banking sector pressures were absorbed by the sovereign sector and led to sovereign debt pressures for few countries in euro area. The tensions in the sovereign debt market and the banking sector increased the fragmentation within the euro area bank funding market. This led to significant funding strains for the banks residing in the countries facing stress during the sovereign debt crisis resulting in debt markets and credit markets in the countries less affected by sovereign crisis to focus more on domestic participants. This affected the credit intermediation in the euro area. Further, there was a deposit outflow from the stressed countries to other countries. The combination of the constrained access to wholesale markets, deposit outflow and more structural funding led to deleveraging and reduction in loan supply, resulting in delays in implementation of the regulations which led to regulatory uncertainty. Examples include, delays in clarifying the implementation of MiFID II, as mentioned, and the 2012 Liikanen framework for ring-fencing and proprietary trading limits for banks. The endeavour should be to strive for expedited implementation of the reforms which will supplement the efforts towards financial stability and market efficiency.

Impact of the Regulations on Strategy of Bank

Significant business model and operational modifications were triggered for banks and the banking sector in light of the experience of the GFC and in view of post-crisis regulatory reforms, and these have impacted banks' profitability. There was a marked shift in the sectoral and geographic exposures of banks, wherein banks again started focusing on less capital-intensive activities with stable funding resources including commercial banking and moved away from complex products such as exotic derivatives, trading and market making activities. Economies which suffered from crisis saw credit declining significantly relative to economic activity. The costs of implementing and complying with regulation are among the trade-offs for achieving greater financial stability and this should find mention. For example, in 2013 (even before the full regime of new regulations was in place), the six largest US banks spent an estimated $70.2 billion on regulatory compliance, doubling the $34.7 billion they spent in 2007.

Recent Debate about the Need for Stringent Regulations

It is being observed that as memory of recent financial crisis and disruption it brought are becoming somewhat distant, some are raising questions about the need for higher capital and liquidity requirements. These voices are gathering momentum in the USA which was the epicentre of the crisis by saying efficiency is as important to public as safety (Jeffery 2018). It has been reported that Randal Quarles, vice chairman for supervision of Federal Reserve Board of Governors, said Fed supervisors 'ought to be taking a fresh look at everything'. And, therefore, the argument goes that there is a need to have a relook at the recent regulatory reforms which impose too much burden on banks. The concept of proportionality, that is, application of rules in different banks in a differentiated manner is being invoked to provide relief to certain kinds of institutions. The financial reforms—especially capital and liquidity standards for internationally active banks—are being addressed simultaneously in multiple settings around the world under different environments and legal regimes, but reinforced by a shared commitment to consistent application. Other areas of financial regulatory reform are not subject to the same degree of coordination: in some areas, coordination is less; in others, it is essentially absent. This also makes it imperative to have a stringent coordinated regulation.

Strengthening Regulation and Supervision—Improving the Capital and Liquidity Standards

The BCBS in its effort to improve resilience in the banking sector has always continued to enhance risk capture requirements in various activities of the banks.

Immediately after the crisis, the market risk framework was revised and concept of stressed VaR was introduced in 2009 which provided for incremental risk charge beyond the conventional VaR estimates. Considering few shortcomings of VaR as a measure and to better capture market risk, BCBS advised in December 2017 that expected shortfall should be used as a measure to capture market risk. Expected shortfall as a measure is a better statistical tool that avoids few problems of VaR measure like subadditivity and has lesser issues with regard to disregarding the fat tails and the tail dependence than the VaR does.

Prudential Regulation

The GFC has led to the identification of skill gaps towards understanding the increasing complexity and related interconnectedness in the financial world. The notion of independence and incentive to the regulators to overcome pressures from various sections and impose required corrective measures is highly recommended.

On similar lines, the Dodd–Frank Act (DFA) was introduced in the USA which made recommendations to the Federal Reserve for increasingly strict rules for capital, leverage, liquidity, risk management and other requirements proportionate to the size and complexity of banks. The DFA was believed to be a regressive act and the pinch was felt mostly on smaller banks. As the IMF paper concludes, the Financial Choice Act was later introduced to modify some elements of the DFA, leave certain DFA key elements untouched and repeal some parts of it. A key proposal is to introduce a regulatory 'off-ramp' for providing substantial regulatory relief for so-called 'qualifying BHCs'. As an alternative, they propose for banks to choose between the DFA and a leaner regulatory regime if capital levels are sufficiently high. Specifically, banks with a leverage ratio of 10 per cent or more would qualify to become 'qualifying banking organizations' (QBOs) and will be exempted from most DFA and Basel III rules, including risk-based capital and liquidity standards; limits to concentration risk; counterparty risk standards and any law that prevents banks from M&A or similar activities. Also, QBOs would be exempted from the application of Enhanced Prudential Standards (including mandatory supervisory and company-run stress tests; single counterparty credit limits and minimum requirements on liabilities, i.e., TLAC) and the submission of living wills. Despite the stated intention of policymakers to provide regulatory relief for small banks under the proposed FCA, the IMF paper shows that these banks would opt to stay under the existing DFA regime.

Regulating global banks is yet another problem that regulators generally face, given their high interconnectedness and dynamic nature, and the need for single global regulator. For instance, in the UK, which is a supervisor of around 170 international banks from over 50 jurisdictions and includes every one of the 30 G-SIBs (Breeden 2016) and as a host supervisor during the crisis learnt the manifestation of global risks in local entities and the importance of home–host information sharing and coordination. For example, on the wholesale side, Bear Stearns and Lehman, both saw problems occur outside their UK operations where UK supervisors had little sight of developments, but that led to uncertainty, loss of confidence and a flight of short-term wholesale funding.

A suggestion to manage this situation could be that the domestic regulators can work together to not just tame the risks facing their own economies but the risks facing the global one—in the same way that lion tamers can work together. The regulators can create synergy by helping other regulators in case they observe any regulatory issue in their domain and other regulator immediately responding to it.

Supervisory Issues Related to Banks Considered as Systemically Important or TBTF

It is generally considered that trading of bank's equity and bonds in financial markets provides an important tool to enforce market discipline on banks. BCBS has also introduced Pillar 3 of Basel regulations which rely on enforcing market discipline on banks by mandating banks to disclose detailed information on riskiness of bank's portfolio. However, a recent research (Kolaric, Kiesel and Ongena 2019) has questioned this assumption in the case of banks considered as TBTF. This research analysed the impact of rating downgrades on the credit default swap (CDS) spreads of the banks. While rating downgrades led to significant widening of credit spreads for non-TBTF banks, the spreads of TBTF banks were not impacted by news of credit rating downgrades. This result raised serious questions over the traditional belief that market discipline can play an important role for TBTF banks. This raises the importance of appropriate regulation and intense supervision of these banks as the main tool for controlling the risk-taking of large banks in view that markets cannot effectively discipline larger and globally interconnected banks/financial institutions.

Debating on Effective Supervision

Effective and prudential supervision is all about understanding the risks, the risk management, creating the right incentives to control these risks and intervention wherever required (Bailey 2016). It is a continuous activity and needs to guard against the peril of falling in the light-touch and deep-painted ends.

Supervision depends on the institutional structure of banking sector. The periodicity and tools of an off-site surveillance to identify the areas of concerns are counter-verified by way of mandated portfolio-specific/risk-specific on-site examination by the examiners taking into consideration the ideas impinged upon by the statutory auditors. A constant upgradation of tools of supervision is required such as shifting from the CAMELS-based approach to the risk-based rating approach (regulation could be light but all pervasive based on ground realities while supervision should be intensive and rigorous).

Considering the fact that global financial stability hinges on strong supervision of systemically important financial institutions which is particularly challenging given their size, complexity and influence on other institutions, quality of supervision has acquired a prime place in financial sector reforms. The major learning points in this area as enshrined in the BCBS Core Principles (especially the revisions in 2012) and as identified by the IMF and World Bank in their recent FSAP study (February 2019) are (i) a clear mandate for proper supervision, (ii) adequate resources and (iii) strong governance structures.

Unfortunately, intensity of compliance in these areas has been observed to be tapering off during the period mid-2013–2014 and mid-2016–2017. Out of the 29 Basel Core Principles, reforms-inertia was observed to be the maximum in the areas on 'independence' and 'resources'. This trend is seen not only in developing economies but also in advanced economies. Further, it is visible across supervisory institutions, be it within or outside the central bank.

It is, of course, true that supervisors cannot be given unlimited operational independence even while their accountability for actions/inactions is expected as a 'given'. But what should necessarily be guarded against is conscious dilution in regulatory framework by way of less intensive supervision and/or deliberate indifference to take timely and corrective supervisory actions against perceived vulnerabilities.

Need and Efficacy of Countercyclical Regulation/Supervision

The financial instability hypothesis associated with Hyman Minsky states that a long period of financial tranquillity, economic growth and stability leads market participants to believe that this benign period will prolong and they become overconfident. This overconfidence leads to less than reasonable assessment of riskiness of financial contracts. This ultimately manifests in increase in their leverage and invest in riskier portfolios. This build-up of risk sows the seed of financial instability and future financial crisis. This view has been well analysed in newer concept 'volatility paradox' proposed by Brunnermeier and Sannikov. In the financial realm, innovative products such as securitization and derivatives' contracts designed for risk sharing led to higher leverage and more frequent crises. Therefore, long periods of economic growth and financial stability require financial regulation and supervision to be vigilant to build-up of such risks and have an ex-ante framework to respond to risks getting built up in the system.

The BCBS has come out with a number of tools to introduce counter-cyclicality in the banking regulation. Basel III has introduced a specific CCCB which will depend on how aggregate credit to GDP at a particular point of time deviates from its long-term trend. This will enhance bank's capacity to build adequate buffers in times of excessive credit exuberance. This will ensure that bank's capacity to absorb losses in periods after excessive credit growth is enhanced and they keep on lending during difficult periods. Further, International Accounting Standards have come out with an expected loss-based loan loss provisioning framework which is in the process of replacing present incurred loss-based provisioning which is highly procyclical. Expected loss-based provisioning framework will introduce some element of counter-cyclicality in the loan loss provisioning by requiring banks to compute expected losses over a longer horizon.

In a recent IMF working paper (Basak and Zhao 2018), the issue of factoring business cycles in macroprudential policies has been examined. A longer history of financial peace builds the investor confidence and increases acceptability of risks. However, future probability of crisis is dependent on the degree of aggregate risky asset position in the system. The investment decision of each trader to increase his/her allocation to risky asset without analysing its true riskiness increases the systemic crisis probability. This leads to the decentralized equilibrium which is characterized by constrained inefficiency and excessive risk-taking. The extent of constrained inefficiency and increasing investor confidence or rather overconfidence sets the stage for requirement of imposition of countercyclical macroprudential policies. These policies by nature of increase in capital and provisioning requirements, thus lead to constrained efficiency and reduce systemic risk. The degree of countercyclical capital and provisioning requirements should be higher as the market tranquillity persists. The resilience of financial system to withstand bouts of market exuberance and development of inherent risks in the system during periods of financial stability needs to be examined thoroughly. Therefore, it is important to highlight that optimal macroprudential policies depend on the trade-off between the resilience effect and risk-taking effect which may increase the degree of countercyclical regulations in case of underestimation and stifle financial innovations.

In one of the BoE staff working papers (O'Neill and Vause 2018), a macroprudential buffer as a countercyclical buffer in addition to the initial margin for the derivatives is suggested which can be used to reduce the fire sale externality during the crisis if adequate precautions are taken before release of such a margin.

Supervisory Colleges: Supervision of Cross-border Banks

As a means to improve the international financial legal framework for financial supervision of global institutions, a notion of supervisory colleges has been advocated. These colleges are *ad hoc* groups which have been made out as a platform for information exchange among supervisors. The goal of this initiative is certainly to ensure safe and sound banking practices being able to be followed by the supervisor fraternity, thereby reducing the requirement of governmental assistance to such financial institutions. This would additionally lead to building confidence in the respective domestic and international financial system. The G20 and the EU have been particularly active in developing these colleges and codifying best practices for their operation.

Light-touch regulation with weak and diminished supervision was the major culprit of GFC which not only prevented the irregularities from coming to the fore but also ensured that no policy corrections could happen midway. When we look back at the reasons of GFC and try to relate the issues with the supervisory work, the basic tenet of supervision, that is, 'trust but verify' was considerably diluted. The fundamental principle of good supervision is through asking pertinent questions even during the good times. Additionally, lack of proper understanding of the developments ongoing in the financial world had further made the supervisors to lag behind the market manoeuvres. This lack of understanding made them oblivious to the building stress in the system. Such a lackadaisical approach to regulation and supervision proved to be dangerous in respect of global banks. The fact that when banks started dealing in complex products or when banks started relying excessively on short-term funding sources for their operations, the supervisors must have raised an alarm and dealt the situation with alacrity.

With the aim of increasing the effectiveness, rigour and intensity of supervision, the Basel Core Principles (BCPs) for Effective Banking Supervision—the global standards against which supervisors are assessed as part of the IMF—World Bank Financial Sector Assessment Program (FSAP) have been revamped. The Joint Forum has also published principles for supervision of financial conglomerates. Several other issues such as model risk, management and corporate governance structure, role and enhanced scrutiny of boards and senior management are also being addressed in different forums.

However, this experiment is not taking off fast in the face of inadequate acceptance of the idea of sacrifice in times of crisis by way of sharing of information and resources. Lack of confluence in legal conclusions across the participating jurisdictions is another impediment. Further, the skills and capacity of supervisors and even the supervisory approach may vary widely.

Concentration, competition and stability can coexist in a financial sector with the support of an appropriate regulatory and supervisory framework. Competition can also 'endanger stability if mixed with the wrong kind of regulation' (World Bank Report 2013). To promote banking stability, policymakers should design and apply better regulations and supervisory practices rather than limit bank competition (OECD Report 2010). In Canada, 'capital regulation is stricter than the requirements of Basel agreements. Banks' foreign and wholesale activities are limited. The mortgage market is also conservative in terms of the products offered, with less than 3 percent being subprime and less than 30 percent being securitized' (OECD Report 2011). The adequateness of the regulatory and supervisory framework is assessed on the basis of risk reduction in the ecosystem, carving out detrimental effects of competition and injecting market discipline. It also needs to adapt to the market structure so as to be able to properly address risks and dangers in banking and prevent any potential crisis. As per the Pillar 2 of the Basel agreement, the supervisors have the authority to intervene and check for imprudent practices, macroprudential tools should be considered to counter asset price and credit booms and take into account the interaction between financial institutions as also covariation between banks' risk profiles. These can contain fragility risk out of herding which is usually encouraged by competition.

Corporate Governance

A fair corporate governance boosts competition and helps markets function properly. Banks as intermediaries in the financial world play a crucial role and hence need to function properly. Creditors/managers of banks carry strong incentives to engage in high pay-offs activities giving possible downside risks to the depositors. What makes corporate governance in banks more important is the relative opaque nature of balance sheet by way of short-term liabilities funding through long-term assets leading to probable mismatch in resources. Ethical standards, governance of executive remuneration, implementation of effective risk management mechanism, quality of board practices, exercise of shareholder rights, etc., are therefore necessary ingredients of a sound corporate governance framework. The Governor of Bank of Mauritius (Roi 2017) observes that

> rules alone, no matter how well written and how consistently implemented, will not be enough to maintain the financial health and stability of the banking system… On-going vigilance in respect of corporate governance of banks as another over-arching priority in the supervision of banks is critically important. (Rameswurlall 2017)

A study of the characteristics of the liabilities and assets as also of the management and working results of the banks over the past few years after the GFC provides useful insights. It calls for an evaluation system to measure the management ability which is required to run and monitor large and complex banks. A more careful consideration of the risk management models and systems put in place in banks needs to be looked into. Risk Management Committee (RMC) of the Board is a prerequisite and the bank's board and management should be made responsible for the level of risk taken and the regulator, on the other hand, must be made accountable for formulating unambiguously clear and rational logical directions that are in sync with changing times and business nature of the banks. The on-site examinations need to be made more dynamic. Further, well-validated, bank-specific, business-specific models for VaR and stress tests, etc., should be in place. Assets Liabilities Management (ALM) Committee should be taking those decisions on a 'cost–benefit' and 'independent profit centre' basis. A careful scrutiny of off-site reports and on-site examination visit by supervisors should ensure adherence to rules. The banks' internal and external audit system may also capture this area for validation.

The implementation of Basel III standards called for a consistent implementation at least among the G20 members seems to be desirable. The Basel guidelines are accordingly customized by respective member countries and issued to their regulated and supervised entities. This may lead to an incoherent implementation of similar standards and could create fault lines for the coming future. A concerted effort in this regard is required and the implementation constantly reviewed for a minimum divergent application.

Conclusion

Going ahead, the financial sector continues to face a challenging environment. Even though the economic outlook looks bright, the reduction in interest margins and other structural forces such as technological innovation and consolidation pressures are major issues for the sector. Achievement of the stringent capital and liquidity standards has opened up the space for banks and other financial institutions to further increase resilience (Bank for International Settlements 2017 Annual Report).

The GFC has made us realize that a well-functioning intermediation function that efficiently provides financing to borrowers through business cycles which will be achieved by financial system is a sine qua non for a vibrant economy. A robust and resilient financial system post-GFC has been created and it is important that its sustenance be maintained by remembering the lessons learned (Dudley 2017).

For a deeply complex and continuously evolving financial industry, what is of prime importance is the ability of the supervisor. If the supervisor is able to act quickly and flexibly, based on their judgement and expertise, the financial system would be greatly benefitted. The proposals that limit the independence of the supervisor will limit its ability to act quickly. Further, in areas where the reforms deviate from global standards in liquidity and capital rules, it needs to be ensured that the deviations do not increase risks as the banks generally shift their operations to lightly regulated jurisdictions. There must be more harmonized rules corroborating a level playing field across the world.

Rules governing behaviour of institutions in the financial industry seem to oscillate between tightening during and after crises, and subsequent relaxation once-normalcy has been attained and maintained. Are we about to enter the next stage of the cycle: a new wave of deregulation? As George Bernard Shaw said: 'If history repeats itself, and the unexpected always happens, how incapable must man be of learning from experience!' (Lautenschläger 2017).

The reforms implemented so far have led to safer financial system by making banks less leveraged and more liquid. Efforts are on to develop international cooperative structures to resolve cross-border systemically important institutions. However, there are still some gaps which need to be filled. Capital levels are still not sufficiently adequate for banks to remain solvent under stress in many jurisdictions. Systemic risk assessment and tools of macroprudential regulation and supervision are still evolving and there is a need to do a lot of work in this area. While global OTC derivatives markets appear safer due to requirement of central clearing, we need to be vigilant that these central counterparties do not become another TBTF type of institution going forward. The focus on regulating the banking sector more comprehensively and strongly may induce shifting of credit intermediation to shadow banking institutions which may not be as tightly regulated. Global policymakers need to remain vigilant, and potential risk developing in shadow banking area needs to be dealt with appropriately. Tensions and uncertainty around global trade, geopolitical risks mainly driven by rising nationalism aspirations, rising global debt and high asset valuations are few other significant risks which the regulators need to be wary about.

However, there are other areas apart from the liquidity and capital concerns that need further assessment from a global perspective, particularly arising from the interplay of political economy with the real and financial economy, disruptive challenges from the Fintech revolution, cryptocurrencies and cyber security threats, uncoordinated inflation targeting frameworks across world economies, lingering sovereign debt crisis for many countries, coordination and cooperation framework across countries for macroprudential crisis prevention. As Karl Marx said, 'Last words are for fools who haven't said enough!' Some potential crisis from unknown unseen forces are always probable. We take a delve in these issues as we move ahead.

References

Admati, Anat R. 2015, December. *The Missed Opportunity and Challenge of Capital Regulation*. Stanford, CA: Stanford Graduate School of Business.

Anginer, Deniz and Asli Demirgüç-Kunt. 2016, April. *Bank Capital and Systemic Stability*. Available at https://openknowledge.worldbank.org/bitstream/handle/10986/19377/WPS6948.pdf?sequence=1&isAllowed=y (accessed on 21 January 2019).

Bailey, Andrew. 2016, 9 March. 'Bank Capital: Debating Again' (Speech given at Barclays' 2016 Financial Conference). London.

Banerjee, Ryan N. and Hitoshi Mio. 2014, October. 'The Impact of Liquidity Regulation on Banks'. BIS Working Papers No. 470. Basel: BIS.

Bank for International Settlements. 2017, 25 June. 87th Annual Report (1 April 2016–31 March 2017). Basel: Bank for International Settlements.

Basak, Deepal and Yunhui Zhao. 2018, May. 'Does Financial Tranquility Call for Stringent Regulation?' IMF Working Paper. Available at https://www.imf.

org/en/Publications/WP/Issues/2018/05/31/Does-Financial-Tranquility-Call-for-Stringent-Regulation-45908 (accessed on 22 January 2019).

Basel Committee on Banking Supervision. 2010a, August. 'An Assessment of the Long-Term Economic Impact of Stronger Capital and Liquidity Requirements'. Basel: BCBS.

———. 2010b, December. 'Assessing the Macroeconomic Impact of the Transition to Stronger Capital and Liquidity Requirements'. Available at https://www.bis.org/publ/othp12.pdf (accessed on 21 January 2019).

———. 2018, November. Implementation of Basel Standards—A Report to G20 Leaders on Implementation of the Basel III Regulatory Reforms. Available at https://www.bis.org/bcbs/publ/d453.htm (accessed on 22 January 2019).

Bostandzic, Denefa, Felix Irresberger and Gregor N. F. Weiss. 2017, 5 October. *Do Higher Bank Capital Requirements Really Decrease Systemic Risk?* Available at https://ies.keio.ac.jp/upload/20180417_econo_Gregor-Weiss_wp_manuscript-1.pdf (accessed on 21 January 2019).

Breeden, Sarah. 2016, 22 March. 'Taming International Banks—Time for Some New Tricks?' (Speech).

Bui, Christina, Harald Scheule and Eliza Wu. 2016, 29 June. *The Value of Bank Capital Buffers in Maintaining Financial System Resilience.* CIFR Research Working Paper No. 089. Melbourne: CIFR.

Caballero, Ricardo J., Takeo Hoshi and Anil K. Kashyap. 2007, September. *Zombie Lending and Depressed Restructuring in Japan.* Available at https://www.nber.org/papers/w12129 (accessed on 21 January 2019).

Caruana, Jaime. 2014, 26 November. 'How Much Capital Is Enough?' (Speech).

Cecchetti, Stephen G. and Kermit Schoenholtz. 2017, November. 'Regulatory Reform: A Scorecard'. A CEPR Discussion Paper. Available at https://papers.ssrn.com/sol3/papers.cfm?abstract_id=3082291 (accessed on 21 January 2019).

Chami, R., T. Cosimano, E. Kopp and C. Rochon. 2017, July. *Back to the Future: The Nature of Regulatory Capital Requirements.* IMF Working Paper. Washington, DC: IMF.

Deli, Yota D. and Iftekhar Hasan. 2017. 'Real Effects of Bank Capital Regulations: Global Evidence'. Bank of Finland Research Discussion Paper. Available at https://ideas.repec.org/p/bof/bofrdp/2017_023.html (accessed on 21 January 2019).

Dudley, William C. 2017, 7 April. 'Principles for Financial Regulatory Reform' (Speech).

Fischer, Stanley (2017), An Interview with Financial Times, published on August 16. Fender, Ingo and Ulf Lewrick. 2016, November. *Adding It All Up: The Macroeconomic Impact of Basel III and Outstanding Reform Issues.* BIS Working Paper. No 591. Basel: BIS.

Ingves, Stefan. 2014, 6 November. 'Implementing the Regulatory Reform Agenda—The Pitfall of Myopia' (Speech).

————. 2016, 10 November. 'Necessary Reforms for a More Stable Financial Sector' (Speech).Stockholm: Sveriges Riksbank.

————. 2018, 29 January. 'Basel III: Are We Done Now?' (Speech). Frankfurt: Institute for Law and Finance Conference at Goethe University.

Jeffery, Christopher. 2018, 17 May. *Regulatory Efficiency or Rollback?* Available at https://www.centralbanking.com/central-banks/financial-stability/macro-prudential/3511151/regulatory-efficiency-or-rollback (accessed on 21 January 2019).

Kolaric, Sascha, Florian Kiesel and Steven Ongena (2019). 'Market Discipline through Credit Ratings and Too-Big-to-Fail in Banking?' Swiss Finance Institute Research Paper Series, Zurich: Swiss Finance Institute, No 17-09, March. Swiss Finance Institute Research Paper No. 17-09 (Revised version, 11 January).

Lautenschläger, Sabine. 2017, 13 March. 'Walled off? Banking Regulation after the Crisis' (Speech). Available at https://www.bis.org/review/r170314b.htm (accessed on 22 January 2019).

Menon, Ravi. 2017, 20 April. 'Financial Regulation: The Way Forward' (Speech). Available at http://www.nas.gov.sg/archivesonline/data/pdfdoc/20170420006/MAS%20MD%20Ravi%20Menon_%20Speech%20at%20OMFIF%20City%20Lecture%20in%20Washington%20DC%20on%2020%20April%202017.pdf (accessed on 21 January 2019).

O'Neill, Cian and Nicholas Vause. 2018, November. 'Macro-Prudential Margins: A New Countercyclical Tool?' Staff Working Paper No. 765. Available at https://www.bankofengland.co.uk/-/media/boe/files/working-paper/2018/macroprudential-margins-a-new-countercyclical-tool.pdf (accessed on 22 January 2019).

Peterson Institute for International Economics. 2016, March. *Benefits and Costs of Higher Capital Requirements for Banks.* Working Paper No. 16–6. Washington, DC: Peterson Institute for International Economics.

Pohl, Michael. 2017, October. *Basel III Liquidity Monitoring Tools—Possible Application of the Additional Tools.* Occasional Paper No. 14. Bern: Swiss Financial Market Supervisory Authority.

Powell, Jerome H. 2017, 22 June. 'Relationship Between Regulation and Economic Growth'. Available at https://www.bis.org/review/r170630a.htm (accessed on 21 January 2019).

Ratnovski, Lev. 2013, 28 July. *How Much Capital Should Banks Have?* Available at https://voxeu.org/article/how-much-capital-should-banks-have (accessed on 21 January 2019).

Roi, Rameswurlall Basant. 2017, 21 August. 'Evolution of the Basel Capital Adequacy Requirements' (Speech). Ebene: International Monetary Fund, Africa Training Institute.

Rule, David. 2015, 2 March. 'What is Left to Do on the Post-Crisis Bank Capital Framework?' (Speech).

Weidmann, Jens. 2014, 21 November. 'Banking Union and Regulatory Reforms—Mission Accomplished?' (Speech).

Yellen, Janet L. 2015, 3 March. *Improving the Oversight of Large Financial Institutions* (Speech).

———. 2016, 28 September. *Supervision and Regulation before the Committee on Financial Services*. Washington, DC: US House of Representatives.

CHAPTER 2

Regulatory Framework Beyond Capital and Liquidity

The post-regulatory reform of strengthening of the capital and liquidity standards alone cannot lead to a safer financial system, and there is a need to identify and manage evolving risks and take additional steps. One such step is reduction of information asymmetry. This will lead to better understanding of risks among market participants, discouraging financial institutions from taking excessive risk leading to a sound financial system, and will act as a deterrent for misconduct. The strengthening and convergence of accounting standards will further lead to international comparability of banks' balance sheets. Stringent regulatory stipulations on banks have led to regulatory arbitrage and shifting of the risks to shadow banking leading to the need for increasing the monitoring of shadow banking activities. Another area which led to the build-up of risks prior to the GFC was the lack of transparency in over-the-counter (OTC) and commodity derivatives, which has been addressed by shifting of trading to organized exchanges through central clearing counterparties. Executive compensation practices also need a revisit to ensure that inappropriate risk-taking is not encouraged and rewarded. Further, a case has been made to develop a system to deal with sovereign bankruptcy and regulation of banks' exposure to sovereigns. To sum up, all this cannot be achieved without a strong risk architecture and culture within the financial institutions. Banks should develop strong governance, risk management compliance (GRC) ecosystem.

Introduction

The focus of post-crisis regulatory reforms has been on tightening the capital and liquidity prescriptions to ensure banks are less leveraged and more liquid. However, it is also recognized that tightening of capital and liquidity frameworks alone will not lead to a safer financial system if other aspects of the regulatory framework such as market discipline, shadow banking activities, OTC and commodity derivatives and so on are not given their due importance. A regulatory framework in addition to mitigating the probability of a crisis should have additional safety net elements to it. Lack of transparency led to an underestimation of counterparty credit risk and concentration of risks. The interconnectedness in the financial system resulting in contagion transmitted rapidly through the system. This necessitated the need to put in place shock absorbers in other segments of financial system along with enhanced transparency to properly ascertain the interconnectedness. In 2009, a comprehensive programme of financial reforms was started by the G20 nations under the aegis of the FSB. The reform programme has four core elements: making financial institutions more resilient; ending TBTF; making derivatives markets safer; and enhancing resilience of non-bank financial intermediation.

Market Discipline and Conduct

Not withstanding, the shortcomings of market discipline in case of TBTF banks, as found in a recent research, as indicated earlier, market discipline is considered an important tool to regulate bank risk-taking. Information to market participants regarding key risk metrics is essential to promote a sound banking system. It has the potential of reducing information asymmetry and can promote comparability of banks' risk profiles. Ensuring key information access to market participants regarding banks' regulatory capital and risk exposures has been the guiding principle behind Pillar 3 of the Basel framework.

The risk information disclosures must be made in such a way that they are easy to understand for all stakeholders including customers and the public at large. They should be indicative of all major information, must not be biased and should include both positive and negative information in a comparable manner with additional information regarding the cross-subsidization across the various activities.

This aspect was also emphasized by the OECD stating the importance of state-sponsored financial education to foster transparency, remove information asymmetry and support deepening of the markets in the economy, which will help consumers to correctly compare different financial institutions' offerings and switch to the institution providing maximum utility (OECD Report 2011).

Moreover, credit information sharing to limit the risk in banking was also envisaged and was to be implemented across the board. This information availability not only disciplines borrowers as they realize that it will be difficult to borrow from other institutions in case of a default but also reduces similar exposures throughout the ecosystem.

Reducing information asymmetries also helps market participants develop better understanding of relative returns offered by competing financial products. The trade-off between risk and reward is something which has been dealt by both modern society and the ancient one, and the increased risks necessarily inflict harm by creating negative value as some risks do give reward but not all risks are compensated. The concept of risk and reward mostly drives everyday decisions of individuals and everyone understands that unnecessary (or imposed) risk is a 'bad thing'.

While developing the thoughts on the much-used idea of the risk–reward trade-off, the logic almost forcefully leads the mind and consciousness towards other 'R's—requital, which perhaps was as important as the other two 'R's, to better understand the conundrum. Requital means retribution, 'a justly deserved penalty for past acts'. The notion of requital is closely related to another relevant R—responsibility—as it connotes the act of correcting 'one's own wrongdoing'.

The 'greed is good' credo of modern times has been seriously questioned by the GFC. Even as the discipline of economics is engaging in deep introspection and the theory of finance is re-examining many of the basic assumptions, it may be appropriate to take stock of some of the major issues related to the risk and reward, and do some collective soul searching about the 'requital' aspect.

The 'inconclusiveness' and 'incompleteness' of the risk–reward trade-off make it necessary to explore the other dimensions of human life for the reason that recurring episodes of crisis in financial systems highlight the need for realizing the importance of understanding the very core of human behaviour for explaining the inevitability of financial and economic theories and models falling short in giving a 'complete' picture of the myriad forces playing out there. The ever-growing, strong tilt of human behaviour towards reward and the almost irresistible tendency to take or overlook risks in that pursuit have almost always resulted in inevitable retribution or requital in the long term.

The architecture of international financial regulation has been the subject of much scholarly and regulatory debate since the financial crisis. Previously limited in its power and aims, that framework has been deployed to coordinate—and in some cases harmonize—domestic approaches to reduce systemic risk. A few areas of cooperation stand out. First are the capital requirements imposed on firms, and especially those imposed on the largest most internationally active institutions. Domestic regulators have largely agreed to adopt international standards along with accompanying restrictions on leverage.

Second, G20 leaders have also agreed to coordinate the domestic regulation of derivatives trading and together have set down a path of more central clearing and increased transparency. Third, major economic powers are coordinating on the issue of cross-border resolution. The post-crisis architecture of international financial regulation that has emerged from these efforts has several laudable features. For one, it reflects domestic regulators' shared desire to reduce systemic risk. It also demonstrates their growing awareness that unilateral approaches to regulating risk are not effective.

There are three main reasons why international coordination is superior to a unilateral domestic approach to activate the private market as a means to the end of reducing systemically significant misconduct. The first and perhaps the most obvious reason is that financial fraud and crime is a cross-border issue. Systemically significant financial misconduct affects markets, which do not observe territorial boundaries or constraints. Part of the informational asymmetry that inhibits public regulation stems from this very feature, as regulators in one jurisdiction cannot often access information about private actors in another, even though their markets are equally affected. In this market-based, deterritorialized economy, information must flow not only from private markets to public authorities but also across jurisdictions. A coordinated approach is thus in each nation's self-interest. A second reason in favour of coordination over unilateralism is to avoid regulatory arbitrage, which makes the whole system weaker. Third, a unilateral approach would have serious legal, political and logistical flaws. For one, in the absence of international coordination, states will be prone to an extraterritorial approach (Skinner 2015).

The keystone of regulatory reform in the wake of the financial crisis has turned out to be an effort to pair substantive changes to the financial industry with an effort to get bankers to behave more ethically. Regulators have emphasized the importance of 'culture' set by a 'tone at the top' that makes 'ethical conduct' a primary organizational value—although they have not given much content to any of these terms. Taking cognizance of the inherent moral hazard and adverse selection issues related to the executives' pay structure, the FSB issued post-crisis guidelines on sound compensation. Banks in jurisdictions which implemented the FSB's principles and standards (P&S) of sound compensation in national legislation changed their compensation policies more than other banks.

The two-phased development of FSB's work on the use of governance frameworks to mitigate misconduct risk analyses the efforts of the international and major national bodies in Phase I and subsequently uses this knowledge in Phase II to develop a toolkit for use by firms and supervisors to strengthen their governance frameworks to mitigate misconduct risk.

In May 2017, the findings of the FSB's two-pronged literature review focused on root causes and scientific insights were published for mitigation of misconduct risk through strengthening the governance frameworks. Avoiding any exhaustive definition of 'framework', and providing only common guidelines, the review included the set of laws, regulations, policies, structures and processes used by firms and national authorities to reinforce corporate governance. Considering the existing knowledge about the framework, the FSB provided a common definition of 'governance' and deliberately avoided an exhaustive definition of 'framework'.

The FSB has developed a toolkit in Phase II for mitigating misconduct risks by doing further work in three areas: (a) cultural drivers of misconduct, (b) individual responsibility and accountability and (c) the 'rolling bad apples (unethical people getting future employment)' from the 10 areas identified in Phase 1 with an objective to develop a toolkit that firms can use to mitigate misconduct risk. The toolkit is summarized as follows:

- Tool 1: Articulation of desired cultural features by the senior leadership of the firm.
- Tool 2: Review of information and use of multidisciplinary techniques for identification of significant cultural drivers of misconduct.
- Tool 3: Shifting of behavioural norms to mitigate cultural drivers of misconduct.
- Tool 4: Culture-focused supervisory programme.
- Tool 5: Prioritize review of such firms or groups displaying significant cultural drivers of misconduct using a risk-based approach.
- Tool 6: Assessment of cultural drivers of misconduct through a broad range of information and techniques.
- Tool 7: Engage firms' leadership with respect to observations on culture and misconduct.
- Tool 8: Identify key responsibilities, including mitigation of the risk of misconduct, and assign them.
- Tool 9: Hold individuals accountable.
- Tool 10: Assess the suitability of individuals to whom key responsibilities are assigned.

- Tool 11: Develop and monitor a responsibility and accountability framework.
- Tool 12: Coordinate with other authorities.
- Tool 13: Communicate and conduct expectations early and consistently in recruitment and hiring processes.
- Tool 14: Enhance interviewing techniques.
- Tool 15: Leverage multiple sources of available information before hiring.
- Tool 16: Reassess employee conduct regularly.
- Tool 17: Conduct exit interviews.
- Tool 18: Supervise firms' practices for screening prospective employees and monitoring current employees.
- Tool 19: Compliance should be promoted for legal or regulatory requirements regarding conduct-related information about applicable employees, where these exist.

As noted by Mark Carney (2017), Chair of the FSB, in his July 2017 letter to G20 Leaders:

> Fines are essential to punish wrong doing and have an important deterrent effect, but it is insufficient and inefficient to rely solely on ex post penalties of institutions and their shareholders. The resources paid in fines, had they been retained as capital, could have supported up to $5 trillion in lending to households and businesses.

Reversing the trend of misconduct and guiding the markets to an uplift would depend significantly on reducing opportunities for bad behaviour, putting in place stronger deterrents and moving in to ex-ante prevention through an ethical risk culture, incentives-inducing ethical behaviour rather than any ex-post punitive actions. A better trade-off between risk and reward needs to be achieved with a clear mapping of responsibilities and accountability keeping pace with market developments.

Ensuring individual and collective responsibility and accountability, alignment of conduct with risk-taking, balance between short-term gains and long-term value creation, taking the industry on board for market-wide common standards, tougher punishments for misconduct, and better background check for employees are some of the measures to improve ethical conduct and achieving ethical uplift. The authorities can further supplement the regulations by conceiving a soft law (standards and codes) and a hard law (legislation) to manage the misconduct risks. The authorities can always implement rules and regulations, but they can also play a broader role by promoting good behaviour (Shafik 2016).

What we also need to understand is that regulation through ethics is soft regulation and comprises guidance, best practices and memorandums of understanding with other regulators, but are serving as growth areas in the administrative law. It is a sort of informal regulation making the formal regulation more meaningful and coordinated. But we are sceptical of these calls for a warm—and seemingly quite fuzzy—culture of ethics (Gordon and Zaring 2017).

With an objective to raise awareness to the tools and approaches for regulating conduct in financial markets, the International Organization of Securities Commissions (IOSCO) published a report in June 2017. The report also contained examples of market conduct tools and approaches that are particularly relevant in the context of wholesale markets. The report comprised of a toolkit for regulators, the common grounds leading to misconduct, description of existing initiatives and a general overview of regulators for managing misconduct.

With the view of encouraging the implementation of IOSCO-compliant risk-free rate (RFR), and to reduce scope for benchmarks manipulation, FSB suggested strengthening of the major inter-bank offered rate (IBOR) benchmarks, providing a greater transactions base and, where possible, by improving the processes and controls around submissions and identifying alternative near RFRs.

The Foreign Exchange Working Group, working under the BIS's Markets Committee established in May 2015 to promote the integrity and effective functioning of foreign exchange markets, developed and released in May 2017 a Global Code of Conduct for the foreign exchange market, together with principles and mechanisms to support adherence to the new standards.

This is a common set of guidelines for good practice in the wholesale FX market aimed at making a robust, liquid and transparent global marketplace, with resilient infrastructure and conforming to acceptable standards of behaviour in which a diverse set of participants can transact with confidence. The global code is neither an obligation for the participants nor a substitute for regulation but is a supplement to them by identifying global best practices. It has 55 principles which cover areas including ethics, governance, execution and client order handling, handling confidential information, risk management and compliance, and confirmation and settlement, electronic trading, algorithmic trading and prime brokerage. The code is intended to be adopted by a broad range of participants, namely financial institutions, central banks, quasi-sovereigns and supranational, asset managers, sovereign wealth funds, hedge funds, pension funds, insurance firms, corporate treasury, brokers and settlement agencies.

This is an important time for the FSB as it is nearing completion of the post-crisis reform agenda, which stands as a major accomplishment. The time is now to focus on the ways in which its functioning can be further improved diligently to enhance transparency and to reach out to maximum possible stakeholders and be prepared for any next crisis. The existent vulnerabilities to financial stability and the subsequent pace of reforms must be ensured for improvement wherever possible.

Strengthening the Oversight and Regulation of Shadow Banking

The shadow banking sector—a set of financial institutions which perform functions very similar to traditional banking functions (the same maturity transformation functions) but which are largely unregulated—saw a phenomenal growth in their operations even surpassing the growth in banking sector leading to a rise in risks and a contagion into the banking system intensifying the crisis. Shadow banks were largely a by-product of regulatory arbitrage, and though they tended to pose similar risks to financial stability, they remained outside the explicit government backstop, namely deposit insurance protection and access to the lender of last resort (LOLR) facility and were rarely backed by any other discretionary support in the eventuality of adverse events.

Post-GFC, measures such as monitoring the exposures of banking system to the sector, more stringent disclosure requirements and a strict vigil on the maturity transformation and leverage for the shadow banking sector activities have been discussed.

The estimates of the shadow banking reach and growth have been measured by various organizations. In 2015–2016, the FSB in its Shadow Banking Monitoring Report of 2016 (Financial Stability Board 2017a) estimated this based on economic functions (EFs) as per its own policy framework. The entire sector was classified with reference to five EFs, which involved non-bank credit intermediation posing risks to financial stability. Across the 27 jurisdictions, a total of $34.2 trillion of non-bank financial entities' assets were reported.

Another study which defined shadow banking as institutions carrying out credit transformations through wholesale funding by issuing tradeable securities and which are outside the purview of the banking regulator in the USA has observed that shadow liabilities reached a peak of $10 trillion in the USA in 2007, while traditional liabilities amounted to about $12 trillion based on Dynamic Stochastic General Equilibrium (DSGE) model. The study has also suggested to base regulation on the EF of a financial institution, rather than on its legal form (Fève, Moura and Pierrard 2017). The study has analysed the interaction between traditional and shadow banking and has shown that in the presence of shadow banking, a countercyclical buffer rule should react to total credit in the economy rather than to a narrower measure represented by credit supplied by the traditional banking sector.

The growth of shadow banking has been attributed as failed enforcement of regulations and light touch regulations by other study (Admati 2015) which states that the exposures of the biggest institutions kept in shadow banking system to hide risk exposure can be viewed as 'shadow hedge funds' given their enormous scope and complexity.

The global regulatory standard-setting bodies have taken a number of steps to eliminate toxic forms of shadow banking and also transforming shadow banking into resilient market-based finance. In 2011, the FSB carried out an assessment which showed that the policy responses accorded to the shadow banking sector risks after the GFC has led to resilience in market-based finance including reduction of risks and reinforcement of benefits.

In the earlier assessment of FSB, the importance of asset management has grown rapidly. FSB has noted that collective investment vehicles which are susceptible to bank-run like funding withdrawals now account for almost two-thirds of identified shadow banking, up from less than one-third prior to the crisis. However, asset management is growing positively from the perspective of creating new sources of funding and investment, reducing over-reliance on bank funding and these positive aspects do bring diversity to the financial system and helps make the system more resilient. However, FSB has also noted that asset management's vastly increased importance requires management of systemic risk in times of stress.

The recent tightening of bank capital and liquidity regulation may incentivize the growth of shadow banks (Irani et al. 2018). It has been observed that when weakly capitalized banks reduce loan exposure, less-regulated non-banks fill the gap. This substitution process is strongly manifested for loans with higher capital requirements and when bank capital is more costly. It has also been observed that this process resulting in growth of shadow banks may lead to emergence of systemic vulnerabilities.

Strengthening of Regulation and Supervision in OTC and Commodity Derivatives Markets

The opaqueness in the OTC and derivatives markets on account of being traded directly between counterparties contributed immensely to the systemic risk due to their scale of business activity which even exceeded the global banking and economic activity and the interconnectedness between the financial institutions.

Another factor which led to building–up of risks in the system was lack of transparency in the OTC markets. The insurance giant, American International Group (AIG), due to opaqueness of portfolio building process, went into providing huge protections believing it would not be required to settle claims. This gross underestimation of risk led to it having to be bailed out by the Federal Reserve. The opaqueness in this process is troublesome as the amount of protection sold by AIG was not disclosed to market participants who kept on buying further protection from AIG.

Improving transparency in the OTC markets was one of the main requirements for post-crisis financial stability which was also considered by the G20. G20 countries, therefore, showed commitment of enhancing transparency by declaring that they will trade standardized OTC derivatives through exchanges having a central counterparty (CCP) for clearing and reporting these derivatives to the trade repositories (TR).

Significant strides have been made in meeting the G20 commitments through international policy development, adoption of legislation and regulation, and expansion of infrastructure. According to the latest FSB's report on implementation of OTC derivative market reforms, 17 countries have put in place mechanism to determine the central clearing of standardized OTC derivatives. Central clearing requirements are now in force in 11 jurisdictions, mostly for interest rate derivatives. Availability of CCPs has increased to 32, with cross-border CCPs, thereby facilitating seamless cross-border central clearing. Comprehensive frameworks for determining mandatory platform trading requirements are in force in 12 jurisdictions, and requirements to trade particular product types on exchanges or trading platforms are established in six jurisdictions. Almost all the member jurisdictions have trade reporting requirement in place. Considerable work was undertaken to achieve harmonized trade and product identifiers and the governance frameworks for those.

The focus has been on greater exchange-related transactions, TRs and/or CCPs supplemented by a robust reporting system. For example, the International Swaps and Derivatives Association (ISDA) has taken the initiative in the USA and has awarded mandate to the Depository Trust & Clearing Corporation (DTCC) to further consolidate the existing TR for CDS and similarly to TriOptima (a company registered in Sweden which already has a service for trade compression) for interest rate derivatives. Some TRs have also been constituted in EU jurisdiction. The DFA of July 2010 and the European Market Infrastructure Regulation provide for TRs. However, there can be a flip side of this useful initiative that by migrating OTC products to CCPs, we are adding to the list of systemically important institutions as all the risks are now being warehoused in these CCPs. While CCPs are using collateral and netting the payment, the risks can only be eliminated if post-netting risks are redistributed back to their clearing members. Also, as CCPs are getting exposed to incentive of profit-making leading to diluting their public utility characteristics, they should monitor the systemic risks and have suitable risk management policies to manage the feedback and procyclical dimensions.

This opens up CCPs to additional requirements as they are taking on enormous amount of counterparty credit risks, shifting of focus from being public oriented to profit-making, and hence may require a central bank liquidity support. Lin et al. (2013) proposed that CCPS should be mandated to maintain capital corresponding to a stress period calibration instead of point-in-time risk parameter inputs as point in time models can be procyclical. This conservative approach to set initial margins would also result in stability of the initial margin requirement during stress periods which would mean less pressure on Clearing Members' liquidity reserves that can be deployed to meet refinancing gaps elsewhere on the balance sheet during times of stress. Along with this, any systemically important CCP may also require an effective recovery and resolution regime with the provision of potential loss-sharing among clearing participants. Other factors such as global presence, regulatory arbitrage due to operations in different jurisdictions, inconsistent or conflicting regulations need to be assessed as well. Efforts being put in by the Committee on Payment and Settlement Systems (CPSS) and the IOSCO promoting the resilience of the financial system will lead to reduced probability of a financial crisis as suggested by BIS-sponsored macroeconomic impact assessment of OTC derivatives regulatory reforms.

There has also been a discussion on possible adverse effects of involvement of banks in derivatives markets. BCBS has taken a number of initiatives to increase the capital requirements for banks' exposure to OTC derivatives. The capital requirement for OTC derivatives which are not cleared through a qualified CCP has been increased substantially by requiring banks to compute a new capital charge called credit valuation adjustment. Market risk capital requirements have already been increased substantially. The result of higher capital requirements has been that many banks have reduced their exposure to complex trading strategies using derivatives. However, there has also been a criticism that banks' withdrawal from derivatives market may have implications for market liquidity. This may ultimately impact the end users of derivatives which rely on banks to hedge their market risk exposure.

The FSB progress report of OTC market derivative as at the end of June 2017 indicated that 22 TRs or TR-like entities have been authorized and operating in all FSB member countries except South Africa and Turkey. Additionally, in some jurisdictions, reporting of OTC derivatives transactions is facilitated by means of an entity, facility, service, utility, government authority, etc., that are not established as an authorized TR but that are used by market participants to report OTC derivatives trade data or provide TR-like services.

Regarding the swaps, in accordance with the DFA, any derivative swap transaction was subjected to new set of rules, since banks (or branches) registered with the FDIC or with access to the Fed discount window are required to segregate their derivatives business into a separately capitalized legal entity along with reporting all the derivatives trades routed through the CCP clearing houses (eligible swaps will require clearance of derivatives clearing organization, and the reporting of trades needs to be done to a Swap Data Repository, with positions in certain securities subject to quantitative limits set by the Commodity Futures Trading Commission (CFTC) and Securities and Exchange Commission (SEC), which will share jurisdiction over the market).

Margin Requirements in Non-centrally Cleared Derivatives

As regards the non-centrally cleared derivatives (NCCDs) or customized derivative products, BCBS issued the final margin requirement framework in September 2013 with a revision later in March 2015. The full phase-in schedule has been adjusted to reflect this nine-month change in implementation. The revisions also institute a six-month phase-in of the requirement to exchange variation margin, beginning 1 September 2016. As per the twelfth progress report of FSB (Financial Stability Board 2017b), as at the end of June 2017, comprehensive margin requirements for NCCDs were in place for 14 jurisdictions, up from 3 in August 2016. However, 10 jurisdictions do not have requirements in force, and six are not expected to have them in place by end 2018. Margin requirements will make NCCDs market safer by reducing the contagion risk and better management of counterparty credit risk by banks. This will also work to incentivize the central clearing of the derivative trades.

The implementation of margin requirements for NCCDs in EMEs like India requires creating legal and institutional infrastructure for efficient exchange of margins. India has deferred the implementation of margin requirements to provide market participants adequate time to plan and prepare for the new requirements (Reserve Bank of India 2016).

Ratings by Credit Rating Agencies: Need to Reduce Reliability

One of the major contributors of the GFC was the unrealistically high credit ratings assigned to mortgage-backed securities, in particular to the upper tranches of collateralized debt obligations and the major firms and investors who blindly relied on them for risk assessment had to pay a heavy price. This blind reliance lead to 'herd behaviour' and ultimately to the abrupt sell-off of securities when they were downgraded (cliff effects) leading to systemic disruption due to procyclicality effect. To address these issues, in October 2010, the FSB had set up principles for reducing reliance on CRA ratings and bolster them with internal credit risk assessment practices.

Developing alternative risk assessment capabilities would be a big challenge for the standard setters who would be required to find incentives for market participants to develop internal rating methodologies and conduct their own credit risk assessment adequately supplemented by timelines and transition plans. Investment managers should be directed to analyse the risk as per the complexity and other characteristics of the investment instruments and the significance of the exposure; and in case of inability to do so, it should refrain from such investments. Regulations and guidelines should ensure that market participants and central counterparties do not automatically trigger large, discrete collateral calls on margin agreements on derivatives and SFTs based on changes in CRA ratings of counterparties or of collateral assets. It would also require the supervisors to enhance their capabilities to oversee and enforce sound internal credit risk management. Finally, public disclosure about the credit risk assessment approach and process is also required.

The business model of CRAs has some inherent flaws—CRAs are paid by the financial entities, issuers of securities to whom they award a rating, which is a potent conflict of interest. Given the existing financial relationship between CRAs and their rated companies, lack of an unbiased view is only expected.

A regulatory system on the CRAs was desirable. Europe led the way by bestowing European Securities and Markets Authority (ESMA) the exclusive supervisory jurisdiction over CRAs registered in the EU. The G20 also identified and affected amendments to their CRA regulations such as restricting unsolicited ratings of EU sovereign debt to three per year to avoid market disruptions. A central European Rating Platform has been identified on which all ratings are required to be published along with inaction of liability clauses on CRAs for their actions leading to either breaching regulations or causing damage to investors. Disclosure-enhancing rules have also been defined.

The same principles were also echoed in the Dodd–Frank Financial Reform Act in the USA with additional oversight over CRAs being mandated by creating an Office of Credit Ratings within SEC, which has been tasked with the overall oversight and enhanced regulation of the CRAs. Rating agencies are now subject to new regulations on maintenance of data and information on performance and controls, reporting of results and operations, internal governance, conflict of interest and whistle-blowing protections.

Section 939A of the DFA required federal regulators to remove references to credit ratings and find alternatives leading to revision in most rules that relied on NRSRO ratings. Banning the use of ratings in regulation has attempted to address the perverse incentives created by the use of ratings and also to the impression that credit ratings were one of the fundamental reasons for the recent financial crisis (Soroushian 2016). BCBS has also developed a framework for computation of regulatory capital for credit risk which does not make use of external ratings. This alternative approach of computing regulatory capital can be used by jurisdictions like the USA which ban use of ratings in the regulatory framework. Further, in order to reduce the mechanistic reliance on external credit ratings, the revised framework requires banks to conduct sufficient due diligence in jurisdictions which allow use of ratings in regulation (Basel Committee on Banking Supervision 2017a, 2017b).

Executive Compensation Practices: A Revisit

There existed a divergent view between the industry participants, IOSCO members and some securities regulators on linkage between compensation practices in the asset management sector and financial stability wherein generally it is viewed that there is no direct link with few regulators believing that the compensation practices may have potential effects on trust and confidence in the markets and sound compensation practices could assist in addressing them.

The primary focus of post-crisis regulatory reform has been to reduce the risk in financial system through improved regulations by limiting excessive leverage and monitoring the bank's portfolio for any undue risk being taken. However, it is also recognized that there is a need for financial institutions to have a complete relook over incentive-based compensation structures which induce excessive risk-taking within institutions. When regulators and supervisors monitor bank activity but the incentives for risk-taking are still present, executives may find new ways to 'game the system' (Larcker et al. 2014). This may ultimately lessen the impact of reforms. It is therefore considered important to have a thorough relook at the incentives for risk-taking present in the institutions.

Syncing with the risk outcomes, time sensitivity and long-term profitability alignment have been called for as the compensation to be adjusted for all types of risk with each FSB member having clearly defined national regulations and supervisory guidance in this regard addressing any potential regulatory arbitrage as a result of market developments and emerging risks. These guidelines should apply to all significant financial institutions and especially to large, systemically important firms. Supervisory cooperation in the area of compensation practices should also form a part of the agenda of supervisory colleges. As regards the Pillar 3 disclosures, special emphasis has been given to independence and expertise of the institution's remuneration committee, to the independence of risk and compliance functions in the compensation process and to the evidence of real cultural change within the institution.

A report published by the Board of Governors of the Federal Reserve System (2011) on incentive compensation practices mentioned that through risk adjustment of awards and deferral of payments, all firms in the horizontal review discouraged employees from getting the organization exposed to imprudent risks. Another survey by the Federal Reserve showed deferring of more than 60 per cent of senior bank executives' bonuses for the largest US banks (Nasiripour 2011). An idea of a 'bonus pool' was also conferred averaging the manager's performance over the years and creating an escrow account for use in case of losses (Roubini and Mihm 2010). Another interesting recommendation was regarding holding back about 20 per cent compensation of top employees by SIFIs which was to be forfeited if the capital level falls below a benchmark (Baily et al. 2013). Also, the threshold of forfeiture must have sufficient cushion before the firm violates regulatory requirements or bond maturity payments.

Another BIS working paper has concluded that the structure of bank CEO compensation has changed after the introduction of the Principles and Standards of Sound Compensation Practices (PSSCP) by the FSB in 2011. This resulted in shift in the variable compensation which becomes less (positively) correlated with short-term profit and more (negatively) correlated with bank risk. A distinction was also observed between firms with and without a chief risk officer and for investment banks for which the correlation with short-term bank profits remained similar (weak) before and after the introduction of P&S (Cerasi et al. 2017). Another NBER working paper suggested to broad base the compensation practices which has been historically linked to many factors, namely boards and shareholders' attempts to maximize firm value, executives' attempts to maximize their own rents (perhaps in conjunction with entrenched boards and inattentive shareholders) and institutional forces such as legislation, taxation, accounting policies and social pressures (Edmans, Gabaix and Jenter 2017).

BCBS has issued a report, 'Range of Methodologies for Risk and Performance Alignment of Remuneration' in 2011 which analyses and discusses the methodologies used by institutions to adjust remuneration, mainly variable component, to risk and performance and has examined various elements of the compensation process to link it with the practices being followed. The report has concluded that firms are using both the financial and non-financial measures for employee performance assessment with a trend towards using economic efficiency measures like risk-adjusted return on the capital. Reflecting the FSB's objective that supervisors should support compensation practices development, the report is intended to help promote the adoption by banks of sound remuneration practices and to achieve a greater degree of consistency in the implementation of the FSB principles.

As PSSCPs are not international standards, the onus of its consistent implementation by all such institutions relied on the national regulators and supervisors. These principles had also identified compensation as one of the priority areas for implementation monitoring. There is also a need for inter-regulator coordination for mitigating possibilities of any regulatory arbitrage. At the national level, there are different degrees of intervention in case a bank fails to comply.

The national supervisor (a) can exercise moral suasion to convince the bank to comply; then it can escalate using (b) firmer interventions within the range of supervisory actions that are applied, including, where available, increasing the bank's specific prudential requirements, such as capital requirements. At the supranational level, coordination among supervisors has the objective to prevent regulatory arbitrage by multinational institutions.

The FSB Compensation Monitoring Contact Group (CMCG) and the IOSCO Compensation Experts Group (CEG) organized a joint roundtable on 13 December 2016 with representatives from some of the major participants in securities market activities. The CEG conducted a survey of securities regulators in 21 IOSCO member jurisdictions on the various aspects of the compensation policy, practices and risk alignment. The major findings are discussed further.

Compensation Practices at Banking Organizations

The compensation practices adopted by banking organizations are as follows:

- Majority jurisdictions had implemented the P&S guidelines.
- With different approaches, the oversight of compensation was embedded with the supervisor.
- The links between compensation and misconduct was being minutely assessed by the supervisors.
- Increased use of back testing and validation practices in this area.
- In-year adjustments to compensation continue to be the compensation tool of choice. Application of malus is still rare in many jurisdictions, while clawback is subject to more significant legal impediments or enforcement issues in many jurisdictions.
- The identification of material risk-takers (MRTs) and the governance mechanisms around these determinations continue to differ significantly between jurisdictions.

It is also necessary to be mindful of the certain unintended consequences of over-regulation of compensation practices within financial institutions. Over-regulation of compensation practices may lead to talent distortion between regulated and other un-regulated or less regulated financial institutions. Further, if regulation adversely affects level of compensation in financial institutions vis-à-vis other institutions who compete in the same market for talent, financial institutions may start to offer higher fixed compensation structures to their employees which may have implications for efficiency of these institutions. Ultimately it may turn out to be management of trade-off between financial stability and efficiency of financial institutions.

Thematic and Country Level Peer Reviews

FSB gauges the implementation of its advisories relating to supervisory and regulatory concern and various recommendations through a mechanism of thematic peer review, wherein a theme based on international financial standards and policy prescriptions and its implications on systemic financial stability is surveyed and its implementation compared across the FSB membership. These reviews have the objective to encourage consistent cross-country and cross-sector implementation of standards and policies and to make future recommendations. This additionally provides an opportunity for FSB members to engage in peer-to-peer dialogue and knowledge sharing. For example, a peer review of resolution regimes was published in April 2013, which was followed by the publication of second thematic review in March 2016.

Thematic peer reviews complement FSB country peer reviews, which focus on the progress made by an individual FSB member jurisdiction in implementing IMF–World Bank FSAP regulatory and supervisory recommendations. All BCBS members will be assessed over time with priority being given to jurisdictions which are home to G-SIBs.

The reforms of FSB are not in the nature of 'one size fits all' and certain reforms may not be apt or suitable to the financial system of a particular jurisdiction. Andrew Sheng, ex-chairman, Hong Kong Securities and Futures Commission stated that major Asian jurisdictions are caught between the USA and EU when rules are not harmonized between the two. Asian regulators and banks are good citizens. They follow because they are rule-takers and not rule-makers. Emerging markets being rule-takers of whatever is decided between the two cannot really decide on their own regime framework. Hence, issues remain pending until it is decided by the USA and EU. One of the major criticisms of the FSB's work is that its reforms fitted the advanced markets, but it had little clue on how they impacted the emerging markets. Former Federal Reserve Governor Dan Tarullo and European politicians have started saying that they may have to wind back some rules. Hence, it is time for Asians to think for themselves on what is the best fit and they have to realize that the idea of a level playing field is a myth (Alexander 2017a). The FSB should take into account these aspects in their thematic peer reviews.

In 2012, BCBS launched its comprehensive RCAP. The RCAP monitors the timely adoption of Basel standards by its member countries and conducts peer reviews on the completeness and consistency of the standards. Further, it also seeks to assess outcomes of the application of these standards. The RCAP has clearly led to improvements in the consistency of banking regulation across BCBS member jurisdictions. The assessments of the capital framework originally identified more than 1,200 inconsistencies or deviations, and many of them were rectified during the assessment. The process has also led to the discovery that many of the important countries like the USA and EU are lacking in appropriate implementation of many critical areas of regulations which does not promote the consistent implementation across the globe.

Harmonization of Accounting Standards

International comparability of balance sheets is generally hampered due to different accounting treatment accorded to similar items across different jurisdictions. This may lead to distortion in financial regulation, regulatory level playing field and may lead to regulatory arbitrage across jurisdictions. For example, derivatives netting rules are far more lenient in the USA (US GAAP) than Europe IFRS accounting rules, thus allowing for vast divergence in accounting of derivatives between these two jurisdictions. Similarly, the treatment of regulatory balance sheet ratios related to total assets such as leverage ratios differs between the US and European banks leading to a lower leverage ratios for the US banks as compared to the European banks.

The BCBS is encouraging for global convergence of accounting standards between the International Accounting Standards Board (IASB) and the Financial Accounting Standards Board (FASB), especially in the areas which are subject to interpretation. A few issues are under intense debate.

The debate has largely focused on specific issues relating to the role of and valuation challenges associated with 'mark-to-market' or 'fair value' accounting and the related aspect of determining the extent of impairment of financial assets, 'OBS reporting' of assets and liabilities including those arising from OTC derivatives, securitization transactions and involvements with special purpose entities. The 'adverse selection problem' related to the accounting and measurement of the fair valuation of derivatives had a prominent impact in exacerbating negative effect of GFC. Another lesson from the Lehman Brothers case was the treatment of a repurchase agreement as a sale and forward contract to purchase instead of treating it as a financing transaction (under IFRS). This led to a reduction in the firm's apparent leverage and created a misleading balance sheet. Such opportunities for tinkering and loopholes need to be plugged. A third issue relates to netting or offsetting of financial instruments such as derivative contracts and the inability of accounting methods to deal with such transactions. The fourth issue which led to low provisioning was related to impairment of financial assets: whether provisioning for potential losses on loans as under IAS 39 was required to be done on an 'incurred loss' basis as against forward-looking 'expected loss' basis.

What was proposed then was determination of an asset as loan or security based on its cash flow leading to categorization either as amortized cost (for those financial assets which comprised solely of payments of principal and interest that are held for the collection of contractual cash flows) or as fair value through other comprehensive income (for those comprised solely of payments of principal and interest that are both held for the collection of contractual cash flows and for sale) or as fair value through profit and loss (for financial assets that do not qualify for measurement at either amortized cost or fair value through other comprehensive income). Similar treatment would be recommended for financial liabilities as well. For most financial assets and financial liabilities measured at amortized cost, public companies would be required to disclose their fair values.

Considerable progress has been made towards convergence of FASB and IFRS, and most jurisdictions have adopted IFRS. In India, the IFRS converged Indian Accounting Standards known as 'Ind-AS' have been put in place and the financial institutions were mandated to shift their accounting to this standard with effect from 1 April 2018. However, on 5 April 2018, the Reserve Bank of India (2018) through its press release mentioned that the implementation of Ind-AS has been deferred by one year.

Legal Entity Identifier

Legal entity identifier (LEI) is a code that uniquely identifies parties to financial transactions with linking it to the 'business card' information. The LEI is a 20-digit, alphanumeric code that connects to key reference information that enables clear and unique identification of companies participating in global financial markets. This framework whose need was highlighted during the GFC has since been put in place to provide financial companies and global financial regulators a better view of true exposures and counterparty risks across the world's financial system. This initiative will not only save costs on collection, cleaning and data aggregation but will also reduce the regulatory reporting burden, facilitate cross-border exchange of standardized, aggregate supervisory data among regulators, supervisors and financial stability authorities, thus vastly improving the rigours of comprehensive oversight of financial institutions and markets with a global reach.

Based on the recommendations of the FSB and after endorsement of its charter by the G20 countries, LEI Regulatory Oversight Committee (ROC), a group of over 70 public authorities from more than 40 countries was established in January 2013 for coordinating and overseeing a worldwide framework of legal entity identification. In June 2014, the Global LEI Foundation (GLEIF) was established by the ROC to act as the operational arm of the Global LEI System. A major initiative of the foundation is the provision of a database of LEIs on their website along with a search function,[1] wherein one can check if an entity has an LEI, or access the reference data associated with an LEI, including verifying whether the LEI is current and can be used in regulatory reporting.

Entities can obtain LEI from any of the Local Operating Units (LOUs) accredited by GLEIF. To start with, banks have been advised in November 2017 to obtain the LEI for the existing corporate borrowers having total exposures of ₹0.50 billion and above. It will then be introduced for borrowers having total exposures between ₹0.05 billion to ₹0.50 billion in a phased manner.

The benefits from LEI are immense and while the industry use of LEIs has progressed, the benefit can be reaped if it is adopted universally. Its use should be expanded as a regulatory requirement across all financial markets.

Ring-fencing

Another landmark change in the domestic banking space that the UK had planned is a separation of retail business from international and investment banking operations by 1 January 2019. A decade on from the financial crisis, the largest UK banking groups are required to implement 'ring-fencing'—or separation—of their retail business from their international and investment banking operations. This essentially puts in perspective a framework in which retail activities of the banks are being insulated from the risks emanating from the international and investment banking activities. The post-crisis regulatory framework and the ring-fencing regime have been designed to be consistent with the other parts. However, it is unclear what constraints will be imposed on resolution options for internationally active banks operating in the UK, since the ring-fence is a national

[1] https://www.gleif.org/lei/search (accessed on 25 January 2019).

initiative. Correspondingly, at least one other country, notably the US, has adopted structural banking reforms (Volcker Rule and the Intermediate Holding Company structure) that are not necessarily fully consistent with the UK ring-fence, exposing banks operating in both companies to dual set of operational constraints and compliance obligations.[2]

Financial Transaction Tax

Another proposal of creating buffers during boom periods through small token taxation was something proposed as early as 1936 when John Maynard Keynes first made a reference to it in his book *The General Theory of Employment, Interest and Money*. The idea gained further popularity in 1978 by James Tobin through a proposal related to foreign exchange transactions and was known as Tobin Tax. Post-GFC, this idea was implemented by France, Germany and the UK and was also recommended by the IMF. This was done as a means to recoup costs incurred in bailing out crises-ridden financial institutions, accumulate funds for any future bailouts, shrink the size of undertaxed financial sectors and discourage risky behaviour in banks. A small levy of tax on all wholesale capital market secondary transactions is expected to discourage speculative carry trades, short-term transactions which flow into the economy in search of quick gains out of inter-country 'price differentials'.

A regime of FTT of 0.1 per cent on shares and bonds, and 0.01 per cent on the derivatives of shares and bonds will be implemented in the EU by early 2018.[3] The tax base applying to derivatives is the nominal value of the underlying assets. The proposed tax will be levied

---

[2] See, for example: 1. Chow, Julian and Surti, Jay (2011) 'Making Banks Safer: Can Volcker and Vickers Do It?' IMF Working Paper 11/236. 2. Vinals, Jose, Ceyla Pazarbasioglu, Jay Surti, Aditya Narain, Michaela Erbenova, and Julian Chow (2013) 'Creating a Safer Financial System: Will the Volcker, Vickers and Liikanen Structural Measures Help?' IMF Staff Discussion Note 13/4.

[3] In January 2013, the EU voted to allow 11 countries (Austria, Belgium, Estonia, France, Germany, Greece, Italy, Portugal, Slovakia, Slovenia and Spain) to implement this much sooner in early 2014.

according to the fiscal residence of the seller of an asset. Another example is South Korea which was planning to impose a similar but variable tax named 'Spahn tax' on foreign currency transactions to limit speculative inflows of foreign capital at very low rates in normal times but high rates in times of extreme fluctuations in the value of the currency.

Dealing with Sovereign Risk?

The GFC manifested also in several European countries through rising sovereign financial stress and threat of sovereign bankruptcy, notably in Iceland, Ireland, Greece and Cyprus.[4] This may be a reflection of the bailout effects carried out by these sovereigns. Reverse linkage was also visible in the case of Greece where difficulties in government finances tended to cause substantial problems for banks, primarily because of the huge portfolios of government bonds held by them. 'Debt trap' forces these mechanics to develop, but the policy responses to deal with the resultant sovereign bankruptcy are typically long and involve protracted rescheduling negotiations.

Several studies analysing the relationship between debt levels of a country and growth have proved that productivity grows more slowly if the debt levels exceed a certain percentage of GDP. Cecchetti, Mohanty and Zampolli (2011) identified a threshold of 96 per cent of GDP, beyond which public debt becomes a drag on growth. The threshold of debt–GDP ratio above 90 per cent was also shown by Reinhart and Rogoff (2010). For the Euro area, Baum, Checcherita-Westphal and Rother (2013) found a non-linear effect on growth, leading to lower growth above a ratio of 95 per cent. A 10-percentage point increase in the initial debt-to-GDP ratio is associated with a slowdown in annual real per capita GDP growth of 0.15 percentage points per year (Kumar and Woo 2010).

---

[4] According to Standard & Poor's sovereign ratings list 2012, 55 countries had their bonds considered as 'junk bonds', that is, bonds that have a high default risk.

The call for a sovereign bankruptcy regime has historical under-pinnings which started over 200 years ago by Adam Smith,[5] as well as echoed during macro-financial crises of the last few decades—the Latin American debt crisis of the 1980s, the Mexican crisis of 1995 and Russia's 1998 default. In 2001, the IMF formulated a proposal for a sovereign debt restructuring mechanism (SDRM), which was rejected by its shareholders in April 2003. Calls for some form of international sovereign bankruptcy regime had returned with renewed vigour in the wake of the GFC, especially when several countries such as Belize, Jamaica, St Kitts and Nevis and Grenada have restructured their debt, with Greece executing the largest debt restructuring in history in February 2012.

The sovereign-bank nexus is a vicious cycle which can be best managed by way of robust regulatory capital requirement regime for banks wherein sovereign exposures are not treated as risk-free when the situation so warrants. Large and undiversified sovereign exposure in the form of large portfolio of government bonds is also what makes sovereign default a potential systemic event for banks. The answer to this lies in the large exposure framework (LEF) which would cap the investment in one single debtor but the key lies in applying the framework to sovereigns as well. However, what is required is a clear resolution framework in place in order to protect the interests of shareholders and creditors and also helping the government from having to rescue banks with taxpayers' money.

Regulation of Banks' Exposure to Sovereigns

BCBS has taken an important initiative in this regard by setting up of a high-level Task Force on Sovereign Exposures in January 2015 to review the regulatory treatment of sovereign exposures and recom-mend potential policy options. BCBS published a discussion paper on

---

[5] 'When it becomes necessary for a state to declare itself bankrupt, in the same manner as when it becomes necessary for an individual to do so, a fair, open, and avowed bankruptcy is always the measure which is both least dishonourable to the debtor, and least hurtful to the creditor.'

regulatory treatment of sovereign exposures in 2017 which outlines the proposed framework. The proposed framework mentions that all kinds of sovereign exposures would require a capital charge and also it will depend on the amount of exposure banks are having to sovereigns, thereby creating an LEF. However, proposed framework may have certain undesirable impact for EMEs as domestic currency sovereign exposures play a critical role in the overall financial system and bank risk management. In a country like India where there are statutory requirements for banks to hold government securities, such capital requirements and a form of LEF will not be practical. Also, the proposals which depend on external ratings are also questionable as capability of rating agencies to assess sovereign credit risk in their domestic currencies may not be robust. Bias of sovereign credit rating agencies (CRAs) against developing countries has been well documented (Ozturk 2014). The damage caused by this bias has also been analysed in the context of European economies (Vernazza and Nielsen 2015). In view of this, it is necessary that BCBS should revisit its proposals of capital computation for bank exposures to sovereigns in their domestic currency.

Assessment of the Risk Architecture and Culture in the Banks

Supervisory process has generally been ex-post in their assessment through penalties and fines. However, these have not prevented a series of scandals in the banking sector leading to a trust deficit having horrific economic consequences. This has called for moving from an ex-post assessment to an ex-ante assessment in the form of a risk culture. Accountability, incentives, mapping of responsibilities, integrity, collaborative working and broad-based internal and external communication are the boosters in this process. To maximize the potential of people, the bank needs to embrace fully collaborative working in diverse teams that value robust debate. And it will focus on improving how to communicate, both internally and externally. Colleagues must be empowered to raise issues promptly, to challenge and to voice any concerns they have (Carney 2017).

Though measuring and managing of risks embedded in the business and setting up an appropriate risk governance architecture was in vague for quite some time, risk culture assessment has gained popularity only in the aftermath of the financial crises. While the banks' management is responsible for putting in place a strong risk culture, the supervisors' role in helping them doing so is more clearly being articulated now. The whole process is expected to be a top-down and bottom-up approach along with the supervisor assessing this aspect on an ongoing basis.

As pointed out by FSB, there are four indicators of a sound risk culture—tone from the top, accountability, effective challenge and incentives. The FSB's emphasis on the risk culture has ensured this should be discussed as a part of supervisory review conversation with the board and with senior management to define risk culture and communicating it throughout the organization while supervision tests behaviours so as to get a reaffirmation that the prevailing risk-taking behaviour is acceptable at all levels. The Bank of England has been pursuing a series of measures to convert ethical drift into ethical lift.

The staggering amount of fines paid globally has been a major concern regarding the redressal costs related to misconduct risks. Fines paid by the UK banks since 2009 have been roughly equivalent to private capital raised during the same period. Further, globally roughly $275 billion in legal costs for global banks has been used since 2008 which may lead to about $5 trillion of reduced lending capacity to the real economy (Shafik 2016). Another study estimated the fines and legal costs to be of tune around US$320 billion since the crisis (BCG 2017). These costs even though difficult to estimate have been found to be substantial. What is required is bolstering of these deterrents with reinforcing individual accountability. In order to reduce 'misconduct risk' in financial sector, FSB and IOSCO have come up with certain measures and recommendations for strengthening financial institution governance, compensation structures, etc., in addition to recommendations for actions directed towards market structures and practices by 2017-end (Financial Stability Board 2017a, 2017b).

Data Standards, Transparency and Disclosure

The crisis exposed another weakness in the then prevailing system which was the lack of industry-wide standards needed to produce high-quality financial data. This not only hindered transparency but also obstructed in accurate assessment of inter-firm linkages and industry-wide exposures, the most glaring example being that of Lehman Brothers. At that time, it was realized that this weakness in data standards and disclosure not only contributed to the crisis but also tended to hamper official efforts to contain it.

To make the financial system more resilient, such gaps needed to be addressed to improve the ability to spot financial vulnerabilities by looking at designated indicators of say leverage, liquidity, maturity transformation, interconnectedness, complexity, etc. Financial stability monitoring, analysis and research require solid, reliable, granular, timely and comprehensive data for analysis and monitoring. Further, as a complement, a lot of focus is being placed on transparency in data and its analysis in the ongoing regime of regulatory reforms so much so that the word 'transparency' appears at least 80 times in the DFA which has designated Office of Financial Research (OFR) to take on this crucial responsibility of increasing market transparency through sharing required data with relevant financial industry participants and with the public. Not more but better information is essential for transparency which is achievable only through better data standards. Sharing of such information would not only help reduce uncertainty but also foster clarity.

BCBS, in January 2015, has come out with revised Pillar 3 disclosure requirements, which address the shortcomings observed in the Pillar 3 framework during the crisis (Box 2.1). The revisions focus on improving the transparency of the internal model-based approaches that banks use to calculate their minimum regulatory capital and enable market participants to better compare banks' disclosures. The Pillar 3 framework in force at the time of crisis, even its enhanced parts pertaining to market risk and securitization in 2009, failed to precisely capture material risks in a bank and to inform the market participants on the adequacy of capital in the system as also in the individual banks.

Box 2.1: BIS-BCBS Standards: Revised Guiding Principles for Banks' Pillar 3 Disclosures, January 2015 (Extracts)

Principles
1. Disclosures should be clear.
2. Disclosures should be comprehensive.
3. Disclosures should be meaningful to users.
4. Disclosures should be consistent over time.
5. Disclosures should be comparable across banks.

Scope of Application
Applies to internationally active banks at the top consolidated level.

Assurance of Pillar 3 Data
The information provided by banks under Pillar 3 must be subject, at a minimum, to the same level of internal review and internal control processes as the information provided by banks for their financial reporting (i.e., the level of assurance must be the same as for information provided within the management discussion and analysis part of the financial report).

Approval Authority
Banks must establish a formal board-approved disclosure policy for Pillar 3 information that sets out the internal controls and procedures for disclosure of such information.

Revisiting the Issue of Operational Risk

Operational risk has acquired the centre stage as technological innovations have taken over the financial services space and failure to adequately address such risks may not only lead to direct and material financial/reputational losses but also have serious systemic impacts on other banks, customers, counterparties and the financial system. Massive financial frauds have surfaced, while the flash crash of May 2010 exposed the intensity of risks in the high frequency trading, thus bringing back operational risk on the regulators' radar. Drawing on the lessons from the financial crisis, in June 2011, the BCBS enunciated eleven 'principles' for management of operational risk to provide guidance to banks (Box 2.2). To follow up on their implementation, the BCBS had conducted a review covering 60 systemically important banks in 20 jurisdictions through a designed questionnaire by which banks self-assessed their implementation of the principles. It was observed in the review that 'banks are at varying stages of implementing the Principles' but more surprising and unfortunate was the fact that 'many banks had not adequately implemented or addressed the relevant risk management response'.

Box 2.2: BIS-BCBS Review of the Principles for the Sound Management of Operational Risk, 6 October 2014 (Extracts)

- **Risk Identification and Assessment**
  - Increase the use of external data for the purposes of risk management.
  - Ensure that action plans from the operational risk identification and assessment tools are monitored.
- **Change Management**
  - Ensure that their change management programmes are comprehensive and fully implemented.
  - Ensure that post-approval monitoring and post-implementation reviews are fully implemented.
- **Three Lines of Defence**
  - Ensure that effective three lines (business units, risk compliance and audit) of defense model are implemented to appropriately identify and manage operational risk.
  - Assign roles and responsibilities of the three lines of defense to relevant departments, including business units, business unit operational risk management (ORM)), other corporate experts and ORM.
- **Operational Risk Management Framework (ORMF)**
  - Develop the integration of the ORM programme into the bank's strategic decision-making process.
  - Develop a quality assurance programme to ensure that the independent challenge and review applied by the second line of defense result in consistent risk and control assessments.

(Continued)

(Continued)

- **Operational Risk Appetite and Tolerance**
  - o Continue their work to further articulate and implement enhanced and forward-looking operational risk appetite and tolerance statements.
- **Board of Directors**
  - o Consider periodically engaging a benchmarking analysis of the bank's ORM framework with the assistance of independent external advisors, as part of the bank's regular assessment of ORMF's design and effectiveness.
- **Senior Management**
  - o Ensure that the corporate operational risk framework (CORF) has sufficient stature, resources and infrastructure, in relation to other risk management functions, to implement the ORMF.
  - o Develop and implement operational risk training and awareness programmes.
- **Monitoring and Reporting**
  - o Quality and timeliness of information related to external events or environments need to be improved.
- **Control and Mitigation**
  - o Ensure that the bank's risk and insurance management programme is subject to regular board and senior management oversight.
  - o Broaden the scope of outsourcing oversight beyond internal or related party providers.
  - o Consider IT risk within the operational risk appetite and tolerance statement.
- **Business Resilience and Continuity**
  - o All businesses and groups should use a risk-based approach, their participation in disaster recovery and business continuity testing with key service providers.
- **Operational Risk Culture**
  - o Continue their work to further align compensation policies with the operational risk appetite and tolerance statement.
- **Role of Disclosure**
  - o Develop a comprehensive disclosure policy that is subject to approval and oversight by the board, and also subject to independent review.

While finalizing the Basel III reforms, BCBS has streamlined the operational risk framework. The advanced measurement approaches (AMAs) for calculating operational risk capital requirements (which are based on banks' internal models) and the existing three standardized approaches are replaced with a single risk-sensitive standardized approach to be used by all banks. The new standardized approach for operational risk determines a bank's operational risk capital requirements based on two components: (a) a measure of a bank's income and (b) a measure of a bank's historical losses. Conceptually, it assumes (a) that operational risk increases at an increasing rate with a bank's income and (b) that banks which have experienced greater operational risk losses historically are assumed to be more likely to experience operational risk losses in the future. The implementation date for the same has been fixed as on 1 January 2022.

Is Global Regulation Walking a Tight Rope?

FSB, in close collaboration with the standard-setting bodies, and informed by work carried out by its members and other stakeholders (including through a public consultation process), developed a framework for the post-implementation evaluation of the effects of the G20 financial regulatory reforms in July 2017 which analyses whether these reforms are achieving their intended outcomes, and help to identify any material unintended consequences that may have to be addressed, without compromising on the objectives of the reforms. The big question is whether the FSB evaluation could maintain international standards or accelerate their decline (Alexander 2017b). The FSB's final framework sets out three methodologies for studying regulatory impact: examining the effectiveness of individual reforms, identifying the interaction and coherence between reforms and an evaluation of overall effects, including the contribution of the post-crisis rules to the G20 objectives of strong and stable economic growth. The views of a few current and former regulators and policy advisers about whether the FSB can maintain its grip on financial regulation are summarized as follows:

- Paul Fisher (formerly Deputy Governor of Bank of England):

  My overall sense is that most of the work on regulation has been done and what they are doing now is fine-tuning. Some of that fine-tuning could be downwards at the margin, because there is no great desire from the authorities for there to be higher levels of capital overall in the system than we have now.

- David Lawton (the former director of Markets Policy and International at the UK FCA):

  The FSB's strength and legitimacy has been underpinned by the unity of purpose at the G20, but recent developments such as growing tension between the US and China, along with the departure of the UK from the EU, could undermine the cohesion of the G20 itself as an organization. The FSB's evaluation must be convincing. My own sense is the political appetite for changing regulation is waning and the focus will be on asking regulators to review, and adjust, the rough edges.

- Jan Pieter Krahnen (Goethe University):

  A general equilibrium model would allow us to assess the total effect of regulation, which is the sum of several distinct partial effects—some positive, some negative—and you want to see the overall assessment. But this is very difficult and probably not possible. If it is pursued, it is typically done in a very stylised view of the economy and you get only an assessment of possible side-effects, rather than a true real-world assessment.

- Andrew Sheng (an adviser to the China Banking Regulatory Commission and former chairman of the Hong Kong Securities and Futures Commission):

  Post-crisis, there is a belief, which I think is mistaken, that the more rules you put in place, the safer is the system. I am more inclined to believe the reverse is the case. Throughout history, enforcement, not regulation, of key red lines— egregious behaviour tackled early—is what prevents or mitigates a crisis.

- Andrea Resti (associate professor of finance at the Bocconi University in Italy and an adviser to the European Parliament):

  European policymakers would only be willing to introduce new rules in a way that does not really bite and is not really binding and does not really increase the constraints of capital and other constraints that are being imposed on banks.

Rolling Back the Reforms

While there is no doubt that the DFA led to reduction in the systemic risk in the USA, it does not address these risks comprehensively and introduced stringent rules having no bearing on the systemic risks. The Financial Choice Act has been proposed in the USA with an objective that taxpayer bailouts of financial institutions must end, and no company should remain TBTF. The USA has since passed a subset of Choice Act recommendations by enacting the Economic Growth, Regulatory Relief and Consumer Protection Act (the 'Act') in 2018 which roll backs some of the provisions of DFA of 2010. It is also expected that financial regulators will propose revisions to the Volcker Rule regulations that are expected to have a more significant impact on large banking institutions. Alan Greenspan has also mentioned that DFA was a huge mistake as it is replete with dangers, discourages innovation and is merely a box ticking exercise which provides avenues to the financial innovators to outsmart the regulations.

The major changes include removal of certain Volcker Rule limitations on hedge fund and private equity fund naming conventions, the exemption of most small banks from the purview of the Volcker Rule, reduced regulatory burdens for small- and medium-sized BHCs, changes favourably affecting custodial banks' SLR calculations, expansion of public securities offering rules to closed-end exchange listed funds and beneficial capital treatment of certain real estate exposures and municipal obligations that make investments in such assets more attractive to banks under bank capital rules. Two important provisions include increase in the default asset threshold for the designation of SIFIs from $50 billion to $250 billion and no requirement of company-run stress tests for banks with less than $250 billion in assets. Supervisory stress tests for banks between $100 billion and $250 billion in assets can be less frequent than the annual cycle that is currently mandated.

Conclusion

While the shortcomings in the prudential regulation which emerged during the recent crisis have been to a great extent removed or being removed, there is a need to identify and manage new risks. Regulators should not be seen to be failing to recognize evolving risks.

The last crisis was due to inadequacy of bank's capital and liquidity, and inability to recognize macroprudential character of regulation. These shortcomings are being addressed. However, we should also see that technological changes are transforming the banking process. Operational risks being brought by these changes are quite challenging. Potential operational risk shocks due to cyber hacking, crashing of bank's core banking solution systems, large-scale data theft, etc., may acquire systemic proportions. Similarly, risks in shadow banking space, misconduct risk, incentives to take excessive risk due to faulty compensation practices, etc., need continuous monitoring.

References

Alex. 2017. BIS Working Papers No 630: How post-crisis regulation has affected bank CEO compensation, by Vittoria Cerasi, Sebastian M. Deininger, Leonardo Gambacorta and Tommaso Oliviero, April 2017.

Admati, Anat R. 2015, December. *The Missed Opportunity and Challenge of Capital Regulation*. Stanford, CA: Stanford Graduate School of Business.

Alexander, Philip. 2017a, 31 August. *Q&A: Asia Caught in the Basel Crossfire, Says Andrew Sheng*. Available at https://www.risk.net/regulation/5323601/qa-asia-caught-in-the-basel-crossfire-says-andrew-sheng (accessed on 23 January 2019).

Alexander, Philip. 2017b. *In the Balance: Global Regulation Walks a Tightrope.* Available at http://www.finregalert.com/in-the-balance-global-regulation-walks-a-tightrope/ (accessed on 23 January 2019).

Baily, Martin N., John Y. Campbell, John H. Cochrane, Douglas W. Diamond, Darrell Duffie, Kenneth R. French, Anil K. Kashyap, Frederic S. Mishkin, David S. Scharfstein, Robert J. Shiller, Matthew J. Slaughter, Hyun Song Shin and René M. Stulz. 2013, March. *Aligning Incentives at Systemically Important Financial Institutions* (A Proposal by the Squam Lake Group). Available at http://squamlakegroup.org/Squam%20Lake%20Bonus%20 Bonds%20Memo%20Mar%2019%202013.pdf (accessed on 23 January 2019).

Baum, Anja, Cristina Checherita-Westphal and Philipp Rother. 2013. 'Debt and Growth: New Evidence for the Euro Area'. *Journal of International Money and Finance* 32 (C): 809–821.

BCG. 2017, March. *Global Risk 2017: Staying the Course in Banking.* Available at http://image-src.bcg.com/BCG_COM/BCG-Staying-the-Course-in-Banking-Mar-2017_tcm9–146794.pdf (accessed on 23 January 2019).

Board of Governors of the Federal Reserve System. 2011, October. *Incentive Compensation Practices: A Report on the Horizontal Review of Practices at Large Banking Organizations.* Washington, DC: Board of Governors of the Federal Reserve System.

Carney, Mark. 2017, 21 March. 'Worthy of Trust? Law, Ethics and Culture in Banking' (Speech).

Cecchetti, S. G., M. S. Mohanty and F. Zampolli. 2011. 'The Real Effects of Debt'. In *Achieving Maximum Long-Run Growth*, 145–196 (Economic Symposium sponsored by the Federal Reserve Bank of Kansas City). Jackson Hole, WY: Federal Reserve Bank.

Cerasi, Vittoria, Sebastian M. Deininger, Leonardo Gambacorta and Tommaso Oliviero. 2017, April. 'How Post-Crisis Regulation Has Affected Bank CEO Compensation'. BIS Working Paper No. 630. Basel: Monetary and Economic Department, Bank for International Settlements.

Edmans, Alex, Xavier Gabaix and Dirk Jenter. 2017, July. Executive Compensation: A Survey of Theory and Evidence. Working Paper No. 23596. Cambridge, MA: National Bureau of Economic Research.

Fève, Patrick, Alban Moura and Olivier Pierrard. 2017, 24 July. Shadow Banking and Financial Regulation: A Small-Scale DSGE Perspective. Toulouse: Toulouse School of Economics.

Financial Stability Board. 2011, 27 October. *Macroprudential Policy Tools and Frameworks*, (Progress Report to G20). Basel: Financial Stability Board.

———. 2017a, 10 May. FSB Global Shadow Banking Monitoring Report 2016. Basel: Financial Stability Board.

———. 2017b, 29 June. *OTC Derivatives Market Reforms: Twelfth Progress Report on Implementation.* Available at http://www.fsb.org/2017/06/

otc-derivatives-market-reforms-twelfth-progress-report-on-implementation/ (accessed on 23 January 2019).

Gordon, Gwendolyn and David Zaring. 2017. *Ethical Bankers*. Available at https://papers.ssrn.com/sol3/papers.cfm?abstract_id=2932317 (accessed on 23 January 2019).

Irani, Rustom M., Raymakal Iyer, Ralf R. Meisenzahl and Jos´e-Luis Peydr´o. 2018. 'The Rise of Shadow Banking: Evidence from Capital Regulation. Finance and Economics Discussion Series 2018-039. Washington: Board of Governors of the Federal Reserve System. Available at https://doi. org/10.17016/FEDS.2018.039.

Lin, Li and Surti, Jay, 'Capital Requirements for OTC Derivatives CCPs'. *Journal of Shadow Banking and Evidence from Capital Regulation*. Finance, January 2013.

Chow, Julian and Surti, Jay (2011) 'Making Banks Safer: Can Volcker and Vickers Do It?' IMF Working Paper 11/236.

Vinals, Jose, Ceyla Pazarbasioglu, Jay Surti, Aditya Narain, Michaela Erbenova, and Julian Chow. 2013. Creating a Safer Financial System: Will the Volcker, Vickers and Liikanen Structural Measures Help? IMF Staff and Economics Discussion Note 13/4.

Ideas of Order: Charting a Course for the Financial Stability Board, Remark by Randal K. Quarles, Vice Chairman for Supervision, Series 2018–039. Washington, DC: Board of Governors of the Federal Reserve System, Hong Kong 2019. Available at https://doi.org/10.17016/FEDS.2018.039 (accessed on 23 January 2019).

Kumar, Manmohan and Jaejoon Woo. 2010, July. 'Public Debt and Growth'. IMF Working Paper No. 10/174. Washington, DC: International Monetary Fund.

Larcker, David F., Gaizka Ormazabal, Brian Tayan and Daniel J. Taylor. 2014. *Follow the Money: Compensation, Risk, and the Financial Crisis*. Stanford, CA: Stanford University Graduate School of Business.

Nasiripour, S. 2011, 10 October. 'US Banks Defer 60% of Executive Bonuses'. *Financial Times*.

Ozturk, Huseyin. 2014. 'The Origin of Bias in Sovereign Credit Ratings: Reconciling Agency Views with Institutional Quality'. *Journal of Developing Areas* 48 (4): 161–188.

Reinhart, Carmen M. and Kenneth S. Rogoff. 2010. 'Growth in a Time of Debt'. *American Economic Review* (Papers & Proceedings) 100 (2): 573–578.

Reserve Bank of India. 2016, 1 September. *Implementation of Margin Requirements for Non-Centrally Cleared Derivatives*. Available at https://www.rbi.org.in/ scripts/BS_PressReleaseDisplay.aspx?prid=37940 (accessed on 23 January 2019).

———. 2018, 5 April. *Statement on Developmental and Regulatory Policies*. Available at https://www.rbi.org.in/Scripts/BS_PressReleaseDisplay. aspx?prid=43574 (accessed on 23 January 2019).

Roi, Rameswurlall Basant. 2017, 21 August. 'Evolution of the Basel Capital Adequacy Requirements' (Speech). Ebene: International Monetary Fund, Africa Training Institute.

Roubini, N. and Mihm S. 2010. *Crisis Economics*. London: Allen Lane.

Shafik, Minouche. 2016, 20 October. 'From "Ethical Drift" to "Ethical Lift": Reversing the Tide of Misconduct in Global Financial Markets' (Speech).

Skinner, Christina Parajon. 2016. 'Financial Misconduct as Systemic Risk'. *Fordham Law Review* 84.

Soroushian, John. 2016. *Credit Ratings in Financial Regulation: What's Changed Since the Dodd–Frank Act?* Washington, DC: Office of Financial Research.

Vernazza, Daniel R. and Erik F. Nielsen. 2015. '*The Damaging Bias of Sovereign Ratings*'. Available at https://onlinelibrary.wiley.com/doi/10.1111/ecno.12037 (accessed on 23 January 2019).

Part II

Managing Systemic Risk through Macroprudential Policy

The job of macro-prudential policy is to protect the real economy from the financial system, by protecting the financial system from the real economy.

—Alex Brazier

CHAPTER 3

Macroprudential Policy

Strengthening the regulatory provisions for financial institutions, in part by gaining better understanding of human incentives and behaviour, strengthens individual institutions, thereby contributing to macro-financial stability. But, history has time and again proved that the stable individual institutions do not always and necessarily add up to a safe financial system. Increased interconnectedness in financial system, correlations, procyclical nature of leverage and liquidity can very rapidly destabilize a stable looking system. A macroprudential approach is needed to understand this connectedness in risks. The need of the hour is an in-depth insight into systemic risk, its cyclical dimension, its cross-sectional dimension and its various sources. A framework should be developed by the regulatory authorities to understand the movement in macroeconomic variables, enhanced stress-testing framework, robust early warning mechanism (EWM) and countercyclical regulatory provisions. Also the macroprudential policy framework coordination with monetary policy authority is essential for mitigating systemic risk.

Introduction

For all the criticism that crises generate and the negative feelings they evoke, there is at least one silver lining—their ability to impart serious lessons. Lessons that break age-old wisdom, lessons that turn the prevailing 'truths' on their head and lessons that bring about a paradigm shift in the way we perceive the world. The GFC of 2007, notwithstanding all the output losses it caused and the systemic upheaval it generated—the impact of which the world is still unable to recover fully from—certainly brought the policy focus on systemic risk, and macroprudential policy as a means to contain such risk. Like all crises, this one too left the world a lot poorer albeit a tad wiser!

It is not that, prior to GFC, the world was not aware of the pro-cyclical nature of leverage and liquidity or the interconnectedness of financial institutions which could destabilize the financial system. The interplay of financial cycles and the economic booms and busts was also not entirely new. There were lingering questions, even in the pre-crisis world (Schinasi 2006), of the need for financial stability, whether that could be ensured solely through collective private actions and the role, if any, of the regulators in ensuring financial stability. However, the pre-crisis regulation focused predominantly on managing idiosyncratic risks of financial institutions and the monetary policy steadfastly emphasized preserving price stability. It was a fallacy of composition which guided the belief that exclusive microprudential regulation targeting stable, individual institutions would add up to the whole financial system being safe.

The crisis also brought out starkly the difference in perspectives between microprudential and macroprudential regulations. While microprudential regulation focuses on partial equilibrium and individual financial institutions, a 'macroprudential' approach acknowledges the full equilibrium and seeks to safeguard the whole financial system. The crisis helped in the overhauling of the regulatory policies by overlaying the extant prudential framework with a 'macro' focus. Further, the monetary policy too had to re-examine its stance between 'lean' versus 'clean' options to address the issue of systemic risk. In sum, the GFC was not allowed to go waste, as the world got to revise its views on the concepts of systemic risk, financial stability and macroprudential regulation, and the regulators began to design appropriate policies to build resilience of the system. During the crisis, it had become clear that the then existing monetary, fiscal, microprudential tools, even when conducted properly and effectively, do not always suffice to assure financial stability. These need to be combined with macroeconomic and financial policies, aimed at reducing systemic risks arising from cross-sectional factors, namely procyclicality and interconnectedness.

Defining Systemic Risk

Systemic risk was the quintessential elephant in the room as it was always present but failed to be noticed by anyone. A part of the problem could be due to the difficulties in comprehensively defining and identifying systemic risk. One is never fully sure of which risk at which point in time gradually morphs from being idiosyncratic and localized risk, to a systemic risk, impacting a larger number of institutions and a greater part of the financial system. There are many attempts at defining systemic risk each focusing on a particular facet of the risk which is evident from the following references.

De Bandt and Hartmann (2001), for example, defined systemic risk as experiencing systemic events wherein institution(s) affected in a systemic crisis actually fail as a consequence of the initial shock, despite their being fundamentally solvent before the systemic event. As such, systemic risk could be interpreted as a kind of risk propagated by way of shocks spread all over the economy creating diffused distress and disruption all around.

There is also divergence among policy analysts as to the nature of the systemic risk, that is, whether it is exogenous or endogenous. For some, systemic risk is exogenous as the risk emanates from outside, while for some, the risks are internally generated, developing and amplifying over time. According to the Bank for International Settlements (2011), risk emanates from within and is generally an overextension of boom resulting from the interaction between the financial system and real economy which in turn sows the seeds of the subsequent downturn and financial strains.

Not all financial failures could be categorized as systemic risk. For an event to be categorized as systemic risk, its impact should be felt on the other parts of the financial system and on the economy as a whole.

Analysts often draw attention to the examples of stock market bust of 1987 and the dot com bubble of the early 2000s. While the 1987 bust, fuelled by leverage trades, generated systemic risk, dot com bubble bust did not have a systemic impact due to limited financial system exposures. Similarly, not all identified credit booms have been found to be a source of systemic risk. Such ambiguous interpretations pose challenges to policymakers in identifying and managing systemic risks.

Systemic risk can have many dimensions to it. For instance, if we consider the housing market bubble before the GFC, immediately prior to crisis, the credit boom entailed that mortgages were issued to sub-prime house buyers backed by overvalued house-assets as these mortgages naturally had a high market value compared to their intrinsic value. Subsequent downturn in the economy led to a further fall in the intrinsic value of these mortgages which at the point of crisis got reflected in their market prices which started to correct very sharply. Financial institutions which were holders of these securities had no option but to cushion the losses with their minimum capital at hand resulting in these institutions becoming insolvent. Capital adequacy under stress can be used to gauge excessive credit growth for a financial institution and this measure if aggregated for a number of firms can provide an estimate of systemic risk. Such a measure also provides an estimate to the regulators and resources to the supervisors that they will need to stem the crises in case of need and keep the focus of regulators on risky, undercapitalized institution in the economy. A systemic risk measure may also have to take into account the steps that will have to be taken by these institutions to de-risk if risk aversion sets in the market.

Systemic risk in the financial sector manifests itself with a systemic breakdown in the intermediation activity which leads to trust deficit, leading to short-term markets becoming illiquid. These illiquid markets entail that highly solvent institutions cannot take over this intermediation activity from weak firms.

A comprehensive definition of systemic risk (International Monetary Fund Report 2009) is: 'The risk of disruptions to financial services that is caused by an impairment of all or parts of the financial system,[1] and can have serious negative consequences for the real economy.'

Defined in terms of financial stability, systemic risk is 'the risk of threats to financial stability that impair the functioning of a large part of the financial system with significant adverse effects on the broader economy'.

Financial instability is defined as a deviation from the equilibrium of investment–saving (IS) in an economy, mainly originating from the malfunctioning of the financial system which consists of banking, other financial intermediaries, and financial markets together with payment and settlement systems.

Given that systemic risk is the risk of threat to financial stability, management of systemic risk becomes the prime objective of the regulators in their endeavour of ensuring financial stability. Management of financial stability is to be effected through containing volatility in three key rates, namely inflation rate, interest rate and exchange rate, across four segments of the economic system, namely macroeconomy, financial institutions, financial markets and financial infrastructure. The interest rates are determined by the intersection of savings (IS) curve reflecting the demand for the money and liquidity preference–money supply (LM) curve reflecting money available for investing. On the other hand, the interaction between aggregate demand of money and aggregate supply of money determines the inflation rate. The interest rate, inflation rate and the knowledge of foreign interest rate can help us determine the exchange rate. The demand and supply of money get affected by any significant issues in the macroeconomy, financial institutions, financial markets and financial infrastructure. For instance, if we consider the precipitating factor for the GFC, in 2006 when the house prices started falling, it affected the aggregate demand of money resulting in reduction in the output and interest rates. This led to concerns in late 2007 and in 2008 regarding solvency of banks in inter-bank lending markets which led to a run

---

[1] Financial system is taken to be banking, other financial intermediaries and financial markets together with payment and settlement systems.

on the banks and the banks were left with no option but to fire sell their assets. Credit in the system was significantly reduced and credit spreads increased. The resulting credit spread adversely affected the output and the interest rates moved to zero.

Another similar example was May 2013 when the Federal Reserve communicated that they are looking to reduce the stimulus. This led to an increase in the capital outflows from the emerging market economies with pressures on their exchange rates and significant losses to the importers in these countries.

Fallacy of Composition—The System Is Not the Sum of Its Parts

As discussed earlier, one of the significant shortcomings found in the pre-crisis wisdom was the misconception that the stability of the individual institutions was a sufficient condition for the stability of the financial system. This assumption turned out be a fallacy given the feedback loops within the system as the individually resilient entities in the system can still be collectively overwhelmed by the stress scenario. During the GFC also, the supervisors got misled through this same fallacy. The stability, safety and soundness of individual banks left traditional regulators and supervisors to believe that the whole system is stable resulting in them being ill-equipped in preventing the coming systemic collapse.

The 'fallacy of composition' is similar to the 'paradox of thrift' that one observes in economics. Thrift, which is a prudent quality of an individual, if followed by everyone in the system, would be disastrous for everyone in the economy. An increased overall saving will bring down consumption leading to a fall in aggregate demand and the investment activity in the economy further leading to an overall harm to the economy. This can also be called rational irrationality—rational at the individual level but that leads to socially irrational outcomes.

Flipping the concept of 'fallacy of composition', we arrive at 'fallacy of division' which suggests that if the whole system is safe, the individual entities are assumed to be safe. This assumption is also fallacious and needs to be guarded against.

This idea of the system being composed of independent units, each contributing to the aggregate risk, leads to the collective action problems of public policy calling for regulatory intervention. Absence of regulation with a systemic view will not create any incentive to limit risk-taking by market participants for reduction in systemic danger for the other market participants.

Dimensions of Systemic Risk

The concept of systemic risk is better understood if we focus on the twin dimensions of it, namely (a) time or cyclical dimension and (b) cross-sectional or structural dimension.

Cyclical Dimension—What Goes Up Must Come Down

The cyclical dimension of systemic risk relates to the progressive build-up of fragility in the financial system which evolves over time. As we all understand, over the economic cycle, there is an increase in the dimensions of booms and busts which undermines macroeconomic and financial stability. During the economic upturn, when things are looking up, risk appetite of borrowers (both individuals and firms) and the lenders goes up. Credit grows rapidly, both as a cause and as a consequence of higher asset prices. Higher collateral values increase the ability of the firms to borrow, while the apparently higher capital positions of the banks increase the ability to lend, causing further amplification in the economic cycle. On the flipside, when strains in the economy develop and economy gets into a downturn, due to the depressed demand and slump in economic activity, the loans become non-performing requiring the banks to recognize less income and provide more for bad loans impacting their capital levels. Erosion in capital levels constrains banks' lending ability forcing them to delever-age, which further depresses the economic activity. In this procyclical-ity dimension, the systemic risk is largely endogenous, and the risk can be highest precisely when it looks lowest. Complacency regarding risk itself turns into a source of risk. As observed by Minsky, seeds of the crises are sown during the period of tranquillity.

Cross-sectional or Structural Dimension— Individually Rational But Collectively Irrational

The cross-sectional dimension of systemic risk focuses on the distribution of the risk within the financial system at a given point in time. The financial shock in structural dimension can arise in one of the two forms: (a) interconnectedness among firms or (b) common exposures.

- *Interconnectedness:* Given that the financial system is a network of interconnected balance sheets, the failure of any of the firms threatens the stability of all other connected institutions that are otherwise sound and lead to a systemic crisis. The interconnectedness could be inter-bank, inter-firm (among banks and non-banks) and inter-country (among the financial systems between countries), which is increasingly becoming important in the highly interconnected world. Effectively, crisis anywhere is potentially a crisis everywhere.

- *Common exposures:* A shock can have wide ramifications and become systemic because of direct common exposures and common business models of financial firms. Illustratively, if all (or significant number of) the market participants have an exposure to an asset 'A' and if one of the participants chooses to sell the asset due to a small price fall, the selling pressure could lead to further fall in prices breaching the stop loss limits of another participant forcing him/her to also start selling. This further exacerbates the price fall forcing many more participants to join the fray till it snowballs into a fire sale. While it was perfectly rational for any participant to dispose of the asset on account of price fall, a collective sell-off by multiple participants of a common asset can force even the unwilling holder to join the fray and escalate the issue to systemic proportions.

Systemic Risk—The Risk to Be Addressed

Systemic risk disrupts financial services and impinges on the financial stability with serious implications for the real economy. The GFC stands as a painful testimony to the deleterious impact of systemic risk evidenced by extraordinarily high economic and social costs. The debilitating impact of financial crises makes it imperative for policymakers to devise policies to assess, measure and manage systemic risks so as to serve the dual objectives of reducing the occurrence of crises and mitigating their amplitude, if and when they occur.

Management of systemic risk, however, is a very complex process. It is fundamentally unclear resulting from a lack of consensus on an appropriate analytical framework and limited measurement tools along with the infrequent incidence of episodes of financial distress, and especially in measuring the feedback effects both occurring inside the financial system and among the real economy and financial system.

Advanced Tools to Measure Systemic Risk— Sophisticated Tools to Measure Complex Risk

Measurement of systemic risk is extremely difficult, in fact as much as managing it. While there are multiple approaches to measure systemic risk, these approaches, according to Jobst and Gray (2013), can be broadly categorized in either of these two categories—contribution approach and participation approach. While the former looks at the systemic impact of an individual institution's failure, the latter deals with the impact on the individual institution of the common shock. Approaches such as conditional value at risk (CoVaR), systemic expected shortfall (SES), joint probability of distress, etc., have dealt with the contribution approach of systemic risk measurement. There are many other studies which are looking at objective and more reliable quantification of systemic risk, and in this regard, Systemic Contingent Claims Analysis (Systemic CCA) is a forward-looking framework which seeks to quantify systemic risk from market implied interlinkages among financial institutions. Considering the complexity of systemic risk measurement, we need a menu of sophisticated approaches to reliably quantify the risk.

Distress dependence among the financial entities and specifically banks is another area that is gaining momentum in assessing the systemic stability. Given the complex web of interlinkages among banks, the distress dependence, which measures the impact of distress of one entity on others in the system, could be used as a useful indicator. The interconnectedness of banks not only arises directly from exposures to one another but also indirectly from common exposures, that is, exposures of banks to common counterparties, sector or geographies, which propagates the distress of one entity to all others very quickly. The interconnectedness leads to non-linear and significant losses much higher than individual distress due to joint probabilities of distress. Assessing the distress dependence is a key factor in assessing the systemic risk.

Market price-based risk measures such as VaR, CoVaR, etc., have limited utility in estimating systemic risk as they sometimes blind side the regulators by underestimating risk in the run-up to crisis. Holistic models such as financial network models are observed to be more efficient in assessing the systemic risk and also avoid fallacy of composition often observed in other models. In fact, India pioneered these efforts in August 2010 when they built Systemic Risk Analytics (SRA) to model financial interconnectedness in the Indian Financial System. Using the network modelling, the snapshot of exposures among the financial system participants is drawn indicating both the direction and the magnitude of cash flows.

Mechanism for Systemic Risk Management

Macroprudential regulation relies heavily on the instruments used by the extant microprudential policy and has a significant overlap with the microprudential regulation in terms of objectives. Consequently, there is a lot of debate over whether macroprudential policy is just a particular perspective of prudential policy or a new policy area in its own right. While the similarities and the distinction between micro and macro policies are arguable, some argue that to strengthen the stability of the financial system as a whole, a distinction needs to be made, keeping in mind the possibility of occasional tensions between them. As mentioned in the FSB's progress report to G20 (October 2011), the difference between these two perspectives, however, is largely semantic if existing prudential policy frameworks address explicitly systemic risk, adopt a system-wide analytical perspective and target tools at systemic risk.

Given the criticality of systemic risk and the difficulties in its measurement, jurisdictions should ideally have an independent financial stability unit (FSU) or department to offer focused attention to the areas of systemic risk and financial crisis management by way of macroprudential regulation and macrofinancial surveillance. The units should undertake the following activities:

- Collection and collation of data series on various variables in the macroeconomy, financial markets, financial institutions and financial infrastructure (payment and settlement systems).
- Study and assess movements in these select variables and prepare reports—quarterly systemic risk dashboards and annual financial stability reports.
- Enhanced stress-testing framework—'top-down' at Financial Stability Department (FSD) and 'bottom-up' at banks—preparation of quarterly stress test reports.
- Identification, designation and revisit of regulatory/supervisory guidelines for systemically important banks (SIBs) and identification of need for application of time-varying capital and provisioning requirements which are countercyclical in nature.
- An EWM.

Systemic Risk Versus Systematic Risk: How Similar or Different Are They?

These two terms sound so similar that they run the risk of being used interchangeably at times. Systematic risk, on the one hand, is the solvency risk faced by institutions arising out of their exposures to market risk. Systemic risk, on the other hand, is the risk that such failure of individual institutions could impact the overall financial system due to spillovers through various channels. Distinguishing between the two risks is an important requirement in the framework of systemic risk management and the measures such as Conditional Shortfall Probability (CoSP) are stated to be useful for this purpose.

Systemic Risk and Financial Stability— An Alternate View

While financial stability is generally defined to be the absence of system-wide risk, the alternative perspective that is gaining currency (Adrian 2017) in defining financial stability is the absence of sharp movements in financial conditions that arise from large increases in the price of risk and negative externalities created by financial vulnerabilities. There is ample evidence that adverse movements in financial conditions adversely impact GDP growth even in the absence of systemic disruptions. A well-designed cyclical macroprudential policy works towards mitigating sharp movements in financial conditions, even if those do not entail system disruptions in the intermediation capacity of the financial system. Monitoring of financial conditions and vulnerabilities provides useful information about downside risks to GDP to the policymakers in the short and medium run and guides the stance of policy.

Why Did Monetary Policy Not Ensure Financial Stability? Lean or Clean Debate

The great moderation—period of substantial decline in macroeconomic volatility—was viewed as reflecting the improved performance of monetary policy along with other structural changes. Inflation targeting was adopted by many countries and the price stability was seen as a sufficient condition for financial stability. The crisis has turned these assumptions on their head and triggered debate on the role of monetary policy in ensuring financial stability. The 'lean or clean' debate used to be one of the most contentious in monetary policy until the crisis. The question was whether the monetary policy also needs to 'lean against the wind' in the expansion phase or it should solely focus on the inflation target and 'clean up' after the credit cycle contracts. While it is admitted that monetary policy can impact financial stability, as evidenced by the experience of lax or loose monetary policies leading to building up of systemic risks, the debate as to whether to use monetary policy for ensuring financial stability by leaning against the wind, that is, increasing the policy rates pre-emptively and by amounts much more than what is adequate for ensuring price stability, is still not settled.

On the one hand, there is the view that monetary policy may be too blunt a tool to address systemic risks, which go beyond a narrow definition of overvaluation in asset prices and which, therefore, require a more nuanced and targeted approach (Shafik 2015).

The risk-taking channel of monetary policy, in contrast to conventional wisdom, takes the view that monetary policy influences and impacts the economy through changes or shifts in the risk-taking behaviour of market participants (Morris and Shin 2014),[2] therefore having implications for financial stability. This channel of monetary policy works by affecting through the risk premiums directly, impacting the corporate investment and household consumption eventually impacting GDP growth thorough depressed consumption and investment. The interplay of monetary policy and financial stability gets more complex as the monetary policy shock also impacts the risk-taking under this framework. For example, an empirical study[3] by Bank of England suggested that setting bank rate around 200 basis points higher than what it was over the period 2003–2006 would have reduced the growth in household debt to GDP by just 200 basis points during 2003–2007 at a cost of GDP growth over this period being 2.6 percentage points lower.

While there are proponents such as Cecchetti and Borio calling for a more active role of monetary policy in ensuring financial stability, it is increasingly realized that financial regulation and macroprudential

[2] Morris, Stephen and Shin, Hyun Song. 2014. *Risk Taking Channel of Monetary Policy: A Global Game Approach.* Bank for International Settlements.

[3] The Interaction of Monetary and Macro-prudential Policy (October 2015) – Remarks by Minouche Shafik, Bank of England.

policies need to be the first lines of defence against systemic risk and that monetary policy does not have a significant role. Blanchard (2017) argues that it is very difficult to make a real assessment of asset bubbles or unhealthy credit booms. Further, lags in the effects of monetary policy make it harder for the policymakers to act. Finally, interest rate is a very poor instrument to decrease risk since any increase in the interest rate to slow down credit growth may also worsen the position of existing borrowers by increasing their debt burden and lowering their income, forcing them to increase their leverage by borrowing more, thus increasing the risks of financial instability that it sought to address in the first place.

The flexible inflation targeting policy regime adopted by many countries with a dual mandate of price and financial stability may turn counterproductive in the long run. The undoing of such policy acceptance is the fact that they warrant unexpected policy adjustments to transitory shocks. The typical thought process that central banks need to lean against the wind may extend to leaning against a credit bubble instead of cleaning them beforehand. The monetary authorities use various models to cater to their dual mandates. What is pertinent is that these models consider prevalent tail risks behaviour of underlying financial variables in their modelling. In contrast to a flexible approach, a fully discretionary monetary policy would hinder financial stability and undermine monetary policy predictability and credibility in the long run. The tail risk events are further intensified in such scenario.

Costs and Benefits of Using Monetary Policy to Lean Against the Wind

It has always been a matter of constant debate that whether monetary policy should be used with an objective of financial stability. The BIS composite asset price index, relating asset prices with the evolution of credit, as in Borio, Kennedy and Prowse (1994) recommended pre-emptive use of monetary policy to ensure financial stability. Subsequently, Bernanke and Gertler (1999) argued forcefully that monetary policy should only respond to fluctuations in asset prices to the extent that they affect forecasts of inflation or the output gap.

Again, contrary to this view, Cecchetti et al. (2000, 2002), Borio and Lowe (2002) and Borio and White (2003) recommended an active role of monetary policy in addressing financial stability risks.

A lot of empirical research is being done in this area to assess the costs (e.g., measured as the costs of unemployment due to pre-emptive tightening of monetary policy) and benefits (measured as lower probability and reduced severity of crisis) of using monetary policy to lean against the wind to ensure financial stability, and some of the studies, especially by Svensson (2016, 2017), conclude that the marginal costs of using monetary policy far exceeds the benefits. ECB's research on this field for euro area also corroborates Svensson's argument and points to the greater costs of using monetary policy to lean against the wind.

Theoretically, it is assumed that systematic monetary policy can be used to reduce systemic financial stability risks, if macroprudential policies are not available. International Monetary Fund (2016) in its staff Report on Monetary Policy and Financial Stability did an econometric study to find out the relation. The results stated that a surprise monetary policy tightening may not necessarily reduce systemic risk for a fragile economy. However, the negative effects of such a tightening may be mitigated when the financial sector is strong, and the surprise action is small.

Simple systematic monetary policy may improve welfare by striking a balance between inflation and output stabilization, thereby reducing the likelihood of financial stress. However, leaning against the wind requires policies to be procyclical. Mixed sectoral results have been obtained regarding procyclicality. Generally, leaning against leverage leads to asset price correction and may lead to financial stress possibly inducing a full-blown crisis. The results thus suggest that the monetary policy reaction must be beyond the simple rule. Alternative financial variables such as mispricing risk have better preference over simple rules but are less reactive to a monetary policy stance. Hence, it may be concluded that a simple macroprudential rule which acts similarly to a countercyclical capital requirement is substantially more effective than the interest policy rule in limiting the build-up of leverage and preventing crisis.

Laseen, Pescatori and Turunen (2017) point that conventional monetary policy focusing on inflation and output will not be effective in addressing systemic risk, as such variables do not contain information about the state of the economy that financial sector leverage contains and leaning against the wind only marginally improves welfare. Their study indicates that an optimal macroprudential policy similar to a countercyclical capital requirement can enhance the welfare by about 1.5 per cent. They indicate that leverage can increase either due to the concerted actions by the borrowers or even on account of general fall in asset prices, and taking a simplistic policy action of increasing the policy rates to reduce leverage, without clearly distinguishing why leverage is increasing, could exacerbate incipient financial stress.

Considering the growth in the macroprudential policy tools which have been provided in most of the jurisdictions to the financial stability authority which is the central bank in most of the jurisdictions, the monetary policy can be used as a complement to macroprudential tools for financial stability.

Macroprudential Policy— A New Approach to Address Systemic Risk

If one were to examine the crisis episodes closely, it becomes evident that the chief debilitating factor on the economy is the generalized asset shrinkage by the credit institutions in the bust phase. Prodded by the procyclical regulation, financial firms which face mounting losses and the declining asset quality in the aftermath of the crisis would rapidly deleverage, and this would lead to huge economic and social costs. The asset shrinkage has two primary costs—credit crunch and fire sale effects. The financial firms may delever by cutting down on new lending which would lead to contractionary consequences in the economy by impinging on investment and employment. On the other hand, the financial firms may choose to delever by selling of the assets on their balance sheets which could lead to a rapid fall in asset prices triggering further fire sales by other financial firms having common exposures. Both the strategies of deleveraging, that is, credit rationing and fire sales, are intimately connected and costs of fire sales manifest during a crisis leading to further worsening of the credit crunch.

Macroprudential policies seek to address the debilitating impact of deleveraging following credit booms. Macroprudential regulation can be understood as an approach to financial regulation that controls the social costs related with wide-scale balance sheet shrinkage of multiple financial institutions when facing a common crisis shock.

Macroprudential policy can be defined as a policy aimed at maintaining financial stability—even though no standard definition exists for financial stability. In more simplistic explanation of macroprudential policy defines it as a tool looking at the macrosystems in an economy.

Three key steps, namely systemic risk assessment, building a case and motivation for macroprudential intervention, and selecting and implementing the macroprudential instruments, can be identified to the macroprudential policy process leading up to the activation of macroprudential tools.

History of Macroprudential Regulation

Even as the usage of the term 'macroprudential regulation' has caught the fancy only post GFC, the origin of the term 'macroprudential' can be traced back to unpublished documents prepared in the late 1970s in the minutes of the Cooke Committee (the precursor to the present BCBS; Clement 2010). During this period, the term generally referred to a systemic orientation of regulation and supervision linked to the macroeconomy (Borio 2010). According to the Bank for International Settlements (BIS), public references to macroprudential policy surfaced only in the mid-1980s. The Bank for International Settlements Report (1986) discussed it as a policy aimed at supporting 'the safety and soundness of the financial system as a whole, as well as payments mechanism'. In the early 2000s, new impetus was provided to the notion macroprudential approach to regulation and supervision (Crockett 2000).

In the aftermath of the GFC, the G20 regulatory reform triggered the work on macroprudential regulation calling in the coordinated efforts of the International Monetary Fund (IMF), FSB and the BIS.

Macroprudential Policy Framework

The basic elements of a macroprudential policy consist of its objective, scope of analysis, set of powers, instruments and their governance.

The management of the systemic risks is carried out through the macroprudential policy framework. Macroprudential policies primarily use prudential tools as a means to limit systemic disruptions through (a) reducing financial imbalances, (b) containing downswings and their effects and (c) identifying and addressing common risk exposures, concentrations, linkages and interdependencies that may lead to contagion and spillover effects. The first two objectives deal with procyclicality issues. The second objective of building defences may be attained by build-up of buffers during boom times which can be used when risks materialize during busts. The first objective of dampening the build-up is essentially 'leaning against the wind' aspect.

Objectives of the Macroprudential Policy

Contrary to the policies such as monetary policy whose objectives are well defined, there is no such consensus on the objectives of macroprudential policy. While macroprudential policy is seen as aiming at financial stability, the lack of definitional clarity on financial stability itself complicates the issue. There are broadly two divergent views of financial stability. According to the Bank for International Settlements (2011), the first view defines financial stability in terms of robustness of the financial system to external shocks, and the second emphasizes the endogenous nature of financial distress and describes financial stability in terms of resilience to shocks originating within the financial system.

Despite the differences in language and emphasis, the general view about the specific goals of macroprudential policy is that it is all about limiting the risks and costs of systemic crises. Macro-regulation acts as a countervailing force to the natural decline in measured risks during a boom followed by a rise in the measured risks in the subsequent bust.

As per Bank of England Report (2009), the objectives of the macroprudential policies should be financial intermediation services oriented—keeping them aloof from the boom bust cycles. Further, macroprudential policy should also not be geared to avoid bubbles and imbalances in general, as they can signal shifts in (bank) credit supply. As an alternative view, the goal of macroprudential policy may also be to limit episodes of system-wide distress that have significant macroeconomic costs. The objective of macroprudential policy would also be to reduce systemic risk by explicitly addressing the interlinkages between, and common exposures of, all financial institutions, and the procyclicality of the financial system.

Pointing out on how capital regulation and the principle of prompt corrective action (PCA) failed to distinguish whether troubled banks react to shocks by raising new capital or shrinking their assets, Hanson et al. (2010) observed that microprudential regulations have over time aimed at forcing banks to internalize losses in order to protect deposit insurance funds and mitigate moral hazard.

Macroprudential policy is also seen as mitigating sharp movements in financial conditions that adversely impact GDP growth. While the policy need not target financial conditions directly, monitoring of financial conditions and vulnerabilities provides useful insights for guiding the stance of the policy.

In sum, the prime objective of macroprudential policy is to limit build-up of system-wide (systemic) financial risk. According to International Monetary Fund Report (2011), macroprudential policy should primarily address risks arising and getting amplified in the financial system, thereby leaving other identified sources of systemic risk to be dealt with by other public policies.

While the prime objective of macroprudential policy is to maintain the financial system stability, other public policies may have the same as their secondary objective. Further, while the focus of macroprudential policies is prevention, the cure (crisis management) falls in the domain of crisis management frameworks.

According to Haldane (2017), market failures associated with fire sale externalities coupled with the linkage of credit booms to aggregate demand externalities provide a rationale for pre-emptive macroprudential interventions.

In this context, a comparison with objective of monetary policy seems quite tempting. In case of monetary policy, it is easy to define its objective in terms of inflation target and then it is easy to assess success or failure of monetary policy with the reference to achievement of the inflation target. However, in case of macroprudential policy, it is not possible to define the objective in such quantitative terms. While we may suggest that probability of systemic crisis may form one possible objective, its reliable measurement is a challenge at this point of time. Also, due to lack of a quantitative target or objectives, it becomes difficult to assess the performance of macroprudential policy. While inflation is an observable indicator, probability of financial crisis is not.

Due to impossibility of assessing the performance based on unobservable indicators, one can try to identify certain observable indicators which contribute to systemic crises. Therefore, setting an objective for macroprudential policy to achieve has to be based on some observable economic variables like inflation in the case of monetary policy. These observable economic variables may be, for example, growth in asset prices, banks' balance sheet growth in certain segments, increase in interconnectedness in the financial system, etc., which directly contribute to systemic risk. However, there is a need for further research in this area to implement it.

Scope of Macroprudential Policies

International Monetary Fund (2011) specifies that the macroprudential policy perspective should cover all potential sources of systemic risk. It mandates that developments in the whole financial system (regulated and unregulated), feedback loop between the financial system and the real economy, including the international spillovers with the focus on systemic risks, rather than individual institutions and idiosyncratic risks should be included.

Perimeter of Macroprudential Regulation

While many settle for the view that macroprudential policies and financial stability policies are one and the same, there are some dissenting voices (Ellis 2012) that warn against blind bundling of all financial stability policies as macroprudential. For instance, the central bank's provision of liquidity to the market that promotes financial stability by alleviating market's concerns need not be categorized as macroprudential but any steps or directions given to reduce risk in an individual institution is a microprudential policy. Then there are fiscal policies to manage aggregate demand by using taxes, automatic stabilizers. Few countries also impose capital controls to contain the volatility of the capital flows, thereby containing the volatility in exchange rates. Therefore, as the financial stability falls under the realms of more than one public policy frameworks, it would be difficult, but at the same time, extremely important, to delineate the boundaries of macroprudential policy for effective policy formulation and implementation. The macroprudential policy's primary responsibility is to ensure that financial stability and other policies should complement it. Irrespective of the mandate of the policy, financial stability is a common responsibility. The macroprudential policies cannot substitute microprudential policy, monetary policy, crisis management, etc. The buffers provided by one type of stringent policy may act as a cushion for another type of policy.

The gains from international macroprudential policy coordination have been studied by the BIS (January 2019) through a two-region, core-periphery macro-economic model with imperfect financial integration and cross-border banking. It has been found that for the world economy, welfare gains from the macroprudential policy coordination are positive, albeit not large but can be increased with greater financial integration. The macroprudential regulation can also be welfare costing by the use of countercyclical tax on bank loans to domestic capital goods producers. However, these have been found highly asymmetric across regions.

The perimeter of macroprudential policies should include early warning systems (EWSs) to monitor the risks of credit portfolio deterioration from a macro-prudential perspective, communicate views regarding the underlying potential system-wide risks increases, countercyclical capital buffer (CCyB) to prevent the systemic build-up of macro-financial imbalances, systemic risk buffer (SyRB) when the potential systemic risk increases, capital measures aimed at addressing excessive exposure concentrations when systemic risk appears to be building up in specific sectors/asset classes.

Interaction of Macroprudential Policy with Monetary Policy

As discussed earlier, monetary policy alone cannot ensure financial stability as evidenced during the GFC. The question then is whether monetary policy has any role to play alongside the macroprudential policy in ensuring financial stability.

The effectiveness of macroprudential policy depends upon its interaction with monetary policy and vice versa. It hinges on the 'side effects' that one policy has on the objectives of the other. Even while it cannot ensure financial stability on its own, monetary policy can impinge on it through its actions. Since monetary policy stance affects risk-taking of the financial system as a whole, it, as remarked by Jeremy Stein, 'gets in all of the cracks and may reach into corners of the market that supervision and regulation cannot'. By providing ample liquidity and cheap funding, monetary policy may minimize incentives for banks to recapitalize and restructure, and promote the evergreening of non-performing loans and regulatory forbearance. Ill-designed or improperly coordinated monetary policy can thwart the intentions of the macroprudential policy in preserving systemic stability. However, a well-designed monetary policy conducted in coordination with macroprudential policy can provide conducive environment and sufficient headroom for macroprudential policy to operate. Masciandaro and Romelli (2018) suggest that policymakers generally have a short-term perspective while using monetary policy to smooth out different kind of macroeconomic shocks (i.e., real and fiscal imbalances). However, this may lead to macroeconomic distortions if the markets are efficient.

In a BIS working paper based on the analysis of data from Central American countries, it was found that effectiveness of macroprudential measures is usually reinforced using monetary policy and vice versa. Effectiveness of macroprudential tools tends to increase when they work as a complement to monetary policy. Similar observations have been found in the empirical analysis from Asian economies also where it is concluded that macroprudential policies tend to be more successful when reinforced with complementing monetary policy.

On the flip side, macroprudential policy can also thwart effectiveness of the monetary policy as changes in (micro and macro) prudential policy affects banks' risk-taking, financing conditions and balance sheet composition leading to an impact on the real economy and price stability. The fact that the credit growth has still not taken off in Euro area despite unprecedented monetary stimulus, according to some, points to the counteracting impact of macroprudential policy slowing down banks' lending activity.

The conflict between macroprudential policy and the monetary policy can be visualized in the backdrop of their respective remits. Monetary policy operates through interest rates to achieve the requisite shift in households' and companies' spending decisions. This shift, however, has implications for the flow of credit and stock of debt and, more importantly, for asset prices in the economy which has implications for macroprudential policy. If monetary policy is loosened to achieve the desired level of prices and output, unintentionally, this has an impact on the borrowing behaviour of the economic agents and asset prices, with each one feeding back to the other resulting in systemic concerns. The recent extraordinarily loose monetary policy in the EU area after the crisis did not achieve the desired success in increasing credit growth. One explanation could be that monetary authorities were not doing enough. However, the other explanation could be that due to stricter capital and liquidity requirements, supervisory stress-testing requirements and implementation of other macroprudential measures, capacity of banks to lend became restricted.

This weakened the transmission of monetary policy. If this explanation is considered correct, it demonstrates conflict between the two policies.

Despite recent progress made in the area of macroprudential policy research, the models that link financial sector to the real economy tend to be typically stylized. In a staff paper (Aikman et al. 2018) published by Bank of England, the issue of interaction between monetary policy and macroprudential policies have been studied using a quantitative model. The authors developed a model to explore how monetary and macroprudential policies affect the economy and interact with each other by ascribing a clear role for the resilience enhancing benefits of the CCB. The paper concludes that deploying the CCB improves outcomes significantly relative to when monetary policy is the only tool. However, results also indicate that less usage of CCB should be done in case of a lower bound constrained monetary policy. This indicates that there is a greater need for coordination between monetary policymaking and macroprudential policy and suggests for having expanded central bank toolkits to ensure they have powers to influence macroprudential policy. However, the benefits are limited in the sense that similar economic performance can also be achieved by different policymakers pursuing distinct objectives. What is pertinent is that the instruments, when faced with a credit boom, should act like a substitute and should optimally tighten the CCB and cushion its macroeconomic impact by loosening monetary policy. Such a strategy becomes less effective if the market-based finance sector is big or the risk-taking channel of monetary policy is strong. These results do indicate that both the policies need to be coordinated to ensure maximum benefit.

A recent empirical study on efficacy of macroprudential policy done by IMF (Poghosyan 2019) carrying a sample of 28 EU countries, using data on 99 lending restriction measures implemented over 1990–2018 has found that lending restriction measures (such as LTV and DSTI) are generally effective in curbing house prices and credit albeit a delay of three years in its impact. Further, the study found that macroprudential measures can be more effective if they are supported by monetary policy actions.

Architecture of Macroprudential Policy

Systemic Risk Surveillance Architecture

Considering the wide scope and challenging objective of macroprudential regulation, in the interest of efficiency and accountability, it
is preferable to explicitly assign the responsibility of macroprudential
regulation to either a single agency or a committee of agencies. Some of
the key elements that a macroprudential authority should be equipped
with include clear mandate, independence, adequate resources and
powers to define the perimeter for macroprudential surveillance, to
access information from all relevant entities and markets and to operate
or direct the operation of policy tools.

But there is still no consensus on which institutional arrangement
for macroprudential policymaking would be more conducive to effective mitigation of systemic risk. The crisis exposed the weakness of the
extant system wherein no agency or regulator had a definitive mandate
of ensuring macroeconomic and financial stability. Post the crisis,
most jurisdictions have proactively indicated agencies responsible for
ensuring financial stability and the protocol for addressing any threats.

Central banks have a major role in maintaining the safety and
soundness of the economic system due to their role as financial sector
regulator LOLR, monetary policymaker, manager of payments and
settlement systems and also custodian and manager of the foreign
exchange reserves. Central banks with required expertise and analysis
of aggregate and sectoral indicators check procyclicality risks and
thereby reduce the probability and impact of failures. In many jurisdictions, central banks also have financial stability as their responsibility,
either formally or implicitly owing to their central position in the
financial system. Masciandaro and Volpicella (2016) indicate that
central banks who are also supervisors of the banking industry are more
likely to be given more macroprudential powers, and higher central
bank political independence is linked to reduced authority in macro-
supervision and central banks pursuing specific price stability objectives
are more likely to be endowed with macro-supervisory responsibilities.

Even while they carry such responsibilities, central banks in certain jurisdictions (e.g., Peru and Chile) do not have access to necessary tools to discharge such responsibilities. All that they have at their disposal are monetary instruments, while other prudential tools would be under the ambit of financial regulators. Having different regulators discharge different responsibilities (against housing all authority and responsibility in one entity) actually strengthens accountability and preserves the independence of regulators. Further, such dispersed responsibilities also provide for diversity of views. However, such arrangements also call for a coordination among all such policymakers to ensure financial stability.

Thus, it follows that the working agenda of a central bank must include the systemic risk concerns having potential of creating financial instability. However, this does not imply in any way that central banks should be made solely responsible for such an arduous and critical task. The most popular approach, as has been deciphered from a cross-country study, is through a committee approach taking all the stakeholders on board. 'Inter-agency committees can bring together different perspectives on the sources of systemic risk and the potential for regulatory arbitrage, as well as identifying the most appropriate tools (which may be housed in different agencies)' (Financial Stability Board 2011). Such committees are given well-defined authority structure and a clear macroprudential mandate to preserve financial stability. Hence, this leads to an independent central bank which is a prerequisite for maintaining price stability.

Finance ministries play a strong role in such committees, especially when it comes to crisis management and recapitalization or bail out. The inclusion of the Ministry has its own share of benefits and drawbacks. The obvious benefits are that there is an integration between fiscal and exchange rate policies and any legislative change may be undertaken quickly. The drawbacks, however, may include increased political interference. Still, the role of government cannot be negated as it is the ultimate owner and accountable to the citizens and can issue its debt instruments which act as a collateral during crisis management.

Post the crisis, most countries have entrusted their central banks with the responsibility for preserving financial stability. An IMF survey (2011) indicates that 90 per cent of the countries which responded to the survey have given the financial stability mandate to their central banks. Another report on cross-country practices states:

> [C]entral banks may have clear responsibility for both macro prudential and micro prudential policy (as in Malaysia and, prospectively, the UK), or account for a large share of the votes in the committee (as in the European Systemic Risk Board [ESRB]). In the US, the Federal Reserve is one of the 10 voting members of the Financial Stability Oversight Council (FSOC), but it is charged with the regulation of systemically important banks and non-bank financial institutions, as designated by FSOC. (Financial Stability Board 2011)

In India, the FSDC and its subcommittee headed by the Governor of RBI is the main operative wing and has all other members of the FSDC (regulators of capital market and insurance sector and the secretaries of finance and financial services and the chief economic advisor to the finance minister) as the members with almost the same mandate to work on. The FSU at RBI coordinates the working of this subcommittee. However, there cannot be one-size-fits-all approach in this as every country needs to have a structure which serves its interest best.

Successful monetary policy and macroprudential policy reinforce each other. Measures to strengthen the resilience of the financial system give support to the monetary policy by shielding the economy from sharp financial disruptions, while macroeconomic stability reduces the financial system's vulnerability to procyclical tendencies. For example, macroprudential policies influence credit supply conditions and hence monetary policy transmission. The conduct of one policy will need to take account of developments and settings in the other.

Different approaches have been adopted by different jurisdictions to the institutional structure of macroprudential regulation based on the country-specific factors. The experience in Asia demonstrates that in addition to bank supervision, central banks have also been made responsible for maintaining stable financial system using these supervisory tools. Two commonly used approaches include (a) the board of central bank acting as macroprudential authority and (b) a committee of the representatives of different stakeholders like central bank, government, regulators and supervisors of different segments of financial market, etc.

The results of a recent IMF survey in 2018 demonstrate varying preferences for institutional mandates. Among 111 countries that responded to the survey, 80 jurisdictions indicated that the central bank played an important role in macroprudential policy with 39 jurisdictions having central bank as the sole macroprudential authority. About 45 respondents to the survey indicated that the macroprudential mandate was assigned to more than one entity—an additional committee alongside the central bank. In about nine countries, a committee or a council outside the central bank was the sole macroprudential authority, while four countries reported that a supervisory agency other than the central bank was the sole authority. Twenty-two countries (including 14 EMEs) indicated that an agency or body has been assigned a formal macroprudential policy mandate, while 15 (including eight EMEs) indicated a three-year future plan for the same. Of the 22 countries with a formal mandate, the central bank has been assigned this mandate (either singly or with other agencies) in 19 countries (includes 13 EMEs). The Ministry of Finance (MOF) is a part of the macroprudential institutional structure in five of these countries.

Specifically, in the USA, the Financial Stability Oversight Council (FSOC), set up under the DFA, provides a comprehensive monitoring of the financial stability. The Council is chaired by the Treasury Secretary and comprises all the regulators such as the Fed, Commodity Futures Trading Commission (CFTC), FDIC, SEC, OCC, Consumer Financial Protection Bureau (CFPB), etc.

In the UK, the Financial Policy Committee (FPC) set up in 2013 is charged with the primary objective of identifying, monitoring and countering systemic risks and enhance the resilience of the UK financial system. The Committee consists of 13 members, of which 6 are the governor, 4 deputy governors and the executive director for financial stability. Five members are selected for their financial experience and expertise, and are independent experts. The chief executive of the Financial Conduct Authority is also a member. The Committee also includes a non-voting member from HM Treasury.

In the EU, the European Systemic Risk Board (ESRB) established in 2010 is responsible for the macroprudential oversight of the EU financial system and the prevention and mitigation of systemic risk. ESRB is chaired by the Chairman of European Central Bank (ECB) and has representation from ECB, European Commission, European regulators of banking, securities market and the insurance sectors along with national macroprudential authorities.

In New Zealand, the MOU between the government and the central bank sets out the objectives of the macroprudential policy, and requires the central bank to consult the government prior to the use of macroprudential instruments and to regularly report the developments through biannual financial stability reports.

Institutional Framework in India

In 2010, a Financial Stability and Development Council (FSDC) which is a non-statutory body, chaired by the finance minister, including the governor of the central bank, was set up to strengthen the institutional mechanism for financial stability. The FSDC is assisted by a subcommittee chaired by the governor.

It also includes among its members the heads of financial sector regulators (RBI, SEBI, PFRDA, IRDA and FMC) finance secretary and/or secretary, Department of Economic Affairs, secretary, Department of Financial Services and chief economic adviser.

The Council monitors macroprudential supervision of the economy, which also includes large financial conglomerates and addresses any inter-regulatory coordination and financial sector development issues along with financial inclusion.

All the members in FSDC are also the members of the subcommittee. Additionally, all deputy governors of the RBI and additional secretary, DEA, in charge of FSDC, are also members of the subcommittee. Executive director, RBI (in charge of financial stability) is the member secretary, while the FSU of RBI is the secretariat for the subcommittee.

Working groups/technical groups under FSDC Sub-Committee include:

- Inter-Regulatory Technical Group (IR-TG)
- Technical Group on Financial Inclusion and Financial Literacy
- Inter Regulatory Forum for monitoring Financial Conglomerates (IRF-FC)
- Early Warning Group
- Working Group on Resolution Regime for Financial Institutions

Conclusion

Financial systems have a tendency to take high risk during boom periods and become risk-averse during downswing. The result is excessive concentration of risk on asset side and reliance on unstable sources of funding on liability side. There is a consensus among market participants that risk has reduced and market liquidity will remain plentiful. The aggregate risk build-up in the system is not internalized by the individual institutions. Similarly, during stress periods, there is excessive risk aversion in the system. There are also significant moral hazard costs in the system due to existence of institutions perceived as too systemic to be allowed to fail. Macroprudential regulation is needed to address these systemic concerns. However, there is a need to entrust the job of macroprudential regulation to an appropriate authority with specific objectives based on observable variables. It is required that macroprudential authority and monetary policy authority coordinate with each other in order to make both the policies effective. In the long run, both stable inflation and robust financial system tend to complement each other.

References

Adrian, Tobias. 2017. *Assessing Global Financial Stability*. Speech at London School of Economics and Political Economy, UK, October.

Bank for International Settlements. 2011. 'Macroprudential Policy—A Literature Review'. BIS Working Paper No. 337. Basel: Bank for International Settlements.

Bernanke, Ben, and Mark Getler. 1999. *Monetary Policy and Asset Price Volatility*. Proceedings of FRB, Kansas City.

Blanchard, Oliver J. 2017. *Rethinking Stabilization Policy: Evolution or Revolution*. NBER Working Paper No. 24179, December.

Borio C.E.V., N. Kennedy and S.D. Prowse. 1994. *Exploring Aggregate Asset Price Fluctuations across Countries*. BIS Working Paper No. 40, April.

Borio, C., and P. Lowe. 2002. *Asset Prices, Financial and Monetary Stability: Exploring the Nexus.* Paper presented at the BIS Conference on 'Changes in risk through time: measurement and policy options'.

Borio, C., and William White. 2003. *Whither Monetary and Financial Stability? The Implications of Evolving Policy Regimes.* Paper presented at the Federal Reserve Bank of Kansas City's Symposium on 'Monetary Policy and Uncertainty: Adapting to a Changing Economy', Jackson Hole, Wyoming, 28–30 August.

Borio, Claudio. 2010. Implementing Macro-prudential Framework: Blending Boldness and Realism. *BIS Report,* 22 July.

Claessens, Stijn. 2014, December. *An Overview of Macroprudential Policy Tools*. IMF Working Paper. Available at https://www.imf.org/external/pubs/ft/wp/2014/wp14214.pdf (accessed on 25 January 2019).

Cecheti, S., H. Genberg, J. Lipsky and S. Wadhwani. 2000. *Asset Prices and Central Bank Policy*. ICMB/CEPR Report No 2.

Cecheti, S., H. Genberg, J. Lipsky and S. Wadhwani. 2002. *Asset Prices in a Flexible Inflation Targeting Framework*. NBER Working Paper No. 8970.

Clement, Piet. 2010. The Term 'Macro-prudential': Origin and Evolution. *BIS quarterly Review*, March.

Crockett, Andrew. 2000. Marrying the Micro- and Macro-prudential Dimensions of Financial Stability Remarks before the Eleventh International Conference of Banking Supervisors, Basel, 20–21 September.

De Bandt and Hartmann. 2001. *Systemic Risk: A Survey*, ECB, Working Paper No. 35, March.

Ellis, Lucy. 2012. Macroprudential Policy: A Suite of Tools or a State of Mind... Speech at the Paul Woolley Centre for Capital Market Dysfunctionality Annual Conference, Sydney, 11 October.

Gambacorta, Leonardo and Andrés Murcia. 2017. 'The Impact of Macroprudential Policies and Their Interaction with Monetary Policy: An Empirical Analysis

Using Credit Registry Data'. BIS Working Paper. Available at https://www.bis.org/publ/work636.htm (accessed on 25 January 2019).

Haldane, Andrew G. 2017. Rethinking Financial Stability. Speech at 'Rethinking Macroeconomic Policy IV' Conference, Peterson Institute for International Economics, Washington, DC, 12 October.

Jobst, Andreas A. and Dale F. Gray. 2013. 'Systemic Contingent Claims Analysis—Estimating Market-Implied Systemic Risk'. IMF Working Paper WP/13/54. Washington, DC: IMF.

Laseen, Stefan, Andrea Pescatori and Jarkko Turunen. 2017. 'Systemic Risk: A New Trade-Off for Monetary Policy'. Sveriges Riksbank Working Paper Series No. 341.

Morris, Stephen and Hyun Song Shin. 2014. *Risk Taking Channel of Monetary Policy: A Global Game Approach*. Basel: Bank for International Settlements.

Masciandaro, Donato, and Davide Romelli. 2018. *Beyond the Central Bank Independence Veil: New Evidence*. BAFFI CAREFIN Centre Research Paper No. 2018-71, February.

Masciandaro, Donato, and Alessio Volpicella. 2016. *Macroprudential Governance and Central Banks: Facts and Drivers. Journal of International Money and Finance* 61(C): 101–119.

Orlowski, Lucjan T. 2010. *Proliferation of Tail Risks and Policy Responses in the EU Financial Markets*. Fairfield, CT: Sacred Heart University.

Shafik, Minouche. 2015, October. 'The Interaction of Monetary and Macro-prudential Policy' (Speech). Bank of England. Available at https://www.bankofengland.co.uk/-/media/boe/files/speech/2015/the-interaction-of-monetary-and-macroprudential-policy (accessed on 25 January 2019).

Schinasi, Garry J. 2006. *Safeguarding Financial Stability: Theory and Practice*. IMF.

Svensson, Lars E.O. (2016 and 2017). Cost Benefit Analysis of Leaning against the Wind. NBER Working Paper No. 21902 (Issued in January 2016 and Revised in May 2017.

Tigran, Poghosyan. 2019. How Effective Is Macroprudential Policy? Evidence from Lending Restriction Measures in EU Countries. IMF Working Paper/19/45, March.

VolAgénor, Pierre-Richard, and Luiz A. Pereira da Silva. 2019, January. Global Banking, Financial Spillovers, and Macroprudential Policy Coordination. BIS Working Paper no. 764.

CHAPTER 4

Early Warning Systems

Timing is very important in the containment of a financial crisis as rapid contagion can make a crisis spread very fast. A system that can predict crises can be very effective in enhancing preparedness and eventually may even help prevent the crises. While leading indicators are being used as part of an early EWM, they sometimes fail to reveal an impending crisis. Using multiple indicators may prove to be difficult due to different indications revealed by them. Therefore, a composite of the leading indicators is generally used for predicting an impending crisis. The indicators can use the movements in various macrofinancial, macroeconomic, market and banking indicators. A good early warning indicator (EWI) should have high success in prediction ability of a high probability of a distress event conditional of course on the quality of noises on signals from the indicator.

Introduction

The importance of the financial sector in supporting economic growth is well documented in the literature. Equally, financial instability can certainly retard the growth potential of a country. The stability of the financial system is even more important for an emerging market country like India, which requires high rates of growth to lift a large section of the society out of poverty and improve per capita GDP. India's financial sector is large with varied participants, products and markets. Though our financial system has been largely insulated from the adverse impact of the GFC, it is important to learn the lessons so that it is more robust and resilient. Accordingly, the lessons of past crises have generated much interest in many nations to frame country-specific crisis management frameworks (CMFs), of which EWMs are an important pillar. Some of the prominent studies that have significantly contributed to the literature include Kaminsky, Lizondo and Reinhart (1998), Herrera and Garcia (1999), Berg and Pattillo (1999 a, 1999b), Edison (2003), Kumar, Moorthy and Perraudin (2002) and Bussiere and Fratzscher (2006).

The techniques used in developing early warning framework included methods such as qualitative approach, signal extraction approach (SEA), multivariate regression approach, limited dependent modelling approach and duration models approach (Gaytan and Johnson 2002). However, of these methods, two methods, namely SEA and multivariate regression (particularly logit regression), have received wider attention. The choice between the two approaches is largely driven by the availability of long time series data sets. Literature on the topic shows that for developing cross-country early warning framework (for instance, for the EU), studies mostly make the use of multivariate regression approach and in the case of country-specific early warning framework, they have adopted SEA. Some studies also compared the operational performance of the two methods and confirmed that multivariate models generally improve performance of EWM compared to univariate signalling models (see, for instance, Duca et al. 2017).

While formulating cross-country early warning frameworks, Babecky et al. (2012a) found out prediction horizon and most useful leading indicators by applying econometric methods.[1] The authors are

---

[1] The prediction horizon for each potential leading indicator is worked out by adopting vector autoregression approach and to identify the most useful leading indicators they used Bayesian model averaging approach.

of the opinion that domestic housing prices, share prices and credit growth and a few global variables, such as private credit, are risk factors essential in developed economies for monitoring of, and for anticipating crises. Jahn, and Kick (2012) regressed a banking stability indicator on a set of lagged values of macroprudential indicators (such as asset price indicators, leading indicators for the business cycle and monetary policy indicators)[2] and found them to be reliable EWIs. The success of such a framework depends on the choice of variables, long data series and study of movement of the variables with a reasonable periodicity. Assessing the implications of movement in these variables, preparation of assessment reports, stress-testing and recovery/resolution planning are also key elements of this framework. Firming up of a standard operating procedure to act swiftly and conclusively in the event of a crisis really befalling would be the last leg of an ideal CMF.

The EWM should screen the available potential indicators and identify those which have the ability to warn of a crisis at a given lead of all the indicators tested.

Constructing an efficient and genuine EWM for any country could be worth exploring when the financial system is becoming more integrated and connected with the rest of the world and also becoming more and more complex. While such mechanisms are in vogue, their rigour and performance need to be enhanced. Focusing on a select few indicators, which are intuitively featured, may have outlived their utility. It is difficult to premise if financial crises can be prevented. But that should not undermine the effort to predict them so that adequate safeguards can be employed to mitigate the adverse impact of the crisis on the financial system and the economy. The EWM typically evaluates possibilities of crises in the macrofinancial space, that is, it forecasts the likelihood that a crisis will occur based on the trends and patterns of a given set of covariates. This, in turn, is expected to identify critical events the authorities need to be vigilant about.

---

[2] The regression model is estimated by using a database of 3,330 banks (in 1995) and 1,685 banks (in 2010).

Characteristics of EWIs

An EWI would qualify to be called one, if it has the ability to signal impending crises and potential crises even if they fail to materialize. Choice of variables and constructing effective indicators are identified as the basic challenges. The process starts with the identification of variables, which could potentially provide useful early warning about potential imbalances in the system. Using empirical methodologies, the predictive power of these variables will be tested to decide which among them exhibit sufficient predictive ability to be useful in the early warning exercise.

Considering the fact that EWIs are ultimately judged on their efficacy to inform the optimal deployment of macroprudential policy tools, they should satisfy three key requirements: early prediction, stability without noise and interpretability (Drehmann and Juselius 2014).[3] EWI signals should be easy to analyse and interpret, and should make sense for the policymakers to work upon.

Early Warning Literature

Research on devising an early warning framework does not have a long antiquity, it began when financial crises occupied a profound place in the history of financial space. As noted earlier, notwithstanding plentifully many approaches devised in the literature two approaches, those of aforementioned, namely, SEA and multivariate regression (particularly logit regression) have received the widest attention.

By using logit models, Navajas and Thegeya (2013) examined the efficacy of financial indicators, broad macroeconomic indicators and other institutional factors in detecting banking distress. Behn et al. (2013) assessed the usefulness of private credit, macrofinancial and banking sector variables under multivariate econometric model framework. The authors found that apart from credit variables,

---

[3] For instance, the Basel III guidance states that 'the indicator should breach the minimum (critical threshold) at least 2–3 years prior to a crisis' (Basel Committee on Banking Supervision 2010 Report: 16).

equity and house prices help in predicting the vulnerabilities in EU member states more correctly. Under dynamic panel probit regression model framework,[4] Antonio et al. (2016) showed the price index and debt–service ratio are to be better suited as EWI, while the credit-to-GDP gap as a signal has better properties closer to a crisis.

Holopainen and Sarlin (2016) conducted a horse race between conventional statistical methods and modern machine learning methods (*k*-nearest neighbourhoods and neural networks). The authors inferred that conventional statistical methods generally outperform the advanced machine learning methods.[5] The authors also combined several economic indicators and built up a composite indicator. A mix of indicators with different frequencies is useful in giving timely warning signals. The empirical relationship between stock market volatility and financial crises was verified under regression by Danielsson, Valenzuela and Zer (2016). They found that low volatility increases the probability of banking crisis. Further, they added that low volatility significantly increases risk-taking, which eventually leads to a crisis when the riskier investments turn sour. Rancan, Sarlinand and Peltonen (2015) and Minoiu et al. (2013) examined usefulness of financial interconnectedness as a source of systemic risk and as an EWI and found that given a similar continuing macroeconomic situation, an increase in financial interconnectedness and decrease in neighbours' connectedness for a country seem to indicate a probable banking crisis.

By applying logit regression model, Coudert and Idier (2016) found that four indicators, namely the bank credit-to-GDP gap, residential property price-to-income ratio (annual change), three-year real equity price growth and debt service-to-income ratio, carry sufficient explanatory power in predicting the crises. Many proved that credit-to-GDP gap has greater predictability of banking crisis and is very useful in signalling vulnerabilities (see, for instance, Drehmann [2013]). Through his empirical work, he demonstrated that credit-to-GDP

---

[4] The authors used cross-country data pertaining to 28 countries spanning over 1970–Q1 to 2010–Q4 for conducting empirical analysis.

[5] By considering 15 EU economies over the three decades, Virtanen et al. (2016) developed unit root-based early warning systems in ex-ante forecasting of financial vulnerabilities.

gap is the best indicator in detecting crises across many countries for several decades including emerging market economies. Sarlin and von Schweinitz (2017) used statistical procedures such as binary choice model for fixing ex-ante thresholds and setting probability thresholds based on preferences. They were of the opinion that the binary choice approach improved out-of-sample predictions and reduced the positive bias of in-sample performance. Kiley (2018) suggests that house prices, equity prices and current account deficits (CADs) have substantial leading information in econometric models to predict the occurrence of a financial crisis. On the other hand, he found that credit is relatively uninformative in predicting the financial distress. His finding differs from the emerging conventional wisdom focused on debt accumulation.

To anticipate building up of stress in the financial system, Mikhail et al. (2011) designed a Systemic Assessment of Financial Environment (SAFE) mechanism which is a hybrid class of model for systemic risk having structural characteristics of the financial system and a feedback amplification mechanism. The system used micro-prudential information from the largest BHCs. The methodology (SAFE) is useful in predicting certain vulnerabilities that provide policymakers sufficient time to take ex-ante policy actions in the medium-term to mitigate inherent uncertainties.

Some authors argue that using multivariate models while developing EWMs may not be possible in the context of developing countries, primarily on account of non-availability of large time series data sets, which are very essential for empirical analytics. Accordingly, they argue that methodologies planned for preparing EWMs for developed countries could be customized by creating the need for country-specific case studies (Seth and Ragab 2012). Some authors (Krkoska 2000) through their research findings found that early warning frameworks devised by adopting 'SEA' provide valuable insights in assessing the vulnerabilities in the macroeconomic environment, particularly for developing countries.

By using signal approach, Alessi and Carsten (2010) and Betz et al. (2013) worked out the type I and type II errors of major leading macroeconomic indicators. Augmentation of bank-specific vulnerabilities with indicators related to macrofinancial imbalances significantly improves efficiency of early warning framework under SEA. Ndung'u et al. (2012) constructed two indices, namely Index of Speculative Pressure[6] (ISP) and Index of Macroeconomic Vulnerability[7] (IMV), while developing early warning framework for Kenya's economy. Loloh (2015) also constructed banking sector fragility index (BSFI) for identifying the Ghanaian banking sector crisis. Three leading indicators namely private sector credit, foreign liabilities and deposits have been used for building BSFI. By examining its trends and patterns, he identified three episodes of excessive risk-taking and four periods of high fragility in Ghana. He also noticed that high fragility episodes are followed by significant increase in non-performing loans in Ghana's financial system.

For identifying the likelihood of failure of a huge number of financial institutions, Schwaab, Koopman and Lucas (2011) constructed coincident measures and forward-looking indicators under dynamic factor framework. Further, the decoupling of the credit risk conditions from the macroeconomic fundamentals can be used as an EWI.

Lang et al. (2019) proposed d-SRI (domestic cyclical systemic risk indicator) which is a leading indicator and starts to increase four to five years prior to systemic financial crises and is highly correlated with the measures of crisis severity. The indicator is a weighted average of six early warning indicators viz., bank credit to GDP change, current account balance, residential real estate price to income ratio change, real equity price growth, change in the debt service ratio, and real total credit growth.

As seen earlier, SEA looks to be most suitable for framing country-specific EWM and is more robust in signaling crises if the movements in the relevant macroeconomic and financial sector

---

[6] Summation of standardized monthly percentage change in three key variables, namely (a) nominal exchange rate, (b) short-term interest rate and (c) international reserves.

[7] IMV is defined as a summation of (a) real effective exchange rate (REER), (b) real domestic credit growth and (c) M2 as a ratio of international reserves.

indicators are aggregated. The researchers adopted SEA to configure country-specific EWM for Indian financial space. Non-availability of longer time series data sets (particularly baking sector variables in the public domain) remained the constraint to try out other approaches. They chose key variables pertaining to macroeconomic, macrofinancial, banking sector and external sector vulnerability. The task of choosing these variables was largely based on previous research on these variables and also data availability in the public domain (Kaminsky et al. 1998).

Efficiency of EWM—SEA

For assessing the validity of EWIs in predicting the impending crises for formulating country-specific EWM, the 'SEA' has been used extensively—Herrea and Garcia 1999; Kaminsky et al. 1998; Ndung'u et al. 2014). In this framework, a signal is emitted if the value of a particular EWI exceeds the threshold value. The signal is said to be effective if it is followed by a crisis within a certain period. Of course, the indicator can also generate noise, or a false signal, if it emits a signal which is not followed by a crisis within the stipulated period. The possible outcomes of signal approach are summarized in the form of contingency matrix in Table 4.1.

In Table 4.1, 'A' is the number of times a distress event followed a signal (in this chapter they assumed that the crisis may occur within

Table 4.1 *Contingency Matrix*

		Actual Class	
		Crisis	No Crisis
Predicted Class	**Signal**	A (Correct Call)	B (False Alarm)
	No signal	C (Missed Crisis)	D (Correct Silence)

Source: Holopainen M. and P. Sarlin (2015).

Table 4.2 *Characteristics of Good EWIs*

Ratio	Definition	Expectation
Good signal ratio	$\dfrac{A}{(A+C)}$	Good EWI is supposed to have high proportion of good signals
Bad signal ratio (also called noise ratio)	$\dfrac{B}{(B+D)}$	Low noise will always be a noble characteristic of good indicator
Noise-to-signal ratio	$\dfrac{B/(B+D)}{A/(A+C)}$	Low noise to signal ratio is a desired characteristic of good EWI
Probability of distress event conditional on a signal from the indicator	$\dfrac{A}{(A+B)}$	High conditional probability is expected to qualify an indicator as a good EWI
Difference between conditional and unconditional probability of distressed event	$\dfrac{A}{(A+B)} - \dfrac{(A+C)}{(A+B+C+D)}$	A higher difference signifies more usefulness of the indicator

1 or 2 years[8] once the signal is emitted), 'B' is the number of times distress event did not follow (within 1 or 2 years) a signal emission, 'C' is the number of times a distress event took place while the indicator failed to transmit a prior signal and 'D' is the number of times a signal is not emitted and no distress event ensued. If a variable is a perfect EWI, then 'A' should be 100 per cent, while 'B' and 'C' should be zero per cent. In other words, a perfect indicator will have zero noise and seamless signaling of distress events. The characteristics of good EWIs are described in Table 4.2.

---

[8] An attempt is also made to ensure whether results will change if the observation window/tracking period is changed from 2 years to 1 year. We found that most of the indicators behaved in a similar way.

Early Warning Indicators

Various approaches have been used to find out the variables to be used as potential EWIs. However, three approaches stand out. First is a theory-based study working with a relatively small set of indicators but enlarged occasionally as per the data series transformations to identify potential leading indicators (Kaminsky et al. 1998). The second approach has been to rely upon earlier researches and creating extensive data sets by including all established leading indicators and various transformations thereof (Frankel and Saravelos 2010; Rose and Spiegel 2009). The third approach has been to consider all the variables available in a selected database and add various transformations. The risk of missing any important potential indicators always remains as the approaches are subject to researchers' judgement. There are various limitations in these approaches as well. The theory-based studies, on account of model limitations, may become limited in carving out the indicators. Similarly, the systematic literature review may result in omission of indicators and studies relying on single database may miss other indicators.

The potential indicators score over the other identified indicators based on their greater predictability of the impending crisis and their impact. The following chart (Chart 4.1) presents the percentage share of the individual sets of indicators in terms of the explanatory power of the overall model. As can be seen, global variables turn out to be the most important set of indicators. The right-hand diagram illustrates the performance of the individual global variables. What can be inferred from the results is the fact that macroprudential policy should monitor both global indicators (such as global GDP, global credit and global inflation) and selected domestic indicators. Among the domestic factors, house prices represent the most significant source of risk to macroeconomic stability. Other important indicators also include the price of crude oil and internal and external debt.

The problem is further aggravated by the fact that there have been very few researches undertaken to tackle the issue related to non-availability of data (Cecchetti et al. 2010). The recent crisis revealed that due to data limitation, indicators such as liquidity ratios are not

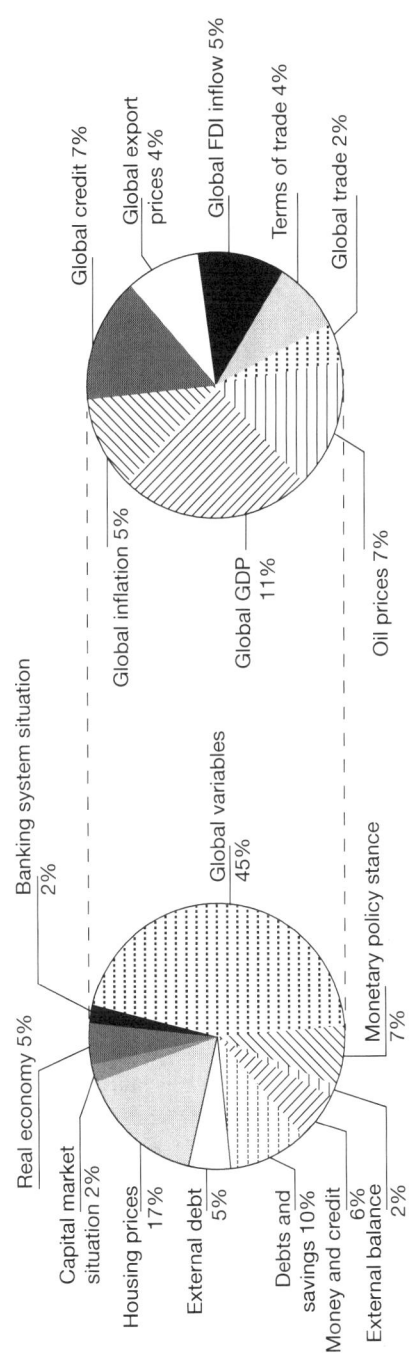

Chart 4.1 The Most Important Early Warning Indicators

Source: CNB Research Project C3/2011.

available, or are only available for some countries and for limited time periods. For example, the ratio of regulatory capital to RWAs (CRAR), credit to households and the deposit–loan ratio for households are few variables that could not be included because of this problem.

Classification of Individual Indicators

Prominent research studies and papers classify EWIs into four groups, namely macroeconomic (including external vulnerability), macrofinancial, market indicators and banking sector. While observing the trends and patterns of the indicators, empirical studies relied on the most commonly used transformations, such as ratios, growth rate, and absolute and relative deviations from the trend value. A brief list of EWIs chosen in various studies is tabulated in detail (Table 4.3).

Table 4.3 *EWIs Chosen for the Study*

Indicator	Definition	Transformation
Macrofinancial indicators		
1. **Credit-to-GDP gap**[a]	Difference between bank credit to GDP ratio and its trend	Ratio
Macroeconomic indicators		
2. **Output gap**[9,b]	Difference between actual output and potential output	Growth
3. **Inflation (Wholesale Price Index [WPI])**[10]	Growth in WPI	Growth
4. **Fiscal deficit**	Gross fiscal deficit as a percentage of GDP	Ratio

[9] Output gap usually captures a lot of risk-taking and it has significant power in predicting the crisis. Output gap (positive or negative) is considered as unreceptive economic indicator. A positive output gap reveals that extremely high demand for goods and services spurs inflation in the economy. On the contrary, negative output gap corroborates a lack of demand and is generally a sign of sluggish economy and the prices of goods generally fall.

[10] WPIs of different base years have been converted to 2004–2005 base year before working out growth in WPI.

Indicator	Definition	Transformation
5. Forex reserves	Forex reserves as a percentage of GDP	Ratio
6. External debt	External debt as a percentage of GDP	Ratio
Market indicators		
7. Lending rate	SBI advance rate	Ratio
8. Interest rate	Call/notice money rate	Ratio
9. Return on stock market (SENSEX)	Logarithmic return	Logarithm
10. Return on stock market (top 100 companies)	Logarithmic return	Logarithm
Banking sector indicators		
11. Credit growth	Year-on-year growth in bank credit	Growth
12. Deposit growth	Year-on-year growth in bank deposits	Growth
13. Credit-to-deposit ratio	Bank credit as a percentage of bank deposits	Ratio
14. CRAR	Capital to RWAs ratio	Ratio
15. Gross non-performing asset (NPA) ratio	Gross NPAs as a percentage of advance	Ratio
16. RoA	Net profit as a percentage of total assets	Ratio
17. Leverage ratio	Total assets as a percentage of equity	Actual ratio (not in percentage terms)
External vulnerability indicators		
18. Exchange rate	Exchange rate of rupee vs US$	Growth
19. CAD	CAD as a percentage of GDP	Ratio

Notes:

[a]Credit-to-GDP gap is calculated as the difference between credit-to-GDP ratio and its trend. Trend in credit-to-GDP ratio is estimated by using HP filter with smoothing parameter (λ) of 1,600.

[b]Output gap is worked out as the difference between the actual output (output is proxied with GDP) and potential output. Potential output can be calculated in many ways, including, for example, by using a Hodrick-Prescott filter with smoothing parameter (λ) on actual GDP 1,600.

Multiple Indicator Approach

As it is difficult to examine the movements of various indicators simultaneously for predicting the impending crises, policymakers, academia and researchers generally synthesize the moments of various macrofinancial, macroeconomic and banking sector indicators and construct composite indices. By studying the behaviour of these composite indices, they try to forecast the probability of a crisis/financial distress much in advance. Though there are many indices that have been documented in the literature, three indices namely, (a) index of speculative pressures (ISP), (b) index of macroeconomic vulnerability and (c) index of banking sector vulnerability (IBSV) have received wider attention in predicting the crises more efficiently.

While constructing the composite indices, it is also a good practice in the literature to discriminate two aspects: (a) risk materialization indicators—generally measured in terms of NPA ratio, CRAR, RoA and (b) the risk accumulation factors—guided by variables such as credit growth, output gap, etc. Empirical research has proved that crises are often preceded by low NPAs and high RoA; these measures generally don't throw any signals before the crisis. On the other hand, high credit growth or output gap usually captures a lot of risk-taking and these indicators have significant power in predicting a crisis.

No discrimination between risk-taking and risk accumulation indicators should be done and both of them should be added together while constructing the composite indices. Having a proper mix of indicators with appropriate theoretical signs (positive or negative) before aggregation generally improves the efficiency of the overall index in signalling the crises.

Index on Speculative Pressure

Previous research corroborates the fact that a crisis is a phenomenon during which there is a significant decrease in exchange rate, although monetary authorities make an effort to stem the currency depreciation by sharply increasing interest rates, and/or by intervening in the foreign currency markets which is characterized by a large decline in international reserves (Herrera and Garcia 1999). The index of speculative pressures, therefore, combines the information on three indicators, namely the nominal exchange rate, the short-term interest rate and international reserves. Although there are many variables that have been suggested in the literature, a good number of studies (see, for instance, Abiad 2003; Eichengreen, Rose and Wyplosz 1996; Frankel and Saravelos 2010; Kaminsky et al. 1998; Krkoska 2000) concur that reserves and exchange rate movements are the most statistically significant variables and are highly reliable estimates of crises events.

Before combining the movements of the variables, they should be normalized by adopting the following min–max rule. Normalization is very essential to ensure that differences in volatility of distinct indicators are standardized. The variable X is normalized by using the following equation:

$$\text{Normalized variable}(X) = \frac{\text{Variable}(X) - \text{Minimum}(X)}{\text{Maximum}(X) - \text{Minimum}(X)}$$

It is generally believed that speculative activities exert considerable pressure on exchange rate. The central bank may normalize the changes in the value of currency by buying or selling international reserves. For instance, central bank may run down reserves to secure the value of domestic currency during the periods of depreciation. Furthermore, as documented in the literature (Eichengreen et al. 1996), the interest rate policy can be used to countervail pressure against the value of local currency. Accordingly, interest rates need to be increased to a certain level which can attract short-term capital flow into the country to protect the value of domestic currency. We have constructed the index of speculative pressures (ISP) on the lines of Herrera and Garcia (1999) and Ndung'u et al. (2014) as follows:

$$\text{ISP} = \triangle\text{NER} + \triangle\text{IR} - \triangle\text{FR}$$

where ISP is the index of speculative pressures, $\triangle$NER is the change in nominal exchange rate, $\triangle$IR is the change in short-term interest rates. Call/notice money has been used as a proxy for short-term interest rate and $\triangle$FR is the change in foreign reserves.

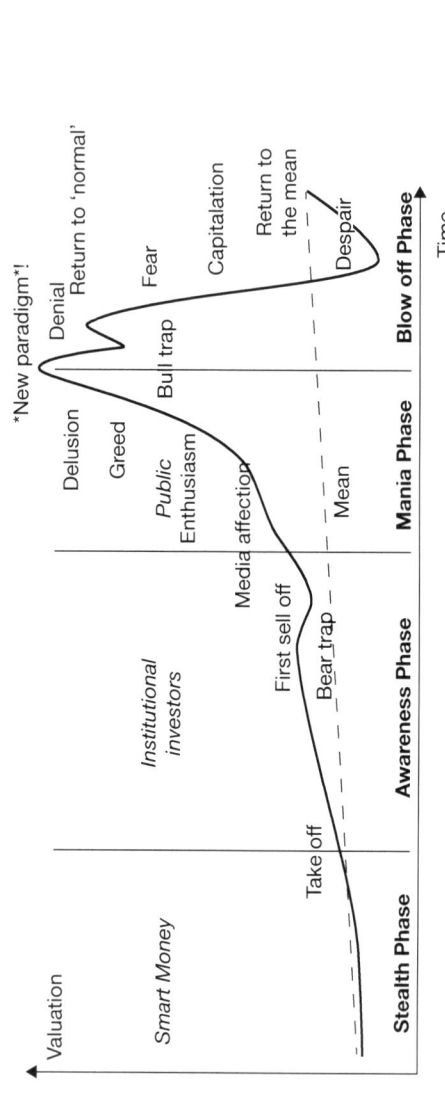

Figure 4.2 *Main Stages in a Bubble*

As mentioned in the methodology, a signal is generated when an indicator crosses a predefined threshold limit; accordingly, a period of speculative pressures is defined as the period during which the ISP crosses the pre-specified thresholds. A crisis period is said to occur when:

$$ISP > \mu + k\sigma$$

Threshold is estimated by adding k standard deviation to the mean value of ISP. The value of k is determined based on two aspects, sufficiently high good signal ratio and low noise ratio.

As money market is generally considered as the fulcrum of monetary transmission policy of any central bank, it forms the key candidate in the financial system. It is generally believed that an increase in the interest rate will decrease the output (generally proxied by GDP) and decrease in the interest rate will accelerate output growth. Output gap (positive or negative) is considered as an unreceptive economic indicator. A positive output gap reveals an extremely high demand for goods and services that spurs inflation in the economy. On the contrary, negative output gap corroborates a lack of demand and is generally a sign of sluggish economy and the prices of goods generally fall subsequently.

The Index of Macroeconomic Vulnerability

Literature highlights that the index of macroeconomic vulnerability is fabricated as the summation of the fiscal deficit, CAD and inflation. Fiscal deficit and CAD are measured as percentages of GDP and inflation is worked out as the year-on-year percentage change in price index (i.e., consumer price index or wholesale price index). In other words, IMV essentially brings together movements in three key macroeconomic imbalances, namely fiscal management, external imbalances and domestic prices. The higher the IMV, the greater the macroeconomic imbalances, and more vulnerable is the economy to distress or a crisis. Accordingly, many researchers through their empirical work have envisaged that the IMV quantifies economic fragility well in advance by emitting signals.

Generally, indicators that measure the macroeconomic vulnerability are constructed based on complex models by making use of sophisticated statistical procedures. In contrast, the IMV is easy to calculate and comprehend. On account of its simplicity in computational aspects, IMV has been considered as one among the excellent EWI and the same has been proven as an indicator which red flags the presence of systemic vulnerabilities as early as possible.[11] The IMV is compiled based on the following equation:

$$IMV = GFD + CAD + INF + RET$$

The economic logic for choosing the variables such as GFD, CAD, INF and RET is explained further. Fiscal deficit arises whenever government spending exceeds its income. Economists and policy analysts envisage that fiscal deficits crowd out private borrowing, manipulate capital structures[12] and interest rates, decrease net exports and lead to either higher taxes, higher inflation or both. One of the factors responsible for Asian crisis of 1997 was that countries were running large CADs and they were financing these deficits by attracting capital flows. When the confidence in the country falls, these flows will dry up, leading to macroeconomic imbalances in the form of rapid devaluation of domestic currency and lower growth of export sector. Price stability or a relatively constant level of inflation allows businesses to plan for the future. Theoretically, it also allows economies to promote maximum employment.

---

[11] However, previous research, particularly studies conducted by Kaminsky et al. (1998), Herrera and Garcia (1999) and Ddung'u (2014), used three leading indicators, namely REER, domestic credit growth and ratio of international reserves, while compiling IMV. However, for improving the efficiency of IMV, some authors also include return on stock market and besides the previously mentioned three indicators (see, for instance, Gavin [1986] and Dornbusch [1983]).

[12] The capital structure is how a firm finances its overall operations and growth by using different sources of funds. Debt comes in the form of bond issues or long-term notes payable, while equity is classified as common stock, preferred stock or retained earnings. Short-term debt such as working capital requirements is also considered to be part of the capital structure.

Inflation is a crucial factor in determining the flow of foreign investments in the economy. Foreign investments are restricted due to a high inflation rate signalling economic uneasiness. In contrast, a low and stable inflation boosts foreign investments as it symbolizes stability and growth.

Banking Sector Vulnerability

The third composite index constructed to measure the crisis periods is IBSV. For constructing IBSV, variables on business performance (credit growth, deposit growth), asset quality, capital adequacy and profitability can be used. As mentioned earlier, the choice of variables is largely determined by the availability of variables for longer time periods in the public domain.[13] Before consolidation, standardization of all variables by using the min–max principle should be done. Previous research on the topic confirmed that high growth in credits/deposits generally accumulates vulnerabilities in the economy. The index is constructed based the following equation:

$$IBSV = GBC + GBD + GNPA - CRAR + ROA$$

where IBSV is the index of banking sector vulnerability, GBC is the growth in bank credit, GBD is growth in bank deposits, GNPA is gross NPAs to total advances, CRAR is capital to RWA ratio and ROA is the return on assets.

After following an iterative process, the value of k, as indicated earlier, is determined.

Early Warning Mechanism for India

In this section, an attempt is made to identify various macrofinancial, macroeconomic, banking and market indicators, which have sound

---

[13] The Reserve Bank of India compiles banking stability indicator by using five indicators: capital adequacy, asset quality, profitability, liquidity and efficiency. We were unable to use liquidity and efficiency variables as the information on these is not readily available.

statistical power of forecasting financial distress/crises. Accordingly, we have chosen 19 key indicators (Table 4.3). The efficacy of these indicators in predicting the crises is assessed through 'signal approach', which has been considered as the most widely used approach in developing a country-specific early warning framework. As it is quite difficult to monitor the movements of each and every individual indicator simultaneously in forecasting the crises events, an attempt is also made to build three composite indices, namely index of macroeconomic vulnerability, index of speculative pressures and IBSV, by aggregating suitable indicators, which have theoretical explanatory power in estimating vulnerabilities in an economy. Such hybridization of inter-sectoral variables has been attempted to justify

> mutually reinforcing processes between the financial and real sides of the economy. For instance, as the economy grows, cash flows, incomes and asset prices rise, risk appetite increases, and external funding constraints weaken, thereby generating potentially large financial imbalances. At some point, these imbalances have to unwind, potentially causing a crisis, characterised by large losses, liquidity squeezes and possibly a credit crunch. (Drehmann and Juselius 2013)

The results showed that few indicators (such as credit-to-GDP gap, output GAP, credit growth, deposit growth, CRAR, gross NPA Ratio and ROA) performed well in identifying the financial distress with good signal and low noise ratios (Annexure 4A.1). However, some other indicators such as gross fiscal deficit to GDP, forex reserves to GDP and return on stock market though displayed reasonably good signals ratio, they also generated notable noise ratio. The results are in line with the earlier findings of Behn et al. (2013) and Drehmann and Juselius (2013). Banking sector variables are seen to exert a significant influence on build-up of financial vulnerabilities. Inadequately capitalized banking sector is a precursor to vulnerability. This is in sync with the Basel proposal of a notion of higher CCB rates in the advent of a possible state of vulnerability. The Credit–GDP gap showing signs of a good EWI would gel well with this policy prescription. Similarly, position of high profitability (ROA) will encourage more lending (credit growth) meaning more risk-taking and thus leading to increased vulnerabilities in the form of higher level of contamination in loans (NPA ratio). The recent episode of severe distress in India's banking sector testifies this. Further, composite indices performed better in signalling the crises well in advance. For example, in case of the composite banking sector vulnerability index, the good signal ratio displays better performance as compared to individual banking sector indicators used earlier. The noise ratio looks better as well.

The analysis suggests that a clear 'quantitative definition of crisis', in respect of banks in India, is possible. For example, the three critical indicators could be credit growth exceeding 21 per cent, CRAR falling below 11.75 per cent and ROA[14] growing by more than 1 per cent. This is what an ideal functional EWM would represent as per Davis and Karim (2008). It tends to satisfy the three pillars of (a) timing, (b) stability and (c) interpretability as proposed by Drehmann and Juselius (2014). All the chosen indicators showed signals of impending crisis 2 years before their occurrence. They are also stable in foretelling crisis with reasonably low noise (being 'no signal' when crisis does not occur). Further, as explained earlier, these results are simple to understand and interpret.

Scope for Future Research

The assessment of performance of two approaches reveals that multivariate logit regression models can improve upon univariate signalling models. It was not possible to attempt logit regression analysis (LRA) in this single country framework due to non-availability of quarterly data series on banking sector variables in the public domain.

The trend of cyclization (financial and business) has come to stay. To that extent, EWM needs further nuancing to be able to smell bubbles. A 'Bubble Threat Warning System' should be a logical extension for future research. Bubbles carry different stages of transformation as

---

[14] The exercise was tried out for the indicator ROE too. The results showed similar trend.

seen in Figure 4.2.[15] As may be clear, the data should allow the policymaker to smell the bubble before the stage of 'take off' when an idea gets brewed into the making of a bubble. It would then be possible to make use of macroprudential tools to soften it. But this would require choicest variables (say leverage ratios across banks and price rises in an important class of assets, namely land, housing, equities, etc.) and sufficient volume of data and may be much finer models to achieve this.

If leverage ratios go off the board (permissible limits as set by the model) and/or prices of the underlying assets tend to rise rapidly (beyond tolerable limits as given by the model), the EWM should flash these as 'red alerts' to signal investing public to keep off and the banks to revert to permissible levels by way of regulatory interventions. These should continue till the threat tends to moderate. The transition across various cyclical phases of a bubble needs to be estimated. The length and intensity of various such phases need to be explained in sync with the state of affairs of the economy. The EWM should be able to differentiate between the acute phase of a crisis and the subsequent recovery period.

This brings to fore another space for attention, namely sectoral credit. If the growth rate in a particular (or sensitive) sector outpaces that of the overall credit growth that could be smelt as a possible bubble in the making. Simple 'industry limits' are prescribed for this purpose without regard to its interconnectivity with other sectors (cement and steel with housing sector) which might be a 'more influencing factor' for a possible overall distress to set in. This is warranted for a more effective EWM but requires complex models to be configured.

It is difficult to measure interconnectedness due to the issues of data unavailability and also due to their nebulous interpretability. Presence of different types of domestic and international imbalances and multidimensional determinants of vulnerabilities to external shocks has made the very process of identification of EWIs cumbersome. The post-crisis effect on GDPs of various countries tended to vary, as also

---

[15] Developed by Jean-Paul Rodrigue, a professor at Hofstra University in January 2006, the chart depicts the stages of bubbles as backed up by 500 years of financial history.

their recovery periods from the end of the most severe phase of the crisis. Separate models are being envisaged to capture their effects.

Stress-Testing Framework (STF) is a robust counter-verification system post EWM. Based on the alerts given by the EWM, it would be desirable to subject the specific sector under question to a stress test to assess the intensity of possible vulnerabilities. STF should be more comprehensive and aimed at identifying stresses which are not observable readily from EWM. It should also indicate the quantified distance from distress (say regulatory capital in case of test of solvency) and create the possibility for focused regulatory attention/response.

One more partly unresolved issue is the characteristic of being 'forward-looking'. A combination of EWM and STF could answer this but an empirical model would be helpful, which, while being able to define the required extent and quality of 'forward-looking–ness', should be able to display the level of required accuracy in 'predicting' distress.

It may be worth mentioning that even in the developed world, the quest for an appropriate systemic risk measurement system, which includes a macro stress-testing model and a forward-looking early warning model, is still on. And going by the progress so far, it will continue for some more time.

Conclusion

Financial crises do not land as a bolt from the blue. Yet, policymakers are at times caught napping while the need to have a pre-emptive mechanism to handle these episodes as and when they occur is well appreciated in literature, financial crisis managers do miss out on them from time-to-time. The Asian crisis of the late 1990s, the failure of Lehman Brothers in September 2008, the Sovereign debt crisis of Europe (Greece, Ireland and Portugal) and the health of Spain's banking sector (collectively, the GIPS countries), all tend to testify the same tendency called in literature as 'disaster Myopia'. Every country invests in firefighting measures despite having not seen even one such disaster episode in decades. In doing so, it tends to discount the severity of possible future losses at present value when comparing them to the current cost of firefighting. It could be beneficial to try, if not to prevent such crises, to at least minimize the extent of damage it might inflict if it ever happens.[16] This could be the best example in defence of why countries should have 'Financial CMFs' of which 'EWM' is a necessary component. The intensity of interconnectedness—inter-economy (thanks to spillover effects of globalization), intra-economy (real and financial sector), inter-sector (banks and non-banks) and intra-sector (bank to bank)—has made the study of predicting and preparing for onset of financial crisis quite intricate but immensely interesting.

Despite the development of large body of empirical literature on early warning framework, accurate forecasting of crises continues to be a very challenging task. For testing the early warning framework, research essentially highlights two approaches: (a) SEA and (b) LRA. It has been cited in the literature that SEA is mostly suitable for developing a country-specific early warning framework, while LRA is basically meant for framing cross-country EWM.

At present, models which measure systemic risk and provide an estimate of probability of financial crises in a forward-looking manner are in their infancy. Even in advanced economies, such models are still being developed and are being tested before policymakers can use them. EWMs provide valuable information to the regulator about the brewing vulnerabilities in the system. An EWI would qualify to be called one if it carries the ability to 'signal all impending crises and does not raise false alarms for crises'. Choice of variables and their seasoning into effective indicators hence is identified as the basic challenge.

---

[16] EWIs could be considered ideal if the crisis they signal does materialize. But they don't happen that way in real world. A few 'false alarms' would be inevitable. It is the trade-off between 'the rate of missed crises against the rate of false positives (i.e., the percentage of signals they emit for crises that do not happen)' (Drehmann and Tsatsaronis 2014). But it should be a policymaker's delight to err on the right side, that is, it is alright to react to a false signal and try to correct a position that would not happen than not to respond to possible onslaught of vulnerability. But sometimes, the cost of reacting to false signals could be too costly especially when the reaction means imposing hard regulations having economy-wide implications. But these are part of the art of policymaking which should be implemented in a calibrated manner after feeling the rock inside water.

The process starts with the identification of indicators/variables which could potentially provide a useful early warning about these costly events with the use of an empirical methodology—which specifies sufficient predictive power of various potential leading indicators—to decide which ones among them exhibit sufficient predictive power to be useful in the early warning exercise.

Given the entrenchment of cyclization of both financial and business, EWM needs significant nuancing to be able to smell bubbles. A 'Bubble Threat Warning System' should be a logical extension for future research.

Considering the fact that EWIs are ultimately judged on their efficacy as suitable macroprudential policy tools, they should satisfy three requirements.

> The first is timing: EWIs must provide signals early enough for policy measures to take effect. The timeliness of crisis detection is of utmost importance to ensure that policy actions can be effective and be deployed in time. This is dependent on the lead-lag relationship between changing a specific macro-prudential tool and the impact on the policy objective. The second requirement is stability: the indicator should not flip-flop between signaling a crisis and being 'off'. EWIs that issue stable signals reduce uncertainty regarding trends and allow for more decisive policy actions. The final requirement is interpretability. (Drehmann and Juselius 2014)

The jury is still out on what should be an effective[17] EWM and whether it resolves the issues for which it is administered. EWM is

---

[17] But, in contrast, it may be argued that an effective EWI may tend to fall into the definitional trap of the usual Lucas critique implying that once these are able to track distress adequately and are able to prevent them to appear (in less harmful state), they may get susceptible to lose their 'leading indicator' characteristics.

> For instance, if banks are forced to build up buffers based on signals issued by well specified EWIs, they would be more resilient toward busts, which in turn could make crises less likely. As Drehmann et al. (2011) argue, however, the loss of predictive content per se would be no reason to abandon the scheme—it would be rather a sign of its success. (Drehmann and Juselius 2013)

being extensively adopted to identify financial distresses in the financial system, primarily to be able to initiate suitable policy actions to contain extent of possible damages. Thanks to many of the forecasts about a mishap having gone wrong, it has incurred enough 'credibility deficit' as well, a trend similarly seen in cases of the meteorologists and economists. Thus, EWM should be effective—fool proof in its prediction—that is, the EWM should be able to predict reasonably accurately an impending crisis. But it continues to be 'better said than done'.

References

Abiad, A. 2003. 'Early Warning Systems: A Survey and Regime Switching Approach'. IMF Working Paper No. 32. Washington, DC: International Monetary Fund.

———. 1999b. 'What Caused the Asian Crises: An Early Warning System Approach'. *Economic Notes* 28: 285.

———. 2012. 'Characterising the Financial Cycle: Don't Lose Sight of the Medium Term'. BIS Working Paper No. 380. Basel: Bank for International Settlements.

———. 2012b. 'Leading Indicators of Crisis Incidence Evidence from Developed Countries'. European Central Bank Working Paper Series No. 1486. Frankfurt: European Central Bank.

———. 2013. 'Evaluating Early Warning Indicators of Banking Crises: Satisfying Policy Requirements'. BIS Working Paper No. 421. Basel: Bank for International Settlements.

———. 2014. 'Evaluating Early Warning Indicators of Banking Crises: Satisfying Policy Requirements'. *International Journal of Forecasting* 30 (3): 759–780.

Alessi, Lucia and D. Carsten. 2010. 'Real Time Early Warning Indicators for Costly Asset Price Boom/Bust Cycles: A Role for Global Liquidity'. Paolo Baffi Centre. Centre Research Paper Series No. 2009–70.

Antonio, R., A. Antunes, Diana Bonfim, Nuno Monteiro and P. M. Rodrigues. 2016. 'Forecasting Banking Crises with Dynamic Panel Probit Models'. Working Paper. Lisbon: Banco de Portugal.

Behn, M., C. Detken, T. Peltonen and W. Schudel. 2013, November. 'Setting Countercyclical Capital Buffers Based on Early Warning Models: Would It Work?' ECB Working Paper Series No. 1604. Frankfurt: European Central Bank.

Berg, A. and C. Pattillo. 1999a. 'Predicting Currency Crises: The Indicators Approach and an Alternative'. *Journal of International Money and Finance* 18: 561–586.

Betz, Frank, S. Oprica, T. A. Peltonen and Peter Sarlin. 2013. 'Predicting Distress in European Banks'. European Central Bank Working Paper Series No. 1597. Frankfurt: European Central Bank.

Bussiere, M. and M. Fratzscher. 2006. 'Towards A New Early Warning System of Financial Crises'. *Journal of International Money and Finance* 25 (6): 953–973.

Cecchetti, Stephen G., M.S. Mohanty and Fabrizio Zampolli. 2010. The Future of Public Debt: Prospects and Implications. BIS Working Papers No. 300, March.

Coudert, V. and Julien Idier. 2016. *An Early Warning System for Macro-prudential Policy in France*. Paris: Bank of France, Financial Stability Directorate.

Danielsson, J., M. Valenzuela and I. Zer. 2016. 'Learning from History: Volatility and Financial Crises'. Finance and Economics Discussion Series. Washington, DC: Divisions of Research & Statistics and Monetary Affairs, Federal Reserve Board.

Davis, E. P. and D. Karim. 2008. 'Comparing Early Warning Systems for Banking Crises. *Journal of Financial Stability* 4 (2): 89–120.

Dornbusch, R. 1983. 'Exchange Rate Risk and the Macroeconomics of Exchange Rate Determination'. *Financial Markets and National Economic Policy* 3: 3–27.

Drehmann, M. 2013, June. 'Total Credit as an Early Warning Indicator for Systemic Banking Crises'. *BIS Quarterly Review*: 41–45.

Drehmann, Mathias and Kostas Tsatsaronis. 2014. The Credit-to-GDP Gap and Countercyclical Capital Buffers: Questions and Answers. *BIS Quarterly Review*, March.

Duca, M. L., A. Koban, M. Basten, E. Bengtsson, B. Klaus, P. Kusmierczyk and J. H. Lang. 2017. 'A New Database for Financial Crises in European Countries'. Occasional Paper No. 194. European Central Bank. Frankfurt: European Central Bank.

Edison, H. 2003. 'Do Indicators of Financial Crises Work? An Evaluation of an Early Warning System'. *International Journal of Finance & Economics* 8: 11–53.

Eichengreen, B., A. K. Rose and C. Wyplosz. 1996. 'Contagious Currency Crises'. National Bureau of Economic Research Working Paper No. 5681. Cambridge, MA: National Bureau of Economic Research.

Frankel, J. and G. Saravelos. 2010. *Are Leading Indicators of Financial Crises Useful for Assessing Country Vulnerability? Evidence from the 2008–09 Global Crisis*. Available at https://econpapers.repec.org/paper/nbrnberwo/16047.htm (accessed on 28 January 2019).

Gavin, M. 1986. 'The Stock Market and the Exchange Rate Dynamics'. International Finance Discussion Paper. Available at https://www.federal-reserve.gov/pubs/ifdp/1986/278/ifdp278.pdf (accessed on 28 January 2019).

Gaytan, A. and C. A. Johnson. 2002. 'A Review of the Literature on Early Warning Systems for Banking Crises'. Working Paper No. 183. Santiago: Central Bank of Chile.

Herrera, S. and C. Garcia. 1999. 'User's Guide to an Early Warning System for Macroeconomic Vulnerability in Latin American Countries'. World Bank Policy Research Working Paper, WPS 2233. Washington, DC: World Bank.

Holopainen, M. and Peter Sarlin. 2015. 'Toward Robust Early-Warning Models: A Horse Race, Ensembles and Model Uncertainty'. Working Paper Series, No. 1900. Frankfurt: European Central Bank.

Jahn, N. and Thomas Kick. 2012. 'Early Warning Indicators for the German Banking System: A Macro-Prudential Analysis'. Discussion Paper 27/2012. Frankfurt: Deutsche Bundesbank.

Joy, Mark, Marek Rusnak, Katerina Smidkova and Borek Vasicek. 2015. 'Banking and Currency Crises: Differential Diagnostics for Developed Countries'. Working Paper Series 1810. Frankfurt: European Central Bank.

Kaminsky, G., S. Lizondo and C. M. Reinhart. 1998. 'Leading Indicators of Currency Crises'. *IMF Staff Papers* 45 (1): 1–48.

Kiley, Michael T. 2018. What Macroeconomic Conditions Lead Financial Crises? Finance and Economics Discussion Series 2018-038. Board of Governors of the Federal Reserve System (US).

Krkoska, L. 2000. 'Assessing Macroeconomic Vulnerability in Central Europe'. Working Paper No. 52. London: European Bank for Reconstruction and Development.

Kumar, M., U. Moorthy and W. Perraudin. 2002. 'Predicting Emerging Market Currency Crashes'. IMF Working Paper 02/07. Washington, DC: IMF.

Lang, Jan Hannes, Cosimo Izzo, Stephan Fahr, Josef Ruzicka. 2019. 'Anticipating the Bust: a new cyclical systemic risk indicator to assess the likelihood and severity of financial crises' Occasional paper series, European Central Bank.

Loloh, W. F. 2015. *Measuring Banking Sector Fragility for an Early Warning System in Ghana*. Accra: Financial Stability Department of the Bank of Ghana.

Mikhail, V. Oet, Ryan Eiben, Timothy Bianco, Dieter Gramlich, Stephen J. Ong and Jing Wang. 2011. 'An Early Warning System for Systemic Banking Risk'. Working Paper No. 11/29. Cleveland, OH: Federal Reserve Bank of Cleveland.

Minoiu, C. Kang., V. S. Subrahmanian and A. Berea. 2013. 'Does Financial Connectedness Predict Crises'. *Quantitative Finance* 15 (4): 607–624.

Navajas, M. C. and Aaron Thegeya. 2013. 'Financial Soundness Indicators and Banking Crises'. IMF Working Paper No. 13/263. Washington, DC: IMF.

Rancan, M., Peter Sarlinand and T. A. Peltonen. 2015. *Interconnectedness of the Banking Sector as a Vulnerability to Crises*. Ispra, Italy: European Commission, Directorate General Joint Research Centre.

Rose, A.K. and M.M. Spiegel. 2009. Cross-country and Consequences of the 2008 Crisis: Early Warning. NBER Working Paper No. 15357.

Sarlin, Peter and Gregor von Schweinitz. 2017. 'Optimizing Policymakers' Loss Functions in Crisis Prediction: Before, Within or After?' Working Paper No. 2025. Frankfurt: European Central Bank.

Schwaab, Bernd, Siem Jan Koopman and Andre Lucas. 2011. 'Systemic Risk Diagnostics Coincident Indicators and Early Warning Signals'. Working Paper No. 1327. Frankfurt: European central Bank.

Seth, A. and A. Ragab. 2012. 'Macroeconomic Vulnerability in Developing Countries: Approaches and Issues'. Working Paper No. 94. Brasilia: International Policy Centre for Inclusive Growth.

Virtanen, T., E. Tolo, M. Viren and K. Taipalus. 2016. 'Use of Unit Root Methods in Early Warning of Financial Crises'. Discussion Paper 27/2016. Helsinki: Bank of Finland.

Annexure 4A.1: EWIs and Its Efficiency

S. No.	Distress Indicator	Definition Adopted	Threshold (Actual Ratio/Indicator)	Critical Region	Good Signal Ratio	False Signal Ratio	Noise to Signal Ratio	Probability of Stress Given a Signal	Conditional Probability of Distress Minus Unconditional Probability of Distress
(1)	(2)	(3)	(4)	(5)	(6)	(7)	(8)	(9)	(10)
Composite indices									
(1)	Index of speculative pressures	Aggregation of nominal exchange rate, interest rate and foreign reserves	0.81	0.81	0.44	0.14	0.32	0.57	0.27
(2)	Index of macroeconomic vulnerability	Summation of gross fiscal deficit and CAD and inflation rate and return on stock market	1.98	1.98	0.56	0.24	0.43	0.50	0.20
(3)	Index on banking sector Vulnerability (IBSV)	Consolidation of credit/deposit growth, CRAR, GNPA and RoA	2.87	2.67	0.36	0.55	0.65	0.60	0.15
(4)	Multivariate super index (systemic financial stability index)	Average of ISP, IMV and IBSV	1.5	1.5	0.30	0.30	1.00	0.33	0.00

Macrofinancial indicator

	Description	Condition	Value					
(5) Credit-to-GDP Gap	Difference between credit to GDP ratio and its trend	Gap is more than 2.05%	2.05%	0.80	0.25	0.31	0.62	0.28

Macroeconomic indicators

(6) Output GAP	Difference between actual GDP and potential GDP	Output gap is more than ₹764 billion or less than ₹1,200 billion	₹764 or ₹1,200	0.70	0.50	0.73	0.41	0.08
(7) Inflation	Growth in WPI	More than 7%	More than 7%	0.44	0.24	0.54	0.44	0.14
(8) Fiscal deficit	Gross fiscal deficit as a percentage to GDP	More than 6.16%	6.8%	0.70	0.55	0.79	0.39	0.06
(9) Forex reserves to GDP (%)	Forex reserves to GDP ratio	Ratio is less than −0.35% or more than 2.19%	7.59% or 14.79%	1.00	0.70	0.70	0.42	0.08
(10) External debt to GDP	External debt as a percentage to GDP	More than 26% or less than 20%	20% to 26%	0.56	0.56	1.00	0.33	0.00

Market indicators

(11) Lending rate (%)	Lending rate is proxied by SBI advance rate	Change in lending rate is more than 2%	2%	0.30	0.05	0.17	0.75	0.42

(Continued)

(Continued)

S. No.	Distress Indicator	Definition Adopted	Threshold (Actual Ratio/Indicator)	Critical Region	Good Signal Ratio	False Signal Ratio	Noise to Signal Ratio	Probability of Stress Given a Signal	Conditional Probability of Distress Minus Unconditional Probability of Distress
(12) Interest rate (%)	Call/notice money rate	Change in interest rate more than 1.5%	1.5%	0.50	0.15	0.35	0.63	0.29
(13) SENSEX	Return on SENSEX	Return is more than 28% or less than 2%	2% to 28%	0.73	0.63	0.87	0.40	0.03
(14) BSE 100	Return on BSE 100	Return is more than 29% or less than 2%	2–29%	0.55	0.63	1.16	0.33	−0.03
Banking sector indicators								
(15) Credit growth (%)	Growth (y-o-y) in credit provided by banks	More than 21.0%	21.0%	0.30	0.20	0.67	0.43	0.10
(16) Deposit growth (%)	Growth (y-o-y) in deposits collected by the banks	More than 19%	19%	0.40	0.25	0.63	0.44	0.11
(17) Credit-deposit ratio (%)	Credit as a percentage to deposits	Less than 54% and more than 73%	52–73%	0.50	0.40	0.80	0.38	0.05

(18) Leverage ratio	Total assets to owned fund	More than 17	More than 17	0.22	0.27	1.23	0.40	-0.05
(19) CRAR (%)	Capital to RWA ratio	Less than 11.75%	11.75	0.50	0.17	0.33	0.67	0.27
(20) Gross NPA ratio (%)	Change in GNPA ratio	Above 7.0%	7.0%	1.00	0.44	0.44	0.43	0.18
(21) RoA (%)	Net profit as a % to total assets	More than 1.0%	1.00%	0.63	0.64	1.03	0.36	-0.01
External vulnerability indicators								
(22) Exchange rate	Exchange rate of rupee against US$	Increase in the exchange rate by more than 13.8%	More than 13.8%	0.18	0.16	0.87	0.40	0.03
(23) CAD	Change in the ratio CAD as a % to GDP	More than 0.5%	2.14%	0.45	0.37	0.81	0.42	0.05

Notes:

1. Trend in credit-to-GDP ratio is estimated by using HP filter with smoothing parameter (λ) of 1,600. As suggested by BCBS, we have also used smoothing parameter (λ) of 400,000; however, there is not much change in the ratio.

2. Potential GDP is calculated by using HP filter with smoothing parameter (λ) of 100.

3. Return on SENSEX is a logarithmic return, that is, return for time period t, $R_t = Ln\left(\dfrac{SENSEX_t}{SENSEX_{t-1}}\right)$

4. Department of Banking Supervision, Reserve Bank of India, also designed a framework of EWIs for measuring vulnerabilities at bank level. The department prescribed thresholds for five indicators: (a) growth in advances (above 18%), (b) CRAR (less than 9%), (c) Net NPA ratio (above 3.35%), (d) RoA (less than 0.40%) and (e) LCR (below 60%).

CHAPTER 5

Stress-Testing Programme

As an adage, the whole system is as strong as its weakest link, and it is during the times of a crisis that the inherent weakness in the financial system surfaces. This is especially so in today's world. The various macroprudential framework and regulatory reforms will ensure a stable financial system if the weakest link is periodically identified and necessary steps taken to ensure that due rectifications are carried out. It is the inappropriate decisions taken during stable times that precipitate and prevent crises. Identifying such decisions is also a key. STFs play an important role in this. An STF should try to be comprehensive and capture all the plausible stress scenarios and should endeavour to consider the role that interconnectedness will play during a stress period comprehensively.

Introduction

The role of stress test which was primarily limited to policymaking changed considerably after the GFC. The credit crisis has exposed the weaknesses amidst techniques applied by the financial institutions for measurement and quantification of risk related to economic capital and formulaic approaches for RWAs. Stress-testing of banks has been designed for plausible severe shocks to test the resilience of banks (Bank of England 2016). Practically, these models assess the impact of hypothetical adverse macroeconomic and financial market scenarios on bank's profitability and balance-sheets. Hence, there is an increased emphasis on stress-testing as an important tool to alert financial institutions and their regulators of their ability to absorb losses through capital should large shocks occur and trigger corresponding contingency funding planning. Moreover, stress-testing supplements other risk management approaches and measures. It plays a particularly important role in:

- Overcoming limitations of models and historical data
- Feeding into capital and liquidity planning procedures
- Informing the setting of a bank's risk tolerance
- Providing forward-looking assessments of risk
- Supporting internal and external communication
- Addressing existing or potential firm-wide risk concentrations
- Facilitating the development of risk mitigation or contingency plans across a range of stressed conditions

Stress-testing refers to an assessment of extreme conditions on the functioning of an organization. Before the financial crisis, stress-testing was conducted to assess the stability of individual institutions under adverse, but plausible economic and financial conditions; such types of stress tests are called 'micro stress tests'. The US and EU supervisors examined the solvency level of the banks through a comprehensive stress-testing programme with the objective of strengthening the banks. This supervisory stress-testing was focused on financial stability, including greater emphasis on macroprudential regulation and its link to supervision by defining remedial actions and also highlighting the enhancements required in the 'micro stress-testing tools'. Stress tests' effectiveness increases if they are designed by keeping the policy objectives in mind. Any stress-testing programme should include, inter alia, the scope and responsibilities, technical tools and communication strategy, and BCBS has published the high-level principles for stress-testing which cover these elements of stress-testing programme.

According to Danièle Nouy, Chair of the ECB Supervisory Board, since 2014:

[T]he supervisory stress-testing is an excellent start in the right direction. It required extraordinary efforts and substantial resources by all parties involved, including the euro area countries' national authorities and the ECB. It bolstered transparency in the banking sector and exposed the areas in the banks and the system that need improvement.

Moreover, as per Daniel Tarullo, member of the Board of Governors of the Federal Reserve since 2014, 'The supervisory stress tests developed by the Federal Reserve over the past five years provide a much better risk-sensitive basis for setting minimum capital requirements.'

The subsequent sections of this chapter elaborate the deficiencies of stress-testing exercise before the financial crises, evolution of stress-testing reforms, especially in the USA, the EU and the UK, newer changes in stress-testing with International Financial Reporting Standards (IFRS) 9 implementation as on 2018 and state of supervisory stress-testing in Asia.

According to Borio, Vale and von Peter (2012), stress test programmes have four components, which are identification of risk exposures (income statements), scenario selection (stress and recession) defining exogenous shocks, models that map these shocks into outcomes (level of capital) and the measurement of outcome.

Stress-Testing—Assessing the System's Resilience

EWM is supplemented with STF to assess the impact of various 'what if' scenarios. STF is a robust counter-verification system post EWM. Based on the alerts given by the EWM, stress-testing informs the policymakers about the system's resilience to various hypothetical shocks and prepares them with adequate policy tools, in case the scenarios actually come true. Stress tests are not a forecast of what is likely to happen to the financial system. Rather, they are a series of (what) (if) exercises. They identify how portfolios respond to changes (stand-alone and simultaneous) in economic variables, such as interest rates, exchange rates and equity prices, to assess the resilience of banks and the financial system to exceptional events.

The steps involved in a typical stress tests are as follows:

- Identify the major risks and exposures in the system, including credit (credit risk, interest rate risk, equity risk and funding risk, among others).
- Define the scope and coverage of the tests.
- Calibrate the shocks and scenarios.
- Implement the methodology and run the tests.
- Interpret the results.
- Public dissemination.

Financial Crisis Simulation Exercises

Financial Crisis Simulation Exercises (FCSEs) have become a useful feature of financial CMF in many jurisdictions. These are practical crisis simulation exercises in forms that are simulated but do resemble reality. They are different from the stress-testing exercises. According to the World Bank:

> While stress-tests assess the quantitative impact of a single or a series of shocks on the financial soundness of institutions and the financial sector as a whole, FCSEs test the adequacy of the financial sector stability arrangements (laws, regulation, protocols, procedures, systems, database, reporting) and the way decision makers utilize them to effectively operate while a simulated crisis unfolds.

A common aim of the exercises should be to test the preparedness of the crisis management setup to handle occurrence of crises as if it has suddenly taken place for some reason or the other. The exercises have also served to test and improve the lender of last resort (LOLR) role and information sharing mechanisms in place. The alertness of all the players to gather information and to use them to manage a crisis as also the effectiveness of the coordination mechanism is put to test this way.

Scenario Selection

The procedure for selection of stress scenarios for assessment of financial risk should include steps to identify combinations of stress to multiple risk factors using a simulation exercise. Various scenarios should be built, differentiated by the degree of severity. The scenario which is consistent with the probable path of the future economic conditions is generally called a baseline scenario. The effect of adverse changes in the various factors both in isolation and in combination is used to define more adverse scenarios. This may also include reverse stress-testing, wherein the endeavour is to find the most likely scenarios leading to losses exceeding a given threshold. Another scenario selection procedure examines the balance sheet structure and risk exposures wherein the balance sheet projections are also allowed to vary over the stress-testing time horizon.

Application of Supervisory Stress-Testing

Microprudential use of supervisory stress tests (Basel Committee on Banking Supervision 2017)

- Reviewing and validating Internal Capital Adequacy Assessment Process (ICAAP) and liquidity adequacy by supervisors
- Wide variety of practices as a result of various approaches to capital assessment
- Setting capital add-ons based on stress tests results
- Review of banks' business plans, though less common

Macroprudential use of supervisory stress tests

- Calibration of the macroprudential policies
- Top-down approach for banking resilience assessment through feedback loops, amplification mechanisms and spillovers

Application of Individual Bank STF (Basel Committee on Banking Supervision 2017)

1. Capital adequacy, liquidity adequacy, enhancing understanding of risk and improved business practices through integration of stress-testing
2. Includes credit risk and market risk and virtually also covers interest rate risk and liquidity risk
3. Areas of application: business and capital planning, risk appetite setting, risk monitoring and limit setting, regulatory compliance, liquidity contingency funding planning and recovery planning

Historical Developments in Stress-Testing

While compliance to the Pillar 2 requirement of the Basel II framework mandated the banks to undertake stress-testing for internal risk management purpose, these were essentially simpler exercises with minimal direct impact on policy.[1] Consequent to the GFC, stress tests have taken on a much more prominent role within the regulatory toolkit. A brief history of developments in stress-testing is presented here as under. Within banks, scenario-based stress-testing first started as early as in the early 1990s on their trading books against both historical and hypothetical scenario. The stress tests' usage was formalized by market risk amendment to the Basel Capital Accord in 1996. This amendment required that the banks using internal model must implement a bank-wide stress-testing programme for market risk. The usage increased by the establishment of FSAP in 1999 after which every country participating in FSAP started conducting stress tests. After 2000, various supervisory authorities began to develop their stress tests. Considering the lag between stress test for market and credit risk, BCBS introduced requirement for credit risk stress-testing in 2004. The financial crisis identified the lacunae in STF

---

[1] For example, simple stress tests were carried out on the French, UK and Finnish banking systems. See De Bandt and Oung (2004), Hoggarth, Sorensen and Zicchino (2005) and Virolainen (2004).

and brought forward the need to improve the stress tests. Regulatory stress tests moved from being small-scale, isolated exercises within the broader risk assessment programme, to large-scale, comprehensive risk assessment programmes. Federal Reserve started the Supervisory Capital Assessment Program (SCAP) in early 2009 and its results were also published. Under the direction of the Committee of European Banking Supervisors (CEBS), EU-wide concurrent stress tests were conducted in 2009. SCAP was aligned with the capital planning process by roll-out of CCAR in 2011.

The uniqueness of various crises has provided banks with a guiding benchmark for future stress calculations based on past events. However, as future seldom exactly resembles the past, the past stress scenarios were required to be augmented with several plausible hypothetical scenarios assumptions. In developed economies, these hypothetical scenarios were often based as stressful changes in overall economic growth, whereas in developing economies these are generally specific to the major issues faced by that economy. These stress tests were at a great variance across the banks with some banks using to quantify the maximum loss while others instil a limit or quantify the capital required to be set aside for a portfolio using these estimations (Committee on the Global Financial System [CGFS] 2000).

Even though credit risk was assumed to be the most significant risk faced by the bank, the process for formalizing the stress tests began with the market portfolio of the banks. By amending the international regulatory capital regime for market risk, the trading portfolios evaluation using stress tests was formalized in 1996. This led to the beginning of firm-wide stress-testing for market risks which was adopted by the large international banks. In banks, credit risk stress-testing found little progress despite credit risk being the biggest risk exposure (Basel Committee on Banking Supervision 1999). In 2005, the CGFS also highlighted this aspect and recommended use of stress tests to capture all the risks of the banks.

Basel II addressed this anomaly between market and credit risk stress tests by making it mandatory for banks using internal models to use the stress tests for both the market as well as the credit risks in 2004. These stress tests were used by the banks to review the robustness of their model-based assessments and the adequacy of capital buffers above the regulatory minimum. Once the Basel II norms were implemented fully, all banks were required to stress test their loan portfolios. Basel II was not implemented by all advanced economies prior to the financial crisis, and banks' stress-testing models for capturing both credit and market risk were still at a developmental stage at that time.

Practices of Stress-Testing—Pre-GFC

Another boost to the stress-testing was provided through the FSAP programme introduced by the IMF in 1999 that recognized the costs of financial crisis on the economic growth and financial markets based on the experience gained in the 1980s and 1990s. This focused both on the stress tests conducted by banks which were focusing on risks faced by the whole institution or at an individual desk portfolio level and the stress tests conducted by policymakers that were aimed at identifying the impact of severe but plausible shocks on the entire economy or the financial system. From its inauguration, FSAP used stress tests as a key component for every country participating in the programme with an objective to quantitatively measure the vulnerability of a country to various macro stress scenarios which will complement insights from other components, namely qualitative vulnerability assessment and review of regulatory and crisis management.

The stress tests used in FSAPs helped several central banks to develop their independent framework by using the inputs of the IMF FSAP as a base and using the banking system as a single entity. These stress tests developed into concurrent STFs which are common at present.

Before the crisis, the stress tests conducted by the policymakers were mainly used for financial stability assessments and did not have a direct impact on regulatory requirement or broader financial crisis.

The deficiencies in pre-financial crises stress-testing are as follows:

- Stand-alone approach: Lack of an integrated enterprise-wide STF due to limited data integration and lack of sophisticated IT systems

- Limited regulatory compliance focus: Single factor focused, that is, capital adequacy
- Insufficiency of data
- Microprudential approach with focus on individual banks rather than a financial system focus
- Subjectivity; principle-based approach
- Lack of awareness

Evolution of Stress-Testing Post-GFC

Post-GFC, many nations started developing country-specific STFs and disclosing the results in public domain to reduce opacity and asymmetric information about financial institutions' positions. This process tends to boost the public perception on the soundness of the financial system. Such a proactive regulatory communication strategy was initiated in 2009 by the US Fed and followed by Europe later.

The DFA made it mandatory for large BHCs to assess whether their capital is sufficient to absorb losses during stressful economic conditions. The tests also assessed interconnectedness in the market, including the risk of a major counterparty default. Liquidity stress test assessments have also been implemented to provide important insights into the adequacy of liquidity positions.

> The consequences of failing to pass a stress test can be severe. If its capital plan has been rejected, the Federal Reserve may, among other things, restrict a bank holding company from paying or increasing dividends on its common stock or increasing any repurchase of its common stock, or both. (Dudley 2014)

A good number of studies envisaged that stress-testing, along with being a key risk management tool during the expansion phase of the economy wherein limited loss data is available, can also be used as an input to microprudential and macroprudential policies to ensure resilience, set capital rules and improve communication. The following is a broad framework that ensures corrective decisions pertaining to the capital adequacy and capital planning are taken.

- *Scenario development and definition:* The key input for stress-testing relates to the scenario development process. The bank should ensure that the scenarios provided by the regulator are translated into real meaning of the business. In other words, banks should be able to customize scenarios to be coherent with any portfolio concentrations (large exposure, industry concentration, market concentration and product concentration).

- *Data accuracy:* The bank-wide data should be reconciled. Banks need to move towards building an integrated risk data mart. This makes it easier to understand the asset correlations, improve consistency in application of STF and also help in forecasting. In addition, BCBS 239 is also pushing banks in this direction for data aggregation and integration.

- *Stress-testing models and methodologies:* Banks should model and be able to understand the methodologies to undertake the calculations of stress-testing exercise. The documentation should accurately describe practices, allow for reviewing and challenging assumption stroke methodology and provide relevant information to decision-makers. The models should capture the link between solvency and liquidity. Modelling contagion from other group entities should also be covered.

- *Integration of stress-testing:* Stress-testing should integrate with bank's risk appetite, business planning, product planning, capital planning, recovery and resolution planning, limit setting and risk monitoring. Establishing group level key performance metrics (KPMs) and key risk metrics (KRMs) for baseline and stressed conditions should figure in the stress-testing exercise and these should be cascaded down to stressed limits and EWIs to the business units and at the product level.

- *Internal audit:* Internal audit should be done periodically to ensure that the end-to-end process is functional in accordance with the internal and supervisory expectations.

- *Capital planning process:* Board and senior management should have strong oversight of capital planning process, to ensure that they are consistent with broader risk management framework and strategic direction of the institution.

Regulatory Practices of Stress Testing Post-GFC

The GFC brought to the fore the significant deficiencies in STFs. The scenarios being used prior to the crisis were revealed to be benign, thereby predicting significantly lower levels of estimated losses which were less than the actual losses suffered during the crisis (Basel Committee on Banking Supervision 2009). The regulatory stress tests which (prior to GFC) were undertaken in isolation within the overall risk assessment programme became more comprehensive and elaborative with the assessments being directly used for policy responses.

This was evident in the promulgation of the US SCAP conducted by the Federal Reserve in early 2009 and the first EU-wide concurrent stress tests that were conducted in late 2009, 2010 and 2011 under the direction of the CEBS and the results were transparently published. These assessments are believed to have contributed to restoring market confidence and resilience in the financial system.

As these focused regulatory stress-testing programmes greatly drove the improvements in the stress-testing capabilities and risk management practices at banks, and with the reduction of the turmoil after crisis, the focus of these stress tests shifted from assessing immediate needs to a system that was developed for an ongoing assessment of adequacy of banks' capital and to provide inputs for micro- and macroprudential policy.

Basel III and Stress-Testing

As was evidenced from the GFC that the capital held by banks and its loss absorbing capacity were highly insufficient to meet the losses generated, it prompted a new capital requirement stipulation by the Basel accord known as Basel III which is being implemented in a phased manner for some of the requirements. There are two marked differences between Basel II and Basel III in the form of quantity and quality of hard minimum capital requirements. These have been substantially increased under Basel III, and further buttressed by including three additional capital buffer requirements in the form of CCB,

CCCB and the global systemically important banks' (G-SIB) buffer. While the first two buffers are expected to be applied across the-board, the third one is applicable to globally systemic banks identified by the FSB. All of them serve macro-prudential objectives.

IFRS 9 and ICAAP Stress-Testing and Capital Planning

In the wake of the 2008 financial crisis, the IASB in cooperation with the FASB launched a project to address the weaknesses of both International Accounting Standard (IAS) 39 and the US Generally Accepted Accounting Principles (GAAP), which had been the international standards for determining financial assets and liabilities accounting in financial statements since 2001. In July 2014, the IASB finalized and published its new IFRS 9 methodology to be implemented by 1 January 2018. IFRS 9 will cover financial organizations across Europe, the Middle East, Asia, Africa, Oceania and the Americas (excluding the USA) and set out new rules for accounting for financial instruments, replacing the rules in IAS 39. The most significant change for banks and building societies relates to the introduction of a forward-looking expected credit loss (ECL) model. Under this approach, the impairment loss would be recognized from the date of origination depending on the credit quality of the asset. Following are the assets which will carry a loss allowance under IFRS 9. The instruments covered under IFRS 9 impairment model are as follows:

- Debt instruments measured at amortized cost or at fair value through other comprehensive income (FVOCI)
- Loan commitments issued not measured at fair value through profit or loss (FVTPL)
- Financial guarantee contracts issued in scope of IFRS 9 not measured at FVTPL
- Lease receivables in the scope of IAS 17

ECL is determined based on a probability-weighted basis as the difference between the cash flows that are due and expected cash flows to the bank. A 12–month ECL requirement is recognized and classified under Stage 1. Similarly, lifetime ECLs for the financial instruments for which there has been significant increase in credit risk since initial recognition are to be assessed. Such assets that undergo significant deterioration in credit quality are defined as Stage 2. IFRS 9 and IAS 39 do not differ in relation to specific provisions (NPA) calculation. The existing specific provision would be classified under Stage 3 as per the IFRS 9 standards.

As per the Bank of England's (BoE) clarification on IFRS 9 for 2018 ICAAP stress-testing and capital planning issued in October 2017:

> Firms should use the initial date of application of IFRS 9 as a starting point for their ICAAPs rather than the closing IAS 39 balance sheet date. For example, firms with a December 2017 year-end should use 1 January 2018 as a starting point. This should allow firms to include Day-1 IFRS 9 impacts into forecasting starting points. Separately, firms should provide an IAS 39-comparable starting point to allow supervision to understand the Day 1 changes between the closing balance sheet under IAS 39 and the opening balance sheet under IFRS 9. Firms should separate out impacts due to ECL provisioning and other elements, for instance, classification and measurement, breaking down this information by material portfolios and sectors where possible. This only applies for the first time a firm switches over to IFRS 9.

> IFRS 9-based forecasts: Firms are expected to submit a full set of forecasts on an IFRS 9 basis for baseline and stress test scenarios. For ICAAPs based on accounts as at 31 December 2017, this information can be submitted on a reasonable endeavour basis.

Stress-Testing Practices Followed in the USA, UK, Euro Area and Asia

In many countries, STF is still in the developing stage. The framework will differ across several central banks and regulators. As discussed in the previous sections, stress tests are now being used as an important regulatory tool in supplementing Basel III capital standards for ensuring adequate resilience. In this section, we review the current use of supervisory stress-testing in the USA, UK and Euro area. Even though the need for procyclical scenarios has been identified in the USA and UK, the supervisory STF in the Euro area still exhibits some degree of incompleteness. Principles of stress-testing followed in the USA, UK and Euro area are documented in the following section.

Stress-Testing in the USA

Since 2011, under the CCAR programme, the Fed runs annual supervisory stress tests to assess the capital adequacy of large BHCs and is disseminating the information through a periodical policy statement. The FRB has advised that the stress scenarios must incorporate the factors that characterized the US post-war recessions with focus on the Great Recession. Unemployment has been the most common negative effect after US recessions, and FRB gives a primary role to this variable in the design of its adverse scenarios, with its expected value rising from 4 per cent to 10 per cent. This band brings in the element of procyclical severity, as during an expansion, a severe shock will be required to attain 10 per cent unemployment and during recession a mild shock can make unemployment rise.

The other macroeconomic variables in the stress test are then modelled to evolve consistently with the predefined target unemployment rate and in line with their typical behaviour in past US recessions. It was observed that supervisory stress tests in the USA exhibit a cyclical pattern. The adverse scenarios are selected based on the path of the unemployment rate preventing the risk of inaction bias by the supervisory authority. The Federal Reserve, however, should take into account a broader set of macroeconomic variables in addition to the unemployment rate for adverse stress scenarios.

The aforementioned stress tests need to be translated into a capital buffer requirement in order to enhance their practical utility. In the USA, it was observed that the country is moving away from 'spreadsheet' and manual consolidation to integrated data platform for finance and risk. Accordingly, strong macroeconomic forecasting capabilities for custom scenarios are built up. They also established a central stress-testing function by moving away from 'silo-based' processes. There is a seamless alignment of capital planning and stress-testing processes. Some of the econometric models used while conducting stress-testing include quantile regression, regime switching regression and panel data models. Neater integration of loss and pre-provision net revenue (PPNR) modelling, creation of challenger models with higher expectations concerning model testing and sensitivity analysis was affected. An important innovation in stress-testing was the recognition that a comprehensive stress test focused on net income was needed to incorporate projections of interest and non-interest income and non-interest expense. While a number of models already existed for making such projections, for instance, those used by banks in their budgeting and planning processes, these were nearly all calibrated to produce projections assuming business as usual conditions, rather than the stressed environment assumed in the SCAP. Supervisors have also enhanced the operational risk management and have mandated BHCs to perform comprehensive operational risk stress-testing as part of the overall CCAR process. Projections of losses arising from inadequate or failed internal processes, people and systems or from external events must be reported by the BHC as operational risk losses, a component of PPNRs. FRB has also mandated the banks to submit FR Y-14M report which collects monthly detailed data on BHCs and intermediate holding companies' (IHCs) loan portfolios. The report comprises three loan and portfolio level collections and one detailed address matching collection. These consist of domestic first lien closed-end 1–4 family residential loans, domestic home equity loan, address matching and domestic credit card data collections. The number of schedules a BHC must complete is subject to materiality thresholds and certain other criteria. There is also an integrated reporting platform for capital planning and reporting. The outcome of the CCAR exercise is seen to bolster the CET1 ratio of the banks from 6.5 per cent to 7.2 per cent in 2017. A constant reduction in the number of banks with weak governance, internal controls, MIS, estimation of stressed revenues and losses is observed. In April 2018, the Federal Reserve proposed to integrate the stress tests of large banks with the regulatory capital rule—known as the stress capital buffer (SCB). Federal Reserve has received comments on the SCB and is expecting to implement it by 2020.

The Federal Reserve has used its stress test programme to assess banks' resilience to stress and used these assessments in their review of banks' business plans. For example, in 2015 and 2016, while 31 large US banks 'passed' their annual stress tests programme, Deutsche Bank US Subsidiary and Santander Holdings annual stress did not, with the Fed noting material weaknesses in their capital planning process. These banks were advised to come up with stress scenarios of their own. Further, in 2016, the Fed also adversely commented on Morgan Stanley's scenario design as they were not truly reflecting the firm level risks adequately.

Stress-Testing in the United Kingdom

The BoE published a widely visible policy document wherein they have described their stress-testing programme from 2016 to 2018 (Bank of England 2018). Two main points of consideration by the BoE are the use of stress test results to set the level of the CCCB and about deciding on a scale for selecting scenario severity. Additional buffer would be stipulated for each bank's stress test losses in excess of the sum of the CCB and the calibrated CCCB, referred to as the PRA buffer. However, this calibration may face issues related to the difference in frequency between the CCCB that are set quarterly and the annual stress tests. The decision regarding the stipulation of scenario severity may hamper the predictability of the overall capital framework. This may be overcome with the use of a simple recession-based measure of scenario severity and a constrained discretion approach to severity choice.

In the UK, scenario is designed as an extension of the EBA tests which incorporates stress factors associated with European recession with UK specific features such as steeper fall in house prices. BoE expects all participating banks to take into account the behaviour of counterparties and of the firm itself, especially as it relates to the exercise of choices embedded in financial instruments or insurance contracts. Government monetary policy responses to the scenario will be permitted, unlike the EBA stress tests. Liquidity risk was only included as an amplification mechanism. Individual bank level results are disclosed which were not a feature of earlier stress tests conducted by the Financial Services Authority (FSA). The results show a constant improvement in the CET1 ratio from 7.6 per cent to 8.3 per cent in 2017 with no failures in 2017.

Stress-Testing in the Euro Area

The ECB has been carrying out annual supervisory stress tests on euro area banks. As clarified by the EBA, the STF needed to be used primarily to develop Pillar 2 capital guidance (European Banking Authority Report 2016). This gave discretion at the hands of the ECB to decide on the capital requirements in a transparent manner. Further, at the time of implementation, it was not clear if it is a one-off exercise or whether the inputs will be used for actual capital stipulation to the banks.

Another issue was the identification of the procyclical components in the stress-testing, as the Euro area is itself a very diverse territory, adverse scenarios were based on each country's individual cyclical position: countries experiencing an expansion should be exposed to more severe adverse scenarios than countries suffering a recession.

EBA/ECB stress tests are very comprehensive and involve a three-step procedure, namely supervisory review, asset quality review and stress-testing. Full disclosure of inputs and outputs of stress-testing exercise is made in the public domain. For undertaking stress tests, EBA collects data pertaining to credit risk and projects credit risk parameters, evolution of RWAs across risk types, detailed evolution of capital including restructuring measures along with profit and loss projections. Detailed disclosures are made pertaining to profit and loss accounts and balance-sheet for areas such as credit risk (exposure, RWA, value adjustments and provisions, default and loss rates). Here also, a marked improvement in the CET1 ratio was observed from 7.4 per cent to 9.4 per cent in 2016. However, an increased capital depletion is observed over the years. Subsequent to the implementation of IFRS, the EBA has run the stress test for 48 European Economic Area (EEA) banks, while the ECB has conducted stress tests for a further 37 directly supervised banks using the EBA's methodology, templates and scenarios.

Supervisory Stress-Testing in Asia

During the GFC, the distress in Asia was less as compared to the USA and Europe. Hence, the Asian regulators were not as motivated to develop robust stress-testing toolkits as compared to the Western regulators. However, few of the regulators like Monetary Authority of Singapore (MAS) asked banks to conduct stress tests annually, using housing price scenarios it developed as part of industry-wide stress-testing exercise. MAS uses a bottom-up stress-testing coupled with the top-down regular industry-wide stress tests (IWST) in their assessments of the banks' safety and soundness. The top-down stress tests also allow for assessment of interlinkages (e.g., inter-bank and macrofinancial linkages) which is reviewed with a view to encourage sound stress-testing practices. Similarly, the Bank of Japan and the Reserve Bank of India conduct outside-in stress tests exercise for financial system stability assessment on a periodic basis.

Methodologies of Stress-Testing

Stress tests may be performed at varying degrees of complexity (simple sensitivity to severe macroeconomic stress) and consolidation starting from the level of an individual institution to the system level. The complexity of stress-testing differs depending on the size and sophistication of a particular financial institution, the diversification and structure of the portfolio and on several other factors. The application of particular principles varies from institution to institution. In general, institutions with more complex portfolios may be expected to take approaches to stress-testing that are more demanding of knowledge and data. Conducting the stress-testing exercises and thereby ensuring stability of financial institutions or system of institutions against adverse but plausible scenarios is actually recommended by the Basel Committee as one of the conditions to be satisfied to use internal models. In general, stress-testing can be conducted by adopting the following two interdependent methods: macro stress-testing, and micro-sensitivity tests and scenario analysis.

Macro Stress-Testing

Macro stress tests are executed by financial sector supervisors and central banks usually with the aid of key financial institutions, to estimate the losses key financial institutions may undergo during adverse macroeconomic developments.

Macro Stress-Testing Methodology

A macro stress test can be either bottom-up, top-down or a combination of the two approaches. In the bottom-up approach, individual stress tests conducted by the various financial institutions themselves add up to the macro stress test. However, they all rely on same future economic developments assumptions as propounded by the supervisor. In contrast, in a top-down approach, the supervisor designs and performs the stress test and the same assumptions and models are replicated by other institutions.

Macro stress tests are being performed for many years under the FSAPs of IMF and World Bank and these institutions produced a lot of literature on the topic (see, among others, Blaschke et al. 2001; Cihak 2007). Regulators of financial sector and central banks also conduct macro stress tests outside the domain of FSAPs as part of their efforts to safeguard financial stability. The key underlying assumptions and results of macro stress tests, both conducted within and outside FSAPs, are sometimes published in financial stability reviews. As banking institutions play a key role in credit intermediation (both short-term and long-term finance), macro stress tests usually focus on banking sector of a country and accordingly, an analysis on credit risk usually forms an important part of macro stress test (a numerical example of stress-testing on credit risk is presented in Box 5.1). Because macroeconomic risk is arguably the main common source of loss for many credit exposures, macro stress tests almost always estimate the impact an economic downturn (or slowdown) would have on banks' credit losses. Generally, in a macro stress-testing, the impact of exogenous shocks on the macroeconomy in terms of change in default rates, asset prices and lenders earning is estimated. The interactions

Box 5.1: Numerical (Hypothetical) Example on Stress-Testing (Credit Risk)

Shock 1: Increase in NPAs by 100 per cent
This can be defined in two possible scenarios: (a) the addition of new NPAs and (b) slippage of standard assets to NPAs.

Case 1: Addition of new NPAs
The new NPAs require additional provisions which are deducted from the capital base. Also, the difference between the total value of the new NPAs and their additional provisions is added to the total RWAs. We assume that there is a proportional increase of substandard, doubtful and loan assets.

$$\text{Capital (Post shock)} = \frac{\text{Capital} - \text{Additional provision}}{\text{RWA} + \text{New NPAs} - \text{Additional provisions}}$$

The example given below is an illustration of approach for calculations

Pre-Shock	Value	Provisions	Post-Shock	Value	Provisions
Capital	500		Capital	500	
Advances			Advances		
Standard	5,000	50	Standard	5,000	50
Substandard	20	5	Substandard	40	10
Doubtful	20	15	Doubtful	40	30
Loss	10	10	Loss	20	20
Total advances	5,050	80	Total advances	5,100	110
			Total additional provisions	110−80=30	

$$\text{CRAR} - \text{Pre-shock} = \left(\frac{500}{5,050} \right) \times 100 = 9.9\%$$

$$\text{CRAR} - \text{Post-shock} = \left(\frac{500 - 30}{5,050 + 50 - 30} \right) \times 100 = 9.27\%$$

(*Continued*)

(*Continued*)

Case 2: Slippage of assets into the NPA category
In the second case, we assume that this increase in NPA is due to standard assets held by the bank becoming NPAs. We assume that there is a proportional increase of substandard, doubtful and loan assets.

Pre-shock	Value	Provisions	Post-shock	Value	Provisions
Capital	500		Capital	500	
Advances			Advances		
Standard	5,000	50	Standard	4,950	49.5
Substandard	20	5	Substandard	40	10
Doubtful	20	15	Doubtful	40	30
Loss	10	10	Loss	20	20
Total advances	5,050	80	Total advances	5,050	109.5
			Total additional provisions	$109.5 - 80 = 29.5$	

$$\text{CRAR} - \text{Pre-shock} = \left(\frac{500}{5,050} \right) \times 100 = 9.9\%$$

$$\text{CRAR} - \text{Post-shock} = \left(\frac{500 - 29.5}{5,050 - 29.5} \right) \times 100 = 9.37\%$$

of these risks in the form of counterparty credit risk and liquidity risk are estimated to guage the impact on the banks.

Regarding the macro credit risk stress tests, Vazquez et al. (2012) made an attempt by presenting a macro stress test model of credit risk based on a division of banks' credit portfolio in terms of size (customers) and economic sectors (corporate loans). They estimated the credit risk of a 21 credit categories-based bank-level data set during 2001–2009. These parameters were simulated and combined using a credit portfolio approach under adverse conditions to estimate the capital requirements. This information is then combined using a credit portfolio approach to estimate the bank-specific capital needs conditional on the realization of the adverse macroeconomic scenarios. The authors suggest that the procyclical behaviour of credit quality varies across credit types. By failing to account for these differences, current macro stress test models may be biased in a material way, underestimating the riskiness of banks that are more heavily exposed to highly procyclical credit types and economic sectors.

Micro Stress-Testing

A micro stress test is designed to assess the resilience of individual financial institution, mainly for compliance for ICAAP as per Basel II. There are broadly two categories of stress tests used in banks, namely sensitivity analysis and scenario analysis.

Sensitivity Tests and Scenario Analysis

There are two main ways to form the adverse shocks that underpin the stress tests. One approach assumes that only a single risk factor undergoes a significant change. These are known as sensitivity tests. An advantage of these tests is that, because only a single variable is stressed or given a shock, they may be relatively easy to implement. Unfortunately, however, sensitivity tests may lack plausibility, because in a stress event it is unlikely that only a single key variable will be significantly affected. Nevertheless, many macro stress tests still rely on a single variable shock as their starting point. A more plausible approach to stress-testing is a scenario analysis that examines the impact of changes in a number of key variables. Because it is more likely to lead to an accurate estimate of the sum of credit and market risk losses under adverse developments, it is the preferred starting point for a macro stress test. Of course, it is more difficult to specify how a number of variables would move together during a stress event. For instance, a typical sensitivity analysis would be to assess the impact on an institution's profitability should interest rates fall sharply in one day. In contrast, a scenario test would consider the impact of, for instance, a 'Black Monday' like event on an institution's profit and loss account. Such a scenario takes into account a combination of changes in different risk drivers being affected by the stress event chosen by the institution.

The use of macroeconomic models can help address this challenge because they can restrict the co-movements of variables to be consistent with economic theory. The variables typically shocked in macro stress tests, in either sensitivity tests or scenarios, are interest and exchange rates, measures of inflation and unemployment, GDP and property prices. A central bank's official macroeconomic forecast, obtained from its macroeconomic model, usually serves as the starting point for deciding on shock sizes. Shocks should be, while plausible, also large. This is because large shocks are more likely to pose a significant threat to financial stability and also because they may not be adequately reflected in firms' internal risk management practices.

While assessing the impact of a shock, whether a single or multi-variable shock underpins a macro stress test, it is important to specify an appropriate time horizon over which the effects of the disturbance will be traced. An appropriate time horizon will balance competing forces. On the one hand, it probably takes a relatively long time for most of the credit losses associated with an adverse shock, such as a significant decline in domestic economic activity, to be realized. Given that most macro stress tests aim to include estimates of losses from credit exposures, this argues for a relatively long time horizon. On the other hand, a shorter time horizon makes it less important to model changes in financial institutions' portfolios. In practice, the time horizon of a macro stress test is usually between one and three years. Another issue is the metric used to evaluate whether a financial institution or system would be able to absorb a particular measure of loss, be it expected loss or the maximum loss with some probability. The standard metric is to assess the measure of loss relative to capital or assets, taking into consideration estimates of current and future net income of financial institutions. Forecasts of net income are commonly based only on past average income. While it would be preferable to model how a large number of components of income would evolve under the stress scenario, this is no easy task. This is because the incomes of financial institutions depend in complicated ways on a large number of factors, including the extent to which income sources are diversified. This is unfortunate because, in the event of losses, net income protects capital.

The combination of top-down and bottom-up approach may also be used to assess the impact of adverse scenarios on asset quality and solvency issues in the banks. The top-down approach based on the aggregated bank credit portfolio data is simulated under distressed conditions (see, e.g., Virolainen 2004; Wong et al. 2006). The top-down approach, however, may lead to limited capability to assess the financial condition of individual institutions. The bottom-up approach addresses this issue by using bank-level data with panel econometrics. The bottom-up approach may also possibly fail due to data constraints.

Sources of Systemic Risk

Systemic risk has been considered as a key determinant of GFC. Systemic risks become evident with large institutions having the common exposures to macroeconomic developments and various sectoral indicators. These are discussed in detail further. 'Short memories' could play an important role in the build-up of large, common exposures (especially after a prolonged period of favourable economic conditions).

Interest and Exchange Rate Risk

Interest rates and exchange rates are the common risks that are faced by the financial institutions. For the interest rates, the financial impacts may be felt because of shifts and parallel movement in the yield curves and the impact is generally approximated, as the product of the interest rate change, Macaulay duration and original value of securities.[2] An estimate of exchange rate risk can be obtained by multiplying the net open FX positions of financial institutions, both on and off-balance sheet, by assumed changes in key exchange rates.

---

[2] In the case of banks, there is also interest rate risk in their loan books which shows up in volatility of net interest income.

Real Estate Price Risk

As we have seen in the case of the GFC, real estate prices may be a potent source of systemic risk as financial losses associated with decline of commercial prices or residential prices may spiral into problems for the whole economy as the exposures are generally spread across the whole range of financial institutions as real estate is preferred as collateral. Also, prolonged increase in real estate prices fuels systemic risk. This is especially the case if real estate markets get caught up in a bubble and prices rise significantly more than justified by economic fundamentals and the bubble burst occurs.

This can easily be related with the inflation-linked housing price bubble existent in the USA before the GFC in 2006. Coupled with the high loan-to-value ratios, the gyration of the events took place in such a way that an unexpectedly large number of homeowners found themselves in a position of negative equity and had no option but to default which spiralled and extended to traditional mortgages as well.

Credit Risk in the Loan Book

The credit risk is the final risk that all individual risks finally pave way to. This is mostly influenced by the growth in various macro indicators. The debt maturity pattern gets impacted in a changing interest rate environment and may lead to an impact on the creditworthiness. Similarly, the denomination of debt whether in domestic and foreign currency may also impact the creditworthiness in a changing exchange rate scenario.

An earlier approach to the measurement of the macroeconomic credit risk modelling was pioneered by Wilson (1997 a, 1997b). This was based on modelling of various macroeconomic variables with PDs for different borrower classes and thus was able to predict the evolution of the PDs in future under various scenarios given a set of starting positions.

This was further supplemented by expected loss for the exposure calculated as a product of the PD, the exposure at default (EAD) and the LGD. Statistical credit rating models include obligor-specific data when generating scores. These can further be calibrated by incorporating macroeconomic variables and computing the 'stressed' scores and PDs for obligors under adverse macroeconomic developments. These stressed losses for individual exposures can be aggregated to obtain total stress losses for the corporate loan book.

Stress-Testing Practices Followed in India

In this section, the stress-testing methodologies conducted for measuring the resilience of Indian financial institutions are presented along with the stress-testing results. The information for this section is largely sourced from *Financial Stability Report* (2017), published by the Reserve Bank of India.

Macro Stress-Testing

This is undertaken through macro shock on GNPAs ratio of banks (at systemic and major bank groups level) and its micro impact on their capital adequacy.

Impact of GNPA Ratio

The slippage ratio (SR) was modelled as a function of macroeconomic variables, using various econometric models. Once SR is projected based on the following models, the GNPA is estimated.

- Multivariate regression to model system level, bank group-wise SR
- Vector autoregression (VAR) to model system level and bank group-wise SR
- Quantile regression to model system level SR

Impact on Capital Adequacy

A two-stage process was used to capture the impact of the capital adequacy of banks: (a) 25 per cent profit after tax accretion to capital and (b) estimating RWAs using IRB formula for additional capital requirements.

Single Factor Sensitivity Analysis—Stress-Testing

Credit Risk

Micro- and macro-level assessment through a shock to the GNPA is levels and assessment of the credit concentration risk through default of the top individual borrower(s) and the largest group borrower(s) for each individual bank. As a result of the assumed increase in GNPAs, loss of income on the additional GNPAs for one quarter is also included in total losses, in addition to the incremental provisioning requirements. The estimated provisioning requirements so derived are deducted from banks' capital, and stressed capital adequacy ratios were computed.

Interest Rate Risk

The interest rate risk on the trading portfolio, that is, namely high-frequency trading (HFT) + available for sale (AFS), is assessed through a duration analysis approach calculated for each time bucket based on the applied shocks. Shocks on interest rates are applied to calculate the stressed capital or CRAR by reducing the impacts from the available capital. For the held-to-maturity (HTM) portfolio, the same mark to market approach was also followed.

Equity Price Risk

Under the equity price risk, impact of a shock of a fall in the equity price index, by certain percentage points, on profit and bank capital is examined.

Liquidity Risk

This is conducted in static mode under the assumption of banks' meeting stressed withdrawal of deposits or additional demand for credit through sale of liquid assets with only 10 per cent haircut on sale of investments assessed as admissible as per norms.

Bottom-Up Stress-Testing: Select Banks

Bottom-up sensitivity analysis is performed by select scheduled commercial banks using their own methodologies. A set of common scenarios and shock sizes are provided to these select banks.

Bottom-Up Stress-Testing: Derivatives Portfolios of Select Banks

The derivatives portfolio of a representative sample of select top banks is assessed on the basis of stipulated stressed conditions consisting of the spot US$/INR rate and domestic interest rates. In the case of domestic banks, the derivatives portfolios of both domestic and overseas operations were included. In case of foreign banks, only the domestic (Indian) position was considered for the exercise. For derivatives trade where hedge effectiveness was established, it was exempted from the stress tests, while all other trades were included.

Disclosure of Results of Stress Tests

Public disclosure of stress test results is a recent innovation. It aims to reduce opacity and asymmetric information about banks' positions and in the process tends to boost the public perception on the soundness of the banking system. Such proactive regulatory communication strategy was initiated in 2009 by US Fed, followed by Europe later. In fact, it is a mandatory rule under the DFA to assess whether large BHCs have a sufficient level of capital to absorb losses during adverse economic conditions. The tests also evaluate market interconnectedness, including the risk of major counterparty default. Liquidity stress test assessments have also been implemented to provide important insight into the adequacy of liquidity positions.

In the past stress test exercise, results of which were announced in March 2015 by the Fed, the only banks which failed the rigours of the exercise were the European banks operating in the USA in the qualitative parameters of deficiencies in their capital planning, governance and risk management, etc. In contrast, the EU tests let the banks carry their own stress tests based on the prescribed scenarios. In Oman, Central Bank of Oman (CBO)'s system carries both 'top-down' (Central Bank of Oman (CBO) assessment on system-wide numbers applying pre-decided scenarios) and 'bottom-up' (individual bank's self-assessed numbers applying the same CBO-led scenarios) approaches and looks for directional convergence to gauge robustness of the results.

Conclusion

Stress-testing has become an integral part of the overall governance and risk management culture of the bank with its outcomes impacting the relevant decision and policymaking. Risk identification and its control, improvement in capital and liquidity management, and communication, and enhancement both internal and external could be assumed to be the main objectives of the stress-testing programme.

The stress-testing programmes must be broad-based with pan organization perspectives and techniques. The stress-testing must be well documented and carried out on the basis of written policies and procedures. The framework of the stress-testing needs to be robust as well as flexible at the same time, with regular updation of the methodologies and periodical independent assessment.

References

Bank of England. 2016. *Stress-Testing of Banks: An Introduction*. London: Bank of England.
———. 2017, December. *Supervisory and Bank Stress-Testing: Range of Practices*. Basel: Basel Committee on Banking Supervision.

Bank of England. 2018. Key Elements of the 2018 Stress Test, 16 March.

Blaschke, W., M. Jones, G. Majnoni and S. Peria. 2001. 'Stress-Testing of Financial Systems: An Overview of Issues, Methodologies, and FSAP Experiences'. IMF Working Paper No. 01/88. Washington, DC: IMF.

Borio, C., B. Vale and G. von Peter. 2012. 'Resolving the Financial Crisis: Are We Heeding the Lessons from the Nordics?' *Moneda y Crédito* 230: 7–47 (Also available as BIS Working Paper No. 311, July 2010).

Cihak, M. 2007. 'Introduction to Applied Stress-Testing'. IMF Working Paper No. 07/59. Washington, DC: IMF.

De Bandt, O. and V. Oung. 2004, November. 'Assessment of "Stress Tests" Conducted on the French Banking System'. Financial Stability Review 5. Paris: Banque de France.

Dudley, William C. 2014, 21 November. *Improving Financial Institution Supervision—Examining and Addressing Regulatory Capture* (Testimony at Washington DC).

Hoggarth, G., S. Sorensen and L. Zicchino. 2005. 'Stress Tests of UK Banks Using a VAR Approach'. Working Paper No. 282. London: Bank of England.

Jones, T., Matthews, Paul Hilbers and Grham Slack. 2004. *Stress-Testing Financial Systems: What to Do When Governor Calls.* IMF Working Papers/04/127, July.

Pesola, J. 2005. 'Banking Fragility and Distress: An Economic Study of Macroeconomic Determinants'. Discussion Paper No. 13. Helsinki: Bank of Finland.

Vazquez, F., B. Tabak and M. Sauto. 2011. A macro stress Test model of credit risk for the Brazillian Banking Sector. *Journal of Financial Stability* 8(20).

Virolainen, K. 2004. 'Macro Stress-Testing with a Macroeconomic Credit Risk Model for Finland'. Discussion Paper No. 18. Helsinki: Bank of Finland.

Wilson, T. C. 1997a. 'Portfolio Credit Risk (I)'. *Risk* 10(September): 111–117.

———. 1997b. *Portfolio Credit Risk (II). Risk* 10(October): 56–61.

Wong, Jim, Ka-fai Choi and Tom Fong. 2006. A Framework for Stress-Testing Banks' Credit Risk, Hong Kong Monetary authority Research Memorandum, 15/2006/October 6.

CHAPTER 6

Tools for Macroprudential Policy

The various tools for macroprudential regulations that can be adopted by the policymaking institutions need to be categorized based on their utility and the identification of timing of imposing them so that in time of need there should be a clear understanding of what needs to be done. The macroprudential framework should aim at a fine balance between rules and discretion, nature of the institutions and should, among other early warning signals, include crisis management mechanism (CMM), resolution and recovery planning.

Introduction

Given the objectives of macroprudential policy, that is, reducing systemic risk, both over time and across institutions and markets, macroprudential instruments are chosen (from existing prudential and macroeconomic tools) and designed afresh to address both these dimensions of systemic risk.

Accordingly, jurisdictions use a variety of instruments based on country-specific factors such as degree of economic and financial development, exchange rate regime, etc. The toolkit available to the policymaker is quite wide and diverse and is fast expanding. It comprises not only existing microprudential and other regulatory tools fine-tuned to suit the macroprudential requirements, but also some of the new tools designed specifically for this purpose. Some of the instruments also serve other policy objectives such as assuring consumer protection or fostering competition, etc. One of the major distinctions among various macroprudential tools is that a few of them are prudential tools having a macro view while the others support financial stability but have other objectives like fiscal policy.

There is significant uncertainty over the definition of what constitutes a macroprudential tool, as it depends on its purpose as much as on its characteristics. Not all the tools used to ensure financial stability are macroprudential tools. It is not clear as to whether and when non-prudential tools such as 'capital flow management measures' can qualify as macroprudential tools.

According to the International Monetary Fund (2011b), the basic premise behind introducing macroprudential tools is to reduce systemic risk. The various tools, namely credit, liquidity, capital regulations, etc., being used by a country depend on the level of its financial and economic development, exchange rate regime and related vulnerabilities. These are also used jointly as 'automatic stabilizers' as these are adjusted to act countercyclically and are combined with other instruments to complement other macroeconomic policies.

Categorization of Policy Tools

There are a multitude of macroprudential tools which could be categorized into various segments based on their character and the objective they seek to achieve. The International Monetary Fund (2011a, 2011b, 2011c) categorized the toolkit as follows:

- Credit-related, that is, caps on the loan-to-value (LTV) ratio and the debt-to-income (DTI) ratio; caps on foreign currency lending; and ceilings on credit or credit growth
- Liquidity-related, that is, limits on net open currency positions (NOPs)/currency mismatch, limits on maturity mismatch and reserve requirements

- Capital-related, that is, countercyclical/time-varying capital requirements, time-varying/dynamic provisioning, higher capital for SIBs and restrictions on profit distribution

The International Monetary Fund (2011b) categorizes macroprudential tools into two categories:

- Instruments designed to reduce the cross-sectional or time-varying dimensions of systemic risk
- Instruments which were originally not developed keeping systemic risk in mind but are suitably modified to act as a part of the macroprudential toolkit provided that (a) they specifically and explicitly address systemic risk and (b) there is no slippage in their use as the chosen institutional framework is supported by the required governance arrangements.

The tools which were specifically designed to reduce the time dimension of systemic risk include countercyclical provisions, and tools designed for addressing cross-sectoral dimension of systemic risk include systemic capital and liquidity charges. Few examples of tools to address time dimension include time-varying LTV, loan-to-income caps, limits on currency mismatch or exposure, CD ratio, dynamic provisioning, etc. Similarly, tools to address cross-sectoral dimension include powers to liquidate financial firms, charging deposit insurance premiums based on risk assessment and regulatory prohibitions on undertaking certain kind of businesses like prohibiting proprietary trading.

The tools are further distinguished based on their response to time series (procyclicality) or cross-sectional (distribution of risk at a given point of time/contribution of individual institutions) dimension.

To address the 'cyclicality' of systemic risk, the instruments need to be time varying or adjusted in a countercyclical manner with a view to lean against the financial cycle. These instruments could be applied either narrowly to specific sectors with identified build-up of imbalances or broadly across institutions and markets when the risks are more generalized. Such instruments should be effective during both the upswing and the downswing of the financial cycle. Considering that there were not many countercyclical instruments in the immediate aftermath of the GFC, the authorities have designed such tools (leverage ratio, capital conservation and CCCBs, etc.) as part of the regulatory overhaul.

Considering the vulnerabilities they seek to address in each of the financial system components, the Committee on the Global Financial System (2010) has categorized the macroprudential tools into three categories, namely (a) leverage, (b) liquidity and (c) interconnectedness, for various categories of financial institutions, namely banks, NBFCs, securities market and financial market infrastructure.

The IMF has categorized the macroprudential tools under six broad categories for collecting the information from various jurisdictions as part of its annual macroprudential policy survey. They are as follows:

- *Broad-based tools:* tools applied to aggregate exposures of the banking system
- *Household sector tools:* tools designed to address risks from household sector
- *Corporate sector tools:* tools designed to address risks from non-financial firms
- *Liquidity and foreign exchange tools:* tools to manage liquidity risks and mismatches in foreign exchange
- *Non-bank tools:* tools to address systemic liquidity risk and fire sale risk in non-bank financial sector
- *Structural tools:* tools to address risks from systemically important institutions and interconnectedness within the system

The overall framework for emerging markets would encompass a different systemic approach, whereby additional aspects such as limits related to open foreign exchange positions, and also, the types of foreign currency which help address currency mismatches across systems may be included in the list of macroprudential tools. However, in complete variance to this situation, it is observed that market-based regulations which act as a barrier for inducing incentives for capital inflows coupled with other macroprudential tools with the objective of controlling large capital inflows that may enhance domestic credit booms are not essentially perceived as macroprudential tools, but rather they are a means to reinforce already existing prudential regulations. Based on the available literature on the subject, it is seen that the phenomenon of procyclicality comes into being from the interaction of various aspects relating to the valuation of collateral. Furthermore, underestimation of loan loss provision requirements can erode banks' balance-sheets and have a magnifying effect on the financial cycle. It is also observed that accounting practices, tax constraints and other techniques for measuring risk cause an increase in provisions during business cycle downswings. Also, another factor relates to haircut setting and margining techniques that are used in concepts relating to securities financing and Over-the-Counter derivatives which are counterbalanced by countercyclical fluctuations in haircuts and margins.

Rules Versus Discretion in Macroprudential Policy Implementation

In order to ensure appropriate measurement of the tools relating to macroprudential policy, there must be a clear differentiation between rules (built-in stabilizers) and discretion. Parallel to monetary policy, rules-based macroprudential tools, like automatic stabilizers may be preferred, and tools like loan loss provisions, capital requirements/capital surcharges or LTV ratios can be designed in a rules-based manner.

With respect to contingent instruments, there have been numerous studies which have analysed their utility as rules-based tools which are dependent upon state action. With respect to differentiation of instruments, it is observed that the contingent instruments can further be divided into two types of instruments namely 'contingent reversible' and 'capital insurance' instruments, wherein the former instrument is linked with debt securities and immediately gets converted into equity based on an index. The latter instrument, that is, 'capital insurance' deals with insurance which a bank can procure in order to make a pay-off during a crisis based on a pre-specified trigger.

The trade-off between rule-based tools and discretionary tools like supervisory review or warnings is also important as every crisis is somewhat different from the other. Speeches or financial stability reports to issue warnings about the building up of the risks in the financial system are commonly used discretionary tools which have the limitation of turning into self-fulfilling prophecies (Martino et al. 2010). Other discretionary tools that could play an important role include supervisory review pressure or quantitative adjustments to the various prudential tools.

Tools can also be distinguished based on quantity restrictions and price restrictions. Perotti and Suarez (2010) provide a theoretical treatment of price versus quantity-based tools based on the Weitzman model (1974), according to which, in the presence of externalities, different policy instruments can have different welfare outcomes given the uncertainty about compliance costs. While price-based tools (taxes) fix the marginal cost of compliance and lead to uncertain levels of compliance, the quantity-based tools fix the level of compliance but result in uncertain marginal costs.

For the quantity restrictions, Hanson et al. (2010) made further distinctions between ratios and absolute values related to PCAs targeted at bank capital. Arguing in favour of an increase in incremental capital amount instead of capital ratio, they suggested that this would avoid inducing banks to shrink their assets, and hence induce countercyclical behaviour.

Addressing Externality—Systemically Important Financial Institutions

Systemically Important Financial Institutions (SIFIs) and, more specifically, SIBs, are the 'TBTF' entities that can pose serious systemic stability issues when they are in a distressed state. They gain an undue advantage of having access to cheaper funding because of their size and systemic importance. This also creates a moral hazard issue as the creditors of such institutions have the confidence that due to systemic stability considerations, these institutions will not be allowed to fail and hence the costs of capital are cheap. The situation is further aggravated when the capital contributor is government.

The financial crisis of 2007–2009 revealed that the failure or impairment of banks having systemic implications had profound damaging implications for the whole economy. The lack of an early warning system (EWS) and the absence of a CMF with an adequate resolution regime, which would have decisively responded to a crisis, led to utter confusion regarding what needed to be done and by whom leading to the aggravation of the GFC.

Understanding the pressing need to identify such entities for more focused regulation, the FSB and BCBS devised the framework to assess the systemic importance of entities (G-SIBs) in terms of not just their size, but also parameters such as interconnectedness, substitutability, complexity and cross-jurisdictional activity. The FSB, in consultation with the BCBS, identified a list of G-SIBs. The latest list was published in November 2018, and 29 banks were identified as G-SIBs. Compared to the previous year's list, the number of banks identified decreased by 1. BCBS has also published an assessment methodology for identification of G-SIBs in 2014. The factors that are used for the identification of SIBs include the following:

- *Size:* Any possible damaging effects in the form of risks for the economy (negative externalities) if a bank fails are likely to increase more than proportionally with the size of the institutions. If a large bank fails, this may, to a greater extent than for smaller institutions, damage public confidence in the financial system as a whole. The size of a bank can be measured in several ways. The BCBS uses the total exposure of the institution as an indicator for size in connection with identifying G-SIBs. In the UK, RWAs as a percentage of GDP are used as an indicator of how systemic institutions are. Switzerland uses an indicator composed of market share for loans and deposits, and the size of total assets in relation to GDP, while Denmark uses total assets to GDP and share of deposits of banks. Thus, at the international level, a uniform measure for the size of an institution in relation to identifying SIBs has not been established.
- *Interconnectedness:* Interconnectedness means that problems in a bank may spread to the rest of the sector, for example, as a

consequence of contractual obligations between institutions. The interconnectedness of the institution with the rest of the financial system may pose a risk that winding up the institution reduces the loss-absorbing capacity of the rest of the sector due to losses on exposures incurred by the D-SIBs. To measure the score of this category, the BCBS makes use of three indicators weighted equally. The indicators are 'intra-financial system assets', 'intra-financial system liabilities' and 'securities outstanding'. An equally weighted set of four indicators vis-à-vis 'inter-bank assets' (including investments and credit), 'inter-bank liabilities', 'deposits from/debt securities issued to non-bank financial corporations' and 'credit to/investment in non-bank financial corporations' can also be used.

- *Substitutability:* If the systemic impact of a bank's distress or failure is greater, the less easily it can be replaced as both a market participant and a financial service provider. As a result, identification of D-SIBs also takes into account the types of roles that banks play in domestic financial markets and in domestic financial infrastructures, which inform views regarding substitutability. For example, this includes share of payments/receipts made through retail and large value payment and settlement systems or providing underwriting services for debt and equity securities. BCBS proposes 'assets under custody', 'payments activity' and 'underwriting transactions in debt and equity markets' as measures of non-substitutability. BCBS primarily projects substitutability as a measure of provision of critical financial infrastructure, although some other aspects might very well be difficult to be substituted by other providers should a big bank fail. For example, if a big bank, which provides 40 per cent of the household loans, fails, others might not be able to easily fill the gap because of their capital and liquidity constraints. However, this aspect should be captured under 'size', and not under substitutability.
- *Complexity:* An institution's systemic importance is higher if the institution has a business model, structure and operations which make it particularly difficult to assess (with respect to risks), hard to resolve and costly to wind up. Assessing building up of risks in more complex banks is more difficult, and winding up of complex

institutions is likely to generate higher costs than winding up less complex institutions, and will therefore, all else being equal, have a greater impact on financial stability. BCBS uses three indictors to measure complexity: (a) notional amount of OTC derivatives, (b) level 3 assets and (c) trading and available-for-sale securities. Factors which complicate winding up may, for example, be the scope of bilateral (OTC) trading with financial derivatives, large trading portfolios or that the institution has many assets in its balance sheet which have not been measured at market value and thus may prove to have a significantly different realizable value. Moreover, significant cross-border activities also add to complexities in operations and resolution.

- *Cross-jurisdictional activity:* An institution having activities across jurisdiction is difficult to supervise and regulate, and may simultaneously affect multiple jurisdictions in case of a failure. Higher the cross-jurisdictional activity, higher is the systematic importance of the institution. BCBS uses two indicators to measure cross-jurisdictional activity: (a) cross-jurisdictional claims and (b) cross-jurisdictional liabilities.

At a national level, the BCBS coined a concept called D-SIBs along with a framework for their identification and formulated a regulatory/ supervisory regime to reduce their probability of failure by increasing their going-concern loss absorbency.

Higher capital requirements for SIFIs address the moral hazard problem associated with the existence of such institutions. The initiatives in this regard, in terms of requiring G-SIBs to hold additional capital and also additional resolution capital (named as TLAC), are quite important to ensure that these institutions internalize the system risk they are generating in the system.

In order to achieve this, SIBs should be in a position to aggregate their risk exposures on a regular basis, across business lines and between legal entities to ensure that both their boards and supervisors are aware of the true extent of risk. During the recent crisis, it was found that many banks which have now been declared as G-SIBs were not able to aggregate the risk exposures to report to their boards and to supervisors. Resolution of such banks proved to be difficult due to this. This had significant consequences for the stability of financial system. BCBS in 2013 (Basel Committee on Banking Supervision 2013) came out with a set of principles to strengthen banks' risk data aggregation capabilities and internal risk reporting practices. SIBs are required to implement these principles. It is felt that effective implementation of these BCBS principles will enhance risk management and decision-making processes at banks.

The DSIBs in particular (in fact, all the banks in general) should have the EWS, stress-testing systems (STS), CMM, recovery and resolution planning (RRP) and the risk appetite framework (RAF) in place. As the EWS and STS have been discussed elsewhere in the chapter, let us look at the other frameworks in detail.

Crisis Management Mechanism

CMM is effective in containing the crisis in case it happens. A crisis management group (CMG) should be formally in place with a bank-specific codified disaster recovery planning. The framework must contain an analysis of possible crisis scenarios supplemented with possible decision-making outlooks to be implemented.

Illustratively, the CMG should work on the following:

- Identify parameters to decipher the onset and evolution of the crisis, along with identifying its distinct characteristics
- Have a decision-making framework involving all the related agencies with clearly defined responsibilities and mechanism for information exchange and coordination
- Have an accountable decision implementation structure with defined roles and responsibilities
- Fructify an effective communications strategy for managing rumours and panic
- Conduct of crisis simulation exercises and disaster drills periodically

Risk Appetite Framework

Banks are in fact special in many ways. Their debtors, creditors and managers have divergent objectives not necessarily aligned with one another. The incentives for the creditors/managers induce them to indulge in high-risk, high-pay-offs proposals, which may result in possible downside risks for debtors. This calls for a framework assessing the risk appetite of the banks as a whole and the mechanism to contain undue risk-taking.

- The risk management policies, the models and a clear under-standing of liabilities and assets with their inherent risks must be reflected in the RAF. Risk management committee/s of the board should be responsible for strengthening GRC as also market monitoring and enforcement by competent authorities.
- Clear and rational internal risk limits on deals, currency, dealer, stop loss, country risk, inter-bank exposures and counterparty (single and group) exposures must be made which are in sync with dynamics of the changes in nature of banks business and as reported by on-site inspection by the supervisor.
- Banks' internal and external audit may assess the independence of the ALM Committee, which should be taking those decisions on a 'cost–benefit' and 'independent profit centre' basis.
- RAF should also be complemented with a broad-based risks disclosures mechanism with all relevant information while being bold enough to indicate which of the activities earn profits, incur losses and the extent of cross-subsidization across various activities. Meant for customers and general public, the assessments should be easily understandable, accessible and meaningful, and bear fully comparable formats.

Banks' board and management should be made directly responsible for controlling the level of risk taken. Fit-and-proper tests for potential management and board candidates may also form the part of an RAF.

How Are the Macroprudential Tools Used?

The challenges faced by the policymakers in deployment of macroprudential tools are numerous. Some of the tools are effective when used in combination with others, while some others could be used singly. Some tools need to be made in sync with time/circumstances to enhance their effectiveness and some need to be deployed targeting certain sectors for achieving better results. Steps should be taken to ensure that there is a coordination between the policies and any conflict is resolved with governance arrangement in which accountability is clearly assigned. A wide array of strategies for usage of macroprudential tools are summarized by IMF (Lim et al. 2011).

Macroprudential Tools: The Timing Conundrum

The real challenge in the implementation of macroprudential policy arises from the issues related to proper identification of timing, the appropriate choice of instruments and their calibration. Imprecision in the usage of macroprudential tools could result in under- or overshooting of macroprudential objectives. Mistimed policy actions, either delayed or premature, could lead to unintended consequences sometimes outweighing the costs of inaction. Too early implementation during the build-up phase could lead to unnecessary regulatory costs and weaken the effectiveness of the policy tool by providing more time for participants to develop strategies to avoid and arbitrage them. Too early intervention in the release phase, on the other hand, might send a wrong signal to the participants denting the credibility of the policy. Too late intervention, obviously, leads to amplification of the very procyclical effects the policy intends to address. Any delay can be termed as being behind the curve decision-making which further amplifies the negative impact.

The stage of financial cycle remains the most important determinant in guiding the activation or release of macroprudential tools. However, considering that the business cycles and financial cycles need not move always in tandem, the policymakers need to exercise abundant caution in administering macroprudential tools, keeping the other macroeconomic variables in policy perspective.

Usage and Effectiveness of Macroprudential Policy Tools

The usage of macroprudential policies has been on the rise, especially post-GFC, though some of the EMEs have been using them much earlier with being more pronounced in case of emerging economies due to their inherent greater vulnerability (Bank for International Settlements 2018).

In terms of the usage of different tools by jurisdictions, the BIS study indicates a more active role by authorities in both Asia-Pacific and Central and Eastern Europe. Real estate mortgage appears to be the most focused segment given its ability to generate asset bubbles. Many economies have introduced measures addressing mortgages of commercial real estate and loans for property development. This is undertaken either by adjusting risk weights for mortgage loans as is observed in most EU member states, or by changing the LTV and DSTI ratios and loan exposure limits as done by EMEs. Further, while the bulk of such measures focus on bank lending, given the increasingly prominent role of non-bank finance, macroprudential authorities have been focusing on such financing channels too.

While some of the instruments are borrower oriented such as DTI and DSTI ratios which seek to reduce the borrower's leverage and enhance resilience, some other instruments are institution-oriented such as countercyclical capital requirements, provisioning rules, etc. Considering the leakages through non-bank channels when the policy exclusively focuses on banks through institution-specific tools, the borrower-oriented policies are being adopted more.

Research indicates that in Spain, provisioning had only a small impact on credit growth, even though it helped strengthen the solvency of banks by building up countercyclical buffers (Caruana 2005; Saurina 2009a). Jimenez and Saurina (2006) suggested that as a regulatory tool, a forward-looking loan loss provision which accounts for credit risk profile of banks' loan portfolios along with the business cycle may be implemented. There has been a view that about half of these banks would not have needed Troubled Asset Relief Program (TARP) support if those provisioning norms were applied to them. Gauthier et al. (2010) suggested the usability of macroprudential capital allocation mechanism as they reduce default probabilities of individual banks as well as the probability of a systemic crisis by about 25 per cent which could substantially improve stability in financial system.

Ireland predominantly uses borrower-based macroprudential policies such as LTV and DTI ratios to mitigate systemic risk emanating from housing. Bank of England places a limit on high DTI lending, as an insurance policy, more as a measure to prevent deterioration in lending standards than to lean against mortgage lending.

Based on the data from 3,177 banks of advanced economies (AEs) as well as emerging market economies, a BIS working paper (Bank for International Settlements Report 2017) found stated that macroprudential measures impact bank risk in a significant manner. This study covered both kinds of macroprudential measures; those which focus on dampening the cycle (like LTV ratios, etc.) and time-varying capital requirements. It was observed that banks react to imposition of macroprudential tools depending on balance sheet characteristics. Smaller, weakly capitalized banks with unstable funding sources react more strongly to macroprudential policies. It was also observed that macroprudential policy instruments impact more during the tightening phase.

An IMF study (Zohair 2019) covering 134 countries from January 1990 to December 2016 has found significant impact of loan-targeted instruments on household credit, and a milder, dampening effect on consumption—one percentage point LTV tightening cumulatively reduces household credit growth by up to 0.65 ppts after one year.

Six principles of Macroprudential Policies

Constancio (2017) lucidly enumerated six principles of macroprudential policies as follows:

- Macroprudential policy should be pre-emptive and strongly countercyclical.
- For targeted early intervention, the macroprudential policy should focus on the financial cycle keeping the time-varying dimension at the heart of policymaking.
- Real estate component is of paramount importance in the financial cycle, and hence the policymakers need to pay special attention to the same.
- Stress tests of the banking and financial system must be covering both the microprudential supervision and the macroprudential dimension.
- Macroprudential policy should complement monetary policy.
- Macroprudential policy must be pan-economy as leaving institutions outside the regulatory perimeter leads to suboptimal and deserted transfer of credit intermediation.

Whether Macroprudential Policies Stabilize Asset Price and Credit Growth?

Many observers assume that the real objective of macroprudential policies and hence their effectiveness lies in stabilizing the asset prices and containing credit booms. However, increasingly it is being observed that macroprudential policies are more effective in building financial system resilience than in containing asset price growth, as there could be many factors driving such growth which the policy may not be able to address. Evidence suggests that during strong upswings, the macroprudential policies have limited effectiveness in curbing the asset price and credit growth.

Challenges in Implementation of Macroprudential Policies

The real challenge in the implementation of macroprudential policy arises from the issues related to proper identification of timing, the appropriate choice of instruments and their calibration. Imprecision in the usage of macroprudential tools could result in under or over shooting of macroprudential objectives. Mistimed policy actions, either delayed or premature, could lead to unintended consequences sometimes outweighing the costs of non-action. Too early implementation during the build-up phase could lead to unnecessary regulatory costs and weaken the effectiveness of the policy tool by providing more time for participants to develop strategies to avoid and arbitrage them. Too early intervention in the release phase, on the other hand, might send a wrong signal to the participants denting the credibility of the policy. Too late intervention obviously leads to amplification of the very procyclical effects the policy intends to address.

Macroprudential Policy: Data Driven

Macroprudential policies require a high-quality, reliable micro-level data in the absence of which the policy formulation will have to rely far more on judgement. Given the serious distributional consequences that macroprudential policies have which lead to public policy concerns, it is advisable to have the policy as objective as possible driven by data. Availability of such data is still a concern for many jurisdictions, thus leaving the macroprudential policymakers acting on discretion which impinges on their credibility and acceptability.

Are Macroprudential Policies Costless?

As is the case with implementation of any policy, there are various costs involved and the benefits of these policies need to be weighed against the costs. Same is the case of the macroprudential policies. There are costs in terms of growth slowdown and other unintended consequences such as spreading of risks into less regulated segments, etc. The balancing between the intended and the unintended distortions needs to be taken into account while deciding on the policy tools for any macroprudential action.

A study by Ayyagari et al. (2017) which looked at the 1.3 million firm level data across 59 countries points to the unintended consequences of macroprudential tools for small firms' financing. The smallest firms (with fewer than 10 employees) are found to be more affected by the macroprudential policies, while younger firms are observed to be more affected in emerging markets.

It is also pertinent to mention that while the costs associated with taking macroprudential measures are quite visible, their long-term benefits are harder to quantify. Indeed, macroprudential policymakers and their policies may never get any credit for preventing a crisis. Macroprudential policies may be quite unpopular, as they put a brake on high credit growth precisely when the general picture looks quite rosy. Under these circumstances, there is a tremendous clamour to argue that this time it is really different, and no action is needed. The positive benefits of macroprudential measures are not easy to quantify due to a number of instruments, their complex interactions and, frequently, the lack of data to prove effectiveness. Therefore, the challenge for future research is to develop models which can quantify the effectiveness of macroprudential policies. At present, models which link financial system to real economy are at their infancy and there is a need to make them robust.

Based on the data for a panel of 64 countries (including advanced and emerging market economies), a BIS working paper (2017) assessed the impact of macroprudential measures on long-run economic performance. This study found that countries which used macroprudential tools tended to achieve higher and less volatile GDP growth. However, these results were influenced by economy's openness and level of financial development. Further, it was also observed that non-systematic macroprudential tools are not conducive for growth.

Issues with Time-varying Tools

Given the difficulty in identifying asset bubbles ex-ante and even greater difficulty in confidently identifying them ahead of their peak, to make the countercyclical policies effective and worthwhile, coupled with political costs of countercyclical policy in the face of such uncertainty, Blanchard and Summers (2017) evinced scepticism about the efficacy of time-varying countercyclical policies. Such scepticism is also shared by others (Berner 2017) as regards the ability of existing tools to detect early the difference between a healthy credit recovery and a dangerous credit boom. However, there is no rush to discard such time-varying tools, as some of such tools, especially LTV ceiling, were found to be effective in certain jurisdictions. This dilemma calls for greater analysis and experimentation to help officials decide whether, when and how to use such tools. Further, dynamic adjustments in these tools may also be needed to maintain the appropriate degree of system resilience.

Communication of Macroprudential Policies— An Art to Be Mastered

Given the lags in implementation of macroprudential policies and the large number of potential instruments, 'communication' seems to assume great significance to achieve the desired impact. While the costs of macroprudential policy (such as costs due to increased capital requirements) are immediate and discernible, the benefits (in terms of averted crises) are not so obvious. This necessitates a clear and convincing communication of macroprudential policies to ensure a 'buy in' from the major stakeholders. Clear and timely communication ensures stability by quelling destabilizing developments and forewarning the market players. However, it is generally observed that the participants do not heed to such alerts till such risks materialize on their radar.

Some of the pitfalls in the communication are that too early warnings may not be taken seriously by the participants, while too late warnings are ineffective and sometimes counterproductive as such warnings at the height of systemic vulnerabilities may trigger and exacerbate crashes. Too early warnings, even when are effective, would be hard to justify in the retrospect since the risks they are trying to address would disappear given the effectiveness of such policies, leaving the participants wondering about the very reason for activating such policies.

Implementing countercyclical capital and provisioning policies face challenges as they are against the consensus view of the market. Higher capital requirements during boom periods lead to shift in the risk-taking to unregulated sectors with linkage to regulated sector. Lower capital requirements during stress periods may not eventually modulate the cycle as banks which may not be willing to take risk expand their balance sheet due to strong risk aversion in the market. Whether will of the market will eventually prevail or not has to be seen; however, macroprudential authority has to overcome the overall will of the market in order to be successful.

Cross-border Spillovers—A Game without Boundaries

Cross-border effects of macroprudential policies can be both positive and negative. It can be positive since macroprudential policy implemented by a jurisdiction leads to enhancement of financial stability which has positive externalities for the other jurisdictions. However, tightening of macroprudential policies by one jurisdiction may lead to shifting of activities to other jurisdictions resulting in regulatory arbitrage. This calls for a greater international coordination among macroprudential authorities, either bilaterally or through international organizations depending upon the extent of spillovers and the distribution of costs and benefits across jurisdictions. Designing coordination mechanisms becomes extremely difficult when the costs and benefits are not aligned among jurisdictions. Conventional channels through which financial spillovers are typically deemed to occur are: (a) spillovers via asset prices and portfolio effects, (b) spillovers via cross-border balance sheet exposures, (c) spillovers through information or confidence effects and (d) policy spillovers that occur when domestic monetary and fiscal decisions in source countries which have the potential to affect foreign financial variables operate not only indirectly but even directly through the channel.

India's Experience with Macroprudential Policies

In India, prior to the crisis, no agency was explicitly granted a mandate for financial stability even though the central bank was perceived to be the implicit systemic regulator. The Reserve Bank of India Act, 1934, mandates the central bank for 'monetary stability, growth and price stability'. In practice, this meant the dual objective of growth and price stability, the relative emphasis being dependent on the context. The RBI, in 2004, taking on board the growing size and importance of the financial sector started assessment of financial stability as well.

Macroprudential Regulations in India

Even before adopting financial stability as an explicit objective, the RBI always had the broader picture of the entire financial system in its mind while framing various prudential policies. It is evidenced in the fact that many of the measures which are being contemplated internationally post crisis were introduced by the RBI years ago. Most notable in this regard is the requirement of higher and better capital for banks and CCP arrangements for OTC derivative trades. Over the years, the RBI has also addressed both the time dimension (procyclicality) and cross-sectional dimension of systemic risks, without christening these policies as macroprudential policies. Since 2004, the use of such policies, more prominently the countercyclical policies, as a tool for ensuring financial stability has become more pronounced, though these policies were used sporadically even earlier.

Policies to Address Procyclicality (Time) Dimension

Due to the predominance of the banking sector, the countercyclical measures adopted in India have essentially aimed at increasing its resilience. In the process, leaning against the wind, that is, the conservative policy framework has had the desired effect of moderating credit booms in the specified sectors through a signalling effect and by affecting the cost of credit (Sinha 2011). Perhaps the biggest objective of adopting such policies was to protect the banking system from a 'bust' were it to occur for any reason.

Even while procyclicality is a largely universal phenomenon within the financial system, its degree varies from one sector to another. Coupled with this is the fact that some of these sectors are deemed 'more sensitive' than others. Monetary policy alone, while dealing with inflation, is a blunt instrument and may not have been able to address the general or sectoral exuberance adequately, with the attendant costs being higher. To address these issues, RBI followed a sectoral approach for the countercyclical policies for building investment fluctuation reserves (IFRs), pre-emptive countercyclical provisioning and differentiated risk weights for certain sensitive sectors. These are discussed as follows:

- *IFR:* One of India's early countercyclical experiments with macro-prudential policy was aimed at countering the impact of fluctuations in interest rates on banks' mark-to-market profits. In the early 2000s, on the back of falling interest rates, banks in India were booking significant valuation gains on their investment portfolio. Since these profits are cyclical and would turn around when interest rates reversed, the RBI mandated building up of IFR to at least 5 per cent of their investment portfolio by transferring the realized gains on sale of investments within a period of five years. The RBI allowed a draw-down of the IFR when the interest rate cycle turned, and treasury incomes started falling—this enabled banks to maintain stable capital adequacy by ensuring that a buffer for 'bad times' was built up during the 'good times'.

- *Time-varying risk weights and provisioning norms:* Sector-specific risk weights and provisioning requirements were mandated by the RBI to cushion against cyclical turns in certain sectors which show a greater growth during the boom phase of the cycle (as was observed for the commercial real estate sector's capital market exposure). For the Indian economy, 2004–2008 was a period of high growth and robust capital inflows, with overall bank credit growing at over 30 per cent per annum. An analysis of various trends, however, revealed that credit growth to certain sectors such as Commercial real estate (CRE) was much higher, exceeding 100 per cent during 2005–2006. The accelerated credit offtake was concomitant with increasing real estate prices. In response, the risk weight for banks' exposure to CRE was increased from 100 per cent to 125 per cent in July 2005, and further to 150 per cent in May 2006. The risk weight on retail housing loans was also increased from 50 per cent to 75 per cent in December 2004. The countercyclical measures were relaxed during the peak of GFC and were reinstated in late 2009 when the credit growth was again accelerating.

- *Limits on exposures to sensitive sectors:* Banks' exposures to sensitive sectors such as capital markets have been capped at 40 per cent of their net worth, both on solo and group bases, while exposures to other sensitive sectors such as real estate and exposures to shadow banking (NBFCs) are closely monitored and suitable regulatory action is taken in terms of fine-tuning risk weights and provisioning requirements when required.

The RBI's countercyclical measures have not been rules-based. They have been largely judgment-based, triggered by multiple indicators and judgemental trends in sector-specific credit growth vis-à-vis aggregate credit, with inputs from the supervisory process and market intelligence. Similarly, the possibility and not the absolute proof of asset bubbles was explored in terms of broad indicators and possible threats (Reddy 2011).

Policies to Address Interconnectedness (Cross-sectional) Dimension

India has a relatively longer history of monitoring interconnectedness within the financial system with a framework in place as early as in 2004 when the term financial conglomerates (FC) was coined. A slew of regulatory measures addresses systemic risks arising out of interconnectedness among banks and between banks and NBFCs, and from common exposures. There are prudential limits on aggregate interbank liabilities and caps on banks' investments in capital instruments of other banks. The access to the un-collateralized inter-bank market is restricted to banks with caps on lending and borrowing by primary dealers. The regulation of NBFCs has been made stringent along with close monitoring of systemically important NBFCs. Even the investments in liquid schemes of debt-oriented mutual funds (DoMFs) as well as to capital markets by the banks are subject to a prudential cap on both solo and group-wide bases. Banks' exposures to sensitive sectors such as real estate are closely monitored along with close monitoring of the exposures of systemically important NBFCs.

The RBI also set up the Clearing Corporation of India Limited (CCIL) to serve as a CCP for settlement of OTC transactions. CCIL offers guaranteed settlement of forward trades in the forex market and trade processing and settlement of cash flows on a non-guaranteed basis for Interest Rate Swaps (IRS) and Forward rate Agreement (FRA) trades in domestic currency.

In June 2004, the RBI, in consultation with SEBI and IRDA, decided to put in place a special monitoring system for the domestic SIFIs, which is referred to as FC. This monitoring framework identifies contagion-like situations at the incipient stage, and also aims at addressing market disruptions issues like assessment of sources of liquidity from a financial stability angle.

Due to associated risks, increased emphasis has been placed on the transparency and risk management of OTC derivatives with periodic regulatory reporting through electronic reporting platform for the secondary market transactions in government securities, which has been extended to other important segments to cover transactions in corporate bonds, Certificate of Deposits (CDs), Commercial Papers (CPs), call/notice money and inter-bank rupee interest rate derivatives. Other major policy measures used to address cross-sectional dimension include the following:

- *Identification of DSIBs:* India has a framework for identifying DSIBs and seeking additional common equity requirements from them to address the concerns emanating from the systemic importance of such entities. The framework is largely based on the BCBS' framework for identifying the G-SIBs, with suitable modifications reflecting the domestic importance. The indicators used for assessment are size, interconnectedness, substitutability and complexity, and the names of the banks designated as DSIBs and additional capital requirements are announced annually. As on date, there are three banks, namely State Bank of India, ICICI Bank and HDFC Bank, which are designated as DSIBs.
- *Limits on inter-bank liabilities:* Considering the interconnected risks in inter-bank exposures, prudential limits have been placed on uncollateralized inter-bank exposures in the call and notice money markets. The borrowings by scheduled commercial banks in the call/notice money markets have been capped at 100 per cent of capital funds (Tier I and II capital), while their lending has been capped at 25 per cent of capital funds.

- *Limits on cross holdings within banking system:* Investment in the capital instruments of other banks and financial institutions is restricted to 10 per cent of investing banks' capital funds, in addition to the stipulation that a bank cannot hold more than 5 per cent of another bank's equity. Though these cross-holding limits are primarily designed to ensure that the capital of banks and financial institutions is contributed largely by investors outside the financial system, reduction in interconnectedness is also a collateral objective (Sinha 2011).

Implementation of Macroprudential Policies in India—Lessons Learnt

- The countercyclical policies had a sector-specific approach, that is, targeting specific sectors such as commercial real estate, capital market exposures, etc.
- Well-coordinated monetary policy and countercyclical policies were in operation during the implementation period on account of RBI's wide regulatory ambit.
- Even though the countercyclical policies dampened the targeted sectors credit growth, its effects were asymmetrical during downturn. And when these were subsequently eased, the credit supply did not increase adequately.
- Varying provisioning requirements were observed to be more moderating in comparison to changing risk weights as provisioning requirements impacted the profit and loss account of banks directly in comparison to risk weights, as average capital adequacy ratio of banks operating in India has been well above the regulatory minima.

Recent Macroprudential Policy Instruments Used in the EU

In the EU, nine countries have taken initiatives to introduce measures like LTV ratio and DTI ratio to reduce excessive credit growth. These borrower-based measures also raise the resilience of financial institutions. In fact, the ECB Governing Council has called upon national governments in all the Euro area countries to introduce legislation to enable the introduction of borrower-based macroprudential measures. In addition to these measures, some countries also increased the risk weights to exposures to real estate to increase the resilience of banks. Slovakia has implemented CCCB, and Lithuania has also stated its intention to implement it. Further, euro area countries have designated about 100 banks as DSIBs.

According to an ESRB document 'A Review of Macro-prudential Policy in the EU in 2017', the most frequently used instruments in 2017 were the systemic risk buffer (SyRB), the cap on the LTV ratio and the CCCB. Mostly, these measures were tightening of existing policy, to address increased cyclical risks including in residential real estate (RRE) markets. In 2017, four EU members activated or increased the buffer rate of CCCB, and with this there are now seven countries in Europe that have adopted CCCB. One specific challenge being faced in the EU is from the higher importance of cross-border banking, which makes it difficult for macroprudential authorities to implement policy as they have national mandate.

Whether the Macroprudential Policy Is Worth the Effort?

The benefits of macroprudential policy do not come without any cost—in terms of (short-term) growth opportunities and also, unintended consequences such as spreading of risks into less regulated segments, of the financial industry. The jury, however, is still out on the balance of costs and benefits of macroprudential policy. Most of the non-financial industry estimates of costs to the real economy—both long-term growth and transition costs in terms of growth—have tended to be small relative to gains in terms of lowering of the probability of financial crises and the associated costs of recessions/lower growth. Unintended consequences are a more thorny issue and are inherently difficult to deal with.

According to the International Monetary Fund (2016), the countercyclical policies which lean against the wind, seeking to reduce the probability and severity of a future financial crisis, however, have explicit costs in terms of a weaker economy with higher unemployment and lower inflation. Further, if ever the crisis were to occur, the costs of such crisis tend to be higher if the initial conditions (the state of the economy while entering the crisis) are weaker. 'Leaning against the wind thus not only has cost in terms of a weaker economy if no crisis occurs; it has an additional cost in terms of higher cost of a crisis if a crisis occurs.' The study also concludes that the costs of leaning against the wind also need to be factored into after considering factors such as effectiveness of macroprudential policy, credit boom, severity or duration of crisis as these generally increase the cost of leaning against the wind making a case against such leaning.

Do the Current Macroprudential Policies Have the Right Focus?

Turner (2017) opines that current macroprudential policies must be supplemented through focusing on the maturity transformation within banks, the behaviour of non-banks and the risks of destabilization from market structures. Unless the macroprudential policy expands its scope to cover maturity mismatches and leverage in non-bank financial institutions, its efficacy in preventing future financial crisis is called into question. This is of particular concern at a time when there is growing trend of credit intermediation through non-banks.

Macroprudential Policies: Challenges

The first challenge arises due to the dynamic nature of the financial sector as macroprudential policies, which are based on system-wide information, need to be flexible, and should analyse risks and evaluate policy responses.

The second challenge which may be envisaged is related to the institutional arrangements that strengthen policymakers' ability and willingness to act. By managing a tail risk, the macroprudential policies can create a strong bias in favour of inaction which may further be exacerbated due to lobbying of the financial industry or by political pressures. Delegation of power to a macroprudential policymaker becomes difficult when available accountability mechanisms are constrained.

What is further a challenge is the requirement of coordination of tools of macroprudential policy with other policy areas, which in case of non-existence will lead to reducing its effectiveness reinforcing existing biases towards inaction.

Another important challenge of macroprudential measures is that they are vulnerable to leaks which reduce their effectiveness. In this context, Bank for International Settlements (2018) defines leakages as migration of the targeted activity outside the scope of the tool's application and enforcement. Leakages may manifest in a number of ways. Sometimes there may be a cosmetic shift in targeted activity into a new guise, without actual reduction in risk. For example, in Malaysia, tighter LTV limits on mortgages to individuals led to an increase in home purchases by firms set up specifically to circumvent the restrictions. Sometimes there may be shift of the exposures to institutions that are outside the regulatory purview or are less stringently regulated, for instance, to shadow banks or to institutions of foreign countries. There have been documented evidences (Bruno and Shin 2017; Cizel et al. 2016) which suggest that an expansion in credit provided by non-banks is perceptible along with external borrowing through offshore corporate bond market due to the effects of macroprudential policies exercised on banks. These limitations on implementation of macroprudential measures may give an impression that riskiness of domestic banking system has reduced; however, the systemic risk has not gone down in the system.

Transmission of Macroprudential Policy and Implementation Delays

Taking up macroprudential policy measures is subject to lags in their implementation. Macroprudential policy tools are difficult to implement in a short notice, especially during tightening phase. This reduces their effectiveness in addressing rapidly changing risks in the tightening phase. Capital buffers for SIBs or CCCB take about a year to get implemented from the time decision is taken. While signalling effect may have some value, actual implementation lags may turn out to be quite a limiting factor. As noted earlier, there are a lot of uncertainties associated with the timing of actual trigger events which may call for macroprudential measures. Another uncertainty associated with lags in implementation may further reduce the effectiveness of macroprudential measures. However, in response to systemic risks' materializing, macroprudential policies can be implemented immediately by releasing the buffers already built earlier. This was the case in the UK, when the CCCB was lowered following the Brexit referendum. This asymmetric nature of implementation lags during tightening, and release phase calls for analysis of instruments depending on the phase of systemic risk build-up (Tobin 2017).

Are the Increased Capital Requirements the Only Game in Town? Way Forward

Most of the post-crisis regulation to address both idiosyncratic and systemic risk appears to be centred on enhancing capital requirements. To obviate the possibility of crisis-like situation, the capital cushion requirements need to be supplemented by instilling an appropriate risk culture within the bank. This should be used as an incentive in a manner that capital surcharge could be made lighter if compliance to risk management-related regulations is of very high calibre in the considered evaluation of the systemic regulator.

'A sound risk culture will provide an environment that is conducive to ensuring that emerging risks that will have material impact on a firm, and any risk-taking activities beyond the firm's risk appetite, are recognised, escalated, and addressed in a timely manner' (Basel Committee on Banking Supervision 2013). It is to be noted that while capital adequacy may be a necessary condition, overall risk governance of SIBs is equally important. So is their quality of management of sources and uses of funds.

Multiplicity of Non-systematic and Local Macroprudential Policies

While each jurisdiction formulates macroprudential policies suiting its best interests, multiplicity of such policies, sometimes, could lead to spillovers leading to reduced global welfare. In the interest of global financial stability, it is imperative to have an increased coordination on Macroprudential Policy packages between major EMEs (having substantial share in world economy) and the major AEs. While the gains from such coordination appear sizeable, their magnitude could be asymmetric with such gains being much larger for peripheral EME vis-à-vis core AEs leading to limited willingness for international coordination. However, AEs could look forward to benefit from reduced spillbacks from EMEs, and such pragmatism is envisaged to lead to a more optimal strategy of international coordination.

Like cross-border transmission of monetary policy in an open macroprudential economy, macroprudential policy implementation is also transmitted across jurisdictions through international trade and financial linkages. Due to globalization of banking and cross-border bank lending, these channels work as conduits for cross-border transmission. Cross-border bank lending channel becomes important when borrowers in a jurisdiction substitute domestic sources of credit with foreign sources when domestic macroprudential policy is tightened, and vice versa for a loosening. In a working paper published by IMF, cross-border macrofinancial spillovers from macroprudential policy measures were quantified (Kang et al.). The broad results of this exercise were that macroprudential policy measures in general have significant effects on cross-border bank credit. However, the effect was found to be strong during tightening phase and less during accommodative phase, and also the cross-border impact has been regionally concentrated. These results indicate the need for having international coordination for macroprudential policies to be successful.

Macroprudential Policies and Its Impact on House Price Synchronicity—An Empirical Study

Macroprudential tools, since the GFC, gained more prominence in policy actions and aimed at curbing leverage and vulnerabilities for checking any future domestic asset bubbles and financial crises. Countries with deeper financial integration, intertwined business cycles at the regional and global levels, have their house prices driven by other factors, such as capital flows from global investors and by housing prices global financial conditions. Using various proxies for global financial conditions, the IMF, Alter et al. (2018) working paper confirms that the accommodative financial flows has positively impacted house price synchronicity at country and city levels. The countries with lower house price synchronicity with the rest of the world, on average, have been found to be more sensitive to macroprudential policies aimed at reducing domestic vulnerabilities, with unintended effect of reducing house price synchronicities compared to high synchronicity countries.

Conclusion

While the debate as to what defines macroprudential policy and what could be the possible contours of the policy framework persists, there has been a broad agreement on three basic tenets, namely (a) the objective of macroprudential policy is to address systemic risks, (b) the focus of macroprudential policy is on the financial system as a whole and (c) it should primarily use prudential tools calibrated to target the sources of systemic risk. Macroprudential policies should not be used as a substitute to microprudential, monetary or other policies.

Financial markets are prone to 'Minsky' moments. They have a natural proclivity to exaggerate and experience cyclical stability. Seeds for financial instability are sown during times when it is least expected. Macroprudential policy in conjunction with other macroeconomic policies needs to play a significant role in assessing and addressing such risks to financial stability. Macroprudential policy is still an amorphous and an evolving area. The objectives, the scope, the toolkit and its effectiveness are still being explored and redefined. Many jurisdictions are experimenting with various macroprudential policy tools in their efforts to ensure financial stability, and the empirical evidence regarding the effectiveness of various policy options is being gradually built up. It would certainly be some time before it reaches a definitive stage as that of monetary policy and till then it is an interesting journey for the policymakers in finding out optimal mix of policy prescription.

References

Alter, Adrian, Jane Dokko and Dulani Seneviratne. 2018. 'Moving Forward with Macro-Prudential Frameworks'. BIS Annual Report. Basel: Bank for International Settlements.

Ayyagari, Meghana, Asli Demirguc-Kunt, Vojislav Maksimovic. 2017. *SME Finance*. World Bank Policy Research, Working paper No. 8241, 14 November.

Basel Committee on Banking Supervision. 2013. *Principles for Effective Risk Data Aggregation and Risk Reporting*. Basel: Basel Committee on Banking Supervision.

Berner, Richard. 2017. Globalisation and Financial Stability. IMF 18TH Jacques Polak Annual Research Conference. Washington, DC: International Monetary Fund.

Blanchard, Olivier and Lawrence Summers. 2017. *Rethinking Stabilisation Policy: Back to Future*. Washington, DC: Peterson Institute for International Economics.

Bruno, V., I. Shim and H. S. Shin. 2017. 'Comparative Assessment of Macro-Prudential Policies'. *Journal of Financial Stability* 28: 183–202.

Caruana, J. 2005. Implementation of Basel II. *Financial Markets, Institutions and Instruments* 14(5, December).

Cizel, J., J. Frost, A. Houben and P. Wierts. 2016. 'Effective Macro-Prudential Policy: Cross-Sector Substitution from Price and Quantity Measures'. IMF Working Paper No. 16/94. Washington, DC: International Monetary Fund.

Committee on the Global Financial System. 2010, May. 'Macro-Prudential Instruments and Frameworks: A Stock Taking of Issues and Experiences'. CGFS Paper No. 38. Basel: Committee on the Global Financial System.

Constancio, Vitor. 2017. Macro-prudential Policy in a Changing Financial System Remarks at the second ECB Macroprudential Policy and Research Conference, *Frankfurt am Main*, 11 May 2017.

Dombret, Andreas. 2017. *Too Little, Too Much, or Just Right? Reforming Banking Regulation after the Financial Crisis*. Speech by at the 21st Colloquium of the Institute for Banking and Financial History (IBF) 'Ways to a stable financial system', Frankfurt am Main, 23 November.

Gabriel, Jimenez and Jesus Saurina. 2005. *Credit Cycles, Credit Risk and Prudential Regulation*. Bank of Spain Working Papers.

Gauthier, Céline, Alfred Lehar and Moez Souissi. 2010. *Macroprudential Regulation and Systemic capital Requirements*. Bank of Canada working Papers 2010–4.

International Monitory Fund. 2011. *Macro-Prudential Policy: What Instruments and How to Use Them*. Washington, DC: International Monetary Fund.

International Monitory Fund. 2016. *Elements of Effective Macro-Prudential Policies—Lessons from International Experiences*. Washington, DC: International Monetary Fund.

Kang, Heedon, Francis Vitek, Rina Bhattacharya, Phakawa Jeasakul, Sònia Muñoz, Naixi Wang and Rasool Zandvaki. 2017. *Macro-Prudential Policy Spillovers: A Quantitative Analysis.* IMF working Paper 17/170. Washington, DC: International Monetary Fund, July.

Lim, C., F. Columba, A. Costa, P. Kongsamut, A. Otani, M. Saiyid, T. Wezel, and X. Wu. 2011. Macroprudential Policy: What Instruments and How to use them? Lessons from Country Experiences. IMF Working paper Series WP/11/238, October.

Martin, Weitzman. 1974. Prices vs Quantities. *Review of Economic Studies* 41 (4, October).

Martino, Giuseppe De, Massimo Libertucci, Mario Marangoni. 2010. Countercyclical Contingent capital (CCC): Possible Use and Idea Design, Bank of Italy, Occasional papers No. 71, September.

Perotti, Enrico and Javier Suarez. 2010. 'Liquidity Risk Charges as a Primary Macro-prudential Tool'. DSF Policy Paper No. 1.

Saurina, Jesus. 2009a. Crisis Response: Public Policy for the private sector, Note No. 7, July.

Schinasi, Garry J. 2006. *Safeguarding Financial Stability—Theory and Practice.* IMF.

Shafik, Minouche. 2015, October. *The Interaction of Monetary and Macroprudential Policy*, IMF Policy Paper.

Sinha, Anand. 2011, June. *Macro-Prudential Polices: Indian Experience.* Available at http://www.bis.org/review/r110617d.pdf (accessed on 11 February 2019).

Tobin, Adrian. 2017. 'Macro-prudential Policy and Financial Vulnerabilities'. European Systemic Risk Board Annual Conference. Frankfurt: European Systemic Risk Board.

Turner, Philip. 2017. *Did Central Banks Cause the Last Financial Crisis? Will They Cause the Next?* National Institute of Economic and Social Research (NIESR) Discussion Papers 484, National Institute of Economic and Social Research.

Weitzman, M.L. 1974. Prices vs. Quantities. *The Review of Economic Studies* [Internet] 41 (4, October): 477–491.

Zohair, Alam, Adrian Alter, Jesse Eiseman, Gaston Gelos, Heedon Kang, Machiko Narita, Erlend Nier and Naixi Wang. 2019. Digging Deeper—Evidence on the Effects of Macroprudential Policies from a New Database, IMF Working Paper, WP/19/66, March.

Part III

Managing Financial Crisis

A banking crisis resembles a battlefield. Loss-generating banks wounded by open deposit runs are serious casualties. Supervisory personnel resemble emergency medical personnel ("paramedics") required to administer first aid to wounded banks under continuing hostile fire. Containment strategy, like battlefield medicine, seeks to locate the wounded, alleviate their suffering, and temporarily stabilize their condition.

—Kane et al. (2014)

CHAPTER 7

Financial Crisis Management Framework

While the measures discussed so far aim at avoiding a crisis, it would be naïve to think that stable and strong financial system and institutions will never encounter a crisis. A financial CMF should always be kept in readiness to control a crisis and prevent contagion. This framework should be properly documented, have roles and responsibilities clearly defined, contain a clear communication strategy and information sharing between decision-makers. The four main requirements that should be addressed immediately at the times of crisis include boosting confidence in market infrastructure, increasing liquidity, supporting viable projects with additional financing and strengthening the financial institutions which might include weeding out the weak institutions from the system.

Introduction

An episode of stress in the financial sector starts with serious malfunctioning at a certain point warranting immediate decision and action without which the ailment may spread and/or deteriorate further with disastrous consequences. It may erupt unexpectedly or may spring up due to delayed action/inaction on a potential issue waiting to come to the fore. Policy intervention to be followed is characteristically complex, unfolding at unreasonable speed and, most importantly, the malady it can spawn on the economy being large, and therefore, usually followed by significant policy intervention.

Crises in the financial sector could be natural/manmade disasters or could be arising out of sudden shocks—external, internal or both—to the balance sheet, manifested in rapid erosion in the value of an asset or a class of assets of an institution or a group of institutions. Since, on the one hand, financial transactions are forward-looking and premised on confidence about the expected outcome and, on the other hand, investors and lenders are subject to the sequential servicing constraints, any erosion of confidence can result in a herd behaviour resulting in market crashes and bank runs. In this interconnected world, as learnt from the 2008–2009 GFC, any financial institution can expect spillovers from other institutions, sectors as well as jurisdictions. Whatever may be the level of preparedness, internalizing perverse externalities *in toto* would be difficult. But putting in place robust systems to face them bravely without chaos should be the bare minimum for any jurisdiction to imbibe.

The importance of laying down a comprehensive contingency framework, including all possible crisis situations and the responses to be accorded in such situations along with the decision-making tools to address the basic issues underlying the crisis with the intent to counter the forces of crisis, is huge as the loss caused due to a crisis is enormous and instantaneous. Central of central bank's interventions to counter episodes such as the global financial crisis, particularly liquidity support on a more massive and widespread scale than in the past crises is a testimony to the fact that the task of managing such crises has turned more complex. The duration of liquidity facilities had to be extended and counterparty/collateral requirements considerably eased with new facilities established to alleviate liquidity shortfalls in specific institutions/markets. Coordinated central bank policy responses across the globe, unprecedented in many ways, then followed, thanks to the interconnectedness among the entities including central bank swap facilities.

Mishaps in financial landscapes are not so uncommon. In the USA, barring only two years (2005 and 2006) since 1934, episodes of bank failures are common. What is more interesting to observe is that such episodes keep on recurring with regular frequency, with almost similar intensity and with ascribed reasons that are characteristically similar (Reinhart and Rogoff 2009). While some attention then gets laid on who was responsible and, of course, what were the costs, what is essentially underemphasized is how best it could have been avoided. The probable reason for the same being the fact that there is an inherent risk of repeating mistakes as past experiences are overlooked in good times, increasing probability of the crisis. Another reason is that crisis seems to follow one another with merged end and starting points.

The objectives of the concept of managing a financial crisis are (a) to avoid failure 'ab initio' and (b) to stop it somehow, and if these two are partially successful or unsuccessful, to prevent it from affecting the real economy. The simplest measure may cynically be to let the affected institutions fail but that could be an extreme idea with complex implications. The aim should essentially be to restore market confidence in the system and in the various individual market participants. Specifically, in the case of banks, this could be through reduction of risk of bank runs. What probably accentuates the problem is the fact that these issues get a wide publicity in the media and once publicized sustaining market confidence in the retail customers becomes very difficult. It is normatively argued that the behaviour of the stakeholders in other sectors (especially non-banking and the various markets) could be paramount in determining the decisions during containing a crisis. The fact is that markets have become transnational and thus require a proactive and coordinated decision-making process with all the stakeholders to orchestrate a response which is considered acceptable without setting off a panic.

A well-designed financial safety net (FSN) system should have a tailor-made set of extraordinary measures to manage a systemic crisis and restore financial stability—considering the fact that crises dampen investor/depositor confidence, potentially to an extreme state of a panic. This would require a blend of micro- and macroprudential measures that take on board 'emergency liquidity assistance', 'deposit protection schemes' and 'exit policies', all of which could promote the containment of a financial crisis. This is because a successful financial regulation programme needs to be holistic in its approach.

A distinction needs to be made between a bank experiencing insolvency or illiquidity—a difficult task considering the razor thin wall separating them and a very little time at hand to diligently evaluate that—while laying out a programme of ELA or LOLR facility/ies. A decision to rescue a bank experiencing liquidity problems that would otherwise needlessly collapse entailing avoidable losses to the stakeholders posing the risk of infecting other stable banks—the 'sine qua non' of a programme of ELA or LOLR—would not be an easy one. Such steps may bring in issues of moral hazard as well. This may invite the central bank to play its 'constructive ambiguity' card carefully so as to ensure that banks seek, and the central bank gives, LOLR only in the most exceptional circumstances, at their own discretion. Such ambiguous, discretionary and non-transparent stances of the central bank are meant to de-intensify the urge of moral hazard and of course the possible sense of complacence. Rights issue or mergers may also be assessed as this may reduce the burden on FSN.

For episodes of financial crisis which are generically complex by nature, no single policy prescription is going to succeed, and hence very little agreement on best practices has been achieved. These support operations should be used infrequently only in the case of threat to the financial stability to prevent run causing wider financial instability which will also minimize moral hazard in the private sector and thereby use of taxpayers' money for support operations.

CMF—The Prerequisites

Policy actions need to be developed in advance of the outbreak of the crisis. In the immediate aftermath, given its specific features, there will be little to no time to develop a CMF ex-post. As such, policy prescriptions for normal/stable times would widely diverge from those during the onset of crisis. One of the critical distinguishing inputs being easing or hardening policies as the crisis unfolds and coming back to normalcy after the offset.

Readiness with a Clear Standard Operating Procedure Document

Financial crisis comes with a very short notice with the danger bells ringing. If unheeded, it appears with a bang holding potentials of wide-scale damage to the economy. An effective CMM hence should spell out well in advance with minute details a clear SOP. This document should be dealing with financial crises, damage preparedness and control mechanism for handling an episode of crisis should it really happen and essentially define the decision-making architecture explaining the responsibilities of each of the units involved. The objective being to halt the crisis from the brewing stage so as to contain the intensity of the negative effects of the crisis, speed of action is the essence. That would require documenting a clear-cut process flow based on the possible events and stress triggers that might unfold. Further, the SOP should clearly define the different options to recover financial strength and viability under severe crises. The responsibilities of the entities involved, for example, the central bank, the MOF, the regulators/supervisors of various institutions/markets, the institution/s in charge of resolution of banks and the deposit insurance agency. 'Who should do what' 'under what situation' in an event of a crisis should be well documented in advance to avoid confusion at the material moment. Supervisors need to be involved in the framework in case of important foreign players.

Legal Jurisdiction Should Be Unambiguously Clear

Jurisdictions should have legislative frameworks defining and delineating roles and responsibilities of various regulators and policymakers. Moreover, there should be transparency in the operating structures of the legal entities involved which includes clear demarcation of financial and operational dependencies between significant legal entities and also within critical banking products and services. This clear demarcation of jurisdictions and operating structures would help the crisis management immensely as it saves valuable reaction time when responding to a crisis. Where such clear delineation of jurisdiction is not unambiguously clear, policymakers are forced to waste 'golden hours' of reaction time in finding out who does what and who should do what. Lack of jurisdictional clarity also exacerbates the crisis by denting the confidence of the market players when they find that no regulator is in clear control of the crisis management.

Crisis Communication Strategy Should Be Well Laid Out

When a crisis occurs, there should be clear strategy on internal and external communication that is very vital to manage information flow. For instance, if it involves a bank failure that becomes the focus of media attention, it is important to maintain confidentiality so much so that the information about a bank's request to the central bank for liquidity support should not be allowed to get leaked. It would otherwise culminate in a bank run with people panicking in fear that they would not get their money back. This had happened in case of Northern Rock as 'Panic was prompted by the very announcement designed to prevent it'. This reflects the importance of an effective and prompt 'crisis communication strategy' with various stakeholders for effective crisis management. It would be always useful, if possible, to carry the media on board with a mission of social responsibility.

Such a strategy should be conceived in accordance with past episodes. To avoid confusion, which could worsen the situation, it is imperative to appoint a dedicated spokesperson who should only make any public announcement on the onset of crisis. This is all the more important considering the fact that an inter-institutional group usually handles crisis management. One high-level spokesman should be appointed and only that spokesman should make announcements as per consensual decisions made by the group. There should be frequent communication to constantly reassure the public about the fate of the affected banks, and depositors, as well as about the state-sponsored arrangements made at the government and central bank ends to safeguard interests of the citizens. This should be able to minimize 'runs' on the banks. Should there be an occasion to share information on possible failure of any bank; the communication should be educative, more nuanced and crystal clear.

But this is easier said than done. Financial crises hardly move along pre-planned designs. There could be unanticipated turn of events, newer developments could emerge and set policies could fail to show desired results. The group should analyse them as and when they occur and inform the public wherever desired. No worthwhile outcome would emerge if the truth is suppressed. Setbacks should be acknowledged; reasons explained, and policy options/effectiveness of the stabilization policies indicated so that trust is maintained on the policymaking institutions and the legitimacy of the government remains well respected.

Operating Entity/Arrangement for Systemic Risk Assessment

There should be an independent FSD to offer focused attention to the areas of systemic risk and financial crisis management by way of macroprudential regulation and macrofinancial surveillance. They should undertake the following activities to earn the inherent ability to forewarn a financial crisis.

- Collection and collation of data series on various variables in the macroeconomy, financial markets, financial institutions and financial infrastructure (payment and settlement systems): This also includes data pertaining to the operational, credit, market risks and ICAAP/periodic stress-testing of financial institutions and forecasted loan loss provisioning in order to study/review the impact on the financial system.
- Study and assessment of movements in these select variables with their correlated impacts on the financial statements of financial institutions, financial market and financial infrastructure and preparation of reports—quarterly systemic risk dashboards and annual financial stability reports.
- Enhanced STF: 'Top-down' at FSD and 'bottom-up' at banks— preparation of quarterly stress test reports. This also includes stressing on the systemic and idiosyncratic risk factors. For instance, the idiosyncratic risk factors can be major counterparty default,

percentage change in liquid assets, system failures, etc. The systemic risk factors would be the cause of any market-wide event like FX rate, crude price change, etc.

- Identification, designation and revisit of regulatory/supervisory requirements for DSIBs: This also includes independent periodic review of their risk management systems, accuracy of the data collected, assumptions applied on their data/parameters and validation of their models.

- An EWM which involves identification of suitable variables having characteristics of signalling of early warning on impending distress. This needs to be done by computing empirically the thresholds for each variable, which if breached either way can forewarn possible vulnerabilities in the system and also what the recovery options available with the steps/action points need to be undertaken to address breach of the indicators.

- Contingency plans: The FSD is required to define the clear contingency plans with the actions points. This also includes roles and responsibilities of key departments of supervisor, financial institution and government.

- Governance structure: FSD to develop the governance process, including developing the monitoring process of EWIs, identifying the responsible committee and developing the escalation procedures should the triggers be set off.

With all the aforementioned mechanisms at place, the authorities could remain alive to potential vulnerabilities to the system. But sometimes, random events—national or external or both—may trigger a crisis. Certain events—small or insignificant or both—can erode public confidence as they befall from the blue. This requires that a constant watch must be kept on liquidity and contagion-related data and their movements. A review of central bank cash holding and the arrangements to disburse cash among currency chests in times of sudden needs should be made. Banks' preparedness to replenish ATMs with cash should be kept on radar. Accordingly, the central bank's perennial preparedness to meet the eventuality of cash shortage in the system is a paramount requirement for the damage preparedness programme.

There should be an apex body for management of systemic risk (macroprudential authority), with representation from government and the other regulators for the financial system. This will be the coordinating body for policy responses of various authorities, and hence is empowered to manage financial instability (as also crisis management whenever they occur). The department dealing with FSD should be its coordinator.

Such well-established analytical framework is meant to meet the challenges posed by financial crises, namely acute time pressure and incomplete information.

Institutional Reforms for Crisis Management

Financial stability management deals with financial institutions, financial markets and financial infrastructures and their inter-relationship with the macro-economy. These four sectors are interconnected. Financial crisis would have bearing on one or all of these sectors. Accordingly, it would not be practical or effective to entrust this to a single agency. A committee/group approach with the knowledge/ information sharing among all these sectors is essential. It is more so during the onset of a crisis. Such a group/committee having nomination from each of the concerned sectors should have high level of consultation, coordination and cooperation among them while thinking of policy responses.

In distress, the requirement of a solid legal basis for exchange of confidential information will be a requirement. If any of these stakeholders identified a situation that might soon transform into some sort of crisis warranting mutual support operations, they should immediately inform the other authorities and invoke the coordination framework. Interagency coordination and cooperation arrangements, however, need to be formally backed by a memorandum of understanding (MOU) on crisis management, an explicit description of legally backed designated responsibilities and tasks even while policy dialogue on financial stability issues among stakeholders would be helpful especially during normal times. This will be useful during crisis times as potential issues relating to sharing of confidential information, areas of conflicts of interest and state of preparedness may crop up. This should also be tested regularly with FCSEs.

Financial crisis policies may be determined by the macroprudential authority (whether a council or a committee or any other form) overseeing financial stability in the jurisdiction. This authority, composed of the top management of the central bank and other financial regulators and the senior executives of the MOF, will jointly take a holistic approach to the onset of the crisis, and possible response therefore, and would ensure that all government agencies work together to resolve the crisis. The macroprudential authority may take stock of brewing vulnerabilities in the system on a biannual basis. During the crisis, it should meet more often, may be once a month. Unhindered and continuous information flow to the key stakeholders such as central bank and the MOF may need to be ensured.

The macroprudential authority may be assisted by a Sub-Committee on Crisis Management (SCCM) with nominees from the central bank and other financial regulators and the government departments. This would be the second tier of policymaking group dedicated to crisis management issues. The SCCM should meet every quarter during normal times and every fortnight during the crisis with the assigned responsibility of having an up-to-date analysis of the emerging risks firstly. As information emerges, they will evaluate the information and set the policy direction for the macroprudential authority. It is imperative that this SCCM should meet regularly with required seriousness and coordinate with involved agencies, ensuring consistent policy direction and have a standard operating procedure (SOP) in place.

The field level assessment and recommendation on crisis management would be assigned to specialized CMG created at the central bank, other financial regulators and the government. The periodicity of the meeting depends upon the state of the economy with the meeting being conducted less frequently, say quarterly, during stable times to being daily during the crisis to guide the response to the crisis. These groups should give technical inputs to the SCCM with practical solutions in respect of their own jurisdiction.

The macroprudential authority should maintain a contingency contact list of key personnel (Contingency Contact Group [CCG]) at a senior level for systemic market participants which will be regularly updated to facilitate quick sharing of information and market intelligence.

The CMG for banking system should be formed at the banking supervisor. Where the banking supervisor is also the central bank and the market regulator, they will also address deposit insurance issues (being the central bank) and the money market, government securities market and the forex market (being the regulator).

The CMG at the banking supervisor should have the heads of various operational departments including legal and FSD as its members with the head of banking oversight in the chair. The head of FSD will be the member secretary. This group will have quarterly meetings to assess any potential crisis-like vulnerability and will keep on exchanging notes in this regard.

The macroprudential authority, at the onset of a financial crisis, should have an emergency consultation on the following:

- Enumerate the crisis situation in the given context based on the inputs provided by the members on the basis of their own framework and the potential of contagion impact of the crisis from one segment of the financial sector to another.
- Crisis assessment and its evolution management through simulations and scenario analysis to identify parameters that characterize the crisis.
- Collective decision-making framework with coordination and exchange between other agencies.
- Implementation of an accountable decision-making with clearly defined roles.
- Communication plan formulation to allay panic and fears.

Regular monitoring by the FSD notwithstanding, during the real onset of crisis, will require certain additional emergency measures. Intensified daily monitoring of deposits (including daily deposit balances) in all the banks should be done. It is necessary to establish direct contact lines with senior management and other key counterparts at the banks most affected by any potential shocks, as well as the weakest ones and the D-SIBs, in order to fully understand the situation and needs of the banking system and to ensure that this understanding is up-to-date on a continuous basis. The contingency plans of the affected banks should be reviewed and understood. CMG should hold emergency meetings every morning to study the information at hand, and at this stage a decision needs to be taken regarding identifying the immediate short-term problems requiring immediate resolution and the medium-term issues that must be resolved if financial stability is to be returned. Examination teams should be sent to banks having the identified short-term problems for intensive on-site visits to ascertain the appropriateness/efficacy of each such bank's response to the nature of problem confronted there as also take a considered view about the viability of the banks going forward. They would look for possible signs of asset stripping in the banks.

FCSE Should Be Undertaken

FCSEs have become a useful feature of financial CMF in many jurisdictions. These are practical crisis simulation exercises in forms that are simulated but do resemble reality. They are different from the stress-testing exercises.

> While stress-tests assess the quantitative impact of a single or a series of shocks on the financial soundness of institutions and the financial sector as a whole, FCSEs test the adequacy of the financial sector stability arrangements (laws, regulation, protocols, procedures, systems, database, reporting) and the way decision makers utilize them to effectively operate while a simulated crisis unfolds.

A common aim of the exercises should be to test the preparedness of the crisis management setup to handle an occurrence of crisis as if it has suddenly taken place for some reason or the other. The exercises have also served to test and improve the LOLR and information sharing mechanism in place. The alertness of all the players to gather information and to use them to manage crisis as also the effectiveness of the coordination mechanism is put to test this way.

Such exercises should be organized by the SCCM at least once a year.

Non-Market Events and Financial Crisis

It is possible that a crisis in the financial sector can emerge as a by-product of natural calamities such as floods and earthquakes, unexpected events such as terrorist attack, war and so on. It is imperative that a codified business continuity plan is kept ready for such specific purposes. Besides that, it should be made mandatory to have off-site and off-city facilities under the disaster management protocol.

Since the macroprudential authority is an adequate mechanism for coordination between the central bank, the market regulators, the payment and settlement systems providers and also the government (which alone can declare a holiday), such episodes may also be included under the CMF as discussed earlier with the macroprudential authority being the decision-making authority. Going by the circumstances and severity of such episodes, the authority should be competent to decide if the financial markets should be kept functioning or even to declare their closure.

There could also be episodes of operational risk—sudden failure/disruption of computer networks/central server or even incidences of cyber frauds. There should be SOPs in place for such emergencies and contingency plans for meeting logistical challenges[1] which are more important than policy responses. There could be abrupt man-made crash[2] in market index culminating into a crisis-like situation in the financial system. Those should also be a part of the CMF.

[1] A similar situation involving management of logistics can be imagined when there is a run on a bank that is otherwise solvent, and the central bank were to make available large quantities of currency to the bank branches and ATMs.

[2] On 6 May 2010, a 'flash crash' happened in the Dow Jones Industrial Average which plunged by 1,000 points (about 9%) only to recover within minutes. High frequency or algorithm traders who use computer models to trade according to predetermined strategies are generally believed to have played a role in the crash.

Geopolitical developments leading to social unrests, violence or even war, etc., could also be a propagator of financial crisis. The CMF should also keep such eventualities under its purview.

The Four Pillars of Policy Formulation for Financial Crisis Management

Pillar I: Market Confidence—Enhancing Market/ Investor Confidence to Stop Panic to Spread

As a financial crisis unfolds, public confidence crashes and expectations run very high from relevant authorities. Accordingly, the immediate priority becomes to devise policies that should meet public expectations and will not allow public confidence to degenerate. The first measure is to devise a strategy to show up determination to limit public discussions showing uncertainty and panic. The public must have confidence in the authorities in charge of policymaking that they understand the problems and are addressing them with all earnest. The next is to identify the immediate causes of the crisis and devise ways to redress them. Illustratively, announcement on increasing deposit insurance coverage and shortening the payout period cools down depositors' urge for withdrawal of deposits. An announcement on the robustness of public financial resources and the determination of the authorities to use them to fight the crisis head-on and that such incremental expense would not stop/defer public expenditure programmes could be the other.

Whatever may be the intensity of preparation, since crises emerge over time and are triggered by some often marginal event, it is difficult to visualize the exact mix of measures required and the extent to which each measure will be required till the crisis unfolds and its nature and volume understood. These elements of unpredictability warrant suitable flexibility provisions, thus allowing the implementing authorities the maximum latitude of operation.

An MOU between the MOF, central bank, banking supervisor and other regulators defining information sharing and coordination

in times of crisis should be signed under the aegis of the macroprudential authority.

Clear and unequivocal announcements on deposit and liability
guarantees with various degrees of cover should be put in place. There
was no clear and uniform policy in Europe during the 2008 crisis.
Different countries ran their insurance programmes, from being minimum level of insurance to blanket unlimited insurance. Clear policy
helps in alleviating fear in the depositors (especially retail) and reduces
the liquidity pressure in view of withdrawals. In many countries,[3] blanket guarantees with various degrees of coverage of deposits and other
liabilities were announced and were successful. Public confidence in
the authorities' commitment to act head-on to avert financial meltdown and the financial wherewithal to do so contribute mainly to their
success. Such guarantees[4] could be by way of public announcements
or still better backed by adequate legal provisions.

Guarantees look simple to implement without immediate direct
fiscal costs but have certain drawbacks. Contingent liabilities of the
fiscal would tend to balloon even while such prior announced state-
sponsored financial arrangements would lead to moral hazard over
time. To overcome this, some countries[5] had opted for sunset clauses.
Additionally, costs and impacts associated with explicit and implicit
guarantee types must be assessed.

---

[3] Finland, Indonesia, Japan, the Republic of Korea, Sweden and Turkey in the
crises of the 1990s. In the context of the current global crisis, all affected countries
(the USA, UK and all EU countries) effectively guaranteed all deposits.

[4] Proclaiming blanket/individual bank guarantees by the government; liabilities of Freddie Mae and Fannie Mae were guaranteed in the USA or by making
available firm-specific loans and other support programmes (loan facilities plus
assumptions of control [AIG], arranged mergers and sales [Bear Stearns, Abbey
National and Bradford & Bingley]).

[5] These include Australia (three years), Denmark (two years), Greece (initially
blanket, then up to €100,000 for three years), Hong Kong (until 2010), Ireland
(September 2010), Malaysia (December 2010), Mongolia (five years), New
Zealand (two years), Singapore (December 2010) and United Arab Emirates
(three years). *Source*: World Bank Crisis Response Notes 1 and 4; IMF Global
Policy Responses to Financial Crisis.

A foolproof mechanism may be devised for reimbursing depositors in case of any bank coming to the verge of failure. While banking supervisors' avowed policy may be to help such banks to revive, it would be always useful to have smooth systems of deposit reimbursements to avoid generation of financial pressures/panics. What is additionally required is a framework in place for transfer of funds to other banking institution, special debit cards or direct payout by central banks during the crisis with unsophisticated depositors being provided with limited depositor protection during the stable times.

Adequacy of accumulated funds in case of default of a bank needs to be kept under watch. There should be explicit backup arrangement to access additional funds to ensure the credibility of the scheme in a time of crisis. The test of its efficacy is reflected in the ability to ensure that payouts can be made within an acceptable time frame (within seven days). As observed in Australia, a competitive bidding process may be envisaged for assuming a failed bank's insured deposits.

Market confidence also depends on the quality of functioning of the payments and settlements system. For the working of the payments system, every bank is systemically important as if any bank with large payment turnover fails the payment system would get impacted. In order to manage liquidity risk while handling large volume/value transactions, fully collateralized intraday credit to individual banks should be provided and queue management and gridlock resolutions mechanisms should be in place.

A system should be in place to conduct surprise testing of the disaster recovery arrangements. Settlement guarantee funds for retail payments and securities settlement should be adequately funded based on a detailed risk assessment. Ongoing watch should be kept on the level of concentration in liquidity and payment in few banks as the failure of few banks can lead to a contagion and affect the whole banking system leading to more bank failures.

Additionally, market confidence is primarily determined by the financial institution's ability to pay its debts. These debts are generally short-term maturity, whereas the financial institution assets are long term. This leads to imbalance/mismatch in the ALM. Therefore, in order to enhance the market confidence along with the guarantees, the regulators/supervisor is also required to impose sufficient capital and liquidity reserves requirements for the financial institutions. Moreover, with the implementation of IFRS 9 guidelines, this would lead to provide more transparency in the financial statements of the financial institutions. Since the assets of the financial institutions which are taken as going concerns both on-balance sheet and off-balance sheet would be required to be forward-looking, the supervisor is required to ensure the robustness of this estimation and also undertake periodic back testing/validation of the models developed by the financial institutions. These steps would ensure adherence to the guidelines and also would provide more consistent approach while assessing the risks in the balance sheets of the financial institutions.

Pillar II: Liquidity Enhancement

Provision of liquidity assistance to the solvent banks[6] and/or if required to non-banks and sometimes special liquidity schemes on a market-wide basis to enable them to meet depositor demands for withdrawal is the most critical policy in the early days of a crisis. The news of illiquidity in any one bank could spread uncontrolled to other banks prompting 'run' on them.[7] For that reason, there must be clarity on

---

[6] Even banks perceived as solvent, as we saw in the fall of 2008, were fed with such liquidity backstops or otherwise markets could have, it was thought, seized up completely. A tendency to hoard liquidity during times of stress sets in, possibly because banks may not engage with one another as each bank feels uncertain that others will do so. But such credible liquidity backstops are supplemented usually with steps to restore the banking system to health as soon as possible even by forcing banks to cut their capital distributions early and to raise new capital in a timely way even if such capital-raising results in the forced dilution of existing shareholders. Ideally, in a time of stress it may be necessary to overcapitalize the banking system relative to the base case scenario to uninterrupted supply of credit to the real economy. As was the case in the USA in 2009, banks should be required to meet their stress scenario capital ratio standards by adding equity capital with no credit given for reducing assets. This leans against the incentive to deleverage to meet higher capital ratio requirements.

[7] For example, the banking crisis in the UK was triggered by illiquidity in one of the smallest banks in the system (Northern Rock).

the mechanisms for emergency lending facilities available to all the banks. Usually, the lending rate is set well above the interest rates that prevailed prior to the crisis, but well below the rates then posted in strained markets,[8] and such lending must be backed by suitable collateral. But there should be flexibility available in the provisions to lend without/unprescribed collaterals in emergency. Most importantly, it must be ensured that that there is an adequate supply of currency in ATMs and banks. This way the banks will not be allowed to go illiquid and as such this message would assuage public fear and restlessness.

The LOLR may also be useful in situations where providing liquidity urgently would help stopping the situation spiralling out of control. There should be a well-defined ELA/LOLR framework with explicit backing of the law to operate it. Standing credit facility (in the form of treasury bills discounting, commercial papers rediscounting and repos in government securities) to the local money market is usually in practice. Reserves requirements are also used for this purpose during crisis. However, LOLR does come along with the issue of moral hazard for large financial institutions.

The official safety net players (the members of a typical CMG) should, by definition, be the core stakeholders in the financial system. These traditionally include the central bank as a LOLR, supervisory authority entrusted with prudential regulation, a treasury and explicit small deposit insurance provider. A committee/group approach is essential since during a crisis there needs to be a high level of consultation, coordination and cooperation between the various interested parties.

Usually, considering the fact that central banks are responsible for safeguarding the payments system and providing emergency liquidity assistance (ELA)/LOLR, the most immediately needed interventions designed to nip panic in the bud, they tend to take on the lead responsibility. Jurisdictions where central banks also are the regulators/supervisors of the predominant sections of the financial space (banks and money/debt/forex markets), they are expected to bear the cross.

---

[8] In Bagehot's view (1873), it should be made available only to avoid panics, to solvent institutions and at a commercial rate against good forms of collateral.

In a macroeconomic scenario warranting tightened monetary policymaking, such requirements of liberal liquidity provision to stem the onslaught of a financial crisis could appear tricky. Accordingly, care must be taken while using open market operations in conjunction with liquidity provision while keeping an eye on the overall monetary aggregates to remain within targets.

Detailed arrangements for an LOLR facility and additional facilities for liquidity provision should be devised. The LOLR facility can be extended at a rate higher than the policy rate to only illiquid but solvent banks against eligible liquid collateral and has a maturity of up to one year. Given the tightness of liquidity conditions, as deemed necessary, a decision could be taken to consider introducing additional liquidity measures such as an extended RO liquidity facility with maturities of, say, up to a year, and a foreign exchange (FX) swap facility with, say, a two-week maturity and an implicit rollover guarantee. For this to be effectively operational, a designated pool of funds may need to be put in place.

Those solvent banks not having sufficient eligible collaterals by way of government securities would need special relaxations. Government liquidity support can be given against bank collateral that includes mortgages (say, up to 70% of book or market value—whichever is lower), receivables (say, up to 60% of book value) and acceptable securities. This may also be extended to significantly undercapitalized systemic banks. Such dilution in quality of collateral should be done as an extreme case that too backed by specific clause under the law meant for 'systemic crisis'.[9] The law should ask for a specific recommendation on existence of a crisis based on consensus among all the relevant authorities.

In addition to the enhanced LOLR facilities, establishment of FX swap facilities, and relaxation of mandatory reserves, the illiquid bank

---

[9] Such special clauses are not unusual. They are specifically meant to be used only in times of financial crisis. State funding for recapitalization of banks was allowed in Lithuania; the USA had waived the least-cost test for bank resolutions in certain circumstances; different levels of guarantees on deposits or other liabilities were invoked in Brazil, Lithuania and the United States.

should also source funds by identifying in fungible capital and liquidity available in the group (such as dividend payment from subsidiaries, surplus liquidity above regulatory requirements) and exercise standby or other facilities from third parties. It should create short-term funding resources by issuing covered bonds, securitizations, FRNs, CDs or other short-term papers, rights offering, manage banking book by targeting key client relationships for deposits, high-value retail deposit growth, restricting generation of new assets and minimize rollover of maturing assets and sale of asset portfolio.

A well-calibrated financial sector support programme with the affected banks should be announced. The programme should involve a mix of commitments and incentives. Commitments could be in the nature of (a) obtaining specific commitments from parent bank groups to keep their exposure vis-à-vis the home country at a specified level for specified number of future years without creating incremental exposures subject to periodic review (this applies only to foreign subsidiaries); (b) keeping sufficient level of capitalization and liquidity; and (c) participating in a supervisor-stipulated stress test exercise. Further, avoidance of blockage of solvent borrowers' accounts based on voluntary conversion of FX and FX-linked loans into local currency loans along with the banking supervisor may be considered.

Pillar III: Loan Restructuring

Incentives for loan restructuring may be given as means to address the asset quality concerns. These are usually in the nature of relaxation in loan classification norms. Banks can restructure their loans by stretching the remaining loan maturity or reducing monthly payments. For such loans, lower loan loss provisioning is permitted. In the light of new IFRS standards relating to financial instruments, there would be higher requirements of provision on such restructured/stressed assets and hence classification can play an important role in lowering the absolute provisions required. Additionally, managing bad assets separately with the backing of the regulator/government would also reduce the stress. The banks would be required to maximize the recoveries from such assets and not just write off to further compound the problem.

In the light of the importance of foreign banks, it is paramount that MOUs on both 'peace time' and 'crisis time' management of instability with the home jurisdictions of the largest investors in the country should be devised. It would be useful if such arrangements are put in place in normal times and are implementable in times of need considering the prevailing legal issues/state of affairs of that country. In any case, regular and formalized exchange of information and cooperation between home and host supervisors are a prerequisite. There should be direct communication channels defined with relevant home country supervisors which could be used officially and authoritatively during onset of crisis. There should be predefined, written and clear division of responsibilities between host and home supervisors and among home and host country entities involved in crisis management (such as the MOF, central bank, deposit insurance funds and resolution agencies). A channel of communication between the respective financial stability committees/councils would be the most practical in this regard. Principles of burden sharing for liquidity and solvency would be documented clearly.

Pillar IV: Bank Diagnosis and Restructuring—Balance Sheet Strengthening of Undercapitalized Banks

This restructuring phase in a CMF may lead to certain hard decisions, the severest being closure of the weakest banks and certain other consolidation measures. But such issues need to be resolved before the emergence of the crisis so that concrete steps can be taken without delay.

Such evaluation and restructuring exercise starts soon after the crisis is perceived to be contained. It starts with an evaluation of bank performance especially their ability to meet prudential norms and, if not, what steps should be taken. Based on performance indicators and bilateral discussions of the supervisor, the banks would be given monthly/quarterly monitorable targets and restructuring action plans. Supervisors get an idea about the strength and going concern status of the banks from implementing such plans. Should need be, pre-course or mid-course corrections in the business model should be required.

There may arise the requirements for certain regulatory forbearance in the form of non-compliance of specific prudential norms. These should be well thought out, explicit, quantifiably monitorable and most importantly for a limited period of time conditioned by positive performance. Penalties should be assessed for banks consistently failing to meet targets.

Assessment methodology should be giving ongoing information on the level of capital of the banks. Those identified as undercapitalized would require steps to strengthen their balance sheets. This identification process hinges on on-site examination by the supervisor or external special audits to re-evaluate the value of items of the balance sheet which get reflected in the adequacy of CRAR. Stress tests can be conducted by both these entities independently based on a downside scenario on the adjusted bank statements to get concrete conclusions. Actionable steps can be initiated to improve things immediately or an MOU can be signed and operationalized to get it improved within a predetermined time frame.

Those for which it cannot be mended at this level, a resolution roadmap will be required to be prepared.

Based on the study of balance sheets, banks needing assistance could be categorized into four types (however, this may be a very difficult classification exercise).

- *Type 1:* Those banks that can prove that they qualify for recapitalization by the shareholders/private funding to increase their capital adequacy ratio (CRAR) in a time-bound programme for meeting minimum capital levels, say to 12 per cent.
- *Type 2:* Those banks that can apply for capital injection from the state; usually, those banks are systemic banks, defined as those if failure would have wide-scale ramifications. Those would have been prior defined as per FSB guidelines or could be so done by way of certain rule of thumb, for example, banks with a market share of more than 2 per cent of total assets of the system and 1 per cent of retail deposits of the system. It could be useful also to have a clause to include non-systemic banks in such state-sponsored

recapitalization programmes provided that they are deemed viable by the regulator/supervisor and to certain extent (say, only up to 50%) of the capital required. In any case, conditions for any use of public money to support recapitalization efforts need to be identified and codified. However, individual bank recapitalization from state assistance may not stop the slide as has happened in the UK. The final value at which the price settled was way less than their previous value, but they did not go bankrupt.

- *Type 3:* The balance sheet management of the bank can also include sale of non-core subsidiaries, sale and lease back of fixed assets (e.g., office building), swap debt for equity, raise new debt capital and raise new equity capital. Cancellation/delaying of dividend payouts for shareholders, write-down of liability instruments with capital characteristics.

- *Type 4:* Those banks which cannot be revived need necessarily to be liquidated. In such cases, being extreme, there should be more stringent legal provisions. There should be specific declaration by the state on 'systemic crisis'. Under such circumstances, deposits and liabilities guarantees with varying degree of coverage beyond the established norms can be extended. The cost test for bank resolution can be waived. Government securities, acquired as a result of providing financial assistance to troubled banks, are preceded by write-down of existing shareholders rights and needs to be divested within a year.

Such an exercise of 'bank-by-bank preliminary contingency plans' is essentially meant to identify those banks which are likely to become a profitable institution after the crisis (viable) or otherwise (non-viable). This is done by assessing also the level of shareholder support, possibility of private investors' interest, quantum of likely capital restructuring needs, extent of protection of depositors' interests and finally 'if it is fit and proper' to pump in any public capital support. This is done formally by way of a 'multiyear business plan' which shows the workings of the number of years to recoup minimum required capital subject to specific policy actions. Quantifiable targets are set for operational restructuring in a prescribed time horizon. An element of 'carrot and stick' policy could be imbibed into this framework. For those who could implement policies within agreed time table to successfully improve profitability and stabilize financial conditions should get further regulatory forbearance while the laggards should confront pre-specified penalties including suspension of dividends and bonuses. It is also expedient to assess the quality and capability of the management to implement policies in right earnest.

Regulators are trying to conceive few trigger points to identify growing vulnerabilities in the banks to ensure that corrective actions are being undertaken promptly. This framework is known as Prompt Corrective Action, or PCA. Regulators are identifying regulatory trigger points, as a part of PCA framework, in terms of various indicators, namely capital, asset quality, earnings and leverage, etc., for initiation of certain structured and discretionary actions in respect of banks hitting such trigger points. The restrictions that can be imposed include from non-declaration of dividend, plan to increase capital, reducing loan portfolio concentration to steps to change the management of the bank, etc.

The obvious challenge would be to collect and collate right data during a crisis. But such policies would have a definite 'time lag' to get fructified into results. The state of crisis cannot wait that long. This would warrant unconventional wisdom in the review of the contingency plans. Supervisor's experience, understanding and sharpness of decision-making would be invaluable as well.

The Supervisory Review Report should also consider other market developments while assessing the strength of banks. It should draw a scenario analysis indicating probable development and the likely response to each scenario. This report should be studied and recommended by the CMG for banks by the bank supervisor for consideration by the subcommittee of macroprudential authority. Response time is the crucial element here. With negative news spreading in line with deteriorating financial situation, crystallization of policy direction that too by the highest authority is essential. The subcommittee should act as fast as possible and let the macroprudential authority announce steps so as not to allow delay giving rise to confusing policy debates which may only worsen the situation and further undermine public confidence. Any forbearance for meeting prudential regulations must be explicitly authorized by the subcommittee/macroprudential authority.

Need for an Independent Resolution Authority and Bankruptcy Code

Resolution authorities are created by the law to handle cases of resolution smoothly and expeditiously in line with rules enshrined in a documented bankruptcy code. This authority and code usually service the whole system in a holistic manner. Generally, bank supervisors are vested with the powers to handle bank resolution and the supervisors of the securities markets with the powers to handle resolution of its regulates. Government approval is needed for state-supported financial bailouts. Since all these three agencies are members in the macroprudential authority, the macroprudential authority or any agency as delegated by it can act as the resolution authority for the jurisdiction.

Resolution Plans—An Inherent Requirement

While regulation and supervision of banks have the objective of minimizing the bank failures and systemic banking crises, it cannot guarantee against failure of banks. When a bank or financial institution which is considered to be TBTF or too systemically important to fail is on the verge of collapse, governments normally have to use public money to save them leading to significant amount of moral hazard problem in the system. Capacity of the authorities to ensure an orderly resolution of such banks is highly critical. Having an ex-ante resolution regime, therefore, becomes critical.

In the financial crisis, as the banks could not be allowed to fail, the taxpayers had to step in. The largest bank resolution by regulators in the GFC in the USA, that of Washington Mutual in September 2008, involved assets of US$302 billion and the bankruptcy of Lehman Brothers, the largest bankruptcy in history, involved assets of US$639 billion (Jarque and Price 2015). This amount estimated by the National Audit Office was around £1,162 billion in the UK.

It includes both a direct cash injection of £133 billion and total guarantees and other non-cash support of £1,029 billion (Cunliffe 2016).

Debtor in possession (DIP) financing is required for firms other than SIFIs for short-term financing to ensure sufficient resources are available in the event of bankruptcy to avoid destabilization and risks to taxpayers. This financing has to be approved by the bankruptcy court and is generally senior to the firm's already-existing debt. The area of contention is whether an ailing bank can obtain sufficient DIP financing.

Taking a cue from the requirements of orderly liquidation through the use of prudent bankruptcy laws, bail-ins and coerced sales, the DFA proposed an Orderly Liquidation Authority (OLA) to formulate a viable resolution mechanism of banks whose failure could cause systemic problems. Another strategy is the mandated bankruptcy laws, which, however, leaves much of the decision-making in respect of key issues like when to commence the process, which process to adopt, sale of the firm's assets or negotiate the terms of a reorganization with its creditors, etc., to the parties themselves, subject to statutory rules and judicial oversight. Bail-in[10] is another strategy for resolving the financial distress of a large financial institution conceived by the European lawmakers and other countries. Unlike OLA which is a full-blown, administrative resolution, bail-in is designed to serve as a mid-course correction to preserve a troubled financial institution with the intervention of the regulators at a time determined by them. The process would also be dictated by regulators on which claims to be altered or not as was seen in the GFC—the sales of Bear Stearns and Washington Mutual to JP Morgan Chase and Wachovia to Wells Fargo brokered by the federal regulators.

The USA formulated a comprehensive resolution regime under the bankruptcy code through the DFA which mandated all BHCs with total consolidated assets of US$50 billion or more and all the designated non-bank financial companies to develop, maintain and periodically submit resolution plans. Additionally, the FDIC requires

---

[10] Passes the cost of meeting losses and of recapitalizing a failing bank on to creditors by writing down the value of their claims or converting them into equity.

depository institutions with assets of US$50 billion or more insured by FDIC to file plans for their orderly resolution under the Federal Deposit Insurance Act. The framework required banks to have a sufficient amount of long-term debt that the FDIC can convert into equity to guarantee that the new bridge company is adequately capitalised. The FDIC and US FED began joint assessment of the submitted resolution plans and if found not sufficient it was required to be resubmitted, failing which more stringent capital and liquidity requirements were imposed. Prior to development of the living wills, the banks should enter a dialogue with the regulator to clearly understand the expectations and desired state. They may then create plans (not having any fiscal support from government) which identifies short-term and long-term actions. This may create opportunities to de-risk business without significantly losing on the rewards.

The government understandably was reluctant to directly get involved in resolution process of big firms as this may give an indication of unfair advantages to such firms. On the other hand, OLA provided a vent of support to distressed firms from the regulator (Dudley 2017). In a 2013 paper (Acharya, Anginer and Warburton 2013), Viral Acharya of New York University, Deniz Anginer of Virginia Tech, and Joseph Warburton of Syracuse University analysed bond credit spreads of 567 financial institutions and found that the passage of the DFA does not appear to have reduced expectations of public support for the largest institutions. These processes put in place have led to substantial improvement in the overall resolvability of the US banking firms and G-SIBs.

US banks today are as strong as any in the world, as shown by their solid profitability and healthy lending over recent years as the resolution planning process has improved their internal structures, governance, information collection systems and allocation of capital and liquidity with improvement in their resolvability by ensuring that they meet their long-term debt and TLAC requirement (Powell 2017).

The EU had also applied such regulations through their Bank Recovery and Resolution Directive (BRRD). This framework has been completed within the banking union with the establishment of the single resolution mechanism, a system comprising a central authority, the Single Resolution Board (SRB) which adopts the relevant decisions for significant banking institutions and the national resolution authorities that participate in the SRB and retain direct responsibility for the less significant institutions. A Single Resolution Fund which is endowed with contributions from the industry to enable financial support to resolution processes is present in this mechanism, though its practical implementation is subject to major challenges and the BRRD will shortly be revised on the basis of a recently submitted legislative proposal by the European Commission (Restoy 2016).

UK also launched its 'resolvability assessment framework' on 18 December 2018. The framework has broadly two components. While one component sets Bank of England as the resolution authority, the other component defines the requirements for banks to assess their own preparation for resolution. Banks are judged on their financial resources, ability to do business throughout the process of resolution and restructuring and co-ordination abilities with authorities and markets during resolution.

Resolution and Insolvency Regimes

In the absence of a proper framework for bailing out distressed institutions in times of crisis, taxpayer's money was used not only to bail them out but also to ensure systemic stability. Thus, it became imperative and at the instance of the G20, both the FSB and the BCBS have proposed the creation of a resolution regime for SIFIs. FSB in its 'Key Attributes of Effective Resolution Regimes for Financial Institutions' has characterized a well-defined resolution regime as one which enables separation of core activities from non-core activities, continuation of core activities followed by an orderly resolution of the institution (Box 7.1). In July 2017, the 'Key Attributes' (KAs) was also included in the FSB's list of 'Key Standards for Sound Financial Systems' for which assessments are carried out by the IMF and World Bank of their member countries under the Standards and Codes Initiative. The FSB's 'Key Standards for Sound Financial Systems' forms part of the FSB Compendium of Standards. The Compendium aims to provide

Box 7.1: The Twelve Key Attributes of Effective Resolution Regimes for Financial Institutions

1. *Scope:* Any financial institution having systemic significance.
2. *Resolution authority:* Administered by a resolution authority (or authorities) having a statutory mandate to promote financial stability and ensuring continued performance of critical functions.
3. *Resolution powers:* Powers to transfer the critical functions of a failing firm to a third party; powers to convert debt instruments into equity and preserve critical functions (bail-in within resolution); powers to impose a temporary stay on the exercise of termination rights under financial contracts (subject to safeguards for counterparties) and impose a moratorium on payments and on debt enforcement actions against the failing firm and powers to achieve the orderly closure and wind-down of all or parts of the firm's business with timely payout or transfer of insured deposits should be provided.
4. *Set-off, netting, collateralization, segregation of client assets:* The segregation of client assets should be effective in resolution. Financial contracts including netting and collateralization agreements should be enforceable. However, entry into resolution and the exercise of any resolution powers should not, in principle, constitute an event that entitles any counterparty of the firm in resolution to exercise acceleration or early termination rights under such agreements provided the substantive obligations under the contract continue to be performed (as would be the case if the contracts were transferred to a sound financial firm or bridge institutions).
5. *Safeguards:* All creditors should receive at a minimum what they would have received on liquidation of the firm. Resolution powers should be exercised in a way that respects the hierarchy of claims, subject to some flexibility for authorities to depart from the general principle of equal treatment of creditors of the same class where necessary to contain the potential systemic impact of a firm's failure or to maximize the value for the benefit of all creditors as a whole. Rights to judicial review should be available for affected parties to challenge actions that are outside the legal powers of the resolution authority.
6. *Funding of firms in resolution:* Resolution regimes should include funding mechanisms that can provide temporary financing to continue critical operations as part of the resolution of a failing firm. Such funding should be derived, or recovered, from private sources.

(Continued)

(Continued)

7. *Legal framework conditions for cross-border cooperation:* Resolution regimes should empower and encourage resolution authorities wherever possible to act to achieve a cooperative solution with their foreign counterparties. Authorities should be able to give effect in their jurisdiction to resolution measures taken by a foreign resolution authority.

8. *CMGs:* Home and key host authorities of all G-SIFIs should maintain CMGs with the objective of enhancing preparedness for and facilitating the resolution of a G-SIFI.

9. *Institution-specific cross-border cooperation agreements (COAGs):* COAGs should be in place between the home and relevant host authorities that need to be involved in the preparation and management of a crisis affecting a G-SIFI.

10. *Resolvability assessments:* Resolvability assessments should be carried out for all G-SIFIs. Authorities should have appropriate powers to require the adoption of appropriate measures to ensure that a firm is resolvable under the applicable regime.

11. *RRP:* Recovery and resolution plans (including high-level resolution strategies) should be in place for all firms that may be systemic or critical in the event of failure.

12. *Access to information and information sharing:* Jurisdictions should remove legal, regulatory or policy impediments that hinder the domestic and cross-border exchange of information in normal times and during a crisis, necessary for RRP and for resolution.

Source: Key Attributes of Effective Resolution Regimes for Financial Institutions (updated in October 2014).

a one-stop, easy-to-understand reference for the various economic and financial standards that are accepted by the international community as important for sound financial systems.

While creating a bank resolution regime, it is important to understand the differences in the objectives of a corporate insolvency regime and a bank insolvency regime. Corporate insolvency laws attempt to reach 'a fair and predictable treatment of creditors and the maximization of assets to satisfy creditors' claims', while for a bank insolvency regime the aim is to 'ensure the protection of (insured) depositors and the continuity of banking and payment services' and minimize the contagion of a bank failure. As long as this objective of bank insolvency is achieved, a bank should be allowed to fail in order to avoid moral hazard.

The safety of G-SIBs and the retail segment of the banking system has come to prime importance after the GFC. There are three well-known reports in this regard: Vickers' report in the UK which proposes ring fencing the retail business from the investment banking activities; the Volcker rule under the DFA in the USA which imposes restrictions on proprietary trading with some exceptions and puts limitations on banks sponsoring hedge funds, venture capital funds and private equity funds; and the Liikanen report for the Euro zone which is similar to the first two. An idea of a SIFI Stability Fund (SSF) has also been floated for the institutions considered to be G-SIBs by the international authorities (Esposito 2013). This fund can be an escrow account wherein every year, 20 per cent of the net profits of identified G-SIBs should be transferred. The fund could be managed by the IMF or another international institution (a self-managed structure) audited by the IMF. If 'problems' arise and an SSF participant needs recapitalization, the fund can be tapped, else after 5 years, the oldest contribution to the fund can be given back to the respective banks.

Even though many guidelines have been issued regarding G-SIBs, however, the issue of how cross-border assets and liabilities would be handled in different jurisdictions in case of failure of an international bank still remains unclear.

Living Wills

A living will is a recovery and resolution plan for a financial institution. The living will of a bank covers all of its operations in a single plan and simplifies legal structures for global financial institutions. The living wills should be reviewed by the home and key host supervisors. What is essential for a living will to succeed is inclusion of a burden sharing plan within various supervisors maintaining the value of financial stability formalized through a burden sharing agreement. However, lack of harmonized insolvency procedure may lead to ineffectiveness of living wills. The living wills further need to include firm's detailed strategic plan for rapid and orderly resolution in the event of distress and the action plan to achieve the same. Living wills promise to be highly useful complements to safety and soundness regulation (Jarque and Price 2015).

Contingent Convertibles

CoCos are debt instrument having features that can trigger their conversion into equity at a pre-specified level of stress. These triggers may be either systemic or related to the specific entity. The CoCos being a form of contingent capital may not lead to actual cash outlay and may only lead to a change in the existing liability structure.

The effectiveness of the CoCos as an instrument to enhance loss absorption was noticed to be limited in the sense that investors were found unwilling to take on losses and started hedging, undermining the value of banks' equity and thus increasing banks' costs of debt finance. This pattern if observed on a large scale may generate a vicious spiral. Thus, with the improvements in loss-absorbing capacity, there are also new dynamics that should be understood better (Caruana 2016). In India also, even those banks which had been under RBI's PCA framework and were in losses found it difficult to enforce losses on investors of such instruments.

There have been concerns on prescription of use of CoCos in the regulation since the financial crisis (Heckinger 2016). It is argued that supervisory and resolution authorities have made CoCos central of regulation, supervision and resolution of banks without understanding the true nature of market dynamics. These instruments have not been tested during crisis times and may be quite inflexible in their operations. Additionally, it is feared that there may be negative events during time of market volatility due to CoCos. Due to these reasons, enhancement of loss absorbency using common equity may be a better option.

There is a panic dynamic associated with the instrument, as witnessed in the recent episode of Germany's Deutsche Bank (Cline 2017). Because of heavy losses in 2015 and the imposition of heavy penalties in 2016 by US authorities for mis-selling mortgage-backed securities, shareholder panic resulted in the steep fall in the price of convertibles and equity. Potential contagion risk emerged. Therefore, a heavier dose of equity is required for G-SIBs with minimal reliance on these untested instruments. In India also, banks on which PCA has been imposed found it difficult to continue with these instruments and many of them recalled these instruments at the time when they needed the capital most.

FSB has initiated a review to monitor implementation and identify any technical issues or operational challenges in the implementation of the standard. This will lead to better understanding of the issues being faced in the implementation of CoCos issuance and maintenance by banks.

Bank Creditors' Bail-Ins

Bail-in is essentially objectively a contingent capital; however, it applies to a larger part of banks' liabilities, existing debt and is expected to take place close to the point of non-viability of the bank.

Several European countries such as the UK, Switzerland, Cyprus, Denmark and the Netherlands have chosen these as an important element in the resolution and restructuring of banks. In Europe, to be able to carry out the bail-in, all institutions, liable to be subject to resolution, are required to hold a minimum volume of loss-absorbing instruments known as the minimum required eligible liabilities (MREL) requirement. The stringency of the MREL requirement is determined through the nature of the eligible instruments and their minimum required volume thereof, which, at present, is at variance in different member states specifically, as regards the status of senior debt in relation to deposits. This has acted as a hindrance to the development of an integrated market and has hampered the homogeneity of the MREL requirements.

The operational aspects of executing a bail-in transaction need to be addressed by the FSB KAs and the TLAC standards. However, FSB has issued a guidance document on a set of principles to assist authorities as they develop bail-in resolution strategies and make resolution plans operational for G-SIBs.

Resolution of SIFIs

As desired for the DSIBs and G-SIBs, for the identified G-SIFIs and D-SIFIs RRP or living wills should be made mandatory with an objective that in the eventuality of EWS and CMM not being able to deliver desired results, a self-propelled recovery may be envisaged for the institution. The plan should inter alia list down bank's operations, the inherent risks, the possible measures to mitigate these risks and re-establish financial stability without official support within a realistic timeframe. Such plans inter alia should cover the following:

- Ex-ante resolution fund from annual profits to be created
- Provisions to raise capital, bail-in provisions and power to undertake asset sale or merger
- Reduce staff costs (e.g., loss of headcount through attrition and limited hiring, compensation in kind rather than cash)
- Reduce deposit with central banks, eliminate excess collateral with payment systems and manage deposits/placements with other financial institutions
- A list of actions that may be required to raise capital and sell subsidiaries and/or other businesses or portfolios in case of a financial shock
- Information/action plan on contractual obligations; cross-guarantees tied to different securities; counterparties to whom the collateral of the bank is pledged
- Plans for rapid and orderly shutdown should the company go under
- The 'bankruptcy code' containing a strategic analysis approved by its board of how it can be resolved in a way that would not pose systemic risk to the financial system

Recovery and Resolution Planning

Even though many jurisdictions have put up RRP processes, their supervisory acceptance has not been so easy. Consultative documents on TLAC implementation have been published by many G-SIBs. Banks have issued substantial amounts of TLAC-eligible liabilities, which would impose losses on investors other than shareholders to avoid government bail outs in case of resolution. The key question is: will TLAC instruments work as intended? There is a flaw in these regulations and it tries to 'economize' on equity by requiring the largest banks to issue debt securities designated as 'loss-absorbing capital'. The TLAC instruments are meant to provide an alternative to bailouts by 'bailing-in' some creditors, while the contingent capital or CoCos use various trigger points to convert debt to equity. The idea behind these securities is to create mechanisms other than bankruptcy (Admati 2015).

Important challenges remain in the area of deposit insurance. As recommended by the Core Principles of International Association of Deposit Insurers (IADI), the seven-day payout rule is still implementable in very few countries. The Emergency Liquidity Assistance (ELA) facilities need to be more deep and explicit. With regard to coordination and communication related to system-wide crisis preparedness and management, there is need to strengthen the role of the deposit insurer in the safety net (Caruana 2016).

Bank Resolution Options

An ideal way to deal with the issue of resolution is to evaluate all possible alternatives available and going in for that option of resolution that ensure minimal cost for the deposit insurance fund and minimal losses to uninsured depositors and other creditors. This method involves evaluating several variables including the following:

- The differences between the book value of assets and liabilities
- The level of insured and uninsured deposits
- Losses on contingent claims
- Any premium paid by an acquirer
- The expected realizable value of liquidated assets

Such an exercise of evaluation of 'least cost' becomes complex during an episode of crisis due to sudden uncertainty imposed on the value of asset and liability, the expected level of recovery in asset values and most importantly the pressure put on policymakers to keep banks alive for the functioning of the economy, which adds to further costs by way of public funds required for this objective to materialize. This has broader implications for the government both in terms of current investment avenues as also those potential foregone future revenue and growth.

To contain depositors' panic resulting in bank runs, often blanket state guarantees are also issued. This is usually done to help viable banks tide over temporary liquidity problems in the immediate term with the objective of continued financial stabilization in the long run. Accordingly, a short-term higher cost element is incurred to gain long-term benefits of stability. The latter not being quantifiable, the cost–benefit analysis could be cumbersome. But what is important is to have the priority right.

Initiating a Purchase and Assumption Transaction

Purchase and assumption transaction (PAT) involves a healthy bank acquiring a potential insolvent bank by way of outright purchase of some or all of its assets and assuming its (insured) deposits. There is usually a premium element attached to such a transaction. In cases where the value of liabilities (insured deposits) exceeds the size of the realizable value of acquired assets, 'assistance' element is also tagged to make the PAT happen. This way, disruptive effects of an otherwise 'liquidation' exercise get avoided.

The valuation exercise involving liquidation value calculation is tricky as it requires the use of valuation models based on statistical sampling. To save time, the bank examination team should do this exercise as they are better aware of the happenings in the bank. If the value of assets is determined correctly vis-à-vis their carrying book value to the satisfaction of both, then the task becomes easier to package the offer with an offsetting amount of (deposits) liabilities.

There remains an underlying load of 'moral hazard' in PAT. The general feeling is that all the depositors of the failed bank including the large sophisticated ones who are not supposed to be protected under deposit insurance schemes are also protected under PAT. This might erode market discipline. But the model wherein uninsured depositors receive the same treatment as in a straight liquidation could be a bit more operationally complex to execute.

Creating a Bridge Bank Out of an Infected Bank Especially a DSIB

Another option is establishing a bridge bank by way of ring-fencing the deposits and good assets and/or taking over some or all of the regular business, such as providing new credit and rolling over existing loans, etc., of one bank or a number of banks. The bridge bank takes up the banking activities which are running profitably and is also allowed to disburse new credit and even rollover existing credit which are possibly performing by nature. In such an arrangement, usually loss assets are liquidated/written off and are transferred to an Asset Management Company (AMC) created specifically to take over the contaminated assets and deal with them separately in a focused manner. The concept of this AMC or the bridge bank becomes an efficient option when it is sold to a solvent counterparty without capital injection by the government. For such an AMC, the OBS items and contingent liabilities including pending law suits, etc., may also move to the AMC so that the new bridge bank may operate unencumbered with such costs, and hence it may find it easier to attract buyers. The bad assets of the bank must not depend on any government support and look to extract maximum value out of these assets.

Ideally, the new bank can be privately owned and created by private investors (who have met the fit and proper requirements of the bank supervisor). During crisis period, however, to meet the eventuality of containing panic, the government can create the bank either for a temporary period or even permanently by making it a state bank. In case the new bank is government capitalized, the recovery for this strategic investor needs to be ensured in the future.

Selling the bridge bank to a solvent bank is a better option vis-à-vis creating a state bank. However, there could be a lurking risk of increasing the concentration risk in already concentrated jurisdictions exacerbating moral hazard further. The potential way could be through a divestiture process wherein the government may offer 20 per cent ownership rights in annual offerings spanning five years or, alternatively, the bridge bank could be resolved via a multi-acquirer process.

Creating good bank–bad bank out of a failed big bank, especially a DSIB, is another popular model to split a failed big bank into two banks, namely one with good assets and the other with the bad ones. Part-nationalization and part-privatization ownership pattern may be used for resolution of a big bank as there would be disruptions typically associated with the insolvency of large banks, and this framework minimises disruption. The segment converted into a bad bank could be sold to the AMC. This technique is popular as it gets potential new investors interested in taking over the troubled bank sans the contaminated portion, and thus resolution of a seriously troubled, but still solvent problem bank is facilitated. The shareholders of the troubled bank will receive the ownership of the bad bank till its transfer to an AMC and the new investors will capitalize the good bank. This way good bank can solely focus on the business of banking, including developing the franchise, efforts on cost-cutting strategies and refocusing the business plan of the bank, rather than dealing with the contamination or litigations. Further, it results in a one-time clean-up of the balance sheet of the bank, thus turning it into one that is fully capitalized. Borrowers will also be encouraged to sincerely complement the bank's collection efforts as they will be satisfied about the good health of the bank. The tendency of looking for 'forbearance' from a sinking ship would also vanish.

Public Recapitalization Programme for Resolution

Though not an ideal solution, this is often the 'last resort' to manage crisis situations. These are designed in the light of specific circumstances and government policies in line with the availability of shareholder resources, the extent of recapitalization needed and the legal structure. Such programmes are subject to a written operational framework document with a commitment from the bank to strengthen internal control measures (cutting costs, increasing revenues, etc.), risk management architecture and high-quality governance culture which would culminate in reduced non-performing loans (NPLs) in a time-bound manner. As a precondition for eligibility, existing shareholders or new private investors must be willing to inject at least half of the Tier 1 capital needed. No bailout of existing shareholders is allowed. Preferably, the shares held by the government (paid for in tradeable government bonds issued on market terms) should have preferred status to shares held by the old shareholders and government as a shareholder would have a nominee in the board.

Creation of an Ex-ante, Industry-funded Resolution Fund

As recommended for DSIBs in the earlier paragraphs, the concept of an industry-funded resolution fund could be thought of. This can be appropriated out of net profits of each bank and kept as a kind of contingency reserve within themselves or, alternatively, in an escrow account created by the bank supervisor. If the fund's jurisdiction expands to non-banks also, then this account can be managed by the Apex Committee in charge of crisis management. These contingency buffers may be created out of levies in the form of financial transaction tax from the financial institutions during good times to cater for losses during any difficult time losses. It has been discussed in greater detail further in the chapter.

Cross-border Bank Resolution Issues

Cross-border coordination arrangements are vital irrespective of failure of an ordinary bank under ordinary times or of SIB during crisis. Concrete steps may be taken to enhance cross-border coordination arrangements regardless of whether there is any spillover to domestic markets from failure of any ordinary bank or any systemic bank during stable times. It must further guard against the spillover effects of the deterioration in any foreign bank branch or the parent of a foreign bank. Such coordination arrangements should cover the following aspects:

- Bank supervisor should have the powers to direct a foreign bank operating in the host jurisdiction not to increase upstreaming of profits or liquidity, transfer risky assets to or transfer good assets out of the host country, should the need arise to do so.
- Wider level of exchange of information with foreign authorities should be put in place with broadened powers to resolve or facilitate a coordinated resolution of a domestic branch of a foreign bank by extending the framework for compulsory business transfers, statutory management and winding up of such operations.
- Prioritizing payments so as not to discriminate against creditors on any basis or jurisdiction.
- Transparent and immediate plans for identifying and enforcement of out-of-court resolution decisions taken by foreign authorities. A foreign court can be added to the list of prescribed courts, if the host country is satisfied that it will give substantial reciprocity of treatment to the judgements of host country courts.

The liabilities in the home jurisdiction may be covered up using the domestic assets of the foreign banks operating in any home jurisdiction as per the extant statutes or regulations and could generally include the following:

(a) Unpaid monthly salaries within certain stipulated ceilings.
(b) The following claims by the Bank Deposits Insurance Scheme Fund, as a guarantor to the deposits:
    (1) The net amount payable to depositors in accordance with the Law of Bank Deposits Insurance Scheme;
    (2) Premiums payable to the Bank Deposits Insurance Scheme Fund;
    (3) Loans and advances;
    (4) Any other dues to the Bank Deposits Insurance Scheme Fund pursuant to the Law.
(c) Claims of the Central Bank other than those enumerated above.

(d) Claims of other creditors of the bank in liquidation including the depositors' rights which are not covered pursuant to the Law of Bank Deposits Insurance Scheme.

Resolution Models for Cross-Border Banks (Bolton et al. 2018)

Resolving a cross-border banks becomes quite difficult due to different legal and institutional structures of resolving banks in different countries, and also reconciling interests of creditors of different countries is not an easy task. This led to a famous quote that global banks are global in life but national in their deaths. Resolution of a global cross-border bank is dependent on the ex-ante resolution model adopted:

- *Multiple point of entry (MPOE):* In this model, a cross-border bank is split along jurisdictional lines and national regulators perform a separate resolution, drawing on loss-absorbing capital and liquidity held separately
- *Single point of entry (SPOE):* In this model, a cross-border bank is resolved as one entity through a single global holding company that holds banking subsidiaries in multiple jurisdictions.

The difference under two models of resolution is that while under MPOE loss-absorbing capital is not shared across jurisdictions and no cross-jurisdictional transfers occur, whereas SPOE allows for the sharing of loss-absorbing capital and cross-jurisdictional transfers during resolution. While SPOE model may be more efficient for cross-border resolution as a whole, political processes of transfer of resources from one jurisdiction to another may hinder its actual implementation during crisis periods. History tells that cross-border cooperation during crisis periods which involve transfer of capital and liquidity from one jurisdiction to another breaks down and ultimately each country engages in ring-fencing. Under these circumstances, MPOE model appears to be a viable option.

Funding of Firms in Resolution

A key component in the implementation of the resolution plan is an implementable funding plan. The FSB has published detailed guidance in this regard in 2018a, 2018b, 2018c. The firm owns assets and the private fund tapping should be the preferred avenue for arranging funds for resolution. The authorities should finalize a resolution funding plan and the firms should have the capability to support monitoring, reporting and estimating funding needs. Also, there should be seamless coordination and sharing of information between the authorities.

Post Bail-in Restructuring

Another model which was followed in the UK where the parliament enacted a law to ensure retail separation at the time of failure. This required ring-fencing of the retail assets ex-ante. This was further followed by other jurisdictions such as Switzerland and the USA. This can be further supplemented through exploring scope for orderly, solvent wind-down of trading books in investment banks in recovery or resolution (Gracie 2016).

Indian Experience

In India, the possibility of evolving a resolution mechanism was explored in March 2016 when a specialized committee was set up for this purpose. The committee has since suggested a draft Financial Resolution and Deposit Insurance (FRDI) Bill. The current resolution framework in the country is limited to the central bank as the liquidator. The draft bill prescribes setting up of a resolution corporation (RC), based on the FSB's Key Attributes of Effective Resolution Regimes for Financial Institutions. The proposed RC would subsume the role of Deposit Insurance and Credit Guarantee Corporation (DICGC) which currently undertakes only the 'pay box' function, that is, reimbursement of insured amount to the depositors of failed banks. However, the draft bill has been withdrawn by the government following public outcry on the indication of institutionalizing the framework that the deposits of the depositors may also be used for recapitalizing a bank in case of a need. Despite India not having any G-SIBs to align the practices followed by its central bank with the best practices, the central bank has established supervisory colleges for its internationally active banks.

References

Acharya, Viral V., Deniz Anginer and A. Joseph Warburton. 2013, December. *The End of Market Discipline? Investor Expectations of Implicit State Guarantees.* Available at http://pages.stern.nyu.edu/~sternfin/vacharya/public_html/pdfs/End%20of%20Market%20Discipline%20-%20Acharya%20Anginer%20Warburton%202_10_2016.pdf (accessed on 12 February 2019).

Admati, Anat R. 2015, December. 'The Missed Opportunity and Challenge of Capital Regulation'. Working Paper Series No. 216. Stanford, CA: Rock Center for Corporate Governance, Stanford Graduate School of Business.

Bagehat, Walter. 1873. *The Lombard Street: A Description of the Money Markets.* London: Henry S. King & Co.

Bank Resolution and the Structure of Global Banks. Discussion Paper No. 778. London School of Economics.

Bolton, Patrick and Martin Oehmke. 2018, 26 April. Caruana, Jaime. 2016, 6 December. 'Post-Crisis Financial Safety Net Framework: Lessons, Responses and Remaining Challenges' (Keynote address at the FSI-IADI Conference on 'Bank Resolution, Crisis Management and Deposit Insurance Issues'). Basel.

Cline, William. 2017. *The Right Balance for Banks: Theory and Evidence on Optimal Capital Requirements.* Washington, DC: Peterson Institute for International Economics.

Cunliffe, Jon. 2016, 5 December. *Ending Too-Big-to Fail: How Best to Deal with Failed Large Banks.* London: Bank of England.

Dudley, William C. 2017, 7 April. 'Principles for Financial Regulatory Reform' (Speech).

Esposito, Lorenzo. 2013, February. 'Connect Them Where It Hurts: The Missing Piece of the Puzzle'. Bank of Italy Occasional Paper Number 151. Rome: Bank of Italy.

Gracie, Andrew. 2016, 26 May. 'Ending Too Big to Fail: Getting the Job Done' (Speech).

Heckinger, Richard. 2016, 5 December. *Should Banks Hold Cocos or Other Kinds of Buffers?* Available at https://www.centralbanking.com/central-banking/opinion/2479054/should-banks-hold-cocos-or-other-kinds-of-buffers (accessed on 12 February 2019).

Jarque, Arantxa and David A. Price. 2015. 'Living Wills: A Tool for Curbing Too Big to Fail'. Annual Report. Federal Reserve Bank of Richmond.

Powell, Jerome H. 2017, 22 June. 'Relationship Between Regulation and Economic Growth' (Speech). Available at https://www.bis.org/review/r170630a.htm (accessed on 21 January 2019).

Reinhart and Rogoff. 2009. The Aftermath of Financial Crisis. NBER Working Paper No. 14656.

Restoy, Fernando. 2016, 29 November. 'The Challenges of the European Resolution Framework'.

Part IV

Coordination in International Policymaking

No one can whistle a symphony, it takes a whole orchestra to play it.

—H. E. Luccock

CHAPTER 8

Dynamics of International Policy Coordination

While cross-border interconnectedness has increased, the regulatory framework for coordination has not kept pace. The Eurozone is a prime example of the benefits of the coordination at decision-making level which has led to higher growth and greater raise in standard of living. The lessons learned from the Eurozone integration can be used in other regions while avoiding its pitfalls. The basic premise on which the integration should be achieved is that the larger good should be top priority over individual country development goals. Regional integration is a systematic process of economic, political, legal and monetary synergy.

Introduction

Vasudhaiva Kutumbakam is a Sanskrit phrase that inculcates an understanding that the whole world is one family. Humans, the driving force behind this family, are not only made of matter but also of mind, intellect and spirit. Their synergy contributes to an energy which enables humans to innovate. Einstein's fundamental theory of nuclear physics,

$e = mc^2$, which explains the material fact that matter is convertible into energy and energy into matter, is the sine qua non of human progress. The synergy between body, mind, intellect and spirit facilitates this transformation. And that is the intrinsic strength of a human. As also enshrined in the Vedantic philosophy, this synergy has to move from the micro to the macro in the same line as from the finite towards the infinite. This basic philosophy of Vedanta similarly applies to financial innovations. There should be a synergy among nations to reap the benefits of innovations. However, lack of synergy may be likened to a chariot with a non-cooperating wheel being forced to move by a disenchanted horse. Over the years, humans have identified their dependence on various natural products for survival and growth. This dependence has led to lot of interdependence between various communities. As a result, the barriers on water, land and environment have been created by human beings to show off their superiority over their neighbours. This lack of synergy among the natural resources owing to unequal material possession is the mother of environmental chaos. Similarly, a lack of synergy between nations can create world economic chaos. World history has seen times of both chaos and synergy. This synergy among nations has over the years developed into the notion known as 'globalization'. In economic and financial terms, it is the process of opening of the individual economies for goods and services.

Globalization has its own share of advantages and disadvantages. Considering the advantages of globalization, countries cannot afford to remain isolated. Globalization leads to broad, deep and resilient financial markets, which are essential for keeping the wheels of global commerce turning. A resilient financial market helps savers diversify risk and enable borrowers to obtain credit at lower cost. And it confers the benefits of convenient exchange and capital certainty on everyone. However, the disadvantages cannot be overlooked either. Important concerns for countries going for economic, financial and monetary integration are the loss of sovereignty to some extent and the likely impact of external events on the domestic economy. As the economies integrate, there is higher likelihood of the spillover impact of the policies of national governments. The classic examples in this case have been the GFC 2008, the European debt crisis, the Taper Tantrum episode 2013 and the Brexit. Some other recent issues in this regard are the spillover effects of monetary policies of advanced countries on the emerging market economies, large reserve accumulations by China and other Asian countries and capital controls by emerging market economies, etc. The recent spate of tariff war initiated between the USA and China may also prove to be a roadblock for greater world economic and financial integration. The countries must look for ways of economic integration and international cooperation which are Pareto-optimal, that is, it should make some countries better off without hurting others. To deal with this issue, there is a need for greater international policy cooperation push towards economic integration. The need of the hour is to envisage a system for Global Monetary and Financial Stability (GMFS) policy coordination. The current form of globalization has been prompted by the mighty and forced on the others. Or to put it differently, the top conceived an idea and the bottom was obliged to embrace it. Thus, it lacked synergy in the right order and commensurate depth. That could be a reason why benefits could not transcend geographical boundaries and crises tend to crop up at the drop of a hat.

> It is reasonable to assert that in a patently imperfect world experiencing significant financial volatility and multiple sovereignties, monetary unions provide the possibility for shared sovereignty and monetary and fiscal discipline which may have some impact on the overall stability of the international financial system. (Venner 2002)

Economic and Financial Regionalism— The Building Block

The first way for moving towards a GMFS policy coordination is by integrating the various regional economic groups present all over the world into a single multilateral outfit. Regional Economic Integration as a philosophy aims to complement integration of nation states with the world economy. There is a need for regional groups to reap the benefits of globalization, but at the same time guard against the vulnerabilities posed by it. Regionalism should not be perceived to bring undesirable consequences for global welfare. The EU example shows, regional integration does not necessarily mean trading less with the rest of the world. In fact, integration, regionalism and globalization necessitate opening of domestic economies to international trade and financial flows, thereby bringing in competition and efficiency. The opening of economies in a regional setting may lead to more external competition than trade, and financial liberalization as geographic, institutional and cultural proximity is directly proportional to cross-border flows and intensity of competition is inversely proportional to distance.

The process of the beginning of the end of geography is backed by reasons which are not philosophical but financial as it essentially means gradually doing away with internal barriers within mutually organized group of nations with a hope to extend it further and further to reap financial benefits. The creation of the EU is the case at hand—it reflects a process of integration of individual nation's economic policies, on both the micro-fronts and macro-fronts. Regional integration is not just a meeting of mind of the people of the nations, it is a systematic process of economic and political synergy and may involve even 'establishing legal framework, developing agreements, procedures and accords on a regional and supranational basis' (Venner 2002). It may not necessarily be backed by a history of camaraderie; the EU aims to replace peaceful coexistence with age-old rivalry by economic integration. Geographical proximity may or may not be a necessary condition as well, 'Borders arise where differences arise, even if the exact drawing of the border will often run through "grey" areas' (Venner 2002). Similarly, horizontal expansion in terms of number of nations may not be that important. Not only that it may slow down the deepening process, possible lack of synergy may choke the very process to death. To a large extent, the regionalization process is just a step towards globalization, and therefore there is little prospect of discontinuing the integration process at the boundaries of the region. So long as the process is powered by the flow of finance across the globe and is conscious of dealing with the associated systemic risk, such an architecture may be welcome.

The preferential trade agreement is an important block of regional economic integration. While multilateralism has its own advantages, the importance of the preferential trade agreements in terms of its interrelationship with the multilateral systems cannot be undermined. The preferential trade agreements are attempting to act as a building block to wider plurilateralism. The very fact that bilateral, plurilateral and multilateral preferential trade agreements are being sought after by important global players and the developing countries points towards the rewards and benefits of such arrangements.

A creative strategic alliance may be the point of beginning based on constructive collaboration rather than destructive competition. While taking care of the political dimensions, it may offer an opportunity to unleash a system of participative macroeconomic management. The logic behind this argument is that one common currency might be a better option than several weak currencies. A single currency offers the synergy and advantage of scale, and thus the hope that the whole might be greater than the sum of the parts. The other option of allowing a 'local hegemon with the will and capacity to enforce discipline, by means of side-payments or sanctions' is not preferred (under the current global scenario and considering that such systems of joint hegemons trying to do the job globally as hitherto is failing miserably) over an alliance approach of monetary partnership among the bloc members. This will especially be optimal while addressing the issues of systemic risks since damage out of contagion will be all-pervading as against benefits which accrue progressively in order of hegemonic influences.

The race to regionalize for a safer global architecture may have potential to leave porous regions as a by-product like 'glocalization' (the distinctive combinations that emerge from the interaction of global and local factors of economic production), which may leave scope for national processes to intersect with regional ones in different ways that can create either 'deep' or 'shallow' schemes of regional integration. Plastering of the pores will be automatic once the arrogant traditional notion of monetary sovereignty is dusted away by progressively dominating power of competitive market forces and nations learn

to adapt to a dramatic transformation of their status, from monopoly to oligopoly.... The logic of oligopolistic competition suggests

> that many governments will eventually yield to the market power of more efficient producers, replacing national monies with regional currencies of some kind.... National currencies are a phenomenon of the twentieth century; supranational currencies are the solutions of the future. (Hausmann 1999: 96, reiterated by Cohen 2003)

In the wake of the continued trend of deterritorialization of money, various national currencies have tended to 'increasingly getting caught up in an intense Darwinian struggle for survival'. Competition will ultimately justify the existence of any individual currency leading to shrinkage in the number of currencies. Currently, there are many currencies around the globe including several small currencies with very limited circulation, which possibly do not represent a stable equilibrium. Quite expectedly, there had been several successful, partially successful and unsuccessful attempts to achieve regional economic and financial integration. Regionalism has been tried and tested in all parts of the world and also within continents. The European integration is the leading example in this case followed by the partial success in Africa, Asia and South America. Even though this integration has never been easy, the advantages have made efforts towards regional economic, financial and monetary integration attempts to multiply.

Asia being the largest continent has several sub-regional blocks in it: the Southeast Asia Block, the Pacific Block, the West Asia Block and the Central Asia Block. Various forms of regional integration have been witnessed in these areas. Sub-regionalism in Asia is a fait accompli considering the presence of three formidable lions in one forest. Each of Japan, China and India, given their size, complexities, political background and overall economic muscle, is an independent force to be reckoned within the current arena. The historical rivalries between Japan and China and also India and China are well known. Each of them tries to outwit the other to occupy the place of the global pole next to the USA and Euroland. Hence, the idea of pooling their might together to occupy the number one place (instead of competing for the third, fourth and the fifth place among themselves) politically may be hard to bloom soon. However, nothing is impossible in the game of power and due to necessity in the face of palpable systemic risk in the globalized economic scenario, innovative structural configurations.

Since sub-regionalism could act as a 'means' to achieve the same 'end' of being a 'polar-head' while offering possible potentials for economic development that too in a manner which is not politically and legally constraining, it is gaining currency slowly but steadily.

The creation of new institutions such as BRICS, AIIB, etc., parallel to the World bank and IMF, could be attributed to the reluctance by the larger powers in these institutions, to confer greater voting rights, and thus greater power to the emerging economies.[1]

> By founding the AIIB and the New Development Bank, China and other emerging powers have signalled that they will not wait for their voices to be better heard…. And decisions like that of the UK—and France, Germany, and Italy—show that they are not alone. (O'Neill 2015)

This development embraced by close allies of the USA 'is also seen as the further devolution of the U.S.-centric economic order organized under the Bretton Woods agreement in 1944' (Levine 2015). 'Perhaps America's opposition to the AIIB is an example of an economic phenomenon—firms want greater competition everywhere except in their own industry' and/or 'it simply wanted hegemony. In an increasingly multipolar world, it wanted to remain the G-1' (Stiglitz 2015). But it was heartening to note the gentler tone of the US Treasury Secretary Jack Lew (31 March 2015) as he declared: 'the U.S. stands ready to welcome new additions to the international development architecture'.

---

[1] Emergence of AIIB or even the BRICS should usher in a new form of global financial governance that is both fragmented and multi-layered. There may be legitimate concerns about this decentralizing trend, but they may be marking the beginning of an end to the display of the dangers of highly centralized power vested in overarching global institution/s as hitherto. It would sow the seeds of a system of effective coordination—with necessary 'checks and balances'— among global, regional and bilateral institutions to pursue public goods together. 'Moreover, a decentralized system would also resonate with the normative structure of the post-global recession world: namely, general skepticism of one-size-fits-all solutions. Multilayered international financial governance could prove to be compatible with regional diversity and national variations in capitalism' (Sohn 2015).

But necessity is the mother of invention and the USA would well remember Benjamin Franklin's famous warning: 'If we do not hang together, most assuredly we will hang separately'. A lot has changed since then.

> US of the 21st century is unlikely to possess the capacity or the will to shape geopolitical order in the way it did in the 20ᵗʰ ... economic interdependence would soften national competition and that global supply chains would beget more effective global governance.... never signed up to the idea of sharing national sovereignty... As they operate their multi-nation supply chains and just-in-time production processes, businesses should understand that the world has changed. (Stephens 2015)

'The G-Zero' position 'can't last, because it will create too many problems that demand cooperative solutions.... regionalization appears the likeliest result because it's the path we're already on' (Bremmer 2012).

There have been several variations in the extent and the manner of the regional financial arrangements. Factors such as economic aspects of financial cooperation, political leadership, role of international institutions and historical paths could have contributed to this. The economic, political, institutional and ideational thought process are the main building blocks for any regional economic integration, and the various push and pull among these factors have led to the development of different approaches to economic integration in various parts of the world. Therefore, although each contribution focuses on one of these factors, it also addresses interdependent processes and effects.

European Regional Integration: Learning Points for Others

European economic integration is nothing short of inspiration for other regions. The continent which saw several intercontinental wars not only won the Nobel Peace Prize for achieving 'peace and cooperation' in Europe but also ushered a new era of cooperation in the world. While accepting the prize, Jose Manuel Barroso, the president of the

European Commission, said that the EU is 'more than an association of states. It is a new legal order, which is not based on the balance of power between nations but on the free consent of states that share sovereignty'. However, there is a need to handle the lessons from Europe carefully as it has implications for the national sovereignty. The unparalleled supranationality evidenced in the EU was led by EU parliaments, which regularly passed laws even though it was opposed by the respective individual governments.

From the founding of the European Coal and Steel Community in 1952 and the establishment of the European Economic Community (EEC) by way of signing of the Treaty of Rome in March 1957 till the final launch of Euro in 2002, the period saw some defining moments in the European monetary history. In the interim, formation of European parliament, evolution of the Exchange Rate Mechanism (ERM) of the European Monetary System (EMS) in 1979 in the wake of collapse of Bretton Woods system, signing of the Maastricht Treaty in 1991 providing the legal and institutional framework for the launch of Economic and Monetary Union (EMU), the torments in the several waves of enlargement were no less challenging. Today, about 500 million proud people closeted in 27 transparent political boundaries boast of deep trade and financial linkages.

Part of the reason why regional institutions could be developed faster in Europe

> lay in the delicate economic and political balance achieved between the interests of the two states … creating peace between France and Germany after a struggle lasting three quarters of a century. Economic and political integration appeared acceptable and unthreatening to smaller states because it rested on a fundamental bilateral rapprochement of two core states, France and Germany. These states, of roughly equal demographic size (until the 1990 unification of Germany), balanced each other, and the resulting relationship prevented the dominance of any single state in the new regional order. (James 1996)

The Franco-German alliance thus effectively anchored the European political and economic regional grouping.

Most importantly, European monetary integration has been the torchbearer for the initiatives, whatever little they are, for forming monetary unions in the developing world. Gulf Cooperation Council (GCC) and Caribbean Community stand out in this regard. The European experience not only encouraged macroeconomic policy dialogue but also strengthened it with policy surveillance and consultation, liquidity support during crises and exchange rate coordination. Latin America had adopted mechanisms for macroeconomic policy dialogue in the context of its three major integration processes: Mercosur, the Andean Community and the Central American Common Market.

The lessons from Europe also point out the errors to avoid. However, it is noteworthy that Europe had developed the cross-border financial integration to a significant level. While this worked well during the better times, the GFC revealed that there were flaws in the overall design of supervision and support systems.

Economic Regionalism in Southeast Asia: Work-in-Progress

Asia's option to remain a backbencher in the global urge to pool regional resources to score political as well as economic points over each other has been one of the most raging debates in the recent time. Absence of strong motivations towards developing deeper regionalism could be due to the inherent hesitation to delegate national authority in favour of any supranational institution. The major countries of the region namely China, Japan or India have not been able, either singly or jointly, to form a lasting regional organization. As a result, Asian regionalism continues to be led by its weaker states, especially the Association of Southeast Asian Nations (ASEAN). The fruits of globalization were however reaped as they prided themselves as 'tigers', 'cubs', etc. But as an aftermath of the Asian Crisis of 1997, a growing consciousness arose about the necessity of safeguarding themselves from various types of external shocks giving rise to systemic crises across the region. The 1997 Asian financial crisis underscored the potential significance of regional-level collaboration in financial and economic policy. Several countries in the region were also subject to shocks and contagion, which caused volatility and the risk of 'sudden stops' and reversals of capital flows. However, in view of its growth potential, Asian countries are tending to offer itself as a force to reckon with along with the Western Hemisphere and the EU. Lest it gets marginalized by the other two who are fast becoming invincible economic powers owing to steady progress in integration, it is intending to taste the same waters.

The South and Southeast Asian economies have affected six trade agreements between them including the landmark ASEAN–India Comprehensive Economic Cooperation Agreement in 2010. The Master Plan on ASEAN Connectivity in 2010 was a significant initiative to support the ASEAN financial integration. The objective was to enable the establishment of the ASEAN Economic Community (AsEC) by 2015 by enhancing intra-regional connectivity in several areas including tourism, development, trade and investment. Some other initiatives taken to enhance cross-border cooperation among the capital markets in the ASEAN countries including building of capacity and infrastructure as summarized in the IMF working paper (Almekinders et al. 2015) on ASEAN financial integration are mentioned as follows:

- Monitoring of implementation of priority actions for freer flow of capital within the region
- Integration, harmonization and development of equity markets, domestic regulations and market infrastructure, respectively, by the ASEAN Capital Markets Forum (ACMF)
- Working CPSS, which focuses on policy, legal frameworks, instruments, institutions and market infrastructure
- Creation of the task force on the ASEAN Banking Integration Framework (ABIF), to achieve ASEAN-wide banking sector liberalization by 2020
- The ASEAN Capital Markets Infrastructure (ACMI) blueprint was developed in 2013 to enable a cross-border ASEAN equity and bond markets through integrated access, clearing, custody and settlement systems and arrangements

The ASEAN free trade area (AFTA) has progressed significantly, particularly for the trade in goods. However, more needs to be done for reducing the non-tariff barriers and increasing service liberalization. While some developments can be witnessed in the ASEAN investment areas, it is still to catch up with the advancement in liberalization for trade in goods. With the objective of deeper regional integration, ASEAN realized the need to progress towards the AEC by 2015. AEC is expected to offer a single market and production base and keep the region globally oriented and competitive. To achieve this, the AFTA needs to be developed into ASEAN Trade in Goods Agreement (ATIGA). It is a lot more comprehensive, particularly with regard to non-tariff barriers. For free trade in services, ASEAN must still do some groundwork, particularly in Mode 3 of service supply, because of its lack of rules of origin.

In addition to the liquidity financing, the ASEAN has also enabled setting up a regional policy dialogue and a surveillance mechanism to thwart any capital account crises and subsequent contagion. What was interesting that the liquidity financing these regional partners provided was significantly higher than what the IMF agreed to lend. While the funds provided by the IMF to Indonesia, the Republic of Korea and Thailand during the crisis were to the tune of US$111.7 billion, the international reserves held by the members of the Chiang Mai Initiative (CMI) were at the time about US$700 billion.

Asian Integration—Issues, Status and Developments

Regional financial integration initiatives (for emerging East Asia-China, Hong Kong, India, Korea, Taiwan, Singapore, Indonesia, Malaysia, the Philippines and Thailand) towards an Asian Monetary Fund (AMF), including the CMI (establishing swap facilities of about $70 billion between the region's central banks to pool resources against a speculative attack), Asian Currency Union, evolution of the East Asia Economic Community, Asian Bond Fund (ABF1 for investing part of the forex reserves in Asian sovereign bonds and ABF2, a new asset class), may be considered as the precursors in the direction of a global initiative. Asian Currency Unit (ACU), which would help track the relative values of Asian currencies, is being modelled on the European Currency Union (ECU). Further, a common market (CM) and a monetary union are policy goals set by the members of the GCC for which assessments are going on.

The post-crisis decade has been the harbinger of deepening regional integration in Asia reflected in intra-regional trade now accounting for close to 50 per cent of Asia's trade. These efforts corroborate the fact that necessity is the mother of innovation and regionalism may be construed as the new-found innovation by Asia to step ahead in terms of development. While the integration of Asian financial markets with the global financial system is well advanced, intra-regional financial integration has considerably lagged. An IMF working paper (Ananchotikul, Piao and Zoli 2015) discusses some reasons which are holding back Asia's intra-regional financial integration. The paper based on a gravity model argues that the increase in bilateral financial integration reflects increased capital account openness, depth and sophistication of the financial systems and trade integration. The paper finds informational asymmetries, barriers to foreign bank penetration and differences in regulatory and institutional quality as the extant obstacles to greater financial integration. It further concludes that the measures to foster further regional financial integration in Asia could be through increased trade integration and capital market development, reduction of restrictions on cross-border capital flows and foreign bank entry and harmonization of regulations. There are also certain areas where regulatory differences still persist which include investor protection, contract enforcement and bankruptcy procedures. There are other risks which may emanate from greater foreign investor participation in the domestic market and developing financial markets which may raise several regulatory and supervisory challenges requiring cross-border supervision and policy coordination. Further, the regional safety nets, including the Chiang Mai Initiative Multilateralization (CMIM), would help mitigate the impact of capital flow volatility.

Further, the deepening and interlinking of the various financial markets in the region may promote containment of capital account and various other vulnerabilities. A 'virtuous (and growth-boosting) cycle in which larger intra-regional capital flows facilitate the expansion of intra-regional trade–and vice versa' could be a practical possibility. These ideas are ingrained in the ASEAN+3 roadmap to develop a regional bond market and the Chiang Mai network of swap arrangements to support exchange rate stability in the region. The motivation for the inevitability of a sub-regional economic integration in the South Asian landscape initially was to complement the efforts of other unions in the Asian region.

The regional matrix need not be country-based, it could also be sub-region based. Combinations of countries could become homogeneous units on specific areas in a Pareto-optimal fashion and then move on to inter-sub-region coordination to get finally transformed into a regional union. This may have least political cost while bearing the benefits of helping attempts towards international surveillance mechanisms as catalytic addendums.

As mentioned earlier, a significant step towards stronger regional coordination in crisis prevention was taken through the CMI in 2010. The CMIM was formed by merging the various existing bilateral swap agreements. It covered 10 ASEAN countries plus China, Japan and South Korea. A surveillance unit for the CMIM—the ASEAN+3 Macroeconomic Research Office (AMRO)—was also created in 2011 to 'monitor and analyze regional economies and to contribute to early detection of risks, swift implementation of remedial actions and effective decision-making of the CMIM'. In July 2014, Brazil, Russia, India, China and South Africa (BRICS) signed the treaty establishing BRICS Contingent Reserve Arrangement, Registered Futures Association (RFA) which is endowed with $100 billion capital and is composed of multilateral swap lines akin to those of the CMIM.

The Eurasian Fund for Stabilization and Development (EFSD, previously known as Anti-Crisis Fund of the Eurasian Economic Community) was founded in July 2009 by Armenia, Belarus, Kazakhstan, Kyrgyz Republic, Russia and Tajikistan. Uniquely financed by members' capital contributions, the EFSD has a total lending capacity of $8.5 billion; both Tajikistan and Belarus have got benefited from this regional facility.

However, despite all efforts, according to the World Bank, South Asia continues to be among the least integrated regions in terms of trade in the world. The factors restraining regional integration can be listed as follows:

- High trade costs and investment restrictions
- Insufficient policy-relevant analytical work on gains of regional integration in both trade and investment to make informed policy decisions
- Sceptical mindset from previous failures in regional cooperation, misinformation and lack of vocal champions for regional cooperation
- Relative asymmetry in size among the South Asian countries
- Historical political tensions, mistrust, cross-border conflicts and security concerns
- Limited transport connectivity, logistics and regulatory impediments

Economic integration is further increased on account of increased trust and people-to-people interaction. Even though it is evident that a greater momentum of regional integration is seen being built in recent years, more is required to be done. With regional integration, a key part of its strategy, the World Bank Group is supporting 'One South Asia' through a twofold programme.

Twin Objectives of the Programme

The twin objectives of the programme are as follows:

- Lending and technical assistance for the creation of opportunities that would help enhance trade and investment linkages in South Asia towards ASEAN levels
- Shaping the narrative for supporting a more informed policy debate and dialogue on specific regional trade and investment themes in South Asia—cross-cutting pillar of South Asian regional integration strategy

The issue of South Asian landscape (India, Pakistan, Sri Lanka, Bangladesh and Nepal) organizing themselves into a compact sub-region has been the most controversial despite the fact that these economies belong to the historical undivided Indian subcontinent. In order to have a realistic and non-rhetorical line of action in this direction for South Asia, in particular, and the others therein, in general, it would be imperative to look at certain issues microscopically. What should be the ideal composition of countries to facilitate a state of 'homogeny' rather than 'hegemony' would be the initial point of focus. Study of economic interdependence, shared vulnerabilities to external shocks, natural disasters, systemic risks out of financial innovations, possibilities of trade and FDI integration and also potentials and economics for growth triangles is required.

Being closer to each other in technological, geographic and perhaps in cultural terms, which may encourage an efficient sourcing and assimilation of technology, formation of growth triangle/s in the region offering a contiguous area for investment, a pool of all the complementary demographic benefits and an investment zone with a concentration of infrastructural facilities, minimal regulations/restrictions could be a viable idea worth pondering over. This would prevent them to compete among each other in extending fiscal incentives in a war for more FDI, thus offsetting the negative externalities of such moves and preventing losing out heavily in terms of benefits from the FDI apart from gaining the ability to affect sophisticated technological upgradation in their production structure relatively easily.

For inter-regional bloc relationship, its potentials with China, Southeast Asia and Japan as distinct sub-regional bloc may be an idea worth pondering over. Closer ties among these South Asian economies in trade and investment flows as a bloc and correspondingly of this bloc with other blocs will be quite beneficial. It would help better resource mobilization within the Asian region, if Indian subcontinent presents itself as a single unit offering optimum economies of scale. China and South Asia, if configured in terms of their trade and investment needs complementarities, together could be a potentially powerful bloc in terms of economic gains and power of trade bargaining.

ASEAN economies had started off with this kind of a trading strategy for better gains from Japan initially and other global trading partners eventually to become an 'economic power bloc' popularly called as the Tigers. With China and Japan being 'blocs' themselves, it would be persuasive for the Indian subcontinent to homogenize its areas of strength to contain avoidable wastage of both efforts and resources due to trading strategies essentially competing rather complementing each other. This bloc had a history of a substantial share in the World GDP through trade in 1700s and 1800s. While colonial plunder reduced their wealth considerably, a post-colonial political partition has prevented them to think in terms of the possible opportunity gains that could be lurking should they attempt to revive, if not a full-fledged economic bloc, at least, a trading and investment-oriented outlook of economic policymaking. Recent years have seen certain realization in this line having unfolded in the corridors of political power culminated in the signing of South Asian Free Trade Area (SAFTA), and it is the time to analyse the tangible economic benefits so that it would be easier to translate them into realities. But, all these hypotheses, not withstanding, are serious issues for debate and discussion.

Even though there seems to be some serious border conflict between China and India, such as the latest in Doklam and in Arunachal Pradesh, political convergence within the contours of economic bilateralism may not be that difficult. Their common aspirations to get back to their past glory as major economic powers have encouraged them to come closer in understanding, while eyeing on the first slot will leave them with a spirit of constant constructive rivalry. That may fetch the lever for political balance, which will erase the mistrust of the other much smaller members for either of them. The ultimate goal of benefitting from financial globalization and preventing themselves from possible systemic risks will force them to remain together by compulsion if not 'by hearts'. Both China and India have become important markets for each other particularly in India with a slew of China-manufactured products making a beeline.

There are potential points for mutual benefit. China's financial sector and also economic institutions are weak compared to those of India. Chinese are masters in computer hardware, Indians are in software. India has world-class entrepreneurship, China has an abundant supply of hardworking and unskilled/skilled manpower. Both are distress-lending their excess dollar reserves to the USA. And so on and so forth. They need not only strategies of coordination towards either fine-tuning or joint formulation of policy, they should rather remain mutually aware of policy interactions and strive to arrive at mutually compatible medium-term strategies, and internationally consistent responses to short-term divergences. They need to pursue a line of 'cooperation' rather than 'coordination' to imbibe the ability to adjust to what the market might do. This way, the sub-region will feed the impulse required by the Asian region to be an effective spoke in the wheels of the renewed framework of international cooperation. And this will result in 'the creation of a more stable framework of expectations that might diminish the impact of the shocks in financial markets....' (Kato 2005).

The following information on the top five exports from the region to the USA is worthwhile to see in this behalf.

	China	India	Bangladesh	Pakistan
1	Consumer goods	Consumer goods	Consumer goods	Consumer goods
2	Machinery and electricals	Intermediate goods	Textiles and clothing	Textiles and clothing
3	Capital goods	Stone and glass	Footwear	Intermediate goods
4	Miscellaneous and clothing	Textiles and clothing	Raw materials intermediate goods	Miscellaneous and skins
5	Textiles and clothing goods	Chemicals	Intermediate goods	Capital goods

Source: World Bank statistics (Latest Available as on 6 March 2019).

Given the characteristics of these products, it would be conceivable to think in terms of making regional hubs by way of relocation of sites and diversion/pooling of resources together. For example, a regional hub covering a 50-km radius around Singapore including much of the southern Malaysian state of Tohore and handful of Indonesian islands off the coast of Sumatra can be created which can pool each other's factor endowments together for cost-effective production for growth. Investor will use Singapore as their hi-tech base to design market and distribute products made in low-cost factories in the neighbouring economies. Similar such ideas of triangles are seen while linking (a) the Philippines' southern island of Mindanao with Sulawesi in Indonesia and the Malaysian bits of Borneo and (b) southern Thailand with four Malaysian states and northern Sumatra in Indonesia. The process of relocation of industries and the spillover of better production know-how therefrom have made the people of Thailand to move out of paddy fields into mills so as to gain in terms of productivity without increase in skills. Thais have perfected the art of de-assembling other products and to reassemble them into better and cheaper products.

In a union encompassing vastly dissimilar members in terms of size, with limited labour mobility, some capital mobility, colonial history, attitude of mutual mistrust, with one partner (India) quite dominant, there appears to be a need for higher sensitivity towards the position of the smaller countries, which may be unlikely. Thanks to it being a source of supply shocks and that because of its dominant position, the other three countries will have to adjust. Accordingly,

> for the costs of forming a monetary union to be small, the within group cyclical correlations must approach unity and the shocks must have roughly equal variances. [T]he costs for each country will be at least one standard deviation larger than the adjustment costs which that country would have faced with floating exchange rates. A currency union will not come cheap…. (Welfens 1997)

There could be substantial benefits from a closer union in terms of a more efficient structure and production patterns based on competition. However, Chaplygin, Hughes-Hallett and Richter (2006) argue that the larger economies may, simply on account of their geographical spread, natural resource base and sheer economic size get a lower risk premium, thus making it difficult for the smaller states to develop new competitive industries. Thus, there could also be the possibility that the smaller nations, in addition to the typically small gains from reduced transactions costs, lower barriers, economies of scale and increased efficiency through competitiveness might gain considerably from importing the financial market benefits of the bigger economy's diversification and strength. This is clearly the case for India with its considerable geographical spread, natural resource base and sheer economic size.

South Asian and Southeast Asian economic integration through improved trade flows has been increasing considerably over the past two decades, but the level of trade remains relatively lower. The economic integration has played a very important role in the past economic success of South Asia and Southeast Asia and is important for future growth as well. But the question is whether these two outward-oriented regions have integrated well with each other and whether they are able to tap the synergies of such integration. Prior to 1990, there was very less discussion regarding the inter-regional economic integration for South and Southeast Asian economies. The solitary trade agreement covering the two regions was the 1975 Bangkok Agreement that included India, Sri Lanka, Bangladesh, Lao People's Democratic Republic, the Republic of Korea and the People's Republic of China. Bilateral trade and investment among these countries was very less. But the Look East policy adopted by India in 1991 and greater focus on outward orientation marked the beginning of a new phase in the economic relations of South and Southeast Asia. Since then, the process of inter-regional integration has seen heightened policy interest in this area.

The Latin America–North America Intra-Region Integration: Significant Scope of Improvement

The economic integration in the American continent was believed to fructify with the formation of a single currency named the 'Amero'. However, it didn't take off. Another attempt was made through the establishment of a South American Community of Nations, comprising member states of the Mercosur (Brazil, Argentina, Uruguay and Paraguay) and the Andean Community, for formulating a single currency on the similar lines as the Euro. However, due to inherent contradictions and by the presence of the USA as the behemoth, the progress in this regard remains grim.

The Pacific Alliance (officially launched by Chile, Colombia, Mexico and Peru in June 2012) had emerged as one of the leading economic integration projects in Latin America. There was an assessment regarding an economic cooperation agenda in response to the failed FTAA with a move to end the destructive cycle of investment treaties and replace it with an alternative economic structure that better respects the sovereignty of nation states (Gabriel 2013).

Faltering growth after the GFC has also made the Latin American countries search for new drivers of growth Lanau (2017).

> Traditional measures of economic integration, such as trade openness, do not capture the complexity of interactions between trade partners and make it more difficult to parse various dimensions of connectivity. We, therefore, turn to the rapidly developing literature on networks (e.g. Barabási 2016; and Newman 2003) to disentangle the sources of integration, explore their network and growth effects, and understand how central the region is in the growing world trade networks (WTN).

The presence of the large localized behemoths such as Mexico and Brazil has appeared to be a hindrance to the cooperation among the LACs. This leaves significant scope for larger countries to position themselves for a more central role in the regional subnetwork and boost regional integration. The paper further finds that LAC countries are relatively well integrated in terms of links to diversified markets, but the strength of those links is weak.

The African Safari for Regional Integration

Regional integration in Africa region was initiated through a political federation West African Economic and Monetary Union (also known by its French-language acronym UEMOA) established in 1994 mainly by the French-speaking countries in French West Africa, and was intended to counterbalance the dominance of English-speaking economies in the bloc (such as Nigeria and Ghana). Similarly, in 2004 in East Africa, an East African Customs Union protocol was signed. The UEMOA has also been formed which is an organization of eight, mainly French speaking, states within the Economic Community of West African States (ECOWAS) and are sharing a customs union (CU) and currency union.

Another feature of African unity is evident through the existence of regional economic communities (RECs), which are regional groupings of African states. These had been formed with a purpose to facilitate regional economic integration between members of the individual regions and through the wider African Economic Community (AEC), established under the Abuja Treaty (1991). This has been formed as a development to the 1980 Lagos Plan of Action for the Development of Africa, and the Abuja Treaty proposed the creation of RECs as the basis for wider African integration, with a view of regional and eventual continental integration.[2] The following are the various RECs in Africa:

- CEN-SAD: Community of Sahel-Saharan States
- COMESA: Common Market for Eastern and Southern Africa
- EAC: East African Community
- ECCAS: Economic Community of Central African States
- ECOWAS: Economic Community of West African States
- IGAD: Intergovernmental Authority on Development
- SADC: Southern African Development Community
- UMA: Arab Maghreb Union

Even though the formation of these regional integration communities has led to exceptionally strong economic growth and performance, it has not resulted in significant and commensurate declines in poverty levels or such commensurate job creation. The main contributors to the same may be on account of low intra-African trade, limited integration and infrastructure connectedness. What needs to be done

---

[2] Source: African Union.

is an acceleration of efforts towards continental integration, boost intra-African trade and improve connectivity through infrastructure development.[3]

Economic Regionalism to Monetary Unions

The main distinguishing factor of a monetary union from a real union is the fact that in a monetary union, only a common currency is accepted as a single currency, that is, a common monetary authority, while a real union encompasses the integration of goods, capital and labour markets among two or more countries belonging to the same geographic area as measured at a given point of time. It depends on the degree of interpenetration of economic activity (includes both real sector [trade, labour mobility] and financial sector [financial flows and exchange rate developments]). It could also include fiscal harmonization and the synchronization of business cycles. Institutional integration is an intrinsic part of this process, which refers to mobilization of cooperation in the matter of deepening and/or widening the spheres of intergovernmental agreements on sectoral cooperation to EMUs with transfer of sovereignty to supranational institutions.

There are strong motivations to transform economic regionalism to grow into monetary unions, including in particular, a reduction of transactions costs and efficiency savings on all exchanges and investments within the group (simulation results in a study by IMF working paper [Tahari et al. 2007] for the European Commission found that the cost of equity and bond financing could fall across Europe by about 50 basis points each), such a structure tends to recoup what all are generally accused to be sacrificed at the national level, namely monetary monopoly or even political sovereignty. In a monetary union set-up, authority is not given up. Rather it is shared and collectively managed by the countries involved. While it obviates the possibility for nations to take unilateral decisions, every nation has a say in the combined decision-making process. In this process, all the participating nations gain as a monetary union acts like a cartel to improve

[3] Ibid.

the market position of its members, thereby being advantageous as compared to the situation of having individual currencies.

In the background of the recent GFC which has brought forth the importance of financial stability, countries are exploring ways of mitigating the impact of external shocks without inhibiting the internationalization process. This has led to calls for monetary union arrangements on a regional basis, and in fact, several parts of the world in Africa, Asia and Latin America have seen initiatives in this direction. While the slower trend in this direction in earlier years was reflective of the overwhelming political inclination in favour of national sovereignty even at the cost of economic welfare, the current positive inkling is motivated by the potential for collective bargaining power for better economic gains they carry. It also carries hopes for reduced social costs of access as it projects scope for better economies of scale. Financial integration fetches better diversification and sharing of risk, thus fulfilling the conditions for the optimality of a currency area. It promises better resource mobilization and allocation from the current 'global financial hub', which Asian economies are discovering lately as they (8 out of 12) do not have even a threshold size of bond investment of US\$100 billion individually 'that would tend to be required for a deep and liquid government bond market' (Gyntelberg, Ma and Remolona 2005). While it boosts opportunities for diversifying investments, it improves the ability to absorb intra-regional and external shocks and hence strengthens the stability and resilience of the economic system.

The benefits from the integration of European bonds and equity markets have been observed to be around 1 per cent of GDP growth over a 10-year period or approximately €100 billion Trichet 2006. It has been evidenced that the EMU member countries disproportionately invest in one another relative to other destinations and more interestingly, at the aggregate level, it is those countries physically closest to the Euro area that are both the most important destinations and sources for external bond investment vis-à-vis the Euro area. This may be the reason why EMU has had a substantial impact on global bond portfolios. This also lends support to the notion that financial globalization is not a uniform process and that financial regionalization is, at least now, a relatively stronger force (Lane 2005).

Regional Integration

What should be the ideal roadmap for an 'integration' into a monetary union to take shape has been a topic of debate in the last few decades. While Europe has experimented with this 'transformation' during the last few decades, others are trying to learn from its experience. What essentially we can learn from Europe's experience is the fact that there have been consistent efforts leading the way to formation of Euro currency. Since its foundation in the 1950s, EU members have continuously reduced their internal barriers to trade and factor movements parallel to lowering external barriers to trade. In short, the old colonial phrase saying that 'trade follows the flag' was reversed in the sense that the flag followed trade. The four-classical stages of integration (free trade area [FTA], CU, CM and economic union [EUN]) were made public and a credible plan with these as medium-term targets was formed. Further, the harmonization and removal of risk premiums across the region were achieved through continuous cooperation and removal of impediments through legislation.

The experience from Europe suggests that a monetary union can be achieved while the process of political integration is on. It will take time for nations to build consensus for giving up power over their own monetary policy and to accept to be bound by fiscal rules. If countries find at least some advantage of such integration, they would find desirable and have the political will to follow through on such arrangements.

The best narration of such a process as quoted by Mongelli, Dorruci and Agur (2005) was by Bela Balassa (1961) who had identified the following five main stages of regional integration:

- *Stage 1. FTA:* An area where tariffs and quota are abolished for imports from area members, which, however, retain national tariffs and quotas against third countries.

- *Stage 2. CU:* An FTA setting up common tariffs and quotas (if any) for trade with non-members.
- *Stage 3. CM:* A CU abolishing non-tariff barriers to trade (i.e., promoting the integration of product and service markets) as well as restriction on factor movement (i.e., promoting the integration of capital and labour markets).
- *Stage 4. EUN:* A CM with a significant degree of coordination of national economic policies and/or harmonization of relevant domestic laws.
- *Stage 5. Total Economic Integration (TEI):* An EUN with all relevant economic policies conducted at the supranational level, possibly in compliance with the principle of subsidiarity. To this aim, both supranational authorities and supranational laws need to be in place.

But it may also be pointed out that there is nothing sacrosanct about such a definitive stages-based transformation. An Optimum Currency Union Area (OCU) may not necessarily be a precondition for monetary union; it may also be its by-product. It helps developing the financial system towards greater and more sustainable non-inflationary growth. The positive impact on potential output via trade and financial integration, as well as the experience with currency unions, has raised optimism on the possibility of a country joining a currency union even before full integration is achieved (Sanchez 2005). The causal link between institutional integration and trade deepening before currency union may also matter and it runs both ways, although the link from institutional integration to trade deepening is far more pronounced. This has been verified in the case of ECU and could be applied to the institutional arrangements in other regions of the world (e.g., Latin America, East Asia and sub-Saharan Africa). Referring to 'endogeneity of Optimum Currency Union (OCU)', the financial and economic integration of which is a resultant of both monetary union and regional institutional integration as a generalized trend, has benefited the European integration (Mongelli et al. 2005). Though 'market integration has been furthered by the single currency and the stability-oriented monetary policy' (Draghi 2006) in Europe, tangible steps towards money market/liquidity management (TARGET settlement system), government securities market (common platform MTS), investment funds, Undertakings for Collective Investments in transferable securities (UCITS). Essentially, UCITS[4] template was also taken in consonance. Financial Services Action Plan, a large, deep and well-functioning Euro bond market, a common European framework rules for accounting, prospectus, capital adequacy, market abuse, transparency and investment services, Single Euro Payments area by 2010, new legal framework for payments, etc., are few other steps as ingredients of a holistic approach towards integration.

As is well known, an optimal degree of economic integration within a region hinges on a substantial degree of financial integration. While it is not easy to prescribe a one-size-fits-all set of actions in this direction, an illustrative bunch of action points are ventured here. Needless to reiterate, they are not in order of priority nor the list is exhaustive but would warrant sufficient emphasis depending on the level of sophistication that the economies in the proposed region have already accomplished in the respective area of action. 'But they must have a few things in common: let competition work; let businesses innovate; let capital find the best opportunities' (Draghi 2006). The aim should be for a well-designed cross-border consolidation that can prevent suboptimal functioning in the financial sector and encourage emergence of business leaders in the world league (Draghi 2006).

- Harmonizing national infrastructure, laws and regulation as well as integrating clearing and settlement and post-trading systems.
- Creating an integrated financial market by way of relaxing statutory restrictions on cross-border capital flows with concurrent steps to evolve risk management systems to meet any unforeseeable contingencies that it might give way to. A mechanism of regional/international regulatory/supervisory edifice would be a crying need. It would be to address, on an ongoing basis, issues relating to currency mismatches, exchange rate fluctuations and credit risks arising from cross-jurisdictional branches/subsidiaries as also business cycles.

---

[4] These are investment funds regulated by the European Union.

- Upgrading supervisory capacity in a coordinated manner based on increased reliance on market discipline, embedding risk sensitivity study in prudential regulation measures and recognizing the complex two-way relationship between monetary and financial stability.
- Chipping in coordinated efforts towards homogenization of financial institutions and infrastructure across the region. Audit and accounting practices, reconciliation procedures, insolvency/bankruptcy arrangements, corporate governance standards, etc., need to be thought of under a comprehensive approach.
- Relaxing non-supervisory restrictions against access by foreign financial intermediaries to the domestic financial markets to usher in competition, hence better efficiency.
- Integrating capital markets towards popularizing use of novel financial products.
- Integrating retail financial markets by way of establishing a homogenous set of rules for provision of consumer credit.
- Establishing linkages between jurisdictions across the whole spectrum of financial infrastructure.
- Harmonizing international codes and standards, and implementing them across the regional financial system to improve investor confidence as also to enrich the flow of capital in the region.

In his speech on 16 November 2017 (de Galhau 2017) on the topic 'Economic Union, Financing Union, Banking Union' in Amsterdam, Mr François Villeroy de Galhau, the Governor of the Bank of France, suggested that to make progress on EUN, there is a need to trigger four accelerators: a macro-accelerator with a collective economic strategy; a micro-accelerator for Financing Union for Investment and Innovation; a fiscal accelerator with common area budget; and the fourth could be processes for facilitating the first three in terms of institutional support.

Conclusion

The regional integration process can be considered fully complete only if both the economic and monetary components are developed. Even in the case of the EU, the Economic and Monetary Union (EMU) is incomplete. While the role of the ECB demonstrates that 'monetary' component of the EMU has been achieved, the 'economic' component has still to catch up. The incomplete integration at the EU level is hindering its ability to fully support not only the monetary policy of the Euro areas, but also the individual countries' economic policies. There is a requirement of strong political will among member countries and institutions to strengthen EMU architecture. The governance of EU financial services has progressed from the individual country level to the European level with internationalization of capital. Experience from the European sovereign debt crisis also revealed that the supra-national regulation of financial services can be considered the best solution to deal with these challenges.

References

Almekinders, Geert, Satoshi Fukuda, Alex Mourmouras and Jianping Zhou. 2015, February. 'ASEAN Financial Integration'. IMF Working Paper No. WP/15/13. Washington, DC: International Monetary Fund.

Ananchotikul, Nasha, Shi Piao and Edda Zoli. 2015, June. 'Drivers of Financial Integration—Implications for Asia'. IMF Working Paper WP/15/160. Washington, DC: International Monetary Fund.

Bremmer, Ian. 2012. *Every Nation for Itself: What happens when No one Leads the World.* Penguin Publishers.

Chaplygin, V., A. Hughes-Hallett and C. Richter. 2006. 'Monetary Integration in the Ex-Soviet Union: A "Union of Four"'. *Economics of Transition* 14 (1): 47–68.

Chirathivat, Suthiphand and Piti Srisangnam. 2013, April. 'The 2030 Architecture of Association of Southeast Asian Nations Free Trade Agreements'. 16. ADBI Working Paper Series: The 2030 Architecture of Association of Southeast Asian Nations Free Trade Agreements, Suthiphand Chirathivat and Piti Srisangnam, No. 419, April 2013. Tokyo: Asian Development Bank Institute.

Cohen, Benjamin J. 2003. 'Monetary Governance in a Globalized World'. In Goddard, Cronin and Dash (Ed) International Political Economy: State-Market Relations in a Changing Global Order.

de Galhau, François Villeroy. 2017, 16 November. 'Economic Union, Financing Union, Banking Union'. Speech at the Annual General Meeting of the Foreign Bankers' Association, Amsterdam.

Draghi, Mario. 2006. 'Financial Market Integration and the Intermediation of Savings'. Speech at the 12th Congress AIAF–ASSIOM–ATIC FOREX, 4 March. Cagliari.

Gabriele, Galati and Richhild Moessner. 2013. *Macroprudential Policy – A Literature Review. Journal of Economic Surveys* 27 (5): 846–878.

Gyntelberg, Jacob, Guonan Ma and Eli M. Remolona. 2005. 'Corporate Bond Markets in Asia'. *BIS Quarterly Review* (December).

Hausmann, Ricardo. 1999. 'Should There Be Five Currencies or One Hundred and Five?' *Foreign Policy*, 116 (Fall).

James, Harold. 1996, 15 June. *International Monetary Cooperation Since Bretton Woods.* IMF.

Lanau, Sergi. 2017. The Growth Return of Infrastructure in Latin America. IMF Working Paper No. 17/35, 14 February.

Lane, Philip R. 2006. 'Global Bond Portfolios and EMU'. IIIS Discussion Paper No. 168, June.

Levine, Gregg. 2015. US treasury secretary in China on eve of Asia bank deadline. The Scrutineer, 30 March.

Mongelli, Francesco Paolo, Ettore Dorrucci and Itai Agur. 2005. 'What Does European Institutional Integration Tell Us about Trade Integration?' ECB Occasional Paper Series No. 40. Frankfurt: European Central Bank.

O'Neill, Jim. 2015. US-UK friction over China is unwarranted. Project Syndicate, 18 March.

Sánchez Marcelo (2005), Is Time Ripe for a Currency Union in Emerging East Asia? The Role of Monetary Stabilisation, ECB Working Paper Series No. 567 / December.

Sohn, Injoo. 2015. AIIB: A Plank in China's Hedging Strategy. Available at https://www.brookings.edu/opinions/aiib-a-plank-in-chinas-hedging-strategy/ (accessed on 15 April 2019).

Stephens, Philip. 2015. Why the Business of Risk Is Booming? *Financial Times*, 12 March.

Stiglitz, Joseph E. 2015. Asia's multilateralism. Project Syndicate, 13 April.

Tahari, Amor, Patricia Brenner, Erik Der Vrijer, Marina Moretti, Abdelhak Senhadji, Gabriel Sensenbrenner and Juan Sole. 2007, May. 'Financial Sector Reforms and Prospects for Financial Integration in Maghreb Countries'. IMF Working Paper WP/07/125.

Trichet, Jean-Claude (2006), *The Process of European Financial Integration: Where do We Stand?* Speech at the campus for Finance 2006, WHU Otto Beisheim School of Management, Vallender, 13 January.

Venner, K. Dwight. 2002, 16–17 September. 'How Can Monetary Policy Be Conducted in the Union?' Conference on Challenges to Central banking from Globalized Financial Systems at IMF, Washington, DC.

Welfens, Paul J. J. (ed.). 1997. *European Monetary Union: Transition, International Impact and Policy Options.* Springer.

CHAPTER 9

New Approaches to International Policy Coordination

There are various approaches to achieving the international financial stability coordination architecture. The prerequisite is to start with integrating real economies and moving towards integrating the monetary authority, financial services regulator, governance framework, payment system and financial technology infrastructure. This coordination can be initiated with global financial stability councils, international monetary systems (IMSs) and a global central bank. The policy coordination can be successful if the member countries are adequately represented and the benefits are reaped by them equally.

Introduction

There are several approaches and theories about achieving a GMFS policy coordination. In this chapter, we would focus upon the various theories about transiting towards global integration. Given the current state of institutional development concerning regional financial integration and capital controls constrained financial market integration, strong political support would be the necessary motivator to push regional integration efforts forward. This includes efforts towards increasing intra-regional trade, more synchronized business cycles, financial market integration, nominal convergence and financial and investment interdependence as these reinforce each other over time, resulting eventually in deeper economic integration. Considerable discord exists in the present structure which is seen to be fragile as, time and again, the nationalist notions have emerged and taken steps backwards towards individualistic approaches. To overcome these limitations, regional financial cooperation mechanisms will have to be evolved while shaping monetary and exchange rate policies. A multitrack approach towards strengthening liquidity provision mechanisms, enhanced economic surveillance systems, multilateralization, exchange rate policy coordination and joint activation of the currency swap arrangements would also have to be followed. Part A of the discussion covers some of the prerequisites towards evolving a GMFS policy coordination, and Part B covers the various approaches to achieve this.

PART A

The Prerequisites

Building a Regional Bloc

The major issue is the choice of membership for an effective configuration of the 'pool' or 'club' of countries. A major role is played by historical and cultural affinity which is quite evident with the European integration taking place despite diversity. However, this affinity may not be sufficient to ensure the integration as in the case of Latin America which did not move further regardless of the said affinity. The 'trade-off between diversification benefits and monitoring costs' is an essential element for such considerations. A 'club in club' structure involving a limited number of countries with the objective of sharing macroeconomic risks as they emanate has been the most popular in this direction. As regard to the current time, international arrangements such as the CMI, the Latin American Reserve Fund (FLAR) or networks of bilateral swap arrangements among the G10 in the 1960s–1970s and among the European countries during the run-up to the establishment of the Euro are few pooling arrangements.

A study by the IMF (Working Paper June 2007) emphasizes that the sizable welfare gains from pooling risks among countries can deliver results. The membership should remain low as 'marginal gains decline quickly for groups beyond six or seven members' and the eligibility criteria of members for pooling could range from heterogeneity in economic and business cycle characteristics to geographical congruity and income level as also the quality of institutions and debt crystallization record.

No doubt, such a bloc will depend on political homogeny besides potentials of benefits likely to accrue to all. The ideal size that will optimize benefits from the arrangements will remain a crucial issue. Accordingly, a bloc should leave enough scope for its horizontal expansion in terms of incremental joining members to act 'as a building bloc toward multilateral freeing of trade' (Albertin 2007), and hence to enhance possibilities of both competitive and comparative advantages in the business of trade. A bloc professing to remain stagnant in terms of membership will be devoid of the evolving scope for such advantages and hence will act as a 'stumbling bloc to the goal of multilateralism' (Albertin 2007).

What should be an optimum size in this will hinge on the equilibrium of political forces that remain on either side of the idea of the creation of such a bloc. The enlargement of the bloc beyond a certain size, labelled as the 'supply-side implied maximum size', will surely be discouraged as it would amount to breach of the contours of political consensus. Till this limit, whoever demands for membership will get granted. Thus, 'the equilibrium size of the regional trading bloc cannot exceed but could be smaller than its supply-side implied maximum size'. 'Higher degree of regionalization is more likely where states are small, economic and political linkages are strong, and domestic politics is heavily influenced by tradable-goods producers and financial interests' (Kahler and Lake 2003).

Regional/Global Money

Polar opposite to the idea of Hayekian private currency, postulation of a single global currency is gathering momentum. This would be a monetary translation of deepening economic integration. Euro is beginning to show the feasibility of a single currency in multinational framework. Mundell had advocated a composite global currency, initially backed by gold combining the euro, dollar and the yen and could be termed as 'geo'. This would be facilitated by creating a single clearing and settlement system built on the RTGS adopted by all major central banks and the TARGET system of the ECB. While with a 'world currency', the number of independent central banks will be reduced, there will be difficult issues emerging relating to the instrument/s that super central bank will require to use and how it will be controlled.

> As a result of proliferation of currencies and a renewed emphasis on price stability, the sanctity of 'one country one money' has come into question. As the number of countries increases, their average size decreases, and the volume of international transactions rises. As a result, more and more countries will find it profitable to give up their independent currency. As the number of countries increases, the number of currencies may not only increase less than proportionately but may even fall. This result highlights an important empirical implication of this model. An increase in the number of countries—such as the one seen in the post-World war II period—implies an increase in number of countries adopting other countries' currencies. (Alsenia and Barro 2002)

Trend of the emergence of local currency unions, a form of medium of exchange that is used by a community for their convenience, has already set in. Local exchange trading system (LETS) is one of the most well-known forms of local currency where a group of people usually residing within the same geographic community joins a formal system for keeping track of the value of goods and services exchanged between the members of the group. An accounting system is evolved to keep track of people's contributions and withdrawals, and a registry is maintained that enables people to find the goods and services they seek. This started in Canada in the early 1980s (by Michael Linton) but has since spread across the USA, Australia, New Zealand and the UK. With recent emergence of digital signature and the Internet, it is possible to envision LETS to spread beyond geographic communities.

Electronic currencies are changing the form of conventional national currencies (smart card, e-purse, etc.). More importantly, it is also creating new kinds of currencies. Complementary currencies have emerged. They do not challenge legal tender status of national currencies, but create new opportunities for payment innovations as they complement the functions of conventional currencies. Japan addresses elderly care crisis with 350 health care currency systems since 1995. China has also started that. Over 2,000 complementary currency systems create local work in over a dozen countries. In Ithaca, New York, HOUR system created by Paul Glover is a US$10 bill. These HOUR notes, in four denominations, buy plumbing, carpentry and thousands of other goods and services. The local credit union accepts them for mortgages and loan fees. People pay rent using HOURs. Eco-money projects creating work by preventing actions against ecological disasters. Together these complementary currencies can provide safety net under conventional monetary systems.

An International Integrated Financial Services Regulator (IIFSR)

Financial innovations were meant to circumvent the 'world of finance' from avoidable risk. Globalization was meant to catalyse this process through geographical diversification. However, thanks to the lack of synergy among people and processes, both financial innovations and globalization are manifesting themselves in an ugly form. The questions remain: How do we handle this conundrum? The answer to this is simply creating a synergy among the nations in a calibrated manner. If the global architecture has helped financial risks to proliferate rather than diversify, then revisiting the very same architecture will fetch its solution as well. This line of thinking is in sync with medical innovations. Through the innovation of penicillin, bacteria were used to kill bacteria. Vaccine for rabies is made of saliva of mad dogs. Snake venom is used to cure snakebites. It may hence be apt to take the position that interconnection among nations will cure the evils that it has given birth to. But the interconnection needs to be synergistically hierarchical in a 'bottom-up' manner. Nations may connect themselves as sub-regions, sub-regions as regions and eventually regions as global.

Such a global synergy based on global cooperation would look for 'the globally optimal set of monetary policy rules' (Engel 2015) to avoid 'unconventional policies with large adverse spillovers and questionable domestic benefits' (Rajan 2014a, 2014b), which could be found in an 'optimal design of a cooperative agreement' (Engel 2015). This could address the resurgence of the ugly 'beggar-thy-neighbour' policies manifested in competitive devaluations or even 'gamed' oil price declines. Such a goal of optimal policy cooperation would mean bringing all concerned to the table and derive a set of solutions in the best interests of all. The design should meet the real ethos of democracy so that necessary momentum and urgency can be generated to internalize a greater portion of the negative effects of spillovers. It will also encourage the general spirit of managing systemic risk of the global whole. The coordination mechanism should be able to inculcate a sense to 'compensate potential losers or even those countries that stand to gain less than others' (Engel 2015) so that most of the constituents should gain.

This alignment and coordinating body could be in the nature of a 'neutral assessor playing a useful role in helping to bridge the divergent views of national policy makers' (Ostry and Ghosh 2013). But such a mechanism needs to have inherent characteristics to reflect 'credibility and neutrality of the assessor' so much so that all the involved countries should feel inclined to appreciate or even accept 'the alternative strategies and the resulting tradeoffs' as also 'reasonable quid pro quos' it might offer. They have also suggested having in place a few 'guideposts' to limiting 'policies that give rise to misaligned currency values or external balances leading to cross-border instability in financial flows'. They find G20 heterogeneous,[1] and hence lack the effectiveness

---

[1] As of October 2014, the membership of the Group of 20 Nations (G20) comprised 19 countries plus the EU. While not formally a member, Spain has

to coordinate optimally an agreement on 'a set of guideposts for each country'. As such, the task is enormous as it involves identification of trade-offs that are welfare-enhancing for the larger set of economies and believe that the 'Integrated Surveillance Decision' conducted at the IMF can foot the bill.

Such dreams have been dreamt even quite a while ago. In an article titled 'Get Ready for the Phoenix' (Jerome Corsi, *The Economist* 1988), it was conceived that

> Thirty years from now, Americans, Japanese, Europeans, and people in many other rich countries, and some relatively poor ones will probably be paying for their shopping with the same currency. The phoenix zone would impose tight constraints on national governments. There would be no such thing, for instance, as a national monetary policy. The world phoenix supply would be fixed by a new central bank, descended perhaps from the IMF. The world inflation rate—and hence, within narrow margins, each national inflation rate—would be in its charge. Each country could use taxes and public spending to offset temporary falls in demand, but it would have to borrow rather than print money to finance its budget deficit. With no recourse to the inflation tax, governments and their creditors would be forced to judge their borrowing and lending plans more carefully than they do today. This means a big loss of economic sovereignty, though the trends that make the phoenix so appealing are taking that sovereignty away in any case. Even in a world of floating exchange rates (more-or-less), individual governments have seen their policy independence checked by an unfriendly outside world.

'Pencil in the phoenix for around 2018, and welcome it when it comes', the article concludes.

participated in all G20 meetings thus far. The current membership includes Argentina, Australia, Brazil, Canada, the People's Republic of China, the EU, France, Germany, India, Indonesia, Italy, Japan, the Republic of Korea, Mexico, the Russian Federation, Saudi Arabia, South Africa, Turkey, the United Kingdom and the USA.

In fact, when Harry Dexter White launched his proposal on new international mechanism in January 1942, he had envisaged a concept of world central bank that would 'issue notes' and would 'function as a sort of central planning agency for the whole world … eliminate possible financial crises….' (James (1996, 40). Even the choice of venue in July 1944 in favour of a 'contemplative wooded retreat in Bretton Woods' from the earlier one in 1933 at the Geological Museum in London was symbolic of the openness and progression of ideas in this direction.

A Central Global Government?

The world is besieged by a lack of symmetry, and stability has seen threats of breakdown. Quantitative asymmetry in shape, size and divergence of interests and advantages between the pivot and the rest of the world tends to facilitate that. It may be correct to presume that imaginative central banking and close cooperation among national and international monetary authorities could prevent such a state. There has been a growing feeling in favour of the development of global money and central banking. But the paradox is that while everybody talks about it, he who listens about it dismisses it as a fantasy, and hence he who proposes to conceptualize a structure starts believing himself as having mild bouts of insanity. Reality follows dream, the cobweb of fantasy germinates scope for innovations. In the realm of insanity, a philosophy takes birth. Reality and philosophy are related, at best distant cousins. Such vigorous engagement, at both official and academic ends, for such a widely dismissed idea is neither a random development nor a crazy riddle. The world is in real search of a metamorphosis of its own structure. It is so much entrenched in its subconscious that it can no more afford to weed it out. When the idea of a 'global parliament' was mooted by Alfred Tennyson in 1842, it became a term to be ridiculed. But the idea never sank. It had been raised time and again.

A central global government having higher authority than the 'regions' as also a regional government having more authority than individual states is an inescapable necessity if the need is to achieve sustained cooperation in the current international system. Pursuit of state interests without cooperation often leads to states treading on each other's toes in the international system, hurting each other and other involved parties for short-term gain. This will be in sync with the concept of 'collective goods dilemma' in which states deplete a shared resource, such as fish stocks, and are unwilling to cut back their use for sustainability because they believe other states will not do the same, leaving them at a disadvantage and their rivals at an advantage.

Regional/Global RTGS System

Linking of payments system interfaces among several countries or regions may provide them with the advantage of scale and enable them to exploit the benefits of international economic and financial integration. Such interoperability would enable easy payment and settlement of funds among the citizens of such unions and provide cross-border access to international markets at lower end-to-end transaction costs. Cross-border transactions can be enhanced by linking the large-value transfer systems between national Payment System Infrastructures (PSIs). In order to develop and implement regional RTGS between central banks, a lot of efforts are being undertaken. One such model for establishing interlinkage between national payment systems is through the central bank bilateral accounts, in which settlement accounts are held by the participating central banks either with a common commercial bank or with one another. However, a unified scheme along with a common technical–operational facility provides a more advanced solution for PSI interlinking. The two basic architectures followed by common technical–operational facility are the fully centralized model and the decentralized model. In the centralized platform model, a single international system replaces the individual country payment system infrastructures. This system allows seamless processing of both cross-border and domestic payment transactions. In a decentralized model, the regional/global systems are interconnected to an existing national settlement system mostly in a 'hub-spoke' structure.

TARGET, which became an integral part of the launch of the euro, served as an important milestone for establishing an integrated

European financial market. In fact, the later version, TARGET2 has enabled the payment services facility in euro beyond the geographical boundaries of the euro area countries. Even the central banks which have not yet adopted the euro currency have the option to facilitate settlement of transactions by participating in TARGET2. However, participation in TARGET2 is mandatory when new member states join the euro area. Any euro operation involving the Euro system has to be necessarily on the TARGET2 platform. Till February 2016, 25 central banks of the EU and their respective user entities were participating in, or connected to, TARGET2.

In view of the likely advantages which accrue from linking the payment and settlement systems, attempts are being made in that direction in various regions across the globe. Some integration models currently operational are 'Many States, Single Currency'—the EU uses Euro and Central America uses US$, SADC uses South African Rand; 'Many States, Many Currencies'—Hong Kong SAR, etc. Some RTGS systems designed to facilitate economic integration are 'RTGS-RTGS—Interlink Model'—Hong Kong, ASEAN 5 and 'RTGS-RTGS-SSP Single Shared Platform model'—the EU.

An International Financial Technology Infrastructure

As nations integrate regionally and globally, they share technology platforms and data networks to facilitate payment and settlement of funds and sharing of information. In the current environment, the breaches of sensitive data, cyber espionage and attacks on critical infrastructures have emerged as an important threat. As the cyber vulnerabilities have proliferated in the recent times, an integrated and cooperative approach in this regard is required. An international financial technology infrastructure will be a necessary requirement. This can be evolved in the lines of European Union Agency for Network and Information Security (ENISA), set up in 2004, meant to ensure cooperation in network security. It has been formed for enhancing the cyber resilience of the EU member states. The same is needed among the law enforcement authorities to fight cybercrime.

The character of transnationality (ability to flow freely across national borders) of flying over the Internet will intensify its need further. The ENISA framework can also be considered from the point of view of regular updates of its objectives, tasks and mandate with the changing scenario, on both the threat and policy sides.

Another aspect is the formation of the permanent Computer Emergency Response Team (CERT-EU), a team comprising the IT experts from member EU institutions, for the EU institutions, agencies and bodies in 2012. CERT-EU cooperates closely with other CERTs in the member states as well as with specialized IT security companies.

Asia also has formed an Asia Pacific Computer Emergency Response Team (APCERT), which is a coalition of Computer Security Incident Response Teams (CSIRTs), from 13 economies across the Asia-Pacific region. The steering committee of the APCERT has also formed a Forum of Incident Response and Security Teams (FIRST) which is a network of individual computer security incident response teams representing government, law enforcement, academia, private sector and other organizations with justifiable interest that work together voluntarily to deal with computer security problems and their prevention.

A Regional Statistical Think Tank

The need for good-quality statistics to support a single economic and monetary policy framework cannot be underemphasized. There would be a need to harmonize the individual country-level statistical standards and also integrate regional statistics. While there had been ongoing attempts to harmonize and disseminate statistics by global bodies such as the World Bank and IMF, regional bodies seeking economic and financial integration have also taken initiatives in this regard. Some examples are discussed as follows.

In the EU, the harmonization of statistics along with national statistical authorities is being done by the European Statistical System (ESS). The ESS has been entrusted with the responsibility of developing, producing and disseminating statistical information. Eurostat is the statistical office of the EU which produces reliable and comparable data. AFRISTAT is the economic and statistical observatory for sub-Saharan Africa. It is an international organization founded in 1993 with 19 member states (Benin, Burkina Faso, Burundi, Cameroon, Cape Verde, Central African Republic, Chad, Equatorial Guinea, Gabon, Guinea-Bissau, Ivory Coast, Mali, Mauritania, Niger, Senegal, Democratic Republic of the Congo, Republic of Guinea, Union of the Comoros and Togo) with an overall goal: to strengthen, develop and support the national statistical systems of AFRISTAT member states. The six member states of the GCC—Bahrain, Kuwait, Oman, Qatar, Saudi Arabia and United Arab Emirates (UAE) had also envisaged a 'Gulfstat'—a regional statistical agency to operate within a 'Gulf States System of Statistics', in the lines of Eurostat and Afristat with an eye on a CM and monetary union.

PART B

Financial Stability Councils—Harnessing the Idea of Synergy, Coordination and Neutral Assessment

This concept leverages on the concept of a global super central bank (GSCB) which was mooted while presenting my paper 'Financial Innovations and Systemic Risk: In Search of an Ever-Elusive Global Super Central Bank' at the International Conference on Business, Banking and Finance held at the University of the West Indies, Trinidad and Tobago, during 1–3 May 2006. With amended scenarios, the concept has been dovetailed into the current emerging 'start-ups' in the nature of financial stability councils, which are generally coordinated by central banks. In the earlier structure, the central board of a central bank would have four independent boards to address various issues, whereas in the revised structure, financial stability councils would have four independent subcommittees to address potential vulnerabilities in four different areas of national financial stability management. Other dynamics would remain the same.

The fundamental focus is on 'committees' whose time has since come to replace 'countries'. With the power of 'hegemony' whether benign or malign no more getting to work, with the voyage of the world from unipolar to bipolar to multipolar (G24) grouping nearing to complete, the need has arisen to expand ideas keeping global systemic risk in consideration. The ingrained area of concern is that 'difficulty in any country could pose threat to any other as also the globe'. Such committees will address specific global issues bearing on the economics of individual countries irrespective of geopolitical differences. Representation by central bank, government and regulators would lend required legitimacy to the decisions taken by the representatives for each participating country. Implementation accordingly will be mandatory on each country as opposed to being voluntary as has been the practice in respect of recommendations of the IMF, BIS and FSB.

The network of financial stability councils (or systemic risk boards) could, in fact, work together

> to foster this fine-tuning of monetary and regulatory measures—to be applied not uniformly across the board, but according to the problems of each country—then we could improve stability. The absence of an international monetary system could, to a certain extent, be mitigated by a serious macroeconomic oversight regime. (de Larosiere 2014)

With increasing recognition of systemic risk as the target variable inviting redress, this network can be used to overhaul the regulatory architecture, with increased coordination and centralization of regulatory powers lying at the national, regional and global space (in that order). This will be capable of addressing the contagion risks built up by the segmentation of regulatory authorities. Thus, the inherent trend of the regulatory authority to neglect potential negative spillovers on the parts of the system it is not responsible for can be monitored.

Illustratively, remaining on the current point, for example, the surging episodes of 'competitive devaluations' or 'taper tantrum', it should be imperative on the part of each economy to ensure its immunity from the after-effects of reversal of *quantitative easing* (QE) by the USA or an invitation to QE by Europe. Although the mechanics could be made simpler and *Pareto optimal* (beneficial for all with little or no harm to any one), if countries sit together and steer policies in their favour. Taking clue from the well-known story of the two cars crossing each other at a narrow road, it is not difficult to surmise that if both the drivers are careful about each other's body and try to proceed through mutual consultations, the crossing will be hassle-free. In contrast, if each is selfishly careful of its own body with little care about what might happen to the other, there is a real possibility that the two cars may slide into peril or impair each other's progress. Expanding the explanation to country level, the best example could be those of the illustrated biological neighbours—India and Pakistan. If India raises its defense budget and buys fighter jets from developed countries for the genuine purpose of its border management, it throws bare an (un) intended consequence on Pakistan to replicate the same action at its end. In this way, both get negatively hit without serving any useful purpose. If they opt to put a moratorium on rise in defense budget as the beginning of an economic integration process keeping political/ historical issues aside for some time, both would benefit economically. A smoker while enjoying his/her smoking never realizes the negative effects of passive smoking on his/her innocent neighbours. Hence, the need arose for state-sponsored norm to smoke only at designated zones. In the same vein, the tapering from the USA, instead of being seen or shown as a tantrum of a hegemon, could also prove to be a testimony for ushering in of a decisive mandate generated out of collective wisdom of all if handled in a democratic multilateral fashion.

The sense of sovereignty and independence had always been an important factor for individual countries. Given a choice, no individual country would like to give up an inch of its independence of the monetary and economic policymaking. As long as the decisions taken by the policymakers help contain excesses that do not spillover and affect other countries, no interference is warranted. Given globalization, however, if keeping one's own house clean robotically leads to flinging trash at the neighbours, this would be a problem. This strengthens the need of policy interactions between various economies even for deciding domestic policies. The best example that can be provided for such interactions is the global cooperation in financial regulation and supervision. The Basel guidelines not only standardize the regulation and supervision policies across the globe but also help in strengthening the financial sector in individual countries through its implementation. Such type of cooperation does not impinge or put constraints on the domestic policies while making the financial system more resilient.

> Multilateralism is key for delivering the best outcomes in this respect. The special roles of global financial institutions and global currencies go beyond international trade and the financial interactions directly linked to trade in the first two layers of globalisation. An internationally agreed joint approach helps to ensure that policymakers properly manage global financial risks, not least those associated with the highly pro-cyclical third layer of globalisation. (Caruana 2017)

This was the motivation behind this attempt to rescript the idea (over the earlier version in 2006), when the debate on a doable scheme on IMS looked to be at crossroads. An attempt has been made in the following sections try to run through the evolution of the concept of IMS over the years, present the two versions of the 'bottom-up' framework of IMS under the Garland Makers' Model and discuss some of the thoughts transacted during recent times.

The Evolution of IMS— The Top-Down Approach

The formation of an IMS has always attracted intense discussions. The genesis of such a system could be traced back to pre-First World War period when gold standard guaranteed free capital flows and stable exchange rates. However, after the two world wars, this system ceased to exist due to capital controls being imposed. The Bretton Woods was initiated after the end of the Second World War as a system of fixed exchange rates. The first idea of an IMS in the form of this arrangement was conceived and the shoots of formation of IMF were visible. However, in 1973, this system ceased to exist, and a new system based on three floating currencies, namely the US$, the DM and the yen was formed. This arrangement got impetus from the capital flows liberalization and provided support for quasi-automatic adjustments of current account imbalances. The basic design of the IMF was to assist countries with current account deficits; however, their role was always fiercely discussed. The cyclical economic shifts have resulted in shift in the importance of the IMF in the present world with it regaining some importance during the Latin American crises in the 1980s and the emerging market crises in the 1990s while again losing relevance during the great moderation (Weber 2011).

In the world of finance, 'systemic risk management' has become the buzz phrase. Macroprudential policymaking has come to stay as a supplement to microprudential decision-making. Financial stability is a public good and must be addressed by public policy. The linkage between real sector and financial sector was also exposed. Accordingly, macroprudential authorities have been set up to monitor the potential vulnerabilities that might surface in all sectors, namely macroeconomy, financial markets, financial institutions and financial infrastructure. These authorities also use macroprudential tools in sync with monetary policy tools to contain their intensity of impacting the system. As their responsibilities reflect, such authorities are in the form of 'committees' comprising all the stakeholders of the country, namely the central bank, regulators of financial institutions and markets, and also the government to extend the architecture to cover fiscal space.

Considering the fact that central banks are often also the regulators of the banking sector, the predominant contributor to the financial institutions segment, such financial stability councils are formed with the central bank of a country (monetary policy, LOLR and regulator of the predominant portion of both the financial institutions and markets), regulator/s of the securities related segments of financial institutions and markets. Certainly, the MOF is also listed in the group. In short, post-crisis, the surveillance architecture of financial stability management of a country has taken the form of a committee (not one country or any other institution) including representatives of the central bank, government and the other relevant regulators. The functioning of these committees is generally coordinated by the central banks.

In the context of the macrofinancial domain, macroeconomic policy and financial coordination are being discussed and coordinated via the G20, along with macroeconomic assessment and surveillance in tandem with the IMF. Responsibility for financial stability, international standard setting and coordination lies with the FSB (the successor to the FSF), yet implementation is at the domestic and regional levels. Monitoring and assessment is taking place through the IMF, the FSB and through regional arrangements. But the monitoring and assessment are still in the mode of managing the severity of the last crisis—much in the same nature of managing liquidity crisis through coordination of banks. These initiatives were organized by the central bank in the case of LTCM failure during the late 1990s and again through the coordination of central banks organized by the Federal Reserve to save Northern Rock in 2007. But these are, in fact, not in the nature of a system as they look like 'a patchwork' (Warner and Buckley 2011)—piecemeal reactions to stem the furores of the crisis at hand, though there is an urgent need for arrangements that manage future crisis supported by documented systems and appropriate structures both regionally and internationally. A call for an international coordination mechanism for monetary policy and financial stability essentially looks for an elaborate institutional architecture reflecting an intertwined fabric of national, regional and global context.

It is by far a well-perceived idea that national regulation in an era of internationalization cannot be operationalized in an independent manner. The impact of any decision inevitably transcends across other related jurisdictions. International economic governance would be required towards setting global standards to improve cross-border transparency on financial systems, institutional behaviour, capital/liquidity standards, systemically important institutions, cross-border financial flows, financial CMM and so on. This would enhance possibilities of reducing regulatory arbitrage across major financial centres across the globe.

While the status of the US dollar as a highly acceptable global transactional and financing currency can be viewed as a step in that direction, the dominance of only one currency, creates challenges and problems for not only the IMS but also for the USA. The US dollar now accounts for as much as 90 per cent of the globe's forex transactions and accounts for 60 per cent of the reserves held by other countries. This role, given the size and dominance of the US economy, the depth, breadth and liquidity of the US financial markets, creates a situation wherein the US monetary policy or actions related to balance sheet expansion or compression by the Fed to influence policy actions of other economies and also impact the financial markets in those economies. While a more pluralistic IMS, that is, 'one with more international currencies on a more equal footing', would provide more stability, it cannot be a panacea of all ills that plagues the system. There is a need and scope to improve international crisis arrangements through closer interactions between domestic regimes. 'But, as they say, one ounce of prevention is worth a pound of cure. And, while putting one's house in order is essential, it is not enough (Padoa-Schioppa (2008): there is also a need to put the global village in order' (Borio 2016).

An ad hoc committee for a new Bretton Woods was formed in August 2007 with Helga Zepp-LaRouche, the chairwoman of the Schiller Institute as its head to follow up on the previous calls of 1997, 2000 and 2006, for a reorganization of the world financial system with support from prominent world personalities, former heads of state and others.

The concept of an 'instant world government' was suddenly evolving. While it was warranted by international inequality, it was contested by Richard N. Gardener who advocated a 'brick by brick approach' in building the 'house of world order'. He was emphatic that such a structure 'will have to be built from the bottom up rather than from the top down'. The 'old-fashioned frontal assault' will look like, to use William James' famous description of reality, a great 'booming, buzzing confusion'. 'Progressive regionalization' as an eventual stepping stone to 'genuine globalization' was also vociferously advocated by Zbigniew Brzezinski (former national security adviser and cofounder of the Trilateral Commission) in his address to Gorbechev's State of the World Forum in October 1995 'because thereby we move toward larger, more stable, more cooperative units'. The ideas of global civil society (GCS) and global citizenship (GC) 'as a reflection of the internationalization of the state' were mentioned by Armstrong (2006).

The key problems with such ideas are the agreement and enforcement issues towards democratic governance. Under the current dispensation, the United Nations Security Council, the World Bank, the IMF, the World Trade Organization and the FSB are supposed to oversee, or at the least, to provide a forum to coordinate and converge towards, the formulation and implementation of modalities pertaining to global governance. This is not that they do not care to carry their brief. In fact, decisions are made, or agreed to, at these organizations that affect every nation. The only issue is that the decisions are not taken democratically. They are taken without the consent of the parties who are most affected when they reflect the use of veto powers of their major shareholders and permanent members. 'The question is not whether global decisions need to be made…. The question is how to ensure that they are made democratically' (Kauppi et al. 2007).

An upgraded alternative would be to have 'small groups of nations of regional, ideological or historical similarity—known as regimes—which aims to harness ideas which benefit all the participants at all the time, "making it more in each state's interest to cooperate than fight with each other for short-term zero-sum gain"'. Such economic arrangements ensure that 'states can work together to detect and stop any nation found to be cheating. States, as rational actors, will refrain from selfish short-term gain attempts if the risk is too great—this is the situation regimes try to create'. Such attempts, termed as 'New Global Order by Stealth' by Steve Watson (2007) in his column dated 5 May 2007 (Internet blog), have been in operation ever since.

The USA and the EU signed a transatlantic economic partnership, the cause of which was further pushed by setting up an economic council in May 2017 leading to harmonized regulatory standards in nearly 40 areas including intellectual property, financial services, business takeovers and motor industry, for evolving a single market which was considered a huge step for the globalization.

In the Council on Foreign Relations' (CFR) document, 'Building a North American Community', a mention is given to the Bilderberg group in a recommendation that private bodies be formed to direct policy between Canada, Mexico and the USA. The document states:

> To ensure a regular injection of creative energy into the various efforts related to North American integration, the three governments should appoint an independent body of advisers. This body should be composed of eminent persons from outside government, appointed to staggered multiyear terms to ensure their independence. Their mandate would be to engage in creative exploration of new ideas from a North American perspective and to provide a public voice for North America. A complementary approach would be to establish private bodies that would meet regularly or annually to buttress North American relationships, along the lines of the Bilderberg.

Thus, such 'club-in-the-club' approach (coined by Erik Berglof of Stockholm School of Economics) as practical complement to processes of global integration is not new to human ingenuity. 'Bond of the South' moves towards regionalization of country insurance against economic shocks were propagated by Argentina's President Nestor Kirchner as a first step 'in the construction of a bank, a financial space in the south that will permit [us] to generate lines of finance'. Eventually this may be a mechanism to cope with potential financial crises without involving the IMF. The recently created Asian Infrastructure Investment Bank (AIIB) aimed at 'helping to meet Asia's need for trillions of dollars of investment in energy, power, transportation, telecommunications, and other infrastructure sectors' (Bergstern 2015) led by China with about 50 countries (including the UK, Australia and certain Gulf and European ones) as members should best be appreciated from this point in view. The 'angry response' of the USA could at best be termed as 'a sorry development that reflects the huge mistake the United States has made' (Bergstern 2015). The 'club-in-club' cooperation/coordination mechanisms relate not only to physical proximity of countries or regional boundaries but also to countries that can come together in terms of similarities in their economic model, growth, etc. BRICS countries (Brazil, Russia,

India, China and South Africa) are another group who are clubbed together as the largest emerging markets economies. As a progressive step, setting up of New Development Bank (NDB)[2] was envisaged at the fourth BRICS Summit in New Delhi (2012) to mobilize resources for infrastructure and sustainable development projects in BRICS and other emerging economies, as well as in other developing countries.

The shift in thought process from 'global lending arrangements' to 'global crash prevention mechanisms' in the late 1990s was backed by the perceived potential of systemic risk in the changing pattern of financial flows across the globe.

> What is really needed is not so much a global lender when we get into problems. The need is to prevent problems, to have a supervisory and regulatory process in place that limits damage around the world, rather than to get into damage control. The need is not for a lender of last resort, the need is for improved supervision and regulation over risk-takers and the major markets. (Kaufman 1991)

This 'create a super-regulator' call was, in fact, amply translated into a proposal of creation of World Financial Authority (WFA) by Eatwell and Taylor in 1998 which came in their report in the wake of LTCM crisis.

WFA would be an independent international financial institution with the responsibility of maintaining safety and soundness in international financial markets because interrelated and cross-border financial businesses warrant regulation and supervision on a unified and global basis in line with those of national regulators functions in domestic markets. Its functions would be to take preparatory and preventive measures towards minimizing the spread of financial crisis in other economies, as well as to lessen the impact of these crises internationally. Also, by way of spreading its areas of watch over the speculative activities, a reduction in the destabilizing leveraged activities and systemic risks may be ensured. In short, WFA would be the suitable

---

[2] The NDB came into existence in July 2015 and is actively involved in providing financial assistance for projects in the areas of green and renewable energy and transportation.

reply to the rise in global systemic risk in a scenario of liberalization of the international markets.

Accordingly, the WFA or any other international financial institution that takes on the onerous responsibility to maintain the soundness in the international financial markets should not only be able to provide a cogent analysis of the overall impact on systemic risk but also be able to steer the participants in the right direction by impressing upon them the values of such analysis and policies. The institution should also be able to mediate between various players in case disputes arise (Eatwell and Taylor 2000). They should, hence, have the power to guide and dictate to national financial markets and to tie them with a system of mandated accountability in the matter of violation of its edicts. The ultimate aim of such a senior regulator would be to 'maximize financial stability between the developed and the emerging markets in such a way as to maximize world productivity' (Felsenfeld 2004). Towards this benefit, the possible hesitation to cede national independent powers of control to an international body like the WFA could be tempered through a dialogue for 'consensus and mutual recognition of self-interest...' (Eatwell and Taylor 2000).

The trend of internationalization of financial market regulation has been perceived from time to time. However, these are not done in a formal manner and/or with perfection.

> Authorization is still essentially national, the information function is highly imperfect, surveillance (by the IMF) is as yet experimental, enforcement is national, and the policy function is predominantly driven by an exclusively G10 consensus. As measured against the template of a proper WFA, there is a long way to go. (Eatwell and Taylor 2000)

The institutional mechanism in vogue to look after international regulation to mitigate systemic risk is also slipshod. There is an 'awkward hybrid' in which the predominant rules are made by the BIS, IOSCO and International Association of Insurance Supervisors (IAIS), while the international surveillance responsibility is vested with the IMF. Worse still, the 'Centre' centre-periphery' paradigm, that is, 'rules are made by the rich nations and enforced on the rest' (Eatwell and Taylor 2000) is prominent enough to steal the charm of the show. Devising an appropriate structure is, in fact, the biggest challenge.

The global super regulator approach would not be

either feasible or desirable. It is not feasible, since there is a very little chance of sovereign legislatures ceding powers in the regulatory area to a supranational body. And it would not necessarily be desirable. A single regulator could well be too monolithic, disinclined to experiment with new regulatory approaches. The rules it would create might not take adequate account of the particularities of the financial sector in different jurisdictions. And insofar as all countries had to agree on regulatory initiatives, there would be a risk of converging on the lowest common denominator. (Crocket 2001)

Crocket (2005), however, hypothesizes an umbrella roof and bringing all relevant international supervisory groupings underneath 'in a way that respects their institutional autonomy while exploiting the synergies of a common location, and the ability to discuss and resolve issues of common concern'. This appears to be an even more complex challenge to deal with.

Another strong votary of reforming the international financial architecture in the wake of cross-border financial interdependence, which is both helpful and hazardous, has been Ralph C. Bryant (1999, 2004). His is a holistic approach towards prevention of crises in the direction of optimizing welfare gains for the whole economy, both national and global, in which the role of the international institution would be essentially 'prosperity management' rather than 'crisis management'. The aim of the proposed global institution would be to look after (a) supranational surveillance and lending intermediation; (b) prudential financial oversight; and (c) cooperative crisis management. The efforts should be to let the national governments understand the efficacy of choosing 'to act collectively not because they agree to bend to the will of an independent authority above them, but because achieving their mutual interests requires cooperation'. Such a collective surveillance would have a watch over 'individual nations from deliberately or inadvertently pursuing policies likely to cause economic disruptions for other nations'. Attempt to attract financial activity by deliberately fostering regulatory arbitrage and supervisory laxity by few jurisdictions or abetting financial crime, money laundering, tax evasion by citizens of other nations would have to be constrained through this 'collective governance' mechanism.

It need not act only as a crisis manger as it would mobilize international consensus towards 'mutually beneficial adjustments of policy instruments' even during 'non-crisis conditions' so that possible market failures can be offset/prevented. It should be so designed in the nature of an impartial 'adjustment referee and coordination catalyst' ('a neutral assessor and a few guideposts' conceived by Ostry and Ghosh 2013) for national macroeconomic policies relating to both internal and external financial flows. This may appear ticklish to weave a monetary policy or fiscal policy for a region or for the world.

> Yet the general global stance of macroeconomic policies is a critical feature influencing the global economic and financial environment. Procedures for intergovernmental cooperation among the fiscal authorities and the monetary authorities of the largest nations are in their infancy.… Encouraging national governments to pursue stable, predictable and mutually consistent macroeconomic policies should be the central feature of collective surveillance. (Bryant 1999)

As such, for national governments, persuasion of a global consensus in these matters will increasingly become an inevitability considering the progressive internationalization of domestic balance sheets.

While there is unanimity on the proposal for a global body and a coordinated management of systemic risk, opinions differ vastly on its possible structure so much so that the 'ratio of architects to builders has grown too large' (Gasper 1999). 'The world is not politically ready for a genuine supranational lender of last resort, much less a World Central bank. It would be no easier to establish additional international institutions with greatly enhanced authority' (Bryant 2003) nor the world is 'ready for a WFA' since the 'creation of a new body with senior responsibility for setting regulatory standards for all financial enterprises worldwide would be an almost unreasonably ambitious approach' (Falsenfeld 2004). While some felt that 'IMF cannot take on the deus ex machine role of an international lender of last resort' (Eichergreen and Litan 1998), others recommended its upgradation in the interim (Eatwell and Taylor 2000) or full-fledged and final (Bryant 2004; King 2006) with suitable functional changes. On the other hand, Falsenfeld (2004) felt BIS as the better candidate for the purpose. As a middle path, merger of the two Bretton Woods institutions and the organization of an international LOLR function by the IMF and/or the BIS has also been proposed.

BIS was created not to be a central bank but rather a bank for central banks. As BIS says in its website presentation, it 'does not possess any formal supranational supervisory authority, and its conclusions do not, and were never intended to, have legal force… encourages convergence towards common approaches and common standards without attempting detailed harmonization of member countries' supervisory techniques'. The BIS was established to be having the primary role for creating a progressive and sound banking environment, in a manner of 'cohabitation', with the national financial policies sponsored by the World Bank and the IMF. The purpose of creation of the IMF was 'to promote international monetary cooperation … provide the machinery for consultation and collaboration on international monetary problems'.

> IMF's main governing body, the 24-member International Monetary and Financial Committee (IMFC), represents all 189-member countries via a constituency system. It meets twice a year and provides guidance to the IMF on all aspects of policy. The problem is that the formality of the IMFC has almost always rendered it incapable of innovation or flexibility. Other two issues are that it has not been able to keep pace with the growth of emerging economies like India and China and also the rise of an outside powerful group in the form of G20 which controls 3/4th of the voting rights in IMF has rendered IMF powerless. (Boughton 2016)

Since both an International Lender of Last Resort (ILLR) (to intervene in the market if the risk of crisis becomes endemic) and a WFA function (to undertake surveillance of financial markets on an ongoing basis to be able to smell) to constrain the intensity of crisis and (its ability to spread), which are of course unequivocally a necessity, a hybrid of both IMF (crisis lending and macroeconomic conditions analysis) and BIS (policymaking for national and international financial stability) appears to be the most favoured proposal. But the homogenization of their heterogeneous activities has got to be led in a step-by-step approach with a sense of 'pragmatic incrementalism' (Bryant 2001, 2004), since in the direction of multilateral cooperation in such complex scenario 'too much' should not be expected 'too soon' (Bryant 2001, 2004). The initiative towards this end has to be sovereign-sponsored since it is a 'disservice to argue that markets will sort things out efficiently if governments will just stand aside and let the market "get the price right" (Bryant 2001) as against waiting for its evolution "incrementally in response to pressures from markets and governments, not discontinuously in response to radical visions"'.

The Anna Karenina principle (*The Economist* 2015) states on account of the three problems of imbalances, capital flows and dollar dependence, every country in the dollar system is unhappy in some way. The 'trilemma' that exists in the country can possibly allow the country to achieve either two of the three issues related to a stable exchange rate, openness to global capital flows and the ability to set its interest rates freely to suit its own economy. There is an issue with both large capital inflows and outflows from a country. Any large capital inflow can set-off appreciation pressures on the local currency with consequent impact on bond markets and interest rates. The issues with rate rises in the USA are quite evident the world over, with the consequent impact in the emerging markets related to currency depreciation and imports becoming costlier. Also, it hurts US exports. The global monetary system needs to design smart ways to tame capital flows, stop beggar-thy-neighbour policies, provide a safety net if things go wrong, and an impartial global payments system.

> It is reasonable to assert that in a patently imperfect world experiencing significant financial volatility and multiple sovereignties, monetary unions provide the possibility for shared sovereignty and monetary and fiscal discipline which may have some impact on the overall stability of the international financial system. (Venner 2002)

Ideally, to be operationally effective, the IMS reform should come from a competition of ideas in a 'bottom-up' format

> from different EMEs and within EMEs, a complex mix of inter-action between markets, nations, civil society and enterprises to balance short-term needs of employment and self-interest, and long-term needs of social equity and survival from climate change.... It is the competition of a bottom-up race to solve the key problems of our era that will shape our global economy and our IMS. (Sheng 2015)

However, the reforms in the IMS seem a distant dream as the IMF staff continue to eulogize the current form of the IMS. The lack of synergies and imperfections in the current system is invisible to them. While 'stocktaking' the current IMS, they articulate that 'Today's IMS has displayed great strength'. Though the paper has identified three areas on which to focus, instead of envisaging a structural change in the system as it is today, the emphasis is only more on strengthening the current structure.[3]

The IMS needs to culminate in a structure having real power to make rules for effective adherence by global financial competition entities and regulatory authorities. The IMS as it stands today has been created in bits and pieces with 'little or no intellectual organiz-ing framework. A manifestation of this fuzziness is that, even among economists, there is no consensus regarding the defining features of the IMS' (Farhi and Maggiori 2016). There have been continuous ongoing reforms in the IMS, making it seem like a disjointed jigsaw puzzle, yet to near its completion and yet unable to solve some of the more fundamental concerns.[4]

---

[3] '[R]eforms could focus on three possible areas: (i) mechanisms for crisis pre-vention and adjustment; (ii) rules and institutions for enhanced global cooperation on issues and policies affecting global stability; and (iii) building a more coherent GFSN' (International Monetary Fund Annual Report 2016).

[4] Reform of the IMS has been an 'evolutionary process', as was envisioned by the C20 in 1974 (International Monetary Fund Annual Report 1974). That evolution is continuing much longer than most of the participants in the C20 anticipated. Some elements are new, but the fundamental concerns about

A 'top-down' approach suggests global regulators in this same manner with changes here and there in the face of 'strong sovereignty concerns that the establishment of such regulators' might raise as hitherto is 'highly unlikely' (Warner and Buckley 2011). Similarly, simple juxtaposition of national priorities and positions to redefine the needs of the globe and getting it administered by one of the current institutions like the IMF, BIS or FSB without regard to the realities that 'reflect better the real world, and particularly the growing importance of emerging countries' (de Larosiere 2014) may not also work.[5] Even though G20 accounts for 85 per cent of world GDP, 80 per cent of world trade and two-thirds of world population, its legal foundation is not by national treaty or law, but essentially self-appointed and its ideas are essentially recommendatory. '... the Basel standards are only "soft law," not legally binding' (Ingves 2014). The current edifice of IMS was constructed in bits and pieces with no political will on part of anyone for tougher global standards. So unsurprisingly, the FSF, which was created to examine the financial system as a whole and to identify vulnerabilities, was found wanting. This led to the creation of the FSB, a supposedly tougher model. The Board has since then issued some warnings in the assessments it has made regarding financial vulnerabilities but still lacks teeth as it cannot direct or persuade countries or regulators to follow or comply with its regulations (Davies 2014).

As discussed previously, this has been the practice under the IMS in vogue. However, the fundamental characteristics of the reform proposals—whether the creation of IMF, BIS, G7, G20, G24, FSF, FSB, etc.—have taken a 'top-down' financial architecture. Indeed, each incremental proposal in the wake of fresh problems has been more

asymmetrical adjustment, the failure of exchange rates to adjust appropriately and disequilibrating capital flows are very familiar (Truman 2017).

[5] The question post-2007 global financial crisis is no longer one of best practice and one-size-fits-all regulations, but of 'best fit'. Since the best analysed and most advanced financial systems, and most sophisticated regulation and supervision failed, there is no 'first best'. One of the major criticisms of the FSB's work is that its reforms fitted the advanced markets, but it had little clue how they impacted on the emerging markets (Sheng 2015).

inclusive and better configured,[6] but the enshrined philosophy remains still. Also, the G20 and FSB are more inclusive vehicles relative to UN, World Bank, and IMF .... after all, G20 and FSB reflect both de jure and de facto models wherein a small group of systemic entities coordinate on global rules of play in the macro-financial system, with others usually feeling they have no option but to follow. In the immediate aftermath of their formation, a number of small economies (both advanced and emerging/low income) had voiced discomfort with such exclusion, privately and publicly.

Of course, the counter-argument could be that while the earlier multilateral organizations have universal membership, they have permanent versus temporary memberships in their key decision-making bodies (UNSC) or subject to veto powers (WB and IMF) 'top-down'. The Stiglitz Commission that went into the dynamics of the global crises and looked for reforms in coordination architecture has recommended the establishment of a Global Economic Coordination Council at the level of the UN General Assembly and Security Council, meeting annually. Other recommendation included the establishment of a global financial regulator and a global competition regulator. These are again 'top-down' by nature. Perhaps there was no thinking beyond what is available, and the purpose has been only to create alertness and try to contain any financial fragmentation tendencies (Caruana 2015). Perhaps designs of international coordination were prompted by the urge to avoid a race to the bottom in regulatory standards. The formation of BCBS was mooted in the aftermath of the failure of the Herstatt Bank in 1974 to tackle complex coordination problems.

Another example of a problematic 'top-down' approach has been the G7 coordination for interventions in the FX markets, popularly known as the Plaza Accord, which has undergone a definitional change depending on the requirements of the major economies. While the

---

[6] The new systems at the IMF (FSAP, Article IV discussions with member countries) and FSB (thematic and peer reviews to monitor implementation of regulations, focused commitment of the political leadership of G20 countries) are reflective of this.

G7 coordination in 1985 was meant for joint intervention in the FX markets by the 'Big 7' so as to calibrate the value of the major currencies to suit the economies, now it is meant to protect the currencies against manipulation (Frankel 2015).

Bottom-Up Framework and the Evolution of the Garland Makers' Model

The idea of a GSCB—central bank being entrusted with both monetary policy and regulatory functions—on a global plane has its origin from the experience of the Great Depression of the 1930s, when Charles Kindleberger (1977) commented that 'For the world economy to be stabilized there has to be a stabilizer, one stabilizer'. The same feeling was echoed again in September 1998 by Jeffery Garten, who strongly felt that the 'world needs an institution that has hand on the economic rudder when the seas become stormy. It needs a global central bank'.

The IMF does not know how to deal with a crisis of international dimension, in which all countries' problems occur at once and are linked. World Bank is not designed to handle financial crises. Cooperation among powerful central banks (FRB, ECB) will not help as global responsibility is not in their charter. The only way out could be an independent global central bank that has the direct responsibility of maintaining global financial stability. The central bank would help other central banks in times of need such as injecting hard currency by buying those country's debt, which would inject more money into those countries to boost growth and simultaneously reduce the burgeoning debt. The central bank can also guide and nurture the financial institutions in various countries which are weak and shaky. This bank could also have an oversight role for banks and financial institutions in various countries and prescribe uniform standards across the globe. It would not only help in standardizing practices but also would lead to the availability of independently verifiable information on these institutions and countries so as to allow international investors to make informed decisions regarding their investments. This would help foster a more integrated global economy (Garten 1998).

The Garland Makers' Model

'Excessive concentration of power in a small group of industrial countries', who are no more 'genuine partners in a cooperative enterprise'
and tend to look after their own interests 'acting outside the Bretton
Woods system' (Buira 2004) has led to a decision-making process that
is devoid of practical insights into the happenings of a large contingent
of the globe and hence has rendered itself 'dysfunctional' to address
the issues of financial stability and development. While 'Failure of
the prevailing governance structure in the international monetary and
financial system' is essentially to blame for such an impasse (Buira
2004), the faltering 'spirit of internationalism' is said to be one of the
reasons behind the diminishing effectiveness of the IMF in managing
international coordination on global issues (Rajan 2006a, 2006b). This
is the outcome of a distinct change in economic status of the emerging
economies (for the better) and the developed economies (for the worse)
resulting in a peculiar scenario in which the former are 'unwilling to be
lectured to' as they 'no longer need funding' from the IMF and 'want
influence over the policies of the industrial countries', while the latter,
on the other hand, continue to wish 'to exercise the influence of an era
that is long past' and to discourage dissemination of IMF findings on
their adherence to international norms (Rajan 2006a, 2006b).

The problem in fact lies in taking an honest position on the issue
of 'what facilitated this impasse' and what is the way out 'to steer
clear of that'. It appears persuasive to believe that the playing field in
the IMF regime was never levelled and has had been discriminatory
because they are dictated by 'quotas and shares' and a principle of
'some are more systemically important' than the others, and hence
have a 'more powerful say'. This kind of approach would hardly work
in an era of globalization in which systemic crashes turn global almost
instantaneously, and crashes and ruptures to the system are country-
neutral. Further, in the 'seesaw game of development', it is reasonable
to appreciate the expectations of the 'advanced emerging markets' as
they would naturally not like to lose out even when it is their turn to
win. The restructuring of economic power would have to equilibrate,
of course, at a different point this time, thus fetching the required balance of power. After all, 'Vastly expanded international capital markets

have created new opportunities but their volatility poses difficult challenges that the IMF is currently ill-equipped to address, except at an enormous cost to the countries' (Buira 2004).

> In a complex globalizing world, no fixed, detailed scheme is likely to work, and there are no global institutions with the authority to decide and even less so to implement it. Therefore, policy coherence and cooperative as well as intellectual pluralism are concepts that should be further explored as proposed guiding principles of global multilateralism. Add the rapid onset of the so-called new economy, and the case for creative flexibility gets even stronger. (Lunde 2000)

The time is hence ripe to appreciate and implement the idea that international surveillance needs to be 'multilateral, putting greater emphasis on the linkages between members, the spillover of one country's policy choices on other countries, and the joint risks that this implies'. This is the philosophy behind this model.

The Model (Version 1) (2006)

The idea carries the clue from the discourses of Lord Krishna (the God himself) in the famous Indian epic The Mahabharata. 'Be like a garland maker, O king; not like a charcoal burner'.

The meaning is explained in the following text.

A garland accommodates flowers of many colours and forms that are strung together for a pleasing effect, while a charcoal, which is the by-product of a variety of wood, is reduced to homogeneous dead matter. These two represent different school of sociopolitical thoughts as garland symbolizes heterogeneity, and hence diversity, while the charcoal burner essentially represents a homogeneity, and hence a fossilized society.

The current arrangement appears to be more akin to the 'charcoal burner' variety as it discriminates economies in terms of the 'power' they wield in global political–economic scenario while discouraging genuine feelings of others. Such an approach cannot but be transitory as it would be hardly 'global welfare-enhancing'. However, as sharp contrast, the committee structure of the proposed model of a GSCB would be an emblem of unity, diversity and under no circumstance disruptive. It would imbibe the soul of a garland and could re-engage everyone (not 'both groups' as suggested by Rajan) for the 'much needed multilateral dialogue' (Rajan 2006).

It would be equally worthwhile to use one more parallel narrative from Indian mythology. Lord Shiva's (the God of destruction of what is evil or outmoded) family consists of Goddess Parvati (his wife) and the two sons, Karthikeya (God of physical power) and Ganesha (God of learning and goodwill). Their close associates are a bull, a snake, a tiger, a peacock and a rat. As is well known, the bull is the food of the tiger, the snake is the food of the peacock, the rat is the food of the snake, but in their discharge of duties of guarding their respective masters, they tend to forget their enmity and live in harmony and camaraderie.

In the same way, the proposed structure of a GSCB would cut across political arrogance as it is being prompted by a unique necessity to remain immune from international systemic risk. It would be in the nature of a 'common-friend-of-all-but-enemy-to-none approach'. This may not be difficult now under the current transformation in the dynamics of global economic performance and power. Given the exposures structure, a systemic crisis may harm the developed economies the most, while it would harm everyone indiscriminately. Immediate necessity may prevail over past legacy, while a democratic committee approach of decision-making has more opportunities to be accepted than it has been as hitherto.

The national super central bank (NSCB) will remain responsible for both monetary management and financial market supervision. There would be four different boards to take custody of the policymaking activities of the four major strands of functions. Each board would constitute one member from the NSCB proper (the chief executive in charge of those functions, or deputy governors as in many countries) and four others from the experts' pool in the respective markets. Illustratively, Board A (Regulation and Supervision of entire financial services) would have the chief executive of regulation and supervision functions of the NSCB and experts from the areas of banking, capital markets, insurance, pension funds, etc. This board would evolve all required policies in the direction of financial stability and will be assisted by various operational divisions, which will implement them as and when they would tend to emanate. Similarly, another board, Board D, would discharge the responsibility of policymaking in the area of monetary management with the concerned chief executive from the NSCB and few other experts from the market. This way, independence of thought processes could be maintained while minimizing the impacts of the so-called 'conflict-of-interest' issues.

The next layer would be the regional super central bank (RSCB), a union of few geographically congruous economies with cultural similarities and trade relations. It would also have the same four boards, each having representative members from the respective boards of the NSCBs. Illustratively, Board A-1 (regulation and supervision of financial services) would comprise the representatives from Board A of NSCB1, NSCB2 and so on, while Board D-1 (monetary management) would comprise representatives from the Board D of NSCB 1, NSCB 2 and so on. This way, each board in a region will have an expert member from each economy equipped with the issues of his/her economy in his/her area of expertise and with the aim of assimilating them with the other experts on that area of the economies in his/her region. The Central Board of Directors-2 of the RSCB would have rotating members from the boards with a chairman nominated by them from among them from time to time.

The final and apex layer would be the GSCB, the union of the RSCBs having four boards and similar representation structure as the RSCBs. Illustratively, the Board A-2 (regulation and supervision of financial services) would have nominated members from the Board A-1's of the various RSCBs and the Board D-2 (monetary management) would have nominated members from the Board D-1's of the various RSCBs. This way, each board in the GSCB will have an expert member from each region equipped with the issues of his/her region in his/her area of expertise and with the aim of assimilating them with counterpart from other regions of the globe. The Central Board of Directors-2 of the GSCB would have rotating members from the boards with a chairman nominated by the boards from among them from time to time.

A graphical presentation of the proposed GSCB model is given in Figure 9.1.

In their report 'Rethinking Central Banking' (September 2011), a team of economists of international repute led by Barry Eichengreen had acknowledged 'the cross-border spillovers from monetary policy' but their solution emphasized on 'ensuring compatibility' between national policy framework of smaller countries and those in large countries. They proposed formation of an 'International Monetary Policy Committee' with 'a small group of systemically significant central banks' to periodically 'discuss and assess the implications of their policies for global liquidity, leverage, and exposures, and the appropriateness of their joint money and credit policies from the point of view of global price, output, and financial stability' and submit a report to the G20. But they themselves were sceptical about its efficacy because of (a) their duplicity of being discussed anyway at various meetings at BIS or even G20, (b) these being 'informal' without any 'accountability' and (c) absence of central banks in G20 format, and hence looked for 'a separate forum', which would address these issues and enable central bankers to 'identify and publicly air the inconsistencies in their policies', thus encouraging them to learn to 'internalize some of the external consequences of their policies'.

Further, in their report of August 2013, 'Think Tank 20: The G-20 and Central Banks in the New World of Unconventional Monetary Policy' prepared by another group of economists of international standing led by Atiyas Izak (2013), they too find the 'G20 process' to have 'lost a lot of its initial force and promise' vis-a-vis its initial vigour post-crisis in managing its intensity. The G20 leaders—primarily 'civil servants and bureaucrats'—will remain 'constrained by their own domestic politics' and as such the forum of negotiations needs to 'involve very strong academic, business, labor and civil society engagement'.

These looked partially akin to the proposal given by Mishra (2006) as earlier which involved brainstorming monetary policy strategies of

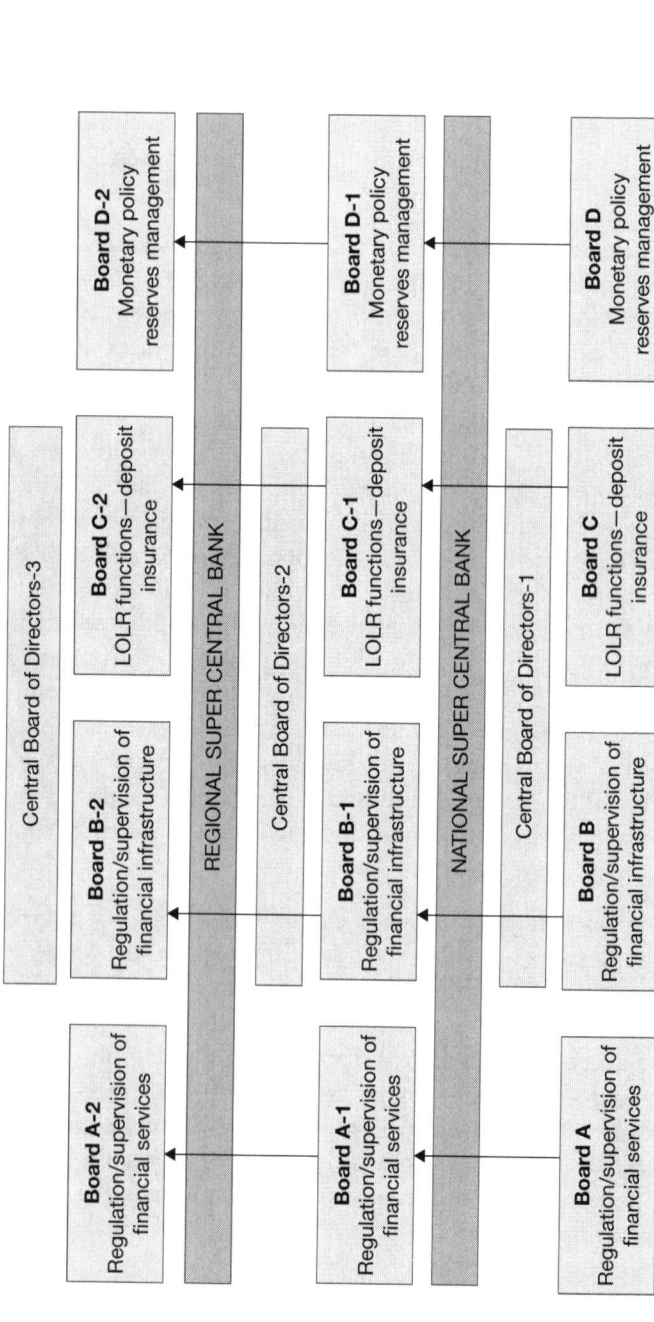

Figure 9.1 *Global Super Central Bank*

individual countries in one of the boards (Board D) of the NSCB–RSCB–GSCB format. But it had addressed the concerns of the Eichengreen group idea even while recognizing the fact that fixing monetary policy issues without regard to those emitted by macrofinancial and fiscal space would create more problems than solving them. Accordingly, formal inclusion of the government and the intelligentsia should be a primary requirement. The elements of democracy and the 'bottom-up' configuration are the other criteria marking their distinct difference.

The Garland Makers' Model— A Modified Approach (Version 2) (2015)

The idea of national macroprudential authority to address systemic risk gained ground in the post-crisis period. These ideas are in the nature of financial stability councils comprising the central bank, financial sector regulators and the government. They deal with all the sectors, namely macroeconomy (including the fiscal space), financial markets, financial institutions and financial infrastructure. They also use macroprudential tools in sync with monetary policy tools to contain the intensity of impact on the system. Considering the fact that central banks are also the regulators of the banking sector, the predominant contributor to the financial institutions segment, such financial stability councils are formed with the central bank of a country (monetary policy, LOLR and regulator of the predominant portion of both the financial institutions and markets), regulator/s of the securities-related segments of financial institutions and markets, and, of course, the MOF as members. There could be subcommittee structures to address each of these matters of concern. In short, in the post-crisis period, the surveillance architecture of financial stability management of a country has taken the form of a council (committee)—not in the form of an institution—with representatives of the central bank, government and the other relevant regulators. These committees are chaired either by the governor of the central banks or the minister of finance (depending on jurisdictions).

This development in the current context inspires confidence to think in terms of replicating such structures into regional and global domains. A regional financial stability council would comprise nominees of each nation in each of the sectors (namely macroeconomy including fiscal place, financial markets, financial institutions and financial infrastructure)—bifurcated into regional subcommittees in order to discuss potential vulnerabilities in each of them on a regional basis. National issues decentralized on the discretion of the region would get escalated in the national platform, while regional issues (depending on global consensus) would get escalated to the international financial stability council through the regional nominees of the respective areas of operation. In other words, monetary policy-related issues across nation, region and globe would have representations vertically levered up for discussion and resolution in an unbiased manner. This process will be followed in a similar way for the other financial stability-related issues. Ultimately, the vertically escalated issues would get converged horizontally seeking regional or global solutions, whatever the case may be.

Such a structural committee approach carries elements of an idea of 'subsidiarity as a principle for collective governance' (Bryant 2003). Each of the four independent boards/subcommittees (in both the approaches) consisting of experts in the respective areas would resemble subsidiaries having an arm's length relationship with the central body of the central bank.

A graphical presentation of the proposed GFSC model is given in Figure 9.2.

There may be an 'international secretariat responsible for administrative and analytical support' with staff brought on deputation from each of the countries. Similarly, there may be a panel of on-site examiners and off-site surveillance analysts drawn from various nations at the regional and global level. In case of need, these experts would take up assignments as independent external members in the teams at the national level. This way, manpower resource cost would remain billed to the NSCB or NFSC, while a type of emergency corpus fund may be created through contributions from all. There is no need of creation of new institutions. Few relevant divisions of the existing set-ups (IMF, WB, BIS and FSB) could be reorganized with the current location at Basel, remaining its headquarters.

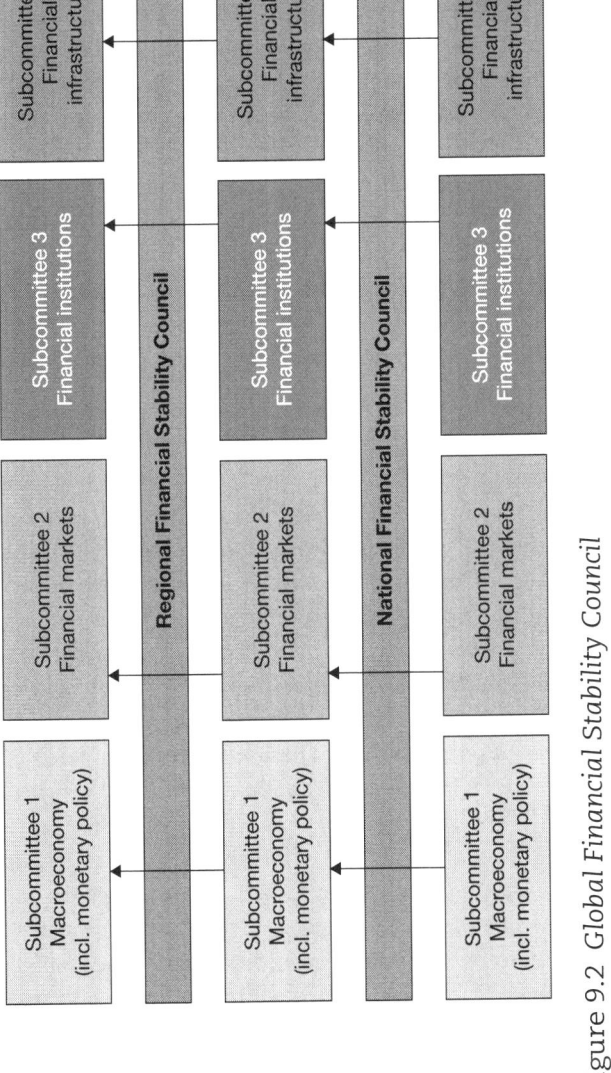

Figure 9.2 Global Financial Stability Council

Many experts in this area have serious apprehensions about central banks being allowed to play the leading role in the act of international cooperation because they are 'unelected' and the 'management of crises involves the actual or potential commitment of public money'. They would just end up mobilizing 'a collective view of the systemic consequences of different means of dealing with crises, then conveying this view to finance ministry colleagues' (Crocket 2005). In the matter of international monetary cooperation, '...we have to talk about more than central banks ... governments will have something to say' (Volcker 2005). Some point to the possible emergence of a sort of moral hazard in the minds of central bankers negotiating in international coordination frameworks. 'Monetary policy makers are accountable to their countrymen, not to a vague "international community." They will likely become more sensitive to whether their actions in the international sphere can be fully defended in terms of bringing benefits to the national economy and its citizens' (Yamaguchi 2005).

The proposed model has scope for overcoming these practical issues. Government is represented in each board/subcommittee, and decisions on public spending, in the event that they do occur, can be taken legitimately in this conclave. As a logical corollary, in the boards or subcommittees at regional or global level in which such decisions are supposed to be taken, a responsible government representative may be the obvious choice to be nominated for. The model leaves enough scope for various wings of the economy being involved in their respective areas, while decisions are taken on them at a regional or global level. The central banker need not necessarily get entangled in all the areas of policymaking. The implementation is left only to its officials for better coordination and homogeneity of action points. In an NSCB/NFSC, all the policymakers are from diverse areas of operations in the economy and are citizens of the nation, including the representative of the central bank. In RSCB/RFSC, representatives of the citizens of various nations sit together to discuss those issues which if taken up on a regional basis could benefit each of the individual nations and such that they would be inclined to take necessary actions at their national ends. A similar process occurs for GSCB/GFSC. It is natural to assume that no representative would like to go in for a decision that may harm its own nation but considering from a regional or global perspective, there could still be an opportunity gain for the representative to get attracted to the notion. While the 'trade-offs' will be many, policy responses and opportunities will be as equally numerous.

William R. White (2006) has voiced an interesting concern in the formulation of an effective macrofinancial framework for managing international systemic risk. The issue of 'the need for closer cooperation on financial stability issues between the various interested agencies in the official sector … agreement among involved agencies that an imbalances problem was emerging … followed by orchestrated statements of concern' would be crucial. Since '… the agencies involved see problems building up but assume that somebody else will do whatever needs to be done', it would be useful to handle this by setting up 'a committee of senior representatives of central banks, regulatory agencies and treasuries to monitor events and identify problems'. The proposed set-up takes care of these issues automatically with independent representatives from all wings of the financial sector, the central bank and the government under one roof, that too on national, regional and global bases deliberate on them on an ongoing basis. This would sound more effective from a practical viewpoint than the piecemeal 'as-and-when-required-get-togethers' organized under the aegis of the FSB at the BIS. If the BIS/FSB gets metamorphosed into the proposed GSCB/GFSC, then the institutional as well as operational issues would tend just to dissolve.

The FSB, which is the post-crisis incarnation of the FSF (established in April 2009), 'at the call of the Heads of State and Government of the Group of Twenty'[7] is meant to promote 'international financial stability' by coordinating national financial authorities and international standard-setting bodies. The interesting dimension akin to what is suggested here is that its membership consists of finance ministries,

[7] Four more countries and territories (Hong Kong SAR, the Netherlands, Singapore, Spain and Switzerland), the ECB and the European Commission, and international financial institutions and standard-setting bodies have been added to the membership.

central banks and financial supervisory and regulatory authorities of the member jurisdictions. Its administrative structure is in a way hierarchical, as suggested in the models (Figures 9.1 and 9.2) in this chapter, the plenary[8] (decision-making), the Steering Committee (taking forward operational work), three standing committees[9] (assimilating country feedback) and various working groups (researching identified technical areas) to facilitate its interaction with a wider group of countries, six RCG[10] have been formed to include 65 non-member jurisdictions, thus covering about 90 countries of the world. By this method, feedback on vulnerabilities affecting regional and global financial systems is analysed with a wider format and initiatives to stem them are taken by the FSB.

However, the FSB's recommendations are not legally binding on its members and it works through the concepts of moral suasion and peer pressure to motivate and commit members to implement its recommendations. Further, the Basel norms at the BIS were seen to be influenced by 'private financial institutions that anticipated being negatively affected by new regulations'. They

were able to enlist their nations' representatives on the Basel Committee to water down the measures. The initial proposal for increasing the ratio of common equity to risk-weighted assets to 8 per cent was scaled back to 7 per cent at the behest of countries

---

[8] The current number of 70 plenary seats.

[9] The Standing Committee on Assessment of Vulnerabilities (SCAV; http://www.fsb.org/organisation-and-governance/members-of-standing-committee-on-assessment-of-vulnerabilities/ [accessed on 22 February 2019]; for identifying and assessing risks), the Standing Committee on Supervisory and Regulatory Cooperation (SRC; http://www.fsb.org/organisation-and-governance/members-of-standing-committee-on-supervisory-and-regulatory-cooperation/ [accessed on 25 February 2019; for undertaking further supervisory analysis or framing a regulatory or supervisory policy response to a material vulnerability identified by SCAV), the Standing Committee on Standards Implementation (SCSI; http://www.fsb.org/organisation-and-governance/members-of-standing-committee-on-standards-implementation/ [accessed on 25 February 2019]; for monitoring the implementation of agreed FSB policy initiatives and international standards).

[10] The Americas, Asia, the Commonwealth of Independent States, Europe, the Middle East and North Africa and sub-Saharan Africa.

whose banks were exposed to Greek debt. The new higher capital requirements mandated under Basel III will not go into full effect for eight years—an eternity from the perspective of financial stability. This works to the favor of countries whose banks are poorly capitalized. The simple leverage ratio that will supplement these new higher capital requirements will similarly not go into effect for a few years and has been set at high levels, which works to the advantage of countries in both Europe and Asia where banks are highly leveraged. The same is true of the new liquidity requirements, which have been watered down at the behest of countries whose banks rely on short-term wholesale funding. (Eichengreen 2011)

In the past, there has been an MOU-based approach to regional/international cooperative structures. An agreement was made on 18 May 2005 towards a MOU among 'banking supervisors, central bankers and finance ministers of the EU on dealing with crises and to enhance practical arrangements concerning cooperation in cross-border crises situations at EU level' (de Larosiere 2005). In our proposed model, they would all be part of the RSCB Board/RFSC subcommittee Europe and would be, as a matter of mandated responsibility, initiating steps on an ongoing basis on any issue of concern in a cohesive and concerted manner.

The GSCB/GFSC in this form can deliberate and formulate on various other issues having bearing on the proposed World RTGS system, International Financial Technology Infrastructure, monetary and real unions as well as regional and global FCs taking inputs from the respective boards of the NSCB. The modalities of creation of lendor of last resort (LLR) and insurance corpus funds can be framed up accordingly on a joint contribution basis.

The distinguishing features of such a model would be as follows:

- It would generate a pool of global experts on each area, who are in the know of the evolving issues on an international plane.
- It would be easier to standardize and implement norms as those would be reflective of economy-specific realties being the brainchild of the expert representatives of the respective economy.

- The issues pertaining to financial regulation, monetary stability and liquidity subventions can be analysed on a holistic manner and on a regional as well as global perspective.
- The market realities on the ground can be captured with lesser wastage of time and human resources and the policy actions can be sharper as they are perceived from a practical point of view.
- The sense of responsibility and accountability of the policymaking would be backed strongly as they are by a sense of support bearing in the interest of individual member economy.
- The hierarchy and economy-specific nomination of market talents (as against public employees) from each economy would lend sufficient sharpness to the teeth of implementation in case of any crises.
- It would be the best bet for smelling and smoothing of systemic crisis of global dimension.
- It would be qualitatively superior to the proposed idea of a WFA as it would profess to take care of both financial and monetary stability with the authority of a central bank. As a LOLR, the central bank also has the fiscal dimension with the government nominee remaining actively associated at each layer of discussion and decision-making. The political strength could be a 'given' since the body of experts is nominated by the sovereign sanction.
- This would be a global body with accountability, and would hence remain focused on its avowed objectives because its functionally diversified activities were looked after by independent bodies of experts (not necessarily from the national governments or central banks) and, thereby, would relax its monolithic physical stature to considerable extent.

It would be worthwhile to reflect upon the ideas shared by Tiff Macklem (the then deputy governor of Bank of Canada in his remarks 'Renewing the IMF—Some Lessons from Modern Central Banking' to the Global Interdependence Center, Philadelphia, on 9 March 2006) on what should be the avowed principles for an internal surveillance outfit in the globalized, market economy of the 21st century. Equally of interest is the evaluation of how the proposed model compares with such expectations to promote 'global financial stability by supporting a market-based international monetary order' (Macklem 2006).

- *Multilateral surveillance against bilateral communication between IMF and a member country:* There is a need for a forum where risks are debated openly, frankly and comprehensively by national policy-makers ... strengthening the analysis of the linkages between the financial sector and the real economy ... potential risks to be identified earlier so that authorities can address any problems, rather than calling on the Fund for financial assistance in the midst of a crisis.

The forum should be effective as the issues that shape the global economy can be discussed 'with candor and good will and in which problems can be resolved' (Macklem 2006).

- *Legitimacy:* 'as a truly global institution, and on a shared sense of trust and responsibility'. 'Global issues can't be effectively addressed if key players feel that they don't have adequate voice as IMF members...quotas and voting powers at the Fund need to better reflect the growing power of Asian and other emerging-market economies' (Macklem 2006).
- *Effective use of markets:* '...to ensure soundness, sustainability, and efficient allocation of resources'. It should be able to establish the 'rules of the game' to address the risk of 'global imbalance' by playing a lead role in 'bringing the right players together, facilitating discussion, and relying on markets to achieve the necessary adjustments' and not doing too much 'exceptional lending' (Macklem 2006).
- *Transparency and accountability:* At IMF, 'Accountability is dispersed and decision-making lacks transparency'.

The IMF would be more effective if the Executive Board focused on setting strategic direction, as well as ensuring that policies are sound and that objectives are met. The Managing Director would then be responsible for policy implementation and be accountable to the Board.... Towards this end, Bank of England Governor Mervyn King had suggested establishing a non-resident Executive Board that meets periodically, rather than almost continuously, which focuses on strategic direction and oversight. Accountability and transparency of the Board's decision-making would also be enhanced with more frequent and more timely reporting. Finally, and very importantly, surveillance and analysis must be, and seen to be, independent of political influence. (Macklem 2006)

A careful perusal would suggest that the proposed GSCB/GFSC meets adequately (and even surpasses in many aspects) all these principles, which have been envisioned for a proposed remodelled IMF. The suggestion given here, as has been made clear earlier, is not too rigid about an entirely new outfit (as it may not be practical to have one fast enough to meet the emergent needs) and as such runs within the wavelength of current understanding of the issues. The proposed model is also in line with the seven-point criteria suggested by Miskin for central banks to ideally execute, especially the crucial last three, namely accountability, transparency/communication and financial stability. All these can be best discharged if we have NSCB/NFSC, RSCB/RFSC and GSCB/GFSC with the necessary characteristics discussed earlier. Thus, the suggestion gets the satisfaction at least of not trying to project something 'weird' or to defend the 'indefensible'.

It would be worthwhile to re-engage a bit more on the functions on the proposed WFA mooted by Eatwell and Taylor vis-a-vis the proposal of GSCB/GFSC. WFA is supposed 'to set regulatory standards for national authorities' and 'assist' them 'to adhere to them' by using a 'carrot' (general market acceptance) and 'stick' (poor ratings for poor adherence) method. With WFA surveillance in place, the

> IMF could be restructured as true lender of last resort, drawing on its own (expanded) resources and coordinating the efforts of national central banks. Its interventions would be infrequent and credible precisely because it would lend only in circumstances in which WFA criteria were satisfied.

Regulatory stances and capital market regimes will be taken by countries 'after due consultations with the WFA'. IMF/WB's 'one-size-fits-all' policy packages 'would become things of the past'. It would also devise better ways of optimizing size and scope of capital flows. It would also be quite useful to draw attention to the currently run hot debate on the status of global surveillance by the Bretton Woods Institutions (especially the IMF and the WB) so as to conceive an appropriate menu of action points, the GSCB/GFSC should be concerned with from the very outset.

For this purpose, a few fundamental issues may be taken for brief analysis. The 'first' is the role of 'an impartial arbitrator' (or a 'neutral assessor'—as envisioned by Ostry and Ghosh 2013—discussed elsewhere) as expected of the IMF by its founders, J. M. Keynes and H. D. White (Rajan 2006). This was amply reflected upon by the remarks of Paul Volcker in as far back as 1992. 'When the Fund consults with a poor and weak country, the country gets in line. When the Fund consults with a big and strong country, the Fund gets in line' (quoted by Buira 2004). Another case in history of IMF reflecting its inability to be unbiased was seen during post-Asian crisis.

> In exchange for providing financial assistance, the IMF required South Korea to raise interest rates and to cut government spending. That is the exact opposite of what the U.S. and Europe have done when faced with a very difficult crisis. One potential reason why this happened is that the IMF is a European and U.S. dominated institution. The head of the IMF up to now has always been a European while the head of the World Bank has always been an American. Asian countries are not represented at the highest levels. (Franklin and Carletti 2010)

'....[T]he [f]und remains reluctant to bite the hand that feeds it; we have yet to see it launch withering critiques of Chinese currency manipulation and U.S. fiscal profligacy' (Eichengreen 2011). It 'should be understood as behaving most consistently not in its commitment to the allocative efficiency of markets, but rather in its commitment to furthering the interests of key groups of economic and political elites'

(Buckley, Macdonald and Pinto 2012)... 'acts as an honest broker between strong political and national interests ... tries to avoid figure-pointing; it tries to avoid putting Japan, China or any other big power in dock' (Pringle 2014).

The system of quota and the way it was decided to be fixed gives ample reason to believe that this was meant to be breached even by definition from the first day. As described by Raymond Mikesell, the person who had been requested by the US Treasury to estimate the first quotas:

> White called me to his office and asked that I prepare a formula for the ... quotas that would be based on the members' gold and dollar holdings, national incomes and foreign trade. He gave no instructions on the weights to be used, but I was to give the US a quota or approximately $2.9 billion; the UK (including its colonies), about half the US quota; the Soviet Union an amount just under that of the UK; and China somewhat less. White's major concern was that our military allies should have the largest quotas ... (Mikesell 1994)

Moreover, countries that wanted to contribute more, such as Australia, Iran and France, were not allowed to do so.

There can hardly be any improvement in such a position now, since any quota increase (the only vehicle for adjusting quota sizes) is required to be approved by 85 per cent of the vote and the US holds over 17 per cent and the EU combined accounts for over 30 per cent of the votes. The collective quota and voting shares of the members of the EU are currently 31.9 and 30.9 per cent, respectively. Even the revised model being considered by the International Monetary Fund (2014) would drop the EU combined calculated quota share to at the most to 22.1 per cent 'illustrating how disproportionate European influence is in the IMF relative to its true economic size' (Truman 2015). The developing countries are apportioned lesser votes, hence lesser say in the decision-making. Moreover, the structure in terms of membership is also perceived to be negatively skewed in favour of developing countries. Though the IMF has 188 members, it is seen to be run by seven of them—the USA, Japan, Germany, the UK, France, Canada and Italy. The bigger a country's financial quota, the more weight it has over the proceedings and deliberation over the running of the IMF. This means that it is run by the countries that are least affected by its policies.[11]

This does not speak well of the standards of corporate governance and the accountability system as they seem to limit themselves to the interests of limited countries and often detrimental to the collective world interest (Nayyar and Court 2002). A committee approach of decision-making is better than a hierarchical one in line with ethics of corporate governance as it relies on more brains than one. If allocated voting power decides the number of brains one individual member can count for himself/herself, then the spirit behind the 'committee approach' gets defeated and the system remains no better than a hierarchical one, because the member having more power in terms of decision-making (by virtue of more voting power) deems to be hierarchically superior to the other having lesser voting power.

[11] Quotas that also determine voting power at the IMF are especially low for rapidly growing emerging markets such as Brazil, the PRC, and India. Kelkar, Choudhry, Vanduzer-Snow, and Bhaskar (2005) found that these three countries had 19% fewer votes than Belgium, Italy, and the Netherlands collectively, although they had 21% more nominal GDP, 400% more purchasing power GDP, and 2,800% more population. On the other hand, Europe controls directly or indirectly 10 chairs out of 24 on the IMF Executive Board, even though it has a common monetary policy and about 30% of quota and voting rights. The charters, quotas, and voting rights of IEIs were designed in the interest of like-minded original core members in 1944 and are inflexible and difficult to change as membership expands. In comparison with the 44 countries that participated in the Bretton Woods conference, membership of the IMF and World Bank now stands at 188.

There have been proposals to reform the quota and voice in the IMF in 2008 and again in 2010. 'The proposal to shift 6 per cent of the quota to dynamic emerging markets and developing countries and to reduce European representation at the IMF Board by two chairs has not yet been ratified' (Rana 2013).

There have been suggestions in the literature of global surveillance reforms to embrace 'globalization' on the back of 'regionalization', thus reflecting the fact on the ground that trade and exchange rate policies are taking on an increasingly regional character with intra-regional business outpacing inter-regional business.

> Regional surveillance can be improved and that spillovers can be addressed better by grouping bilateral consultations by regions, whether or not the region has formal arrangements.... Another useful change in IMF governance ... would be to reconfigure and consolidate the constituencies of the Executive Board around regional groupings.... This is particularly important in the case of Europe and other complete monetary unions but applies well to regions in which monetary and financial integration is less advanced but in which cross-border effects are nonetheless prevalent. (Henning 2005)

This idea gets special focus in the proposed model. RSCBs/RFSCs are supposed to discuss and sort out national issues having regional ramifications on the pedestal of a regional outfit with representatives from all the concerned nations in a democratic manner. Representatives of the regions then carry these regional voices to the GSCB/GFSC, the ultimate altar of discussions on regional issues having international ramifications. The Executive Board of the GSCB/GFSC gets constituted with the representatives of various RSCBs/RFSCs, which by definition would be non-residential in character while carving out policies for international systemic risk management in an ongoing manner. The nominations from the nations and then from the regions being decided in an issue-specific manner, the nominees for specific policy deciding meetings at the RSCBs/RFSCs or the GSCB/GFSC would necessarily be outside-cherry-picked-experts being rotated, thus ensuring impartiality and transparency of decisions 'that differentiate constructive from unconstructive regional financial facilities' (Henning 2005) backed by sheer parochial bias.

As such, the GSCB/GFSC could 'function as a trusted, independent and expert secretariat for policy makers around the globe' as also act as a true 'custodian of global governance' with considerable and well-defined homogeneity in the 'forms of representation, goals and authority'. The proliferation of 'second or third generation emanated institutions', namely, G7/G10/G20 (agenda setting and rule ratification), IMF/WB/IFC/BIS/FSB (rule-making and enforcing), IFAC/IASC/IOSCO/IAIS (rule setting) with inherent 'overlapping jurisdictions', which the current inertia has given birth to, would eventually stop. All aspects of global governance will be taken care of by the NSCB (NFSC)/RSCB (RFSC)/GSCB (GFSC) by way of internal working groups consisting of the well-identified global expert pool available at their disposal. While on one hand this would tend to sharpen the focus of the very rationale of their formation, they would mean restraining the avoidable suboptimal use of man and material resources on a global plane on the other.

The approach to global monetary and financial surveillance in the model proposed in this chapter would rely extensively on the philosophy of 'homogeny' rather than 'hegemony' with little trace of 'democracy-deficit'. Experts in the countries at national, regional and global levels will be sitting together to decide which concept is the best for which country and region and at what point in time so that global imbalances are tackled in a practical manner. There would not be any concept of one authority being superior to another in terms of decision-making and with provision for being mandatorily consulted. In such a system where regulatory guidelines are framed taking the regulated parties within the umbrella of confidence, the possibility of non-adherence and use of 'carrots' and 'sticks' for that purpose may not be needed. Such strategies may be considered at the national level but not at the regional or global level. With the current trend of diluted internationalism and inverted economic power structure, expectations for any involuntary adherence will have chances to be bellied while voluntary compliance will be respected as an exception than a rule. In this respect, the proposed model has better scope for being accepted and because it also involves a metamorphosis of existing structures (and hence minimum tinkering in the men and money availability), it should be a more 'sensible international action' (Eatwell and Taylor

2000). Further, the puzzle of the possible 'governance trilemma'[12] that the current outfits face are well handled by the proposed model.

Kawai and Rana (2009) and Rana (2013) sound optimistic on the slow but steady progress towards decentralized decision-making in the global arena, and, as such, their ideas echo the one proposed in this chapter. Based on their experience with the Asian financial crisis, they argue that efforts 'to prevent and manage a capital account crisis required actions at the global, regional, and national levels or a multilayered global financial safety net'.[13] They go on to envision a multi-layered decision-making structure where national, bilateral and regional initiatives are given cognizance based on 'functional federalism' and 'the principle of subsidiarity' that believe in taking on board decisions made at the lowest possible administrative level for decision-making globally. This will lend flexibility and credibility to international decisions as they are taken out of decisions within countries, which typically involve several layers of government. Such global public goods managed by a regionally decentralized decision-making process would encourage emerging economies to take leadership in the whole process. It would be easier to have national and regional decisions tailor-made to allow for globally coherent measures that act

---

[12] There is broad agreement that IEIs need to become (i) more democratic, (ii) more effective in delivering public goods, and (iii) universal by accepting all countries that apply for membership. These requirements add up to a trilemma; achieving any one two objectives makes achieving the other more difficult. For example, the United Nations (UN) is democratic and universal but suffers on effectiveness. Similarly, the IMF and World Bank are universal and effective but not democratic. The G20 represents 4.2 billion people of the world but not the other 2.6 billion people. (Kawai, Petri and Sisli-Ciamarra 2009: 13). (Rana 2013)

[13] Financial globalization is 'associated with large inflows and sudden reversals of capital flows, the bursting of asset bubbles, and a banking crisis' 'tending to affect an economic entity's balance sheets and solvency positions. The costs of balance sheet recessions tend to be higher and recovery from such a crisis takes longer. They also tend to be systemic, affecting most or all sectors of the economy, with strong contagion to neighboring countries (which may be innocent bystanders).' Rana (2013) (ibid).

as building blocks of a global system. These principles tend to gel quite well with those enshrined in this chapter. The semblance of such a decentralized architecture[14] is getting visible in the ongoing configurations at the currently existing global bodies. They feel that replacing G20[15] by 'the Global Economic Coordination Council (GECC)

[14] In the developmental architecture, the World Bank is complemented by four regional development banks. In the financial architecture, we have the FSB at the global level and the ESRB, the three European bodies for banking, insurance and securities market and the proposed Asian Financial Stability Board (AFSB) at the regional level. In the international monetary architecture, the G20 is at the apex. The IMF has various multilateral safety nets. There are the bilateral financial safety nets (BFSNs) among central banks that were triggered when Singapore and the Republic of Korea faced liquidity problems in late 2008. In Asia, about a dozen and a half bilateral swaps were established between central banks of the region under the CMI in the aftermath of the Asian financial crisis. In March 2010, these were combined and expanded to become the CMIM. In April 2011, the AMRO, an independent surveillance unit for the CMIM, was established in Singapore. AMRO's mandate is to 'monitor and analyze regional economies…'.

[15] G20 is an

extremely differentiated and heterogeneous set of countries, whose conditions and priorities differ both in the short term and over the long run. It would be extremely naive to expect that such a group would be able to reach agreement on anything beyond the immediate crisis at hand, despite their ambition to tackle structural issues (Gokarn 2010).

the G20, the forum in which 19 countries plus the European Union bargain over solutions to pressing international problems … is a dysfunctional institution that will create as many problems as it solves … 20 negotiators never agree on anything of substance unless and until they feel threatened by the same problem at the same time and to more or less the same degree. (Bremmer 2012)

Paul Martin (Canada's finance minister, 1993–2002, then prime minister, 2003–2006)

was the man who created the G20. He didn't put forward the G20 idea mainly to improve global governance. Instead, it was the product of his careful calculation of what was best for Canada. His country had long been a member of the G7, a privileged position. But years before the market meltdown of 2008, Paul Martin understood that the world's balance of power was changing more quickly than many realized and that the G7 was and the Financial Stability Board by a World Finance Organization (WFO)' and 'establishing the proposed Asian Financial Stability Board (AFSB) by involving the region's regulators and supervisors' as in Europe to assist the FSB would be useful.

Schinasi and Truman (2010) also favour a global financial architecture that persuades remedial actions—in times of crises—at the national, regional, continental or global level. While they like to 'establish the conditions for closely coordinated policy development and implementation' and to let the process to start from below—at national levels—and to 'collectively and equitably create, manage, and capture the benefits of global public goods', they do not appear to be in favour of dislodging the applecart of the IMF and FSB whose financial stability roles, they feel, should be enhanced individually and collectively through the means of cooperation and collaboration. While

> the IMF must focus on macroeconomic and macro financial stability and their linkages and implications for the stability of the global financial system, the FSB must focus its efforts on sponsoring the adoption of new international supervisory and regulatory standards that improve the ability to assess, monitor, and hopefully maintain systemic financial stability in addition to the safety and soundness of financial institutions.

To address 'legitimacy issues', FSB should report to the IMF's International Monetary and Financial Committee (IMFC) in addition to the G20 ministers and governors and G20 leaders. Accordingly, they would like to see the IMF having more power and authority 'to facilitate the dialogue between member countries' and to get the FSB to 'call on the IMF to consider and deliver on certain issues'.

This model does see some similarities in the configurations for the NSCB (NFSC)/RSCB (RFSC)/GSCB (GFSC) proposed by

---

fast becoming irrelevant. He became convinced that Canada needed to exchange its first-class seat on a sinking ship for a secure spot on a bigger boat. By leading the effort to build that boat, Martin believed that Canada could win valuable new friends. The G20, dysfunctional or not, is now a fixture of international politics. (Bremmer 2012) it with these proposals. These are, however, not democratic set-ups and are based on hegemonistic principles, while this chapter recommends something quite different in their inherent characteristics. It is, however, in alignment with Hannoun (2010) who feels that the global framework would be effective to handle both 'price stability and financial stability' concerns if it carries policy contributions from microprudential, macroprudential, monetary, fiscal and market disciplines in a holistic manner. It would accordingly need to 'rely on close cooperation between central banks and supervisory authorities, both within and across borders'. The institutional set-up of the mechanism of international coordination must be 'based on precise mandates and clear accountability'. Both versions of coordination mechanism reflect such thoughts.

Macroeconomic stability and financial stability in the various regions may be promoted through coordinated efforts on inflows and outflows to minimize any spillover impacts. This becomes more important in the view of the regional economies sharing common capital inflow or outflow pressures. What can be done is formalizing an informal policy coordination on the exchange rates which could go in a long way to maintain intra-regional exchange rate stability along with each country's macroeconomic stability. They can also bolster regional FSNs. The countries under a group can analyse any international spillover effects together and provide consistent, coherent advice to the global body.

While deciding on macroprudential policies for a nation (or for that matter a region),[16] the financial stability councils would address international issues, including the imposition of negative externalities of their policies on other countries and vice versa. The other related issues, namely cross-border regulatory arbitrage, 'leakage' effects and home-host authority conflicts arising from the supervision of financial institutions that operate in multiple jurisdictions can also be judiciously handled in these outfits. National and supranational authorities in the nature of NFSCs/RFSCs as a matter of their mandate will need to

---

[16] Regional architectures such as ASEAN, ASEAN+6 and the East Asia Summit are among those forums that attempt to create a more resilient regional block with respect to trade, finance and mobility of resources.

spot and contain risks across borders and globally via efficient practices of information sharing and on-the-ground decision-making.[17] By its very preamble for creation, the authorities need to avoid economic nationalism as a matter of rule and especially in the time of crisis. Home bias will harm all the members.[18]

The achievement of unified regulatory harmonization has been elusive on various accounts. Continued changes in the related economies warranting changes in regulation have been a prominent reason. It has also been prudently stated that countries in position to implement best practice regulation promote mutual recognition in areas such as fund management, harmonize market infrastructure and promote cross-border supervisory. MOUs may move on to higher stages of harmonization.[19] These regional regulatory institutions can then strengthen ties with their respective global institutions.

The process by which both the RSCB/RFSC and GSCB/GFSC would be funded for its day-to-day running and also for keeping a 'buffer fund' for unforeseen contingencies would have to be thought of in a serious manner considering the current arrangements in place and their perceived drawbacks. It should neither be on the basis of proportionate share in the capital pool nor should it be on the basis of size and status of the economy concerned. In such a broad approach of decision-making, each member's opinion should be given equal attention. This fundamental difference in structural change should not get

---

[17] The Spanish housing bubble, which affected Spain directly and Germany indirectly, is a good example of a case in which cross-border information sharing and actions would have been helpful.

[18] German banks had lent large sums of money into Greece, Spain and other peripheral European countries. When they pulled their funds back home as a result of regulatory pressure and a short-sighted view of their own self-interest, it severely harmed the borrower countries. That harm rebounded on Germany as the Euro Crisis accelerated, damaging confidence, trade and the overall economy across Europe, including Germany.

[19] The EU has committed itself to shifting financial regulation from the national to the regional level by way of a region-wide regulatory framework which will include the Single Supervisory Mechanism headed by the ECB and region-wide resolution and deposit insurance structures.

compromised on the issue of mobilizing financial wherewithal. Each financial unit can have a deposit with the NSCB/NFSC (to look after the operational expenses of RSCB/RFSC and GSCB/GFSC) and/or can have a floating provision to meet unforeseen systemic crises to be used when an occasion arises or can contribute to central insurance fund based on the size of the business. It should also have a 'provision of bridge finance to stave off particular dangers' (Crocket 2005) or an attractive insurance facility in the nature of a 'global version of the Chiang Mai initiative, where countries offer to lend reserves to each other … or a … formal pooling of country reserves … that would offer far more automatic access in times of trouble….' (Rajan 2006, as a part of an IMF reforms programme).

While thinking of these kinds of means and the available pools of contingency funds, a need would arise to ensure that moral hazard does not work to reduce risk awareness. To this end, regulatory or supervisory policies can be evolved to reduce such behaviour. If the scheme of compensation is linked to supervisory opinion on genuineness or legitimacy of the claims made, such tendencies may be expected to be kept at minimum.

This is in no way an easy task. But given the potentials for collective rewards as along with systemic risk looming large, such edifices need to be erected. While globalization of the economic world is distinctly discernible, the shadows of close-knit geographic zones are visible too. So long as they reinforce each other's vitality, there is no harm. The so-called 'Chairs and Shares' (Rana 2013) mode of global governance must give way to 'CARE and SHARE' mode made up of the 'voice' of all. Let the chronology of monetary history (which has been) driven by 'warfare' be steered in future by 'welfare' of the human race (Noyer 2015).

Another impetus to this idea was given through an empirical study by Bank for International Settlements (2013) which assessed the efficacy of monetary actions for a multi-country system based on empirical estimations. It considered the spillover effects in a Taylor multi-country model (TMCM) which includes the USA, Japan and the other G7 countries (described in Taylor [1993]) and in an

IMF global model (GPM6), which along with the USA and Japan also includes some emerging market economies in Latin America and Asia.

The report concludes:

> As with most forecasting endeavors, predicting the likely course of international monetary policy coordination requires examining recent trends and then determining the state of play today. Empirical research beginning in the early 1980s predicted that the gains from international coordination of monetary policy would be quantitatively small compared to those achieved from each central bank following a monetary policy which optimised its own country's economic performance. This was the implication of empirically estimated multi-country monetary models that assumed market-determined flexible exchange rates, international capital mobility, no arbitrage on the term structure of interest rates, rational expectations, and price and wage rigidities which formed the basis for monetary policy effectiveness. These predictions turned out to be pretty close to actual monetary policy outcomes in developed countries during the Great Moderation period—the 1980s, 1990s, and until recently. Economic performance improved dramatically, especially compared with the 1970s, as central banks moved towards more transparent rules based monetary policies—including through inflation-targeting or flexible inflation targeting—and focused on domestic price and output stability. Attempts to formally coordinate policy choices across countries would probably have added little to macroeconomic stability during the Great Moderation, as the monetary models implied. The international monetary system was operating near an internationally cooperative equilibrium (NICE). What caused the recent departure from the NICE monetary system? The first is that monetary policy deviated from the optimal rule-like policies, which were a prerequisite for the result that the gains from international coordination were relatively small; the theory was not wrong, but rather the policy assumptions that went into the theory no longer held…. The second explanation is that the complaints about spillovers and calls for coordination by some countries are part of a process by which some central banks are adapting their policies to better suit their own domestic situation.

Conclusion

Going forward, the world economies should strive for a more balanced system and rule-based monetary policies taking into account the likely spillover effects it will create the world over. International policy coordination should result in optimization of economic performance in member economies, provide for adequate representation for all members, and create the system to cater to the needs of the all. Only then can a global model be built for pan world policy coordination.

It has been observed that developing regions such as Latin America, Africa and Asia resort to financial arrangements that differ from the Euro Area model since the European Union project is significantly broader and has as its inspiration/aspiration, socio-political and economic welfare goals that go beyond monetary unions and single currency areas. Barbara Fritz and Laurissa Mühlich's (2015) contribution in this regard addresses the question of why Optimum Currency Area (OCA) theory has been the fundamental premise that guided European integration. This theory focuses on the allocative efficiency gains from monetary policy cooperation in developed/advanced countries, ignoring the other fundamental economic incentives that may be reaped through cooperation among developing and emerging market countries which are taken to be the creation of short-term liquidity, increasing regional trade and financial links, enhancing the shock-sustaining ability, thereby protecting from the impact of exogenous global shocks. As we have seen, the small, emerging and developing nations are particularly vulnerable with regard to these shocks. Hence, for these aims, the route adopted by the emerging nations has not been initially envisaged through the formation of a currency union rather through the regional arrangements with a sequencing to monetary union, starting with trade integration wherein monetary union is a last step and is preceded by a significant effort towards economic convergence, free flow of labour, goods, capital and finance, and uniform rules of consumer protection, market and competitive practices (but, not of financial regulation and supervision), nor in the fiscal realm. As we have discussed, a variety of regional economic arrangements across the developing world have been coined in terms of incentives and respective domestic or regional economic structures.

With regard to liquidity support provisions, depending on the type of the financial international arrangement, the support has been found to be varied. The main issue, however, is political. As generally in regard to liquidity support, a surplus country, which may be richer, transfers resources (or takes over risks) to the deficient and broadly poorer economies. Hence, this arrangement works on inequality rather than equality which is the basis of the political risks to the integration process. Liquidity supports in the forms of establishment of institutions such as regional monetary funds, other types of last resort mechanism, bilateral or multilateral swap agreements or in the consolidation of ad hoc bailout agreements are generally found world over. Hence, the choice of a regional leader to participate in the establishment of this sort of a regional financial and monetary arrangement becomes pertinent. The trade-off between short-term costs and long-term benefits in terms of economic and political gains needs to be gauged for the arrangement to be effective. The Garland model discussed earlier essentially takes into consideration all these aspects and provides a sustainable solution for the future world economic and financial cooperation.

References

Albertin, Giorgia. 2007. 'Will a Regional Bloc Enlarge?' IMF Working Paper No. 07/69, April.

Armstrong, Chris. 2006. 'Global Civil Society and the Question of Global Citizenship'. *Voluntas,* 2006. Available at https://ssrn.com/abstract=2589003

Arner, Douglas, W. and Ross P. Buckley. 2010. 'Redesigning the Architecture of the Global Financial System'. *Melbourne Journal of International Law* 11 (2): 1–55.

Atiyas, Izak, Haroon Bhorat, Kemal Derviş, Peter Drysdale, Claudio R. Frischtak, Ippei Fujiwara, Daniel Gros, Paolo Guerrieri, Alan Hirsch, E. Fuat Keyman, Homi Kharas, Miguel Kiguel, Donald Kohn, Xue Lan, Marina Larionova, Wonhyuk Lim, Jacques Mistral, Rakesh Mohan, Yoshio Okubo, Guillermo Ortiz, Galip Kemal Ozhan, Andrey Shelepov, Paola Subacchi, Maria Monica Wihardja, Guntram B. Wolff and Qiao Yu. 2013, August. *Think Tank 20: The G-20 and Central Banks in the New World of Unconventional Monetary Policy.* Available at https://www.brookings.edu/wp-content/uploads/2016/06/TT20-central-banks-monetary-policy-2.pdf (accessed on 25 February 2019).

Bank for International Settlements. 2013. 'International Monetary Policy Co-ordination—Past, Present and Future'. Working Paper No. 437. Basel: Bank for International Settlements.

Bergsten C. Fred. 2015. US Should Work with the Asian Infrastructure Investment Bank, Peterson Institute for International Economics, *Financial Times*, 15 March.

Borio, Claudio. 2016. 'More Pluralism, More Stability?' Seventh High-Level SNB–IMF Conference on the International Monetary System. Zurich.

Boughton, James M. 2016. Is There a Future for International Monetary Cooperation? Centre for International Governance Innovation, 25 April.

Bremmer, Ian. 2012. *Every Nation for Itself: What Happens When No One Leads the World.* Penguin Publishers.

Bryant, Ralph. 2003. *Turbulent Waters: Cross-Border Finance and International Governance.* Washington, DC: Brookings Institution.

Bryant, Ralph. 2004. *Crisis Prevention and Prosperity Management for the World Economy.* Washington, DC: The Brookings Institution.

Bryant, Ralph. 1999, July. 'Reforming the International Financial Architecture'. Brookings Discussion Papers in International Economics No. 146.

Buckley, Ross P., Marshall Macdonald and Pinto, eds. 2012. *Reforming International Financial Governance, New Visions for Market Governance: Crisis and Renewal* (pp. 43–51). Oxford: Routledge.

Buira, Ariel. 2004. 'Can More Representative Governance Improve Global Economic Performance?' Draft of the Technical Group. Available at https://www.g24.org/wp-content/uploads/2016/01/Can-More-Representative-Governance-Improve-Global-Economic-Performance.pdf (accessed on 22 February 2019).

Caruana, Jaime. 2015. Financial reform and the role of regulators: Evolving markets, evolving risks, evolving regulation. Speech at GARP 16th Annual Risk Management Convention, New York, 24 February.

Caruana, Jaime. 2017, September. 'International Arrangements for A Resilient Global Economy'. Keynote Speech—Reinventing Bretton Woods Committee.

Corsi, Jerome. 1988. 'Get Ready for the Phoenix'. *The Economist.*

Council on Foreign Relations. 2005. *Building a North American Community.* Available at https://cfrd8-files.cfr.org/sites/default/files/report_pdf/PDF%20posted%20on%20web–English.pdf (accessed on 25 February 2019).

Davies, Howard. 2014, 16 October. The Spider of Finance, Project Syndicate.

de Larosiere, J. 2005, 27–29 June. 'Reflections on the Future of Cooperation Between Central Banks'. Speech at 4th BIS Conference.

de Larosiere, J. 2014, 12 May. 'The International Monetary Anti-System'. *Central Banking Journal.* Speech based on 'Bretton Woods @ 70', organized by the National Bank of Austria and the Reinventing Bretton Woods Committee, February.

Eatwell, J. and L. Taylor. 1998. International capital markets and the future of economic policy. A paper prepared for the Ford Foundation project International Capital Markets and the Future of Economic Policy. New York: Center for Economic Policy Analysis; London: IPPR.

Eatwell, J. and L. Taylor. 2000. *Global Finance at Risk: The Case for International Regulation*. New York: Policy Press.

Eichengreen, Barry, Mohamed El-Erian, Arminio Fraga, Takatoshi Ito, Jean Pisani-Ferry, Eswar Prasad, Raghuram Rajan, Maria Ramos, Carmen Reinhart, Hélène Rey, Dani Rodrik, Kenneth Rogoff, Hyun Song Shin, Andrés Velasco, Beatrice Weder di Mauro and Yongding Yu. 2011, September. 'Rethinking Central Banking'. Report of the Committee on International Economics and Policy Reform. Waterloo: Committee on International Economics and Policy Reform.

Eichengreen, Barry. 2011, December. 'International Policy Coordination: The Long View'. NBER Working Paper No. 17665. Cambridge, MA: National Bureau of Economic Research.

Engel, Charles. 2015, February. 'International Coordination of Central Bank Policy'. NBER Working Paper 20952. Cambridge, MA: National Bureau of Economic Research.

Farhi, Emmanuel and Matteo Maggiori. 2016. 'A Model of the International Monetary System'. NBER Working Paper No. 22295. Available at https://www.nber.org/papers/w22295 (accessed on 15 April 2019).

Frankel, Jeffrey. 2015. 'The Plaza Accord, 30 Years Later'. NBER Working Paper No. 21813. Cambridge, MA: National Bureau of Economic Research.

Franklin, Allen and Elena Carletti. 2010, February. 'New Theories to Underpin Financial Reform'. Presented at the Institute for New Economic Thinking 2010 Spring Conference, 8–11 April, Cambridge, England.

Fritz, B. and L. Mühlich. 2015. 'Varieties of Regional Monetary Cooperation: A Tool for Reducing Volatility in Developing Economies?' *Contemporary Politics* 21 (2): 127–145.

Garten, Jeffery E. 1998. 'Needed: A Fed for the World'. *New York Times*, 23 September.

Gokarn, Subir. 2010. Policies for Growth and Financial Stability Beyond the Crisis—The Scope for Global Cooperation. ICRIER/InWEnt/DIE Conference, Mumbai, 27 October.

Hannoun, Hervé. 2010, 26–27 February. 'Towards a Global Financial Stability Framework'. Speech at 45th SEACEN, Governors' Conference, Siem Reap Province, Cambodia.

Henning, C. R. 2005, 23 September. 'Regional Arrangements and the IMF.' Speech at the Conference on Reform of the IMF Organized by IIE.

Imbs, Jean M. 2007. Pooling Risk Among Countries, IMF Working Paper No 07/132, 25 June.

Ingves, Stefan. 2014. Basel III Implementation: Progress, Pitfalls, and Prospects. Speech at Peru, 3–5 November.

James, Harold. 1996. *International Monetary Cooperation since Bretton Woods*. IMF and Oxford University Press.

Kahler, Miles and David A. Lake (2003). *Governance in a Global Economy—Political Authority in Transition* 37 (3): 409–414.

Kaufman, G. 1991. 'Lender of Last Resort: A Contemporary Perspective'. *Journal of Financial Services Research* 5: 95–110.

Kauppi, Piia-Noora, Jo Leinen, Graham Watson and Gérard Onesta, eds. 2007. *The Case for Global Democracy—Advocating a United Nations Parliamentary Assembly.* Germany: Committee for a Democratic U.N. Berlin.

Kawai, M., and P. Rana. 2009. The Asian Crisis Revisited: Lessons, Responses, and New Challenges. In *Lessons from the Asian Financial Crisis*, edited by R. Carney. London: Routledge.

Kawai, M., P. Petri and E. Sisli-Ciamarra. 2009. *Asia in Global Governance: A Case for Decentralized Institutions.* ADBI Working Paper 157.

Kindleberger, C. P. 1977. *Manias, Panics and Crashes.* Palgrave Macmillan. King, Mervyn. 2006, 6 February. 'Reform of the International Monetary Fund'. Speech delivered at ICRIER, New Delhi.

Lunde, Leiv. 2000, December. 'Coherence or Dissonance in the International Framework: Overlapping Responsibilities'. ECON Centre for Economic Analysis.

Macklem, Tiff. 2006, 9 March. 'Renewing the IMF—Some Lessons from Modern Central Banking' (Remarks to the Global Interdependence Center). Philadelphia.

Mikesell, Raymond F. 1994. *Essays in International Finance.* Princeton, NJ: International Finance Section, Princeton University.

Mishra, Rabi N. 2006, 1–3 May. 'Financial Innovations and Systemic Risk: In Search of an Ever-Elusive Global Super Central Bank' (International Conference on Business, Banking and Finance). Trinidad and Tobago. Available at http://sta.uwi.edu/conferences/finance/abstracts.asp (accessed on 22 February 2019).

Nayyar, Deepak and Julius Court. 2002. *Governing Globalization: Issues and Institutions.* Helsinki: World institute for Development Economics Research.

Noyer, Christian. 2015, 8 June. Michael Bordo and Angela Redish quoted in 'Spheres of Influence in the International Monetary System' (Speech).

Ostry, Jonathan D. and Atish R. Ghosh. 2013, December. 'Obstacles to International Policy Coordination, and How to Overcome Them'. IMF Staff Discussion Note SDN 13/11. Washington, DC: International Monetary Fund.

Peterson Institute for International Economics, Working Paper 10, 14 September.

Pringle, Robert. 2014. *The Money Trap—Escaping the Grip of Global Finance*, 2nd edition. Basingstoke: Palgrave Macmillan.

Rajan, Raghuram G. 2006b, 10 April. 'The Role of IMF in a Changing World'. Lecture at the Kiel Institute.

Rajan, Raghuram G. 2006a, 8 March. 'The Ebbing Spirit of Internationalism and the International Monetary Fund: The 2006 Krasnoff Lecture'. Stern School of Business, New York.

Rajan, Raghuram G. 2014a, 31 January. *Rajan Warns of Policy Breakdown as Emerging Markets Fall.* Bloomberg. Available at http://www.bloomberg.

com/news/print/2014-01-30/rajan-warns-of-globalpolicy-breakdown-as-emerging-markets-slide.html (accessed on 22 February 2019).

Rajan, Raghuram G. 2014b. 'Competitive Monetary Easing: Is It Yesterday Once More?' (Remarks at the Brookings Institution). Washington, DC. Available at http://rbi.org.in/scripts/BS_SpeechesView.aspx?Id=886 (accessed on 22 February 2019).

Rajan, Raghuram G. 2015, 25 June. 'Going Bust for Growth' (Remarks at the AQR Conference at London Business School).

Rana, Pradumna B. 2013. From a Centralized to a Decentralized Global Economic Architecture: An Overview. ADBI Working Paper Series No. 401, January.

Schinasi, Garry J. and Edwin M. Truman. 2010. *Reform of the Global Financial Architecture.*

Sheng, Andrew. 2015, 23 January. 'Proposal—The New Global Financial Architecture'. BCBS 2015–2016 Programme.

Taylor, John B. 1993. Discretion versus Policy Rules in Practice. *Carnegie-Rochester Conference Series on Public Policy* 39: 195–214 (North-Holland).

The Economist. 2015. *Thrills and Spills.* Available at https://www.global-economic-symposium.org/knowledgebase/the-new-global-financial-architecture/proposals/the-new-global-financial-architecture-1 (accessed on 22 February 2019).

Trauman, Edwin M. 2017, October. The End of the Bretton Woods International Monetary System. Peterson Institute for International Economics Working Paper No. 17-11.

Truman, Edwin M. 2015, 15 January. 'What Next for the IMF?' Policy Brief. Washington, DC: Peterson Institute of International Economics.

Venner, K. Dwight. 2002, 16–17 September. 'How Can Monetary Policy Be Conducted in the Union?' Conference on Challenges to Central Banking from Globalized Financial Systems at IMF. Washington, DC.

Volcker, Paul. 2005. International Institutions in a global Economy. Speech at Cairncross Lecture at St. Peter's College, Oxford.

Watson, Steve. 2007, 5 June. *EU/US Merger: New Global Order by Stealth.* Information Clearing House. Available at http://www.informationclearing-house.info/article17657.htm (accessed on 22 February 2019).

Weber, Axel. 2011. The IMF and the International Monetary System: Lessons from the Crisis. Jacobsson Foundation Lecture, 25 September.

White, William R. 2006, January. 'Procyclicality in the Financial System: Do We Need a New Macro Financial Stabilization Framework?' BIS Working Paper No. 193. Basel: Bank for International Settlements.

CHAPTER 10

Macrofinancial Policy Coordination in the Current Milieu

The ultimate objective of a financial system is to ensure that the real economy grows at an optimum pace, and to achieve this, a stable financial system is a prerequisite. The approaches discussed in the previous chapter to achieve global policy coordination are a way forward. Ensuring this coordination is even more important in the current scenario wherein central banks across the world are looking to reduce the size of their balance sheets. While historically a top-down approach has been favoured for policy coordination, a bottom-up approach can be more favoured as the members feel more inclusive under this alternative. The higher the cooperation, the higher will be the policy coordination and even higher will be the probability of achieving the policy goals.

Introduction

The world has moved from being monocentric to being polycentric. Polycentrism represents a departure from the previous periods.

However, this polycentrism is itself centred around two to three Western countries. Between 1947 and 1995, the General Agreement on Tariffs and Trade (GATT) governed the trading system in the world which was largely dominated by the USA and Europe, with the later addition of Japan. During this period, trade disputes were largely the product of the shifting economic power balances among Western countries, particularly after the creation of the European single market and the rise of Japan in the 1970s and 1980s. The Bretton Woods system was born in 1944, and then morphed into the World Bank, the IMF and the GATT, the predecessors of the World Trade Organization (WTO). The creation of G5, G7 and G8 was prompted by the need to oversee the process of provision of international public goods. The FSF is the product of the Asian crisis. The call for the New Bretton Woods (NBW) system in the wake of the Global Economic Crisis (GEC) of 2008–2009 has, thus far, expanded the G8 to the G20. The group of finance ministers and central bank governors was also moved into the G20 Summit of Leaders—designating it as the 'premier forum for economic cooperation', while upgrading the FSF to the FSB by expanding membership.

Financial innovations were meant to rid the world of finance from avoidable risk and inefficiencies. Globalization was expected to catalyse this process through geographical diversification. But thanks to lack of synergy among the people and processes, it is manifesting itself otherwise. This has been further worsened due to the advent of various economic, financial and monetary crises in the world. Financial crisis begets a call for international cooperation primarily because the international regime remains under great stress as international interdependencies tend to be especially visible. Perceived stakes are also seen to be the highest in such occasions. In history, there has been a pattern evident of financial crises where great efforts are made to cooperate with various stakeholders such as the 1992 EMS crisis to avert the breakdown of Bretton Woods, which was established in response to the 1931 financial crisis, and the threat to gold exchange standard to counter the GFC of 2008 and the subsequent European sovereign debt crisis of 2011–2012.

What these crises led to was an observed trend of trust reduction for prominent institutions. This trend is especially evident in the AEs of Europe and the USA (Lipton 2018). Then, how do we handle this lack of trust conundrum? The answer is synergy among the nations in a calibrated manner. But the interconnection needs to be synergistically hierarchical in a 'bottom-up' manner. Nations may connect themselves as sub-regions, sub-regions as regions and eventually regions as global. This connectedness is more evident in the form of the spillover effects between the economies. These spillover effects are essentially macroeconomic spillovers and financial spillovers. As has been observed in the related discussion throughout the previous chapters, the financial spillovers have been affecting the macroeconomic well-being of various economies.

Macroeconomic Policies and Financial Spillovers

The interconnectedness in the world has reached new heights. With technological innovation and deepening of economic and financial markets around the world and with emergence of new centers of power, the spillovers of discordant policy measures are quite evident. The GFC had established that the financial sector performance has become so pertinent that it may throw up the whole economy in shambles along with percolating effects in the connected economies. The adoption of unconventional monetary policies to combat the negative impacts of 2007–2009 financial crises on their respective economies, reportedly 'to avert a 1930's style of global depression' and its unwinding in the mid-2013 to normalize the system (popularly called the onset of 'taper tantrum'), is another stark example of financial spillovers leading to macroeconomic instability. The interconnectedness had let the money flow to emerging economies in search of yields after the GFC. However, with the unwinding the relative spread appeared to narrow down which lead to wide-scale outflows from these economies. This resulted in panic setting in the emerging economies, leading to substantial market volatility because of capital outflows from these economies. Such risks of monetary policy 'spillovers' are expected in the current interconnected world. However, the dynamics of such transactions are not that simple as 'it prompts a reaction. Such competitive easing occurs both simultaneously and sequentially ... and both advanced economies and emerging economies engage in it ... being pushed towards competitive monetary easing' (Rajan 2014) 'and musical crises' (Rajan 2015).

The channels by which these shocks are transmitted to emerging market economies are via the interest rates, the exchange rate and changes in asset prices. A further channel of transmission for quantitative easing has been through

> the international bank lending channel of monetary policy rates and QE, through foreign banks and their effects on the supply of credit to local firms, the associated real effects in the economy and reach-for-yield risk-taking incentives.... The results suggest that foreign QE affects more risk-taking in emerging markets through an expansion of credit supply to riskier firms rather than improving real outcomes of firms in emerging markets. (Morais, Peydró and Ruiz 2015)[1]

The impact on the emerging market economies was also higher where these economies were more exposed on the liability side to banks in advanced countries. The 'deleveraging of the banks in advanced

---

[1] Several empirical studies examined the cross-border financial market impact of QE policies. The latest being by Chen, Qianying, Andrew Filardo, Dong He, and Feng Zhu (2015). They found that

> QE measures which lower the US corporate spread have had sizeable effects, which vary significantly across regions and individual economies ... have had sizeable and widespread effects on global equity prices ... end to have a greater impact on many emerging economies than on the US economy.

The same work cites Neely (2010), Glick and Leduc (2012) Chen, Filardo, He and Zhu (2012, 2014a) and Rogers, Scotti and Wright (2014) to have contributed to such type of conclusions. Sobrun Jhuvesh and Philip Turner (2015) have concluded that 'globalisation has linked EM financial markets more closely to long-term interest rates in the major centres' and this could result in 'monetary and other policy choices in the Ems' having faced with 'new constraints'.

economies then triggered a run on banks and other entities in emerging economies'. Not only emerging market economies that were directly exposed to banks in advanced countries suffered, other economies who were not directly exposed also experienced financial disruption due to the deleveraging operations. 'Increased global financial network leaves no safe havens from a financial crisis' (Park and Shin 2017). Hence, global inter-bank exposures become a channel for transmission of shock and the impact of the shock on the economy becomes more significant given the high degree of leverage in the balance sheet of the banks. 'Moreover, correlated exposures across banks may lead to the amplification of otherwise small shocks to profitability' (Hale, Kapan and Minoiu 2016).

The unconventional monetary policies by AEs that led to the ballooning of their balance sheets and the subsequent adjustments related to withdrawal of the liquidity from the system and gradual increase in policy rates will continue to have spillovers in the emerging market economies. This process has only gathered pace in the recent past. Further, the impact may be quite different for different economies. The use of only monetary tools by the emerging economies may not be enough to negate the impact. Additional tools such as capital controls and/or macroprudential policy tools would be required to be utilized by these economies to complement the monetary policy tools (Singh and Wang 2017). Emerging economies, therefore, must pay attention to the changing dynamics in the balance sheets of AEs, particularly US Federal Reserve Bank (FED) and ECB balance sheet, as it could result in quite a significant effect on the domestic economy and the financial system. While a limited impact is found in the real economy, the financial markets bear the main brunt of any spillover. This becomes particularly more pronounced in cases of economies which have a greater open capital account and have strong trade and financial linkages with the AEs.

Though most emerging economies have been able to absorb the volatility spillover from the AEs, the end of the story has not yet been written. It has been found that the impact of the spillovers on currency markets can be 10 times greater in the case of a Euro area balance sheet expansion than from a FED spillover. In the absence of any international coordination to minimize the spillover and its impact, emerging market economies could do good to be ready with measures to limit the volatility spillovers. To help insulate the economy, macroprudential policies as well as targeted capital controls can be used (Apostolou and Beirne 2017).

A variety of macroprudential policy measures that are currently being undertaken by various countries to avert spillovers also pose a spillover effect. While 'output and bank credit spillovers from sectoral macroprudential policy shocks are generally small worldwide but are seen to be regionally concentrated and economically significant for countries connected by strong trade or financial linkages'. The CCB adjustments by various economies also have the potential to generate sizeable regional spillovers (Kang et al. 2017).[2]

These varied reasons for the spillover effects have been mostly attributed by economists to the individualistic approaches adopted by various countries. The Asian crisis of the late 1990s, which prompted many economies to build up a substantial quantum of FX to meet future contingencies, led individual countries 'to self-insure by accumulating foreign exchange reserves'. Allen and Carletti (2010) have termed it as 'an inefficient mechanism from a global perspective' as it sowed the seeds of the next global crisis by way of creating global imbalances.

> The remarkable paradox in international finance is that the emerging markets' desire for self-insurance has, if anything, increased global risks on account of the fear that simultaneous liquidation of these holdings at the time of a crisis may accentuate the de-stability during a similar future crisis…. (Prasad 2011)

The obsession of the emerging market economies to accumulate reserves (mostly deemed high quality safe assets and its excess global

---

[2] Event study and panel regression analyses find that liquidity and sectoral macro-prudential policy measures often affect cross-border bank credit, whereas capital measures do not. This empirical evidence is stronger for tightening than for loosening measures, is distributed across credit leakage and reallocation effects, and is generally regionally concentrated.

demand, including safe reserve assets, has contributed to the existent low interest rate environment in the world economy) also brings back to focus the 'Triffin paradox'. Ironically, the desire of these economies to stay safe is becoming instrumental in creation of global risks (Obstfeld and Taylor 2017). As the famous quote goes, 'One often meets destiny on the road he takes to avoid it.'

Internalization by impacted countries of the adverse externalities emitted by crisis origin countries (in terms of both spillover of the direct crisis impact and spillover of the latter countries' crisis fighting policies that were devised while looking solely at their own country's interests) is the theoretical solution to the problem cited earlier. However, does this occur always and is it wholesomely possible, particularly in a global scenario in which economies are interconnected? Well, possibly—as propounded by Ostry and Ghosh (2013) 'no', as 'a policy of undervaluation may spur domestic growth and may even be justified if there are production externalities at home; but the policy may nevertheless force undesirable external adjustments in other countries and curtailing the policy may be costly for the home country'. Rather, it may encourage protectionism to emerge particularly, within the slower growing economies—some which may have the wherewithal to withstand pressures while the others could still be threatened with dire economic consequences. This is precisely the issue at hand. As the US Fed policy impacts the whole world, it is required that the Fed takes decisions based on global outlook or only from domestic outlook perspective. Collective action is incited to resist the intensification of such pressures. Considering the divergence in performance of various economies, such initiatives are bound not to get the wholehearted cooperation of all. Further, 'with several "global public goods" which may require inter-country alignments, some uneven economic prospects across major players may act as a "hurdle" (Gokarn 2015). Rightfully, the need and hence the call for 'a more coordinated global monetary policy … with both high income and emerging countries' (Freixas, Laeven, and Peydró 2015) is being sounded. Whether systemic approach to emerging risks at country level by 'using macroprudential policies can reduce, or even neutralize, the foreign externalities stemming on emerging markets from foreign monetary policy from core economic areas, or whether a more coordinated global monetary policy is the only solution' (Morais et al. 2015) have captured the centre stage of current economic thinking on managing future crises.

The GFC has changed the extent of financial globalization and its perceived costs and benefits in academic circles. Even before the onset of the GFC, several studies had called for a reassessment of the advantages and disadvantages of financial globalization. The two important dimensions for such studies were: (a) the reassessment regarding the stability of capital flows, and (b) re-examination regarding the benefits of financial integration in terms of efficient allocation of savings. Regarding the first dimension, the notion of greater resiliency from financial integration based on long-term capital flows is more persuasive compared to the short-term capital flows. As regards the second dimension, it has been accepted that long-term positive effects on growth of the countries would accrue only if certain thresholds of institutional development are met. If adequate institutional developments are not achieved, capital flows are likely to be used unproductively, leading to unsustainable lending booms and too much short-term capital inflows leaving the countries vulnerable to sudden stops once optimism fades due to local or global factors.

International cooperation was reflected in the lead taken by the USA to stem its intensity

> using US dollar swaps with various central banks instituted by the Fed in order to provide US dollar liquidity. The IMF was not able to act as lender of last resort and its role in the Euro-debt crisis was largely advisory. The Fed extended temporary dollar liquidity facilities to 14 central banks during 2008 and many of which were even renewed in October 2013. (Nakaso 2014)

There was also a coordinated reduction of 25–50 basis points in the policy interest rates by the central banks of six AEs to ease 'global monetary conditions after the Lehmann Collapse' (Board of Governors of the Federal Reserve System Report 2008; Eichengreen 2013b). As a sign of acceptance of the idea that 'coordinated action could be better than unilateral action' (Mohan 2014), the Federal Open Market Committee (FOMC) members went on-the-record, appreciating the actions of 'the policy makers around the globe ... working closely together' and carrying 'a similar view of global economic conditions', with the willingness 'to take strong actions to address those conditions', and thus reflecting the fact that 'coordinated action could help to bolster consumer and business confidence and so yield greater economic benefits than unilateral action' (Board of Governors of the Federal Reserve System 2008b).

What has become apparent in recent times is that the short-term risks to financial stability have increased amidst growing regionalism and economic integration. The rise of nationalist political thought process in prominent countries like the USA, UK, Austria, Hungary, etc., has given new impetus to economic disintegration. The political threat to economic integration has always been the greatest factor for economic disintegration. At this present juncture, this political thought process has got coupled with economic conditions worldwide. There is a view in the developed countries that their further development is being compromised for the growth of the emerging and developing countries. Well, this may be refuted on two grounds, the development of emerging countries will lead to an increased demand for the developed nations' goods, which will lead to further increase in their well-being. The other notion is with great power comes great responsibility and the developed nations must act like the big brothers. The impact on an integrated emerging market meant a stronger dollar, higher credit spreads, weaker equity prices and higher interest rates.

Regarding pertinent economic issues plaguing the current environment, higher inflationary trends may lead central banks to respond more aggressively than currently expected, which could lead to a further tightening of financial conditions. Valuations of risky assets are still stretched, and liquidity mismatches, leverage and other factors could amplify asset price moves and their impact on the financial system. Emerging markets have generally improving fundamentals but could be vulnerable to sudden tightening of global financial conditions. Banks have strengthened their balance sheets since the crisis, but parts of the system face a structural US dollar liquidity mismatch that could be a vulnerability. Crypto assets have features that may improve market efficiency, but they could also pose risks if used with leverage or without appropriate safeguards. Similarly, the corporate credit sector also is a vulnerable spot for financial stability if not catered to properly. It is observed that the riskiness of corporate credit allocation increases during the boom cycle and with the size of credit expansion. Too many lenders lending to potential vulnerable borrowers increases the vulnerability of the financial system for an economy. Also, the domestic credit markets get impacted through the external commercial borrowing route for credit of the corporates. The phenomenon of rising house prices has been a feature of the economic recovery in many countries post the GFC. But they have also been occurring in an accommodative monetary policy environment in many AEs, raising the spectre of financial instability should financial conditions reverse and simultaneously lead to a decline in house prices. The present trends also hint towards slowdown in housing segments certain prominent world economies.

The Economic and Financial Reintegration

As can be seen from the 2007–2008 GFC, the European sovereign debt crisis and the Taper Tantrum episode in 2013, tremors were created in global markets that even policymakers in the advanced countries found difficult to neutralize. These developments marked a stall at the global financial integration process. After this brief pause, the global financial integration process got back on track with the rise in the external balance sheets of major economies. Increasing gross external asset and liability positions suggest greater financial integration, but the downside is in the form of higher volatility in capital flows and currency, because of portfolio rebalancing and larger exposure to other external shocks. Because of these factors, there could be an increase in call for protection from external shocks and balance of payments crises.

The prevailing institutional structure for international policymaking has still a long way to go for dealing with the financial globalization. The European sovereign debt crisis highlighted that if the member countries do not follow the rules in letter and spirit, state sovereignty in fiscal and economic policy decisions can become challenging in a monetary union. However, there is no need for scaremongering and going for a large-scale reversal of the global financial integration of recent decades, as such a reversal would seriously undermine real economic integration and the benefits associated with it. Instead, it would be better to mitigate unwanted spillover effects, which might involve some retrenchment, as it did in this country and many others after the crisis to make global financial integration safer.

However, all these changes and voices of concern fetched peace-seeking solutions which were merely transitory in nature. With the intensity of the crisis blowing over, the regime of mistrust would relapse. Hence, when the prospects for international policy coordination become difficult in this top-down configuration/s attempted so far, it might be better understood working from the bottom-up.

International macro-financial crises such as the Eurozone crisis, East Asia and Latin American crises of the 1980s and 1990s, laid bare, that the key to financial instability was the combination of open financial markets and unregulated international capital flows coupled with procyclical with related monetary and fiscal policies (International Monetary Fund 2012; Krampf and Fritz 2015). Hence, the European pre-crisis model of regional integration, which based financial stability as a by-product of trade-oriented integration, had to search for alternative approaches for regional arrangements specifically designed to ensure financial stability.

Quite curiously and as a counter effect, in crisis situations, with high and mounting financial stakes, collective action failures are very likely to arise, especially because there will be every likelihood of dominant, ex-post efficient and implementable strategies not being able to get germinated. This may get accentuated on the fact of tensions arising due to national authorities acting in isolation endeavouring to minimize own losses without considering losses their policy actions will impose on other authorities leading to a sort of 'prisoner's dilemma' giving rise to a solution 'not ex-post Pareto optimal', that is, at least one player will be losing heavily unnecessarily (Cihak and Decressin 2007).

In the given background, the idea that 'it is unrealistic for EME governments to expect major financial centres to fine tune their economic policies in response to economic conditions in other parts of the world and therefore rather than excoriating about the monetary policy of other countries, the optimal solution rests in each country managing its own economic affairs by delivering a combination of low inflation and financial stability' is likely to give rise to an equilibrium which is sub-optimal. It is observed that the inclination for countries to act unilaterally gets fillip especially during periods of crisis. Also the consequences of the negative externalities which unilateral action can impose rise significantly. Therefore, it is necessary that nations take into account the externality effect of their policies upon other countries and act accordingly rather than just being confined in a narrow manner towards acting based simply on their own circumstances. International coordination and co-operation is generally acknowledged and regarded as a logically feasible and optimal solution. However, this is not correspondingly reflected in the observed commitment and enthusiasm towards this approach, possibly because it is considered unrealistic given the significant bottlenecks perceived to be a roadblock against coordination at an international level. However, it is also noticed that since macroeconomic policies which are implemented in an uncoordinated manner can have an adverse impact and amplify a financial crisis, there is also a growing consensus on the need for having greater coordination at the global domain.

Studies have been able to empirically establish that a partial effect of policies relating to 'quantitative easing' on foreign economies is related to risk and therefore sensible domestic policies and robust domestic institutions can operate for countries as a 'shock absorber' from US monetary spillovers. This fact, therefore, suggests the requirement of greater coordination at a global level in order to deal with the hazards of policy spillovers and externalities. The process of globalization is irreversible and entails nations becoming more and more interdependent with each other. The Nations of the Global North would continue to have negative spillover effects of their domestic policies over other nations. Better wisdom must prevail whereby one could conceive of synergistic benefits that would accrue on a global level on account of intelligent coordination. The critical condition needed for fruition of the dynamics of coordination involves the need for policy reforms at the domestic level to internalize certain unreasonable elements of externalities. The changes required involve a paradigm shift from the present system which places the burden of adjustment on borrowing countries to a symmetric system where pressure is also placed on 'surplus countries'.

An international coordination framework for economic governance will benefit every country including the USA. Apart from raising regulatory standards all over the global financial space, it would constrain

> harmful behaviors in the United States that (it) would wish to limit anyway... Economic activities abroad can have significant negative spillovers on US well-being, as well as present opportunities for (mutual) gain to be unlocked.... Unnecessary financial volatility and misbehavior abroad transmitted to the US economy directly, rapidly, and strongly (can be considerably reduced). (Posen 2015)

There is the rest of the world economy that is kicking in terms of growth and progress. They are increasingly leaving the USA behind by way of incremental growth 'in size and financial depth relative to the US economy' (Posen 2015) and would not bear the patience to continue to pester the USA 'to engage with (them) in discussion of the rules by which it is partially governed' (Posen 2015).

Some time back, it was worthwhile and heartening to note that the USA has started taking 'the potential international implications of Fed policies seriously'. Though their domestic policy mandates are 'out of simple self-interest', they remain actively conscious of the possible 'international effects of Fed policies' to 'spill back onto the U.S. economy and financial markets' as also their special responsibility 'given the dollar's role as the international reserve currency'. They would as such 'remain attentive to the risk that the onset of Fed policy normalization could bring a new round of market pressures on EMEs' (Dudley 2015). They sound to be in sync with the expectation that 'No matter what a central bank's domestic mandate, international responsibilities should not be ignored' (Rajan 2015). Similar views were echoed by Stanley Fischer (2015):

> As we consider the decision of policy rate normalization, we are mindful of possible spillovers to other economies, including emerging market and developing economies. In an interconnected world, fulfilling the Federal Reserve's objectives under its dual mandate

requires that we pay close attention to how our own actions affect other countries and how developments abroad, in turn, spill back into U.S. economic conditions.

While countries are on the path towards greater economic integration, some reversals have been witnessed in the recent past. Among the prominent setbacks are Brexit (which will lead to departure of the UK from the EU) and the withdrawal of the USA from the Trans-Pacific Partnership (TPP) in early 2017. Also worrying was that the trend from the UK and USA elections indicated a popular drift towards nationalism and disenchantment from globalization from the very champions of globalization themselves. However, soon after, a sort of countermovement took place, with pro-European forces holding the upper hand in the elections in France, the Netherlands and most recently in Germany. The important question amid all these discussions is whether the benefits of financial and global integration can be sacrificed for the sake of temporary populism. The European nations are looking forward to reforms and discipline to strengthen their structure. Brexit has catapulted the EU and in the Euro area to expedite the reform process. It may help in completing banking union and building a capital markets union. The European integration has been further strengthened by single supervisory mechanism and harmonized regulation a capital markets union.

With the USA pulling out of the TPP in early 2017, the remaining 11 countries are exploring alternative ways to sustain economic integration in the Asia-Pacific region. Studies have shown that these 11 countries can gain significantly from TPP-like agreements among themselves, even without the USA. Discussions are also ongoing for a Regional Comprehensive Economic Partnership (RCEP) with 16 member countries in Asia. The TPP with five other Asia-Pacific economies is slated to deliver higher benefits than the original one, which will be greater than the bilateral agreements between individual nations and the USA alone. Because of withdrawal from TPP, the USA would have to do without the benefits that would have accrued from the relatively large TPP agreement arrangements. Not only will it reduce US exports to the Asia-Pacific region, but it would also keep trade liberalization on the global agenda and may also entice other large partners such as Europe and who knows even the USA may eventually join as they might observe that it is losing out.

The recent trade war initiated by the USA with Europe, China, India and other nations has led to another blow on the road towards a multilateral system. As new powers emerge to rival the USA, the world should prepare for a future in which global cooperation is no longer an option. The USA *ended* its participation in the Paris Climate Agreement. Also, the USA has launched unprecedented attacks on the WTO by accusing it of infringing upon American sovereignty and by *blocking* the appointment of judges to its appellate body (Laïdi 2018).

However, the immediate crisis of the multilateral system has only a marginal effect on the volume of world trade, which is now more dependent on global value chains—in a sense, the most effective instrument against protectionism—than on international accords. That is why we should not be excessively pessimistic about the future of the trading system, as long as the norms on which trade rests are respected. In fact, despite the repeated failures of multilateral trade negotiations over the past two decades, world trade since 2001 has grown dramatically (Lipton 2018).

One might think that in an international system where power is spread more widely than in the past, the need for consensus through negotiation and dialogue would be commensurately greater. But while that might be normatively true, recent events show that the world is heading in a different direction. For example, Russia, wielding its veto power at the United Nations Security Council, continues to stand in the way of any resolution to the war in Syria. Russian President Vladimir Putin seems completely uninterested in addressing the crisis multilaterally and has instead pursued a narrower peace process alongside Iran and Turkey, with the obvious goal of diminishing America's influence in the Middle East (Subramanian 2018).

The need for innovating structures that can help withstand periodic economic blows will encourage the formation of sub-regional economic blocs as the possible solution. As an example, interconnectedness among India and Bangladesh can significantly reduce the transportation costs and link India with ASEAN via Myanmar. The recent cooperation including using the Ashuganj port in Bangladesh for shipment of Indian goods to Northeast India, expanding of rail links within Northeast India and between the two countries, the BBIN Motor Vehicles Agreement, sharing of Internet capabilities, electricity export from India are steps in this regard (Sanjay Kathuria, in World Bank Blog 2016). Similar steps in the Southeast Asian economies can significantly increase the regional prosperity and benefits to the economy. Further, SAARC development fund, which was developed by the eight SAARC member states in April 2010, is looking to achieve status of lender to raise funds from capital markets as it aims to become a full-fledged regional development bank. An increase in the dialogue can lead to increase in trust, which will eventually increase the interconnectedness among the Southeast Asian economies.

Political dislike may prevent the process from gathering momentum, though the legitimacy of economics and common welfare will pull it out of cold storage. Political confederation will remain in the agenda; however, it may be pushed down as the final item. A case in point is the matter of Euro and also in the case of GCC and East Africa, in which the idea was to plant one market, one single monetary union and then ultimately one political federation in that order. A genuine financial integration programme in the face of a shock (which will be with all probability, reasonably common and well correlated) may even turn into a political package and tool.

> Moreover, what is sacrificed at the national level (monetary monopoly or even political sovereignty) is recouped at the group level. Authority is not surrendered but pooled and delegated to the joint institutions in Partnership, to be shared and in some manner collectively managed by all the countries involved. Each partner's loss, therefore, is simultaneously also each other's gain. The individual state may no longer have much latitude to act unilaterally, but every government retains a voice in decision making for the group as a whole. They are all, in this sense, gainers. Net effects for participants, therefore, could turn out to be distinctly favourable. (Cohen 2008)

Crises will tend to cure the 'economic-attention-deficit disorder' and structural innovations on regional lines will take the centre stage.

Since systemic risk does not recognize geographical borders, with financial activities running on a global plane in order to be viable as a commercial business, arrangements for internationalization of regulatory/supervisory architecture need to look for GSCB/GFSCs to motivate financial innovations to manifest itself in an orderly manner across the global village. Thus, it will help ensure that monetary stability and financial stability remain the order of the day. The complex issue of evolving level playing fields in such a system has been enunciated through the idea of a Garland Makers' Model (Version 1—2006) (Version 2—2015) discussed earlier.

The IMF and the BIS under the current regime are not in sync with the avowed objectives. Role of the IMF in the IMS is limited to applying promoting macroeconomic stability surveillance and economic policy advice, while BIS provides food for thought processes on various emerging international issues to the member countries. The World Bank acts more as a development finance institution.

> Sadly, the American-dominated World Bank cannot serve as a model for the AIIB. It is now well known that the World Bank has served as an instrument of American foreign policy. Joe Stiglitz has documented how the World Bank punished Ethiopia at the request of private American banks, which had lost revenue on loans to Ethiopia. (Mahbubani 2015)

The FSB is evolving into a better fit but not of the expected genre. 'The G20 and the Financial Stability Board do not have the full competences to fulfill the role of the "fourth pillar" of international economic governance' (Constâncio 2015).

The role of global bodies in designing high-level principles and exchange of ideas to flush out/reduce systemic risks cannot be ignored but one should not expect these high-level committees to understand the low or local level risks. One of the major criticisms of the FSB's work is that as the reforms were undertaken with AEs in mind, it had little clue to the impact of these reforms on the emerging markets. Similarly, If 'Basel II did not prevent the 2007–09 crises—what makes you think Basel III or IV will prevent the next crisis?' (Sheng 2017).

> In fact, a paradox of the global system is that global rules are most important for small countries, even though it is precisely said they that have the least influence over the formulation and defense of such rules. This problem can only be solved if the smaller countries organize themselves and if regional institutions are truly made part of a broader international order. (Ocampo 2006)

The IMF is no stranger to distrust. We have been at the centre of crisis and controversy. We have faced pressure again and again to reform and to meet the changing needs and expectations of the international community. We feel it again now in discussions about the global financial safety net (GFSN), which we all need as a bulwark against future crises. We all need to work together to prepare multilateralism for a world where trust and authority are more decentralized. Our multilateral institutions are more critical than ever. We cannot take them for granted. The way we rebuild confidence is to make sure that cooperation leads to concrete gains that benefit all people, and that these gains are widely shared. We can restore trust in institutions and larger purposes if we set out to regain the sense that something concrete can be achieved by working together (Lipton 2018).

Since a universally acceptable financial regime will warrant complex process of negotiating and compromising (where different national interests, industry interests, financial democracy, etc., may be brought to terms), the suggested concepts of GSCB/GFSC could do the job optimally. But now on, they can hardly be 'the band masters' for the international monetary orchestra. The order has changed. Britain had given it away to the USA, and there is no heir apparent in sight. The history of international cooperation arrangements shows that there had been one-off such endeavours based purely on commercial quid pro quo. Perhaps this is the reason that they were so transitory. Centre periphery hegemonic arrangements would find it difficult even merely to take shape let alone gather momentum. The GSCB/GFSC would be in line with that reality of change in international economic order in which the orchestra would be played by many masters with equal stake on the show and without malice to each other.

This idea is in line with the vision of Jose Antonio Ocampo (2006) of the future IMF. He would love to view it

> as the apex of a network of regional and sub-regional reserve funds and swap arrangements—that is, a structure more akin to that of the European Central Bank or the United States Federal Reserve system than to its current centralized structure. In turn, competition among global, regional, and sub-regional institutions is probably the best arrangement in this area.

By global governance, some 'imagine blue helmets and maybe black helicopters', while some others feel 'a ring of panacea and utopia about it' (Talbott 2003). But the real issue is

> to welcome a democratic system in which there are distinct mechanisms for people to make their voice heard and also to make their decision makers accountable. There should also be an agreement about the issue of the legitimacy of the wings of global governance and the extent of transparency they are expected to display. (Florini 2003)

All these can ensure the sort of cooperation needed of 'multiple actors dealing in a common way with problems rather than a system of top-downness' (Steinberg 2003) that the prevailing system propagates. The Garland Makers' Model of global governance seems to meet most of these requirements, though it does not presage major dislocations in the existing physical and human capital systems. Most importantly, it relies heavily on a 'bottom-up' approach of consensual decision-making. Interestingly, Sheng (2015) also shared this idea.

> With financial globalization, increasingly complex financial structures, rapid expansion of balance sheets, and high cross-border financial exposures, surges in capital inflows and outflows are exposing countries and the IMS to much greater risk of financial crises, as balance sheets magnify the effect of these flows, while shocks are transmitted more easily across countries. Gross external

asset and liability positions have significantly increased over the past two decades, and there has been a marked transformation in their composition. Against this backdrop, the resources in the GFSN—a loose knit connection of insurance/liquidity/financing instruments—do not seem to have kept up with the growing external liabilities. (IMF Staff Report 2016)[3]

The reciprocal currency arrangements or the central bank swap lines between Federal Reserve and various central banks[4] emerged as an important tool in stabilizing the financial system by enhancing the ability of these central banks to provide US$ funding to financial institutions in their jurisdictions. However, not many emerging market economies were part of these arrangements who instead built up a large cache of forex reserves to face the crisis. Referring to this, Mr Urjit Patel, the then governor of Reserve Bank of India, at a seminar hosted by the Group of 30 in Washington, had said,

> Some of us would go as far as describing this situation as virtual apartheid, in which systemic central banks protect themselves and their self-interest. Meanwhile, EMEs on the receiving end of global financial turbulence are systematically denied access. The time has come to end this sectarian approach and access to swap lines be made equally available. (Patel 2017)

International cooperation—organized in a bottom-up (nation subregion, region and global) design could be the antidote to the operation

---

[3] The global financial safety net (GFSN) —a set of institutions and mechanisms which provide financial support to countries hit by a financial crisis (often currency, banking or sovereign crisis) —is widely considered to be an essential element of the international financial architecture and a necessary infrastructure to support financial integration and globaliszation. FX reserves, central bank swap and repo lines, funding by international institutions and regional financing arrangements are considered the key elements of the GFSN. (Beatrice Scheubel, and Livio Stracca – 2016).

[4] ECB, Swiss National Bank, Bank of Japan, Bank of England, Bank of Canada, Reserve Bank of Australia, Sveriges Riksbank, Norges Bank, Danmarks Nationalbank, Reserve Bank of New Zealand, Banco Central do Brasil, Banco de México, Bank of Korea, MAS.

of fallacy of composition—financial resilience-boosting national actions could be detrimental to other nations and hence the international system. 'The more cooperation, the more carefully coordinated national policies are in timing and nature, the lower will be the need for international liquidity to finance imbalances'. A global systemic liquidity arrangement may be the need of the hour to supplement the macrofinancial approach to address systemic risk. 'The degree of … international cooperation … influences the amount of liquidity needed to finance imbalances in the face of temporarily divergent and conflicting national policies' (Cooper 1969).[5] The idea of such a cooperative approach to global liquidity provision looks more relevant today. 'A collateral benefit of such cooperation is that it can mitigate other coordination failures in national economic policies' (Obstfeld 2011). Accordingly, such a system would 'likely operate near an international cooperative equilibrium in which each country optimises its economic performance' (Taylor 2013).

Managing financial instability with a global perspective 'is in everyone's interest but it involves solving a collective action problem'. The availability of global schemes of large unconditional insurance pools would dampen the perverse incentive of accumulating precautionary reserves by the emerging economies. This will thus rid them of the associated damaging macroeconomic policies such reserve accumulation tends to force upon them. The risk of spiralling global macroeconomic imbalances and the attendant risks of crises and their spillover effects may thus get automatically mitigated. Further, this method also creates a transparent mechanism taking all concerned on board and the global costs of a country's policies would be internalized to some extent or, at a minimum, made more visible (Prasad 2011).

Homogenizing policy formulations emanating from heterogeneous country units as panacea for global ills would need institutionalization of the spirit of 'spontaneous cooperation' (Baldwin 2010) as displayed in Asia. Even 'Europe's founding fathers … did not start with grand designs … exploited windows of opportunity … national interests

---

[5] Taken from Truman (2011).

permitted establishment of long-lasting institutions that in turn fostered deeper economic integration'.

The relevance of such architecture of global governance of monetary policy and financial stability at the current juncture, not withstanding, is incomprehensible 'to get USA on board' (Engel 2015 e-mail to the author) as the new structure implicitly calls for its consent 'for ceding any decision-making power to an international body'. Going by the current approach of the lawmakers in the USA on quota reforms in the IMF—surrender of its huge share in decision-making—and on the hesitation 'of giving the Fed independence', such an idea that does not envisage special privileges for any country would be difficult to sell to the USA. And he suggests that an 'opt-out' clause—any country who does not find it useful—can be excluded. But the approach will not solve this dilemma and could be self-defeating. The idea needs to take the USA, the star player on board, and to rid the countries of the false signals of the 'fallacy of composition', 'tragedy of the commons' and 'prisoner's dilemma'.

A general view (including in the emerging economies in particular) is gaining ground that the US monetary policy should be implemented unilaterally without regard to developments elsewhere to take care of the possible detriment of the US economy. This could be 'practical' but 'short-sighted' since 'if a change in US policy leads to better performance in other countries it is likely to have positive feedback on the United States, which would certainly be in the interest of the United States' (Taylor 2013). As such, 'international considerations will impinge more directly on the objectives of price and economic stability in the US' (Eichengreen 2013b), and hence the USA 'should worry about the effects of its policies on the rest of the world' (Rajan 2014) and, accordingly, the Fed should 'take into account the external impact of its actions' on others. 'Through trade and financial linkages, financial and economic distress in foreign markets can come home to roost' (Buiter 2014).

Thus, the idea of a possible global financial system requiring an appropriately designed architecture is neither new nor novel. The chorus for an 'effective', 'ongoing' and 'binding' international coordination mechanisms was heard first in the early 2000s. With financial crisis occurring at regular intervals, a need was felt to bring about a complete change in the designs of the structures—domestic, regional and international—in sync with the changing dynamics of global finance. Rajan (2014) initiated the fresh debate on revisiting 'the international rules of the game' calling for 'collective action', with Lagarde (2015) finding 'scope for greater international policy cooperation to minimize the negative spillovers'. Rajan (2015) looks for 'responsible global citizenship' that

> would require a country to act as it would act in a world without boundaries. In such a world, a policy maker should judge whether the overall positive domestic and international benefits of a policy, discounted over time, outweigh its costs. Some policies may have largely domestic benefits and foreign costs, but they may be reasonable in a world without boundaries because more people are benefited than are hurt.

> The need for cooperation in financial regulation is well understood. Yet, when it comes to monetary policy, the dominant view is that keeping one's own house in order is enough. There is a need for international cooperation in the realm of monetary policy. The need for such cooperation is especially pronounced when it provides the backing for financial stability. That is why monetary policymakers need to take further practical steps to complement their domestic analysis with a more global perspective. (Jaime Caruana, September 2017)

Post the GFC, financial stability has started taking the Centre stage in the minds of the regulators as 'countries now become more susceptible to a new species of "capital account crises," fuelled by bank and bond lending, and its sudden withdrawal'. This has led to a focus on a new financial trilemma rather than the classic monetary policy trilemma. The 'financial trilemma' suggests that if you want financial stability and also an open capital account, you have to let go of your autonomy over the domestic financial policy (Obstfeld and Taylor 2017). Similar predicaments have been expressed by many others. One such is the 'Globalisation trilemma'. As Dr Andreas Dombret,

member of the Executive Board of the Deutsche Bundesbank, puts it
in one of his speeches:

> Let's search for answers that are right—and let's expose oversim-
> plified, misleading ideologies—neither nationalist populism nor
> hyper-globalisation will lead to prosperity and security. Global
> economic cooperation has helped us to build a more prosperous
> society. However, it does have side effects. Only by reducing and
> managing these side effects can we foster global cooperation in the
> long term. Focused global cooperation promises a way forward. We
> should all put our minds together to decide how this can be best
> achieved. (Dombret 2017 quoting Henry L. Mencken)

This lesson was in fact learnt the hard way during the most recent
crisis. Central bankers/regulators/supervisors in some of the AEs
were also misled by these fallacies. Individual policy decisions may
spring collateral externalities which are harmful for the entire system.
This was witnessed during the GFC when, in order to preserve and
deleverage, individual banks refused to lend simultaneously, thereby
creating system wide risks (Cunliffe 2015).

In the similar vein, national country-specific policies could prove
detrimental to the interests of other nations and the global economy in general. It need not be intentional as a part of the age-old
'beggar-thy-neighbour' policy but a genuine by-product of a globalized
economy in which countries are intertwined with each other by way of
trade, financial flows and financial institutions. Domestic contingencies will overpower unintended consequences of individual country
actions on others and in the process policymaking will miss the wood
for the trees, resulting in an overall downtrend in global growth. It
comes as no surprise that, as revealed in the long history of financial
crises, a significant portion of countries simultaneously experienced
a crisis including: the Baring-related panic of 1890, the US-centred
international crisis of 1907, the European post-war crises in 1921, the
banking panics at the beginning of the Great Depression in 1930–1931
and the GFC associated with the Great Recession of 2007–2008
(Jordà, Schularick and Taylor 2010). However, what are the gains
from coordination? Whether having countercyclical macroprudential

coordination among countries is a better choice than countries pursuing their own domestic policies? A BIS study to quantify the gains associated with countercyclical Macroprudential Policy coordination in a core periphery DSGE setting, relative to the case where countries pursue their own policies, found out that the gains from coordination were sizable though unevenly distributed across countries with peripheral countries gaining more compared to the larger core country (Pierre-Richard Agénor, Enisse Kharroubi, Leonardo Gambacorta, Giovanni Lombardo and Luiz Pereira da Silva 2017). The aforementioned finding is in line with the conventional wisdom that riskier emerging market countries gain much more from financial integration/coordination than safer or AEs. Conversely, however, studies have also indicated that AEs benefit more than emerging economies from financial integration in the long run as 'riskier countries while benefiting more from risk sharing will also reallocate precautionary savings towards the safer countries, boosting its capital accumulation' (Nicolas Coeurdacier, Hélène Rey and Pablo Winant 2015).

Conclusion

The GFC was a wake-up call for the world that the financial system has become so interlinked that nothing can be looked upon in isolation now. The GFC also showed the fault lines that existed in the regulatory and supervisory dimensions and that the regulators need to pull up their socks. With regard to the changes made in the capital and liquidity frameworks, the reforms initiated after the crisis have so far been concentrated to fill the gaps pointed out by the GFC. But what is required is a forward-looking approach which essentially means rather than any crisis pointing to gaps in the current system, the checks and balances in the system need to be built in such a way that it entails self-assessment on its way and course correction wherever required. While the requirements of central clearing and margining for OTC trades may have made away with these deficiencies, the newer deficiencies need to be identified and addressed in time. Special focus must remain on the systemically important institutions and newer regulatory means to be devised so that their stature does not come in the way of them getting penalized adversely in the form of higher capital.

With regard to other challenges, the technological evolution in the financial world also needs to be dealt in by the regulators. The newer risks in the form of cyberattacks would need global coordination to be dealt in an effective manner. Similarly, risks in shadow banking space, misconduct risk, incentives to take excessive risk due to faulty compensation practices, etc., need continuous monitoring. The other areas pertaining to operational risks as the risk–reward trade-off in the financial sector are immense; hence, the constant vigil needs to be maintained. The special focus on the misconduct risk needs to be maintained and the present system needs to be made more stringent and broad-based. Regulators and supervisors need to be specially focused to identify any new means by which misconduct may creep in the system. The code and rule of ethical imbibed in an organizational culture is the need of the hour.

Even though the risks have reduced after the GFC, however, newer fronts seem to mar the world economy with talks of recession being heard every now and often. The recent developments in the financial world and more importantly in the real and monetary economy seem to be nerving the world on the impending disaster. What is the need of the hour is strengthening the decision-making with regard to the whole framework of macroprudential policy along with stress-testing and EWSs. The greatest issue with the current regime is that there is information, views and counter views on the future, and in this hara-kiri, what is left is inadequate decision-making in a timely manner. Even though several economists have predicted a recession in the coming one or two years, the policy masters today are not willing to concede their ground, and this is the issue which leads to problems.

What is required in such a scenario is what has been suggested in the book, a global coordination mechanism. When views and counter-views are accommodated with reverence and an attitude to learn from each other, the way forward automatically gets easier. Many jurisdictions are experimenting with various macroprudential policy tools in their efforts to ensure financial stability, and the empirical evidence regarding the effectiveness of various policy options is being gradually built up. The thin line between the complex monetary policymaking and the newly born macroprudential policymaking is little blurred.

There is a requirement of strong political will among world countries and institutions to strengthen coordination architecture. Going forward, the world economies should strive for a more balanced system and rule-based monetary policies considering the likely spillover effects it will create world over. Since the monetary policy is the fulcrum of the financial regulation and supervision, a common ground in this regard will automatically lead to a more concerted effort on all other fronts.

Even when the Bretton Woods framework was formalized, in the hindsight, it may seem to be a wishful thinking of the prior thinkers in that regard. Having said that, it is prepositioned (and it is not that infeasible) that the current debate/discussion-oriented decision-making by G20 countries under the aegis of FSB could be a pointer to that fact. Trust deficit would remain an issue. But 'necessity will be the mother of invention' in such situations. The first one could be through economic integration among various economies pursuing the 'club-in-club' approach without waiting for the utopian 'political union'. The second one could be the evolving concept of an international coordination of both monetary policymaking and macroprudential policymaking on a global plane. The current approach of IMF–BIS–FSB coordinating this idea in a 'top-down' fashion is proving to be inadequately effective. There could be a 'bottom-up' approach to this whole idea of global coordination which will be primarily piggyback on the configuration of financial stability development councils already in place. A 'Garland Makers' Model' has been proposed based on the well-established Hindu philosophy. Various issues have been highlighted in this regard. Model 1 gives monetary policy coordination, while Model 2 deals with financial stability policy coordination architecture.

As we have seen, the global coordination is marked by various pulls and pushes. The path travelled so far has been a bumpy ride with its own sets of speed breakers. However, the desire for the destiny to be achieved still remains intact. Concluding, we can say that in a world economy marked by uncertainty, a more stable and cooperative global framework should provide more confidence to allow the real economy to grow and be less corrosive of political life generally. An immediate objective can then be creating a more stable world with less financial turbulence, as central banks traverse down the exceptional monetary measures they had taken to stimulate the economy.

Does it sound to be a wishful thinking?

This idea suggested in the book may still take more time to crystallize but we should not give up as we tend to recall Bagehot in *Lombard Street*: 'I have written in vain if I require to say now that the problem is delicate, that the solution is varying and difficult, and that the result is inestimable to us all.'

Further,

> All truth passes through three stages. First, it is ridiculed. Second, it is violently opposed. Third, it is accepted as being self-evident.

—Arthur Schopenhauer

And finally …

> Yes, we have won the war, but not without difficulty; but now we are going to have to win the peace…

—Georges Clemenceau

References

Allen, Franklin and Douglas Gale. 2006, January. 'Systemic Risk and Regulation'. Working Paper No. 05–24. Philadelphia, PA: Wharton Financial Institutions Center.

Allen, Franklin and Elena Carletti. 2011, February. 'New Theories to Underpin Financial Reform' Presented at the Institute for New Economic Thinking 2010 Spring Conference, Cambridge, England, 8–11 April 2010.

Apostolou, Apostolos and John Beirne. 2017. 'Volatility Spillovers of Federal Reserve and ECB Balance Sheet Expansions to Emerging Market Economies'. ECB Working Paper Series No. 2044. Frankfurt: European Central Bank.

Baldwin, Richard. 2010, June. 'Sequencing Regionalism: Theory, European Practice, and Lessons for Asia'. CEPR Discussion Paper Series No. 7852. London: Centre for Economic Policy Research.

Buiter, Willem. 2014. *The Fed's bad manners risk offending foreigners*, 4 February.

Caruana, Jaime. 2017. International Arrangements for a Resilient Global Economy. Speech at the Conference on 'The uncertain future of global economic integration', jointly organised by the Central Bank of Iceland and the Reinventing Bretton Woods Committee, Reykjavik, 14 September.

Chen, Qianying, Filardo, Andrew, He Dong and Zhu Feng. 2015. Financial Crisis, US Unconventional Monetary Policy and International Spillovers. IMF Working Paper WP/15/85, April.

Cihak, Martin and Jörg Decressin. 2007, July. 'The Case for a European Banking Charter'. IMF Working Paper No. 173. Washington, DC: International Monetary Fund.

Cihak, Martin and Richard Podpiera. 2006, March. 'Is One Watchdog Better Than Three? International Experience with Integrated Financial Sector Supervision'. IMF Working Paper No. 57. Washington, DC: International Monetary Fund.

Coeurdacier, Nicolas, Hélène Rey and Pablo Winant. 2015, December [2019]. Financial Integration and Growth in a Risky World. NBER Working Paper No. 21817.

Cohen, Benjamin J. 2003. 'Monetary Governance in a Globalized World'. In *International Political Economy: State-Market Relations in a Changing Global Order*, edited by C. Roe Goddard, Patrick Cronin and Kishore C. Dash. Lynne Rienner Publishers.

Cohen, Benjamin J. 2008. *Global Monetary Governance*. Routledge.

Constâncio, Vítor. 2015, 13 February. 'Financial Stability Risks, Monetary Policy and the Need for Macro-Prudential Policy' (Speech), Warwick.

Cunliffe, Jon. 2015. *Macroprudential policy – from Tiberius to Crockett and Beyond*, Speech, 28 July.

de Larosiere, Jacques. 2014. 'The International Monetary Anti-System'. *Central Banking Journal* (12 May).

Dombret, Andreas. 2017. The Future of Global Economic Cooperation—Brexit, Basel III and Beyond. Speech at a reception to welcome Olga Wittchen, Financial Attaché, as the Bundesbank's representative in London, London, 23 February.

Dudley, William C. 2015. The U.S. Monetary Policy Outlook and Its Global Implications. Remarks at the Bloomberg Americas Monetary Summit, New York City, 20 April.

Eichengreen, Barry. 2013b. Does the Federal Reserve Care About the Rest of the World? *Journal of Economic Perspectives* 27(4, Fall): 87–104.

Fisher, S. 2015. Monetary Policy in the United States and in developing countries—Speech at the Crocket Governers' Roundtable for African Central Bankers, University of Oxford, UK, 30 June.

Florini, Ann. 2003. The Coming Democracy: New Rules for Running a New World. *Foreign Affairs* (September/October).

Freixas, Xavier, Luc Laeven and José-Luis Peydró. 2015, 22 March. 'Global Divergences—Challenges Will Emerge from the Unevenness of the Global Recovery'. *Business Standard.*

Freixas, Xavier, Luc Laeven and José-Luis Peydró. 2015. *Systemic Risk, Crises and Macro-Prudential Policy.* Cambridge, MA: MIT Press.

Hale, Galina, Tümer Kapan and Camelia Minoiu. 2016. 'Crisis Transmission in the Global Banking Network'. IMF Working Paper WP/16/91. Washington, DC: International Monetary Fund.

International Monetary Fund. 2012, 14 November. Jordà, Òscar, Moritz Schularick and Alan M. Taylor. 2010, December. 'Financial Crises, Credit Booms, and External Imbalances: 140 Years of Lessons'. NBER Working Paper No. 16567. Cambridge, MA: National Bureau of Economic Research.

Kang, Heedon, Francis Vitek, Rina Bhattacharya, Phakawa Jeasakul, Sònia Muñoz, Naixi Wang and Rasool Zandvakil. 2017. Macro-Prudential Policy Spillovers: A Quantitative Analysis. IMF Working Paper No.17/170, Washington, DC: International Monetary Fund.

Krampf, Arrie and Barbara Fritz. 2015. *Coping with Financial Crises: Explaining Variety in Regional Arrangements.* Available at https://www.tandfonline.com/doi/full/10.1080/13569775.2015.1031986 (accessed on 27 February 2019).

Lagarde, Christen (2015). Spillover from unconventional monetary policy— Lessons for Emerging Markets. Speech delivered at Reserve Bank of India, Mumbai, 17 March.

Laïdi, Zaki. 2018, 18 May. *Is Multilateralism Finished?* Available at https://www.project-syndicate.org/onpoint/is-multilateralism-finished-by-zaki-laidi-2018-05?barrier=accesspaylog (accessed on 26 February 2019).

Lipton, David. 2018, 30 April. 'Mahbubani, Kishore. 2015, 16 March. *Why Britain Joining China-Led Bank Is a Sign of American Decline.* Available at https://www.huffingtonpost.com/kishore-mahbubani/britain-china-bank-america-decline_b_6877942.html (accessed on 26 February 2019).

Mohan, Rakesh and Muneesh Kapur. 2014. Monetary Policy Coordination and the Role of Central banks. IMF Working paper WP/14/70.

Morais, Bernardo, José-Luis Peydró and Claudia Ruiz. 2015, March. 'The International Bank Lending Channel of Monetary Policy Rates and Quantitative Easing Credit Supply, Reach-for-Yield, and Real Effects'. World Bank Policy Research Working Paper No. 7216. Washington, DC: World Bank.

Nakaso, Hiroshi. 2014. Toward Innovative Payment and Settlement Systems. Presented at 9th Asia Banking CEO Round Table, Tokyo, 25 November.

Neely, Christopher J. 2010. Unconventional Monetary Policy Had Large International Effects Federal Reserve Bank of St Louis. Working Paper 2010-018G.

Obstfeld, Maurice and Alan M. Taylor. 2017. 'International Monetary Relations: Taking Finance Seriously'. NBER Working Paper Series, 23440. Cambridge, MA: National Bureau of Economic Research.

Obstfeld, Maurice. 2011, December. The International Monetary System: Living with Asymmetry. NBER Working Paper No. 17641. Cambridge, MA: National Bureau of Economic Research.

Ocampo, Jose Antonio (ed.). 2006. *Regional Financial Cooperation*. Brookings Institution.

Ostry, Jonathan D. and Atish R. Ghosh. 2013, December. *Obstacles to International Policy Coordination, and How to Overcome Them*, IMF Staff Discussion Note, December.

Park, Cyn-Young and Kwanho Shin. 2017. *A Contagion Through Exposure to Foreign Banks During the Global Financial Crisis*. Available at https://www.adb.org/sites/default/files/publication/346346/ewp-516.pdf (accessed on 26 February 2019).

Patel, Urjit. 2017. Better Access to Currency Swap Lines: Urjit Patel Says Emerging Markets Largely Have Been Excluded from the Global Network. Speech at a Seminar Hosted by the Group of 30 International Banking Seminar. Washington, DC. Available at https://www.wsj.com/articles/reserve-bank-of-india-governor-calls-for-better-access-to-swap-lines-1508085779 (accessed on 22 February 2019).

Pierre-Richard Agénor, Enisse Kharroubi, Leonardo Gambacorta, Giovanni Lombardo and Luiz Pereira da Silva. 2017, June. The International Dimensions of Macroprudential Policies. BIS Working Papers No. 643.

Posen, Adam S. 2015. Testimony Submitted to the Senate Committee on Banking, Housing, and Urban Affairs Hearing on 'The Role of the Financial Stability Board in the US Regulatory Framework', Wednesday, 8 July.

Prasad, Eswar S. 2011. Role Reversal in Global Finance. Presented at 2011 Jackson Hole Symposium, organized by the Federal Reserve Bank of Kansas City.

Rajan, Raghuram G. 2014, 31 January. *Rajan Warns of Policy Breakdown as Emerging Markets Fall*. Bloomberg. Available at http://www.bloomberg.com/news/print/2014-01-30/rajan-warns-of-globalpolicy-breakdown-as-emerging-markets-slide.html (accessed on 22 February 2019).

Rajan, Raghuram. 2015, 25 June. *Going Bust for Growth*. Remarks at the AQR Conference at London Business School.

Sheng, Andrew. 2015. *Proposal – The new Global Financial Architecture*, BCBS 2015–16 programme, 23 January.

Sheng, Andrew. 2017, August. *Asia Caught in the Basel Crossfire*. Available at https://www.risk.net/regulation/5323601/qa-asia-caught-in-the-basel-crossfire-says-andrew-sheng (accessed on 26 February 2019).

Singh, Manmohan and Haobin Wang. 2017. 'Central Bank Balance Sheet Policies and Spillovers to Emerging Markets'. IMF Working Paper 17/172. Washington, DC: International Monetary Fund.

Sobrun Jhuvesh and Philip Turner. 2015, August. Bond Markets and Monetary Policy Dilemmas for the Emerging Markets. BIS Working Papers No. 508.

Steinberg, James B. 2003, 8 April. The Future of Global Governance. Briefing organized by Brookings Institutions), Washington, DC.

Subramanian, Arvind. 2018, 16 April. *The Globalization Backlash Paradox.* Available at https://www.project-syndicate.org/commentary/globalization-backlash-financial-integration-risks-by-arvind-subramanian-2018-04?barrier=accesspaylog (accessed on 26 February 2019).

Talbott, Strobe. 2003, 8 April. The Future of Global Governance. Briefing organized by Brookings Institutions, Washington, DC.

Taylor, John B. 2013, December. International Monetary Policy Coordination: Past, Present and Future. BIS Working Paper No. 437. Basel: Bank for International Settlements.

The Liberalization and Management of Capital Flows—An Institutional View. Washington, DC: International Monetary Fund. Available at www.imf.org/external/np/pp/eng/2012/111412.pdf (accessed on 26 February 2019).

Truman, Edwin M. 2011, 16 December. Three Evolutionary Proposals for Reform of the International Monetary System. Remarks at the Bank of Italy's Conference in Memory of Tommaso Padoa Schioppa.

Trust and the Future of Multilateralism' (Introductory Remarks for the Eurofi High Level Seminar). Available at https://www.imf.org/en/News/Articles/2018/04/30/sp042618-trust-and-the-future-of-multilateralism (accessed on 26 February 2019).

Epilogue
Potential Concerns for Central Banks

'Would you tell me, please, which way I ought to go from here?'

'That depends a good deal on where you want to get to.'

'I don't much care where—'

'Then it doesn't matter which way you go.'

—Lewis Carroll, *Alice in Wonderland*

Keeping Up with the Pace of Change

Analysis of the past seldom gives us a 20–20 vision of the future. Financial crises of the past have occurred not because central banks were prepared for them but precisely because they were not. The world is changing now at a faster pace than it ever was. If the world around is changing, can central banks be insulated? The role of technological developments in transforming our world needs little reiteration. It is predicted that 50 per cent of today's jobs will no longer be there in 2030 and business cycles today are a third of what they were 30 years ago (Handy 2015). The fundamental understanding of economic activity is shifting, for example, we understand that the Internet, the borderless, amorphous presence of the Internet, without which modern commerce is not possible is not a part of any computation. In these changed circumstances, how does the role of the central banks change? Of course, we have been talking about mechanization for a while now. In the early days of computerization, popular fiction talked about how computers would take over all our functions from making coffee to driving our cars. Today with Internet of Things (IoT) and Google's driverless cars, these are becoming closer to reality, but apocalypse is not here. In most things that matter, despite massive increases in computing power following Moore's law, things have changed only marginally. So, should we be worried?

In ignoring the obvious, maybe central banks could fall prey to the 'technology mudslide' hypothesis of Christensen and notice rapid change below their feet and possibly be dragged away (Brower and Christensen 1995). While much of the hypothesis is for commercial entities for whom innovation is a way of survival, it is easy to see how a parallel can be drawn to central banks retaining their relevance.

The rapid rise of technology in banking has been one of the success stories in the sector. Starting from advanced ledger posting machines (ALPM) in the 1980s to rapid spread of core banking solutions (CBS) to almost the entire banking sector by 2010, the banking sector leveraged available technology to the maximum. The introduction of the various technology products has had a beneficial impact on both banks and customers. For the customers, the important benefits are anywhere banking, Internet banking, ATM banking and mobile banking. It has also facilitated the use of secured debit and credit cards. For the banks, the major benefits are centralization of customer information, centralized transaction process, centralized accounting process, basic Management Information Systems (MIS) reporting and real-time information availability (Rangarajan 2014).

The evolution of banking technology in this period was on predictable lines, the banks continued with banking and technology companies provided the IT solutions. Recent developments, however, seem to be different. The rapid change in scenario where the two industries have started to merge with each other have given rise to the popularity of new terms such as disruptive innovation (Clayton Christensen). Schumpeter). In addition to the established and licensed players in the financial markets, that is, banks, non-bank financial companies (NBFCs) and non-bank payment service providers authorized under the Payment and Settlements Act, today there are infrastructure companies (mainly telcos), IT service providers and a large number of financial start-ups (collectively known as FinTechs) which have started operating in banking or bank-like areas. There is reason to think that the day is not far off when the banks would be viewed more as technology companies offering banking products and services (Khan 2015).

To be fair, technology disruptions are not limited to the financial sphere alone. Don Acemoglu and Pascal Restrepo (2017) argued that in the race between humans and robots for jobs, the robots are convincingly winning. The advent of artificial intelligence (AI)-powered analysis may also be visualized for the financial sector. In March 2018, members of IMF's executive board gave their blessing to a dramatic overhaul of the way the organization gathers, governs and uses data. The 'Overarching Strategy on Data and Statistics at the Fund in the Digital Age', the first of its kind, lays out how the Fund plans to improve the quality of data, boost the ease with which it can be shared and start making greater use of innovations in big data and AI(International Monetary Fund 2018).

The banks have made extensive investments in technology in setting up data centres and equipping them with state-of-the-art software. The next few years are critical as banks focus on making the most out of their technology investments to increase their return on investment. The strategic use of technology to implement a differentiated business model, a transformed customer experience and an optimized cost structure will separate the leaders from the laggards in the industry (Ernst & Young and Indian Banks' Association 2014). Accordingly, any study on financial stability will not be complete if it does not focus on this very core area of development in the banking industry, that is, the effect of technology in transforming banking services.

We look at five new developments in the domain of banking and finance, which could potentially give central banks sleepless nights. The five areas which we would look at in this segment are (a) the evolution of cyber money or digital currency and the demise of physical currency, (b) the rise of FinTechs and alternate financing, (c) the risks to technology-based banking from cyber threats, (d) whether monetary aggregates are relevant for central bank decision-making and (e) whether central banking itself is under threat and central banking as we know it will survive.

The Past and Future of Money

The move from the 'analogue currency' (paper bank notes and coins) to digital currency is destined. The basis of the new monetary universe is sand rather than paper—a computer chip rather than a central bank note (James A. Dorn). Money has witnessed its transformation from physical money in the form of objects, coins and notes into more abstract means of payment such as bills of exchange, cheques and credit cards. The turn of virtual money has arrived. With innovations in ICT and biometrics, its pace of spread is likely to gather momentum. While it will be backed by distinct consumer preference, it may pose challenges in the realm of central banking in its avowed role as the guardian of the financial marketplace.

Over the centuries, monetary geography has changed repeatedly under the influence of economic, technological and political developments. Today it is changing yet again in ways still not fully appreciated. The traditional wisdom relating to monetary geography rests in the premise that money or currency is the exclusive prerogative of the nation state or sovereign entity, that is, government. Barring a few exceptions, governments have the authority to exercise exclusive control over the issue and circulation of money within their territories. 'At the heart of this understanding, reflecting contemporary norms of political legitimacy is the principle of absolute monetary sovereignty' (Cohen 2001). Money in the form of currency is exclusively circumscribed within the territory or boundaries of a country making it a monopoly of the state. The approach of having a territorial currency is a pragmatic one and its advantages are easy to grasp. Indeed, a single currency in circulation leads to maximization of network externalities within a country. Furthermore, it is easy to gauge the underpinnings for the adoption of the concept of monetary monopoly by governments as it is understood that monetary power emanates from the backing of a sovereign entity. Also, in fiscal terms, a territorial currency acts as a valuable source for revenue, seigniorage to underwrite public expenditures which especially proves beneficial during periods of emergency in terms of economic crisis and threats to national security. Also, it is broadly accepted among the body of experts and specialists in monetary economics that a monetary monopoly of the nation state is a powerful tool which aids in managing and directing the conduct of macroeconomic affairs of the economy. This can be construed as monetary policy in the conventional sense of the term and incidentally this is also of paramount importance in understanding the topic at hand. However, it is also to be understood that from a historical perspective the conception of territorial currencies is rather a very recent phenomenon. Territorial currencies have come into existence only during the last 200 years and in fact prior to 1800, the idea of governments claiming a monopoly over the issue and circulation of money/currency never existed and neither had macroeconomics as a subject come up. The era prior to 1800 witnessed rampant and widespread cross-border circulation of currencies, existence of private monies and monetary policy had not been conceived as yet. Eric Helleiner (1999) has mentioned that the notion of absolute monetary sovereignty or state monopoly of money came about only during the 19th century with the strengthening of nation state authority in Europe and elsewhere in the world. Territorial money witnessed its climax phase during the middle of the 20th century and has been on the wane after the Second World War. Today, central banks around the world seem to favour open direct competition among currencies, and capital controls have become less popular. The central bank's intervention in currencies are, by and large, seen as an outlier strategy rather than a regular function. This reversal is making conventional understandings of monetary geography increasingly obsolete.

E-Money

Simply put, electronic money or e-money is the electronic alternative to cash. The monetary value of e-money can be stored electronically on receipt of funds and is used for making payment transactions. E-money can be held on cards, devices or on a server. Examples include prepaid cards, electronic wallets, such as M-PESA in Kenya, or web-based services, such as PayPal. As such, e-money can serve as an umbrella term for a number of more specific electronic value products and services.

The EU has been defining terms related to e-money since 2000, which is much longer than many other countries or regions. Many new terms were defined in the 2008 directive from European Union. An e-money institution is a legal person that has been granted authorization to issue e-money and hybrid issuers are service providers who issue e-money as an accessory activity to their core activity, that is, businesses, such as mobile phone companies, public transport companies, etc.

Both economic agents and policymakers have the latitude to act and to influence both the process and the outcome of the new category of e-money's gestation. New form of governance is the challenge. Role of financial entities, enabling technology providers and regulatory authorities, needs to be redefined. Computer code can be used to define and control the rules and behaviour of a given system and its components. Privacy and decency rules built into the system architecture constitute an efficient alternative to legislation and administrative laws and decrees. Regulators can make use of this.

Private E-Money: A False Dawn?

Discussions about central bank getting out of the business of issue of currency have remained only academic since at least Hayek. The acceptability of private e-money is remote if it is not under the aegis of the banks and through them of the central bank. Ability to redeem and the recourse to emergency sources of liquidity will remain the dominating factor for such a trend to flourish. It is mandatory for private e-money to be finally convertible into government-backed money. For that, the private e-money provider will have to maintain deposit accounts at banks. There is chance that banks may not like to be a conduit to a competing business or will attach strings of a discouraging nature.

The only plausible way private e-money providers can undertake this is by organizing outfits in the form of limited purpose clearing houses or a credit card system to cater to a homogeneous group of potential users. Visa, for example, is actually a member-owned association, where the membership includes banks. Clearly, since private e-money (to the extent that it exists) will be part of the payment system, the central bank must be concerned about the emergence and uses of private e-money and the dangers that a private e-money system poses. Apart from the difficulty in managing price stability in an arena cumbersome and costly. Currency issuing authorities are exploring ways and means of improving the efficiency of currency operations, and reducing the cost of cash handling is not a new idea, but an idea which is gaining prominence recently. In Singapore, Singapore Electronic Legal Tender (SELT) was being envisioned in 1997 as a sequel to their aim to turn Singapore into a cashless society. This was motivated by the high expenditures to manage the currency issue function, that is, to support local currency in circulation and to meet the cost of handling cash.

Even though the fact is disputed now and then, BitCoins have come to symbolize the entire genre of Virtual Currencies (VCs). Bitcoin is a form of digital currency, created and held electronically. No one controls it. Bitcoins aren't printed like dollars or euros—they're produced by people, and increasingly businesses, running computers all around the world, using software that solves mathematical problems. It's the first example of a growing category of money known as cryptocurrency. In addition to Bitcoins, other examples of popular cryptocurrencies include Litecoin, Ethereum, Zcash, Dash and Ripple. Of these, investors have most interest in the Ethereum in addition to the Bitcoin.

In the 2015 white paper on digital currencies, BIS–CPMI have identified eight demand side reasons for the development of these private and VCs.

Are Bitcoins therefore fast replacing traditional payment methods? After comparing exchange traded volume of Bitcoins to total transaction volume within the Bitcoin network, Glaser et al. (2014) conclude that most users (by volume) treat their Bitcoin investments as speculative assets rather than as means of payment. Bitcoin investments seem to offer diversification benefits according to Brière, Oosterlinck and Szafarz (2013), who study correlations between Bitcoin and other asset classes. Gandal and Halaburda (2014) examine exchange rates of different VCs to observe co-movement and identify opportunities for triangular arbitrage. Preliminary results on daily 'closing' prices indicate little opportunity, although this may reflect that the arbitrageurs operate faster than the frequency of data points.

of profitability-oriented issuance of private money, it may pose a huge systemic risk in the eventuality of a run on the private provider, or the scope of a gridlock it could introduce into the payment system if private e-money payments are suddenly refused. Such problems will surely spill over into the banking system and other financial markets, given the various linkages between private e-money, government money and the bond market. Even if it is ever encouraged, it should be coupled with elaborate safeguards against such lurking systemic risks to be covered on supervisory mechanisms to which other financial firms are subject to. Further, coexistence of private e-money with sovereign e-money may reduce the effectiveness of monetary policy, as the overall money supply will become more responsive to interest rates given the economics of private e-money creation.

Issuing e-money is a distinct business activity (issuing payment instruments) that can be regulated separately (Ireland, Denmark, the UK, Sweden) or a business activity that can occur as a part of banking activity (Austria, Germany, Spain, the Netherlands, Portugal). Only if the representation of e-money is located on a device in the physical possession of the hands of the consumer, like Japan's FeliCa smart card or Netherlands, Chipknip card it is e-money, otherwise it is banking, whereas in the UK and New Zealand, it is not primarily relevant if the customer holds e-money in his/her hands, but whether the system functions as an e-money system. Existence of account-based/server-based e-money systems is formally acknowledged/agreed.

Wave Cash Goodbye?

It may not necessarily be proper to envision the digitization process of physical money as something happening behind the curtains of the central banks nor that there exists any apparent threat to their ability to carry out their avowed functions for the economy. A predominantly digital monetary system may be seen to have positive implications for assessing monetary aggregates and the velocity with which money circulates in the economy, considering the fact that the clearing and settlement systems that underpin a virtual monetary space could offer greater transparency. Current efforts to track physical cash are both

The protection of online privacy and personal information arises in many contexts, and Bitcoin offers a specific set of rules and firms like the 'mixers' that seek to offer privacy, though, as we have seen, the privacy protections can be breached in various ways. Several papers analyse the public Bitcoin transaction history (Ober, Katzenbeisser and Hamacher 2013; Reid and Harrigan 2012; Ron and Shamir 2013), finding a set of heuristics that can help to link Bitcoin accounts with real-world identities as long as some additional information is available for a related transaction. Androulaki et al. (2013) quantify the anonymity in a simulated environment similar to Bitcoin, finding that almost half of the users can be identified by their transaction patterns.

Bohme, Christin, Edelman and Moore (2015) tell that the original vision of Bitcoin offers one set of answers, but as new constituents approach the service, it becomes less clear that early design decisions meet prevailing requirements. It is also uncertain whether a single service can serve all needs. For example, those who seek greater privacy may be prepared to accept greater technical complexity and perhaps higher fees. However, recruiting mainstream consumers and merchants seems to call for a focus on simplicity and lower prices. Bitcoin may be able to accommodate a community of experimentation built on its foundations.

Examining how well existing cryptocurrencies fulfil the role of traditional money, Bank of England's Governor Mark Carney opines that 'the long, charitable answer is that cryptocurrencies act as money, at best, only for some people and to a limited extent, and even then only in parallel with the traditional currencies of the users. The short answer is they are failing' (Carney 2018).

Central Bank and Virtual Currencies

Central banks have identified a few concerns with existing VCs in the future. They include risks-to-price stability, risks-to-financial stability, risks-to-payment system stability and prudential supervision.

Central Bank Issued Digital Currency

The aspect of central banks issuing digital currency has been examined by Tolle (2016). A central bank-backed digital currency issuance could have large consequences for commercial and central banking. The issuance of central bank issued digital currencies (CBDCs) could result in the decoupling of payments from bank deposits and put an end to banks' ability to create money. This makes central bank money the ultimate settlement asset (BIS-CPMI 2003). If households and firms were given access to central bank backed digital currencies through accounts at the central bank, banks' dominant role as providers of payment services would be called into question. In effect, retail payments and securities' transactions would no longer have to be mediated by banks, as the funds would be transferred directly from one party's account to another's. A disintermediated payment system could gradually replace the current centralized system and its associated credit and liquidity risks (BIS 2003). The main benefit to account holders would be access to cheap and fast peer-to-peer (P2P) transactions.

Similarly, Bordo and Levin (2017) examining a central bank digital currency find that it serves as a stable unit of account with a practically costless medium of exchange, and a secure store of value. In particular, the CBDC should be interest-bearing, and the central bank should adjust that interest rate to foster true price stability. Goodfriend (2016) has argued that when a CBDC is launched, it is likely to cause an accelerated obsolescence of paper currency. Indeed, once the central bank's digital currency is widely used as a form of electronic payment, the demand for holding paper currency and coins would quickly diminish, especially if deposits and withdrawals of cash are associated with substantial fees by the central bank and private financial institutions. That would leave only people who want to engage in anonymous transactions alone to use VCs and other forms of payment.

Cybersecurity

Being wholesomely technology-based, modern-day financial sector needs to take cognizance of the possible threat of cyberattack to which it is exposed at all times. Considering the vulnerability of core functions in firms and various financial market infrastructures (FMIs) by way of data corruption, data loss or outright damage to systems, there is an acute need for cyber defence codified in a cyber-resilience framework. 'Part of this is active engagement with threat intelligence to understand likely adversaries, their motivations and ways of 'working'. While discussing on cyber resilience, Rameswurlall Basant Roi, governor of Bank of Mauritius, points out that

> [W]ith digital technology, the cycle of obsolescence has accelerated. Just imagine the average lifespan of a phone app is a mere 30 days. We do not have enough time to master anything in today's world before it is displaced. The risks of enterprises and along with them lending institutions going bust are indeed unprecedentedly heightened. It's very difficult for any lender to appropriately assess risks arising out of digital advancement—and more so for any regulator. (Basant Roi 2017)

Increased digitalization brings efficiency gains for financial institutions and fosters financial inclusion, but it also creates a range of new and partially understood risks that evolve quickly and take multiple forms. One of the key risks is cyberattacks against financial institutions.

These are becoming more common and considerably more sophisticated. Virtually, everybody is exposed to cyber risk in some form. The economic aspects of cybersecurity are gaining increased importance and visibility, and the days when cyber risk was understood as a pure IT problem are now gone. Today, many countries set the development of a cybersecurity industry and standards as key policy objectives.

Recent high-profile cyberattacks on financial institutions have focused attention on the need to strengthen cybersecurity. Among financial institutions, banks have the most public-facing products and services. They are also data repositories and are thus significantly vulnerable to cyberattacks. Consequently, cyber risk is a major concern for most bank supervisors. However, only a handful of jurisdictions have specific regulatory and supervisory initiatives on banks' cyber risk; these include Hong Kong SAR, Singapore, the UK and the USA.

Views differ on the need to specifically regulate cyber risk. One view is that the evolving nature of cyber risk is not amenable to specific regulation and that cyber issues can be handled with existing regulation relating to technology and/or operational risk. The other view is that regulatory structure is needed to deal with the unique nature of cyber risk, and given the growing threats resulting from an increasingly digitized financial sector. Testing banks' vulnerability and resilience to cyber risk through tools like penetration testing is a common requirement, as well as the reporting of cyber events. Another common requirement relates to having clear responsibilities and accountabilities at banks as a key component of their cybersecurity framework. Less common regulatory requirements include cyber threat intelligence sharing (although it is generally encouraged).

The security capabilities of third-party providers are a critical element of any cybersecurity framework, but the specific supervisory approaches depend on the extent to which third parties are covered by the powers of bank supervisors. Supervisory approaches specifically developed to assess the soundness of banks' cybersecurity are still evolving. Cybersecurity continues to be assessed largely as part of the ongoing risk-based supervisory framework, and, more recently, this has been complemented by thematic reviews. There is also a scope to increase the level of cooperation and coordination among supervisors from different jurisdictions and financial sectors.

The Committee on Payments and Market Infrastructures (2016) defines 'cyber risk' as 'the combination of the probability of an event occurring within the realm of an organisation's information assets, computer and communication resources and the consequences of that event for an organisation'. By this definition, any organization (or person) with information assets and who uses online communications technology is exposed to cyber risk. Indeed, the advent of information technology (IT) has made interconnections of people and organizations within and across economies pervasive, and with this comes the heightened risk of cyberattacks.

Threat Landscape

Although computer systems can be compromised through a variety of means, it is necessary to understand malicious actions and the attackers that carry them out. The risk to information and computer assets comes from a broad spectrum of threats with a broad range of capabilities. The impact and therefore the harm to the banks will depend on the opportunities they present to an attacker in terms of the vulnerabilities within the systems, the capabilities of the attackers to exploit them, and ultimately their motivation for attacking. For example, an easily guessed password to an online account takes very little technical capability to exploit. With a little more technical knowledge, attackers can also use tools that are readily available on the Internet. They can also bring resources (people or money) to bear in order to discover new vulnerabilities. These attackers will go on to develop bespoke tools and techniques to exploit them; such vulnerabilities enable them to bypass the basic controls provided by systems. To protect against these bespoke attacks, banks will be required to invest in a more holistic approach to security. The motivation of attackers can vary from demonstrating their technical prowess for personal kudos, financial gain, commercial advantage, political protest, through to economic or diplomatic advantage for their country (National Cyber Security Centre 2016).

Responses to Cyber Threats

At the instance of the G20, the Financial Stability Board (2017b) initiated a stock-take study and submitted its report in October 2017. The report found that there were 35 schemes of reported supervisory practices, which covered a variety of content elements. Some of the elements covered by those schemes, listed in descending order by the number of schemes in which they were included, are review of policies and procedures; review of programmes for monitoring, testing and auditing; review of data security controls; review of governance arrangements; review of risk assessment process; review of past incidents and organization's response and recovery; testing by supervisor and/or submission of test results to supervisor; communications by supervisor; review of sectoral impact of past incidents; information sharing by financial institutions; expertise of supervisory team; supervisory review of third parties; and joint public–private testing.

The National Institute of Standards and Technology (NIST; 2014) put out a framework for improving critical infrastructure cybersecurity in 2014. The framework has been widely replicated with regional variations with various central banks. The framework focuses on using business drivers to guide cybersecurity activities and considering cybersecurity risks as part of the organization's risk management processes.

To conclude, we can look at the final communiqué of the G7 meeting held in Bari in 2017 (Ministry of Finance, Japan 2017), finance ministers and central bank governors stated that they 'recognise that cyber incidents represent a growing threat for our economies and that appropriate economy-wide policy responses are needed. No point of cyberspace can be absolutely secure as long as cyber threats persist in the surrounding environment'.

FinTech Regulation— New Financial Intermediaries

Banking has historically been one of the business sectors most resistant to disruption by technology. Since the first mortgage was issued in England in the 11th century, banks have built robust businesses with many concentric circles, including enabling distribution through branches and developing unique expertise such as credit underwriting based on both data and judgement. They have the special status of being regulated institutions that supply credit, the lifeblood of economic growth, and have sovereign insurance for their liabilities (deposits). Moreover, consumer inertia in financial services is high. Consumers have generally been slow to change financial services providers. Particularly in developed markets, consumers have historically gravitated towards the established and enduring brands in banking and insurance that were seen as bulwarks of stability even in times of turbulence.

A new wave of technological innovations, often called 'FinTech', is accelerating change in the financial sector. FinTech leverages the explosion of big data on individuals and firms, advances in AI, computing power, cryptography and the reach of the Internet. The strong complementarities among these technologies are giving rise to an impressive array of new applications touching on services from payments to financing, asset management, insurance and advice. The possibility now looms that entities driven by FinTech may emerge as competitive alternatives to traditional financial intermediaries, markets and infrastructures. The FinTech landscape continues to evolve. In the first nine months of 2016, global investment in FinTech reached $21 billion, marking a five-fold increase over 2013. Much of this investment is occurring in the USA and in Asia, where large and successful FinTech firms operate in the payments and lending space, and new investment is going into insurance, distributed ledger technology (DLT) and wealth management. While there is currently limited evidence regarding risks to financial stability emanating from FinTech developments, change is occurring rapidly and decisions taken in this early stage may set important precedents. Policymakers should continue to assess the adequacy of their regulatory frameworks in an environment of increasing adoption of FinTech, with the objective of harnessing the benefits while mitigating potential financial stability risks (Financial Stability Board, 27 June 2017).

FinTech innovations have led the banking industry to change the way it transacts its businesses. Basically, technology-based online/ P2P lending, payments and settlement (including distributed ledgers), insurance and trading/investment (including robo-advisors) have enabled customers to access financial services without—or with reduced—bank involvement (BIS Annual report 2016–2017). One rapidly expanding area is online/P2P lending. This has created both challenges and opportunities for banks in the sense that these are potentially disruptive sources of competition in a key business line and opportunity if banks can also go for cost reductions, improved customer experience and enhanced efficiency using these platforms.

Regulation of newer types of entities and processes created to deliver financial services poses a number of challenges to regulators. As these types of entities are still evolving, their regulation or supervision may inhibit desirable financial innovation. However, they may have potential consumer protection and financial stability risk considerations. The issues related to money laundering and financing of terrorism are equally important. In this regard, a concept which has emerged is regulatory sandbox.

Reasons for the Growth of FinTech

There are two common and interrelated drivers of FinTech innovations (Dong et al. 2017). First is shifting customer expectations, and another, demand factors. With an estimated two billion global customers without basic banking accounts and services, financial inclusion is also an important issue in many jurisdictions. FinTech in many cases attempts to fill the gap by providing easy-to-understand and convenient services, which tend to lower costs of adoption and lower barriers to access for customers. While a firm can offer an innovation to the market, it will not be successful unless there is demand for the innovation. A number of unique demand factors are driving the adoption of FinTech innovations. Relatedly, there are demographic factors driving demand. These include the growing financial influence of computer- and mobile-savvy millennials, and economic development and convergence factors that tend to ease the adoption of FinTech in some rapidly growing emerging market and frontier economies. Both of these factors have potential to significantly increase the user base of FinTech. Finally, many FinTech innovations may display positive network externalities that influence demand. The ubiquity of the Internet access and the real-time transacting capability of users of Internet-connected devices have given rise to higher customer expectations with regard to convenience, speed, cost and user-friendliness of financial services, which has in turn become one of the most important factors in consumer purchasing decisions. Second is evolving technology. New technologies include big data, AI, machine learning, cloud computing and biometrics. A number of factors which could make these innovations different from past financial services developments include tight integration of different technologies which enable many to be combined to offer single products.

Changing Financial Regulation and Market Structure

Since the GFC of 2008–2009, policymakers and regulators pursued actions intended to reduce the risk of future crises. Prominent actions include: the review of balance sheet requirements, such as higher capital and lower leverage requirements in the banking sector; addressing the risks posed by shadow banking entities and activities; the evaluation of the robustness of resolution and recovery regimes, including additional stress-testing requirements; the regularization of the OTC derivative markets; and the review and enhanced requirements for FMIs (such as payment systems, securities and derivatives market infrastructures). These combined changes in financial regulation may have resulted in many intended shifts in financial activity and related pricing. As a result of this and potentially other factors, such as a low interest rate environment that increase desire for cost-cutting and more efficient use of capital, traditional financial firms, including banks, have reduced or withdrawn from some activities. Concurrently, the GFC has impacted incumbent financial institutions through several channels. Shocks to wholesale funding and repo markets have compelled banks to build sounder funding structures, based, for instance, on stable deposits. This, combined with greater investor risk aversion, may have also forced deleveraging by some banks. Finally, the sale of foreign activities and the (voluntary or policy-induced) restructuring of global banks may have entailed a retreat from some business lines and market segments.

Potential to Undermine Financial Stability

Alongside these benefits, FinTech innovations can potentially have an adverse systemic impact on the financial system, although there is no evidence of such an impact at present. An adverse systemic impact implies a risk to the provision of critical financial services. A major disturbance in these services, or a disintermediation of regulated entities providing them, can have potentially serious negative consequences for the real economy.

Central Bank Response to Regulating FinTech

Financial regulation is thought of as increasingly complex and intrusive, with all significant financial institutions facing multiple regulatory jurisdictions, and regulators requesting increasing amounts of granular data from firms to ensure compliance. These data will ultimately allow the understanding of systemic risks, also enabling better understanding of the behaviour of actors in the system—consumers, banks, intermediaries—and to get a view of best practices. It will also enable an understanding of how entities in financial systems are exposed directly and indirectly to one another via similar exogenous factors and directly via financial instruments referencing those same institutions. Moreover, the data should allow analysis of the degrees to which institutions react to regulation and how these reactions propagate through financial markets.

The complexity of regulation, however, may come at a price. Financial institutions have stringent and detailed requirements that potentially discourage innovation in new financial products. Thus, complexity and stringency in financial regulation raise an important consideration in the continuing support for new FinTech—the challenge of balancing encouragement with regulation. Likewise, if the current trend in financial regulation continues, non-bank entities will emerge to do things that banks cannot or choose not to do.

Smart regulation is the result of a comprehensive review of existing regulatory systems in the light of rebalanced objectives and emerging technology. From the standpoint of application of technology to regulation (RegTech), it involves digitization of systems which in turn supports application of advanced analytical approaches to yield better regulation. It also involves the development of new financial infrastructure, including digital identification systems and frameworks for payments and other transactions. Beyond RegTech, smart regulation requires analysis of existing systems in order to build entirely new approaches which take into account balanced objectives of economic development, financial stability and consumer protection. Smart regulation requires rethinking regulation in all its forms in order to develop new approaches and new systems in order to support the new form of financial system which is rapidly evolving.

Data-driven Regulation and Compliance

There is the possibility that financial regulation and requests for increasing amounts of data are hindering the capacity of traditional financial institutions to operate and, more importantly, innovate. Regulation and data requirements could benefit from being redesigned, simplified and automated. Harmonizing financial regulation across multiple jurisdictions and creating new automated reporting and analytics standards could improve the financial services industry's efficiency, potentially reducing systemic risk and delivering economic benefits.

Need for Greater Tools for Regulatory Infrastructure

The regulators could benefit from a fully integrated analytics infrastructure able to handle an increasing range of financial, economic, retail, spatial, text and social data. As well as historical and streamed data, this could include public sentiment monitoring and sophisticated analytics techniques such as machine learning. The infrastructure to support both the automated collection of data and analysis presents an opportunity for companies using innovative technologies. Some of the technologies, we can see regulators using in the coming years, include database and streamed processing infrastructure, data mining analytics tools, visualization tools and computational platforms.

Models for Central Bank Regulation

Regulation of technological innovation in finance must seek to balance competing objectives, especially of innovation, financial stability and consumer protection (Arner et al., 2017). This is a particular challenge for regulators 10 years after the GFC as that crisis prompted a massive focus on financial stability and enhanced consumer protection. Against this background, the great promise of FinTech has begun to alter regulatory attitudes and approaches to regulation of technological innovation.

In regulating FinTechs central banks can possibly adopt an informal approach discussed below or a well-defined structure for such regulation.

Informal steer: The central bank will provide guidance and advice to the financial institutions or FinTech companies on the modifications that can be made to their proposed business model or solution to fit prevailing laws and regulations. This approach is suitable where the modified business model or solution does not significantly diminish the value proposition of the original proposal.

Regulatory sandbox: Financial institutions or FinTech companies may be allowed to test their innovation in a controlled environment, subject to fulfilling the eligibility criteria specified by the bank. The bank may provide guidance and support in the form of regulatory flexibilities during the testing period where appropriate. Set of rules that allows innovators to test their products/business models in live environment without following some or all legal requirements is subject to predefined restrictions.

Working with Big Data

The financial industry is one of the most data-oriented businesses. For example, the operations taking place on the back of our daily payments and settlements via credit cards, debit cards or deposit accounts can be regarded as data processing. Banks provide financial intermediation services through making complicated decisions and assessments on borrowers, interest rates and assets for investments by collecting and analysing various types of data. Insurance companies design insurance policies and set their fees at appropriate levels by also collecting and analysing data. These insurance schemes allow society to efficiently redistribute risks among various entities and enhance its resiliency against future uncertainty. As such, the financial and insurance industries have indeed promoted economic growth in modern and postmodern society.

Data utilization and the development of the economy have been strongly connected with each other. Today it is not an exaggeration to say that every economic activity is inseparable from collecting and processing data. For instance, demand forecasts, and production planning and inventory management by firms consist of large amounts of data processing (Nakaso 2017).

The widely popular focus paper from *Central Banking* magazine conducted a survey of central banks in August 2018. The study found that there was still some way to go. Despite big data's growing importance, 62 per cent of respondents to the survey said that data governance is not clearly defined within their organizations. The IMF's efforts to upgrade its own data governance and take advantage of big data may provide some useful ideas in this area. The fund is also working with many of its members to upgrade their data capabilities. Several regulatory technology specialists were asked how big data can change the way financial systems are overseen, reshaping and hopefully streamlining the work of supervisors and private sector firms. The forum participants from the Bank of England and Sveriges Riksbank expressed the hope that big data techniques could soon be embedded in the day-to-day operations of central banks.

Relevance of Monetary Aggregates

The external financial environment is an important backdrop in discussions about real activity and financial stability. The sensitivity to external financial conditions is most apparent for economies with open capital markets, but it also applies to economies that have open trade sectors, but not necessarily a fully open and liberalized financial system, as is the case in many emerging economies. Traditionally, bank liability aggregates have been identified with monetary aggregates and have been associated with macroeconomic outcomes through the transactions role of money and the quantity theory of money (Friedman 1956).

How does domestic liquidity depend on global factors? What are the differences across narrow and broad money aggregates? How do countries differ with respect to their sensitivity to global factors? How does global liquidity vary with global economic activity? How does global liquidity affect growth, trade and other measures of economic activity across countries? How useful is global liquidity as a measure of global economic activity? To the extent that measures of bank liabilities also convey information on the size of the banking sector balance sheet, bank liabilities may also serve a useful role as a measure of financial vulnerability. As a measurement exercise, the balance sheet of the banking sector can be measured either in terms of the assets or in terms of the liabilities. Nevertheless, there are factors that may favour measures of the liabilities side when attempting to gauge overall financial conditions.

Bank liabilities tend to be more transparent and homogenous than bank assets. Liabilities tend to be short term—mainly in the form of deposits—and hence the book values of liabilities are close to their marked-to-market values. In addition, liabilities can more easily be organized by category into core and non-core liabilities that have contrasting cyclical five properties. Non-core liabilities exhibit greater procyclicality so that the ratio of non-core to core liabilities conveys useful information as an EWI of financial vulnerability (Hahm, Shin and Shin 2013).

For financial stability purposes, the distinction between core and non-core liabilities of the banking sector is not always captured by the ease of settlement of transactions. Overnight repurchase agreements (repos) between financial institutions are claims that are short term and highly liquid. However, the Financial Crisis of 2008 demonstrated through the near failure of Bear Stearns and the bankruptcy of Lehman Brothers that repos can be highly destabilizing when the collateral requirements on the repos rise through higher imposition of higher margins charged by creditors, setting off a spiral of distress in the financial system as a whole (Adrian and Shin 2010). An important dimension that is not addressed in the traditional hierarchy of monetary aggregates is who holds the claims. The same claim can have very different financial stability implications if it is held by different entities. The cash deposits of a leveraged hedge fund at its prime broker are similar to demand deposits of household savers in the banking system in terms of how liquid the claim is. However, they have very different systemic implications. At the other end of the spectrum in terms of liquidity, a covered bond issued by a bank is an extremely illiquid and long-term claim that is not money-like. However, a covered bond held by long-term investors such as a pension fund is similar to retail deposits in that the funding provided to the banking sector is more 'sticky'—that is, stable—than a mortgage-backed security or a collateralized debt obligation (CDO) held by a securities firm.

Few years ago, the Fed stopped publishing M3, a broad measure of money supply. With this, the whole literature got a false impression to discuss issues relating to M3 without the explicit mention of the word money. This is unfortunate. Just because there is a loss of control of something at a specific point of time does not mean that it should not be monitored any more. The weight that each announcement receives depends much less on the quality of the data than on market commentators and participants beliefs about the weight that the Federal Reserve puts on the announcement. The chairman and other officials give hints and clues about what they watch. These weights shift frequently, and they are not uniform across the members of the FOMC. If there is a hypothesis relating these noisy indicators to long-term objectives, it has never been stated or evaluated. The FOMC watches many different indicators that guide changes in the federal funds rate. If by chance these give signals that do not differ very much from the signals given by money growth, a rule-based strategy relying on money growth would have produced similar results in recent years. Both theory and evidence suggest that the interest rate, at times, has been a misleading indicator when money growth gave a correct signal (Francis et al. 2001).

Even in a regime, where an interest rate is the central bank's policy instrument, attention would need to be paid to any monetary aggregate. This interaction is fundamental to monetary policy. The fact that other variables have bigger and more visible roles in the piece should never cause us to lose sight of this. It might happen, and indeed in the case of contemporary Japan, which has much in common with the USA in 1930–1933, it has happened that the economy still requires monetary stimulus in a situation in which the nominal interest rates under the authorities' direct control have reached zero. Methods such as open market purchases of long-term securities or equities or unsterilized intervention in the FX market are generally tried in such an event. The purpose of such measures would be to increase the quantity of money, in hopes of generating an excess supply thereof, and hence extra expenditure.

To avoid erosion of the monetary base, central banks could be tempted to resort to alternative measures. They could issue digital money themselves in the same way as they provide paper currency right now. They could apply high reserve requirements on digital money balances. Or as an extreme measure, they could limit the proliferation of digital money products. The drawback of these measures is that they would reduce the private sector's incentives to invest in the development of digital money products. Central banks may also like to predominantly encourage digital monetary system for assessing monetary aggregates and the velocity with which money circulates in the economy in a much better way, as a virtual monetary space could offer greater transparency in the clearing and settlement systems. Current efforts to track physical cash are both cumbersome and costly. Switching over to digital money systems which depend on universal accessibility to network clearing and settlement promises the scope for real-time verification of almost all transactions by volume and kind without necessarily abandoning confidentiality. Digital money could in fact facilitate tracking of monetary aggregates, and thereby improve the effectiveness of policy adjustments aimed at meeting macroeconomic objectives.

History shows that the usefulness of monetary aggregate targeting (versus interest rate targeting) depends non-linearly on the inflation/deflation zone the economy is in. For high inflation and deep deflation, monetary targeting appears to be a relatively effective guide for policy. When inflation is low, the usefulness of the monetary aggregates may be exceeded by short-term interest rates, especially if velocity is sufficiently unpredictable. In this way, monetary aggregates open a window on the possibility of macroprudential policy that takes cues from the money stock. Central banks that continue to give some attention to monetary aggregates have emphasized the financial stability properties of monetary aggregates for this reason. For instance, the ECB has shifted in recent years to interpreting their monetary pillar increasingly as a financial stability pillar (Hyun Song Shin and Kwanho Shin 2011). Emphasizing the monetary aggregates appears, from a historical perspective, to be rather important during periods of high inflation and deep inflation. During periods of low inflation, velocity over short periods of time has shown a tendency to be more volatile and unpredictable than variation in the natural interest rate, thereby tilting the balance of arguments towards the reliance on interest rate instruments in the conduct of monetary policy. However, in the zone of low inflation/price stability and low to moderate deflation, the influence of the zero lower bound for short-term nominal interest rates makes reliance on short-term interest rates more problematic; hence, the balance tilts towards the monetary aggregates playing a dominant role as the policy instrument and guide of choice.

A recent study on Gulf economies showed that even the fast pace of financial developments in the three GCC countries has not caused undue shifts in the equilibrium money demand relationships, irrespective of whether money stock is measured narrowly or broadly. All three GCC economies continue to exhibit well-behaving and reliable long-run money demand equations, although simple adjustments in some of these equations are necessary to account for the process of financial innovations. Thus, it appears that targeting either M1 or M2 still represents a proper long-run policy strategy in the three GCC countries. Therefore, it can be supposed that monetary targeting is still alive and well in the GCC region, and central banks in these countries should maintain a close watch on money supply growth as a guide of their monetary policy actions.

Traditional monetary aggregates were defined around their legal form, and how liquid they are in transactions. For the reasons outlined earlier, these traditional aggregates will be less effective as a macro-prudential monitoring tool without further adaptation. The particular adaptations that may be usefully summarized in the following three points are as follows: (a) for countries with open capital markets, international capital flows into the banking sector will be key indicators of financial vulnerability. During a boom, when bank assets are growing rapidly, the required funding outstrips the growth of the domestic deposit base, and is often met by capital flows from the international banks, and is reflected in the growth of short-term foreign currency-denominated liabilities of the domestic banking system. Therefore, short-term foreign currency-denominated bank liabilities can be seen as the volatile non-core liabilities of the banking sector; (b) for countries with relatively closed financial systems, where domestic banks do not have ready access to funding provided by the global banking system, a better approach would be to adapt existing conventional monetary aggregates to address financial stability concerns. The key distinction is not how liquid the claims are, but rather who holds the claims. The distinction between household retail deposits and corporate deposits in the banking sector will play a particular important role in this regard; (c) more generally, invoking the accounting principle that defines core versus non-core liabilities of the banking sector may prove useful in guiding classification exercises of financial systems and economies more broadly. Core liabilities are the claims of the household sector on the intermediary sector. Non-core liabilities are the claims of the intermediary sector on itself (Chung et al. 2014).

Conclusion

Academia and central banks are focusing on the risks arising out of these developments in financial technologies. The common quest among all these researchers is the need for greater transparency in the new developments and the need for greater collaboration among the various regulators.

> The challenge for policymakers is to ensure that FinTech develops in a way that maximises the opportunities and minimises the risks for society. After all, the history of financial innovation is littered with examples that led to early booms, growing unintended consequences, and eventual busts. (Carney 2017)

Central banks are understandably more conservative—they are public institutions charged with maintaining the integrity of monetary policy and the banking system, neither of which allows for risk that is difficult to quantify. However, as the interest in block chain grew into a roar, central banks have no choice but to take note. More commercial banks are experimenting with these technologies to gain competitive advantage and central banks cannot remain mute spectators.

The situation brings to mind the words of one of the leaders of the French Revolution who said: 'There go my people. I must find out where they are going so I can lead them.'

If central banks fall 'behind the curve' and lose touch with the banking sector, they cease to be prescriptive. And in a fiat system, that could be deadly. Also, as Bitcoin enthusiasm infiltrates the hallowed halls of economics, the potential threat of currencies that don't need central banks begins to look more real, as does the intriguing opportunity to rethink the way money works.

Obviously, systemic change is slow and fraught with institutional barriers. Yet central banks are, on the whole, stepping up their innovation game. Most of the work is being done in silos, although some collaborations with the public sector and with other central banks are underway.

What central banks need to do, however, is form their own consortium. While each bears a unique combination of structural, economic and geographic considerations, their goals are similar. Much of the central bank work currently being done is repeated behind gilded doors elsewhere. Collaborating on research and testing, with each other and even including private components of the ecosystem, will advance the work much faster. A central bank block chain consortium would need to do more than test applications. It would need to exchange ideas on the future of the institution itself. It is better to engage in a cooperative fashion, applying a range of experiences and seeking shared solutions. The resulting lessons learned, not to mention successful innovations, will help the central banks jointly bring their respective economies into a new phase of development.

It would also mark a turning point in history.

References

2017, 12–13 May. Communiqué, G7 Finance Ministers and Central Banks' Governors Meeting. Bari, Italy.

Acemoglu, Daron and Pascal Restepo. 2017, March. 'Robots and Jobs, Evidence from US Labor Markets'. NBER Working Paper No. 23285. Cambridge, MA: National Bureau of Economic Research.

Adrian, T. and H. S. Shin. 2006, 14 July. 'U.K. Monetary Regimes and Macroeconomic Stylized Facts' (NBER Monetary Economics Conference). Boston.

Adrian, T. and H. S. Shin. 2010. 'Liquidity and Leverage'. *Journal of Financial Intermediation* vol. 19, issue 3, 418–437.

Androulaki E., G.O. Karame, M. Roeschlin, T. Scherer and S. Capkun. 2013. Evaluating User Privacy in Bitcoin. In *Financial Cryptography and Data Security*, edited by R. Sadeghi. FC 2013. Lecture Notes in Computer Science (Vol. 7859). Berlin, Heidelberg: Springer.

Arner, Douglas W. and Zetzsche, Dirk Andreas and Buckley, Ross P. and Barberis, Janos Nathan, Fintech and Regtech: Enabling Innovation While Preserving Financial Stability (January 1, 2017). (2017) 18(3) Georgetown Journal of International Affairs 47; UNSW Law Research Paper No. 18-41; University of Hong Kong Faculty of Law Research Paper No. 2018/036.

Available at https://files.stlouisfed.org/files/htdocs/publications/review/01/05/23-32Meltzer.qxd.pdf (accessed on 28 February 2019).

Bank for International Settlements (BIS), 87th Annual Report 2016–17

Bank for International Settlements: The role of central bank money in payment systems: August 2003: ISBN 92-9197-654-7

Böhme, Rainer, Nicolas Christin, Benjamin G. Edelman and Tyler Moore. 2014. Bitcoin: Economics, Technology, and Governance (July 15, 2014). *Journal of Economic Perspectives* 29 (2, Spring 2015). Harvard Business School NOM Unit Working Paper No. 15-015.

Bordo, Michael and Andrew Levin. 2017, August. 'Central Bank Digital Currency and the Future of Monetary Policy'. NBER Working Paper No. 23711. Cambridge, MA: National Bureau of Economic Research.

Bower, Joseph L. and Clayton M. Christensen. 1995, January–February. 'Disruptive Technologies—Catching the Wave'. *Harvard Business Review*, 43–55.

Briere, Marie, Kim Oosterlinck and Ariane Szafarz. 2015. *Virtual Currency, Tangible Return: Portfolio Diversification with Bitcoin. Journal of Asset Management* 16(6): 365–373. doi:10.1057/jam.2015.5

Carney, Mark, Governer of Bank of England. The Promise of FinTech – Something New Under the Sun? (Speech). Deutsche Bundesbank G20 conference on "Digitising finance, financial inclusion and financial literacy", Wiesbaden, 25 January 2017.

Carney, Mark. 2018, March. 'Future of Money' (Inaugural Scottish Economics Conference Edinburgh University).

Central Banking. 2018. *Big Data in Central Banks Focus Report*. Central Banking.

Chung, Kyuil, Jong-Eun Lee, Elena Loukoianova, Hail Park and Hyun Song Shin. 2014, January. 'Global Liquidity Through the Lens of Monetary Aggregates'. IMF Working Paper No.14/9 Washington, DC: International Monetary Fund.

Cohen, Benjamin J. 2001. 'Electronic Money: New Day or False Dawn?' *Review of International Political Economy* 8(2): 197–225.

Committee on Payments and Market Infrastructures. 2016, June. *Guidance on Cyber Resilience for Financial Market Infrastructure.* Available at https://www. bis.org/cpmi/publ/d146.pdf (accessed on 28 February 2019).

Dorn, James, ed. *Future of Money in Information Age.* Washington, DC: Cato Institute, 1997, ISBN: 1-882577-52-3.

Ernst & Young and Indian Banks' Association. 2014, January. *Banking on Technology: Perspectives on the Indian Banking Industry.* Available at https:// www.ey.com/Publication/vwLUAssets/EY-Banking-on-Technology/$FILE/ EY-Banking-on-Technology.pdf (accessed on 27 February 2019).

Financial Stability Board. 2017a, 27 June. *Financial Stability Implications from FinTech.* Available at http://www.fsb.org/wp-content/uploads/R270617.pdf (accessed on 28 February 2019).

Financial Stability Board. 2017b, October. *Summary Report on Financial Sector Cybersecurity Regulations, Guidance and Supervisory Practices.* Available at http://www.fsb.org/wp-content/uploads/P131017-1.pdf (accessed on 28 February 2019).

Forum). Tokyo.

Friedman, Milton. 1956. 'The Quantity Theory of Money—A Restatement'. In *Studies in the Quantity Theory of Money*, edited by Milton Friedman. Chicago, IL: Chicago University Press pp 3–21.

Fung, Ben, Scott Hendry and Warren E. Weber. 2017. 'Canadian Bank Notes and Dominion Notes: Lessons for Digital Currencies'. Staff Working Paper 2017-5. Ottawa: Bank of Canada.

Gandal, Neil and Hanna Halaburda. 2014, September. Competition in the Cryptocurrency Market. CEPR Discussion Paper No. DP10157.

Glaser, F., K. Zimmermann, M. Haferkorn, M. Weber, and M. Siering. 2014. *Bitcoin Asset or Currency? Revealing Users' Hidden Intentions.* Tel Aviv: ECIS.

Goodfriend, Marvin. 2016. 'The Case for Unencumbering Interest Rate Policy at the Zero Lower Bound'. *Economic Review.* Speech at Economic Symposium at Jackson Hole Kansas City, MO: Federal Reserve Bank of Kansas City.

Hahm, Joon-Ho, Hyun Song Shin and Kwanho Shin. 2013. 'Non-Core Bank Liabilities and Financial Vulnerability'. *Journal of Money, Credit and Banking* 45 (S1): 3–36.

Handy, Charles. 2015. *The Second Curve.* Publisher: Random House UK (March 1, 2015)

He, Dong, Ross Leckow, et al. 2017, June. Fintech and Financial Services—Initial Considerations. IMF Staff Discussion Note SDN/17/05. Washington, DC: International Monetary Fund.

Helleiner, E. 1999. 'Nation-States and Money: The Past, Present and Future of National Currencies'. *RIPE Series in Global Political Economy.* Routledge.

Helleiner, E. 2010. A Bretton Woods Moment? The 2007–2008 Crisis and the Future of Global Finance. *International Affairs* 86 (3): 619–636.

Hyun Song Shin and Kwanho Shin. 2011, February. Procyclicality and Monetary Aggregates. NBER Working Paper No. w16836. Cambridge, MA: National Bureau of Economic Research.

International Monetary Fund. 2018, March. *Overarching Strategy on Data and Statistics at the Fund in the Digital Age.* Washington, DC: International Monetary Fund.

Khan, H. R. 2015, 3 August. 'IT Governance and IT Strategy' (RBI Speeches).

Nakaso, Hiroshi. 2017, 1 November. 'Big Data—Its Impacts on Economies, Finance and Central Banking' (Fourth FinTech National Cyber Security Centre. 2016, January. *Common Cyber Attacks—Reducing the Impact.* Available at https://www.ncsc.gov.uk/content/files/protected_files/guidance_files/common_cyber_attacks_ncsc.pdf (accessed on 28 February 2019).

National Institute of Standards and Technology. 2014, 12 February. *Framework for Improving Critical Infrastructure Cybersecurity*, Version 1.0. Available at https://www.nist.gov/sites/default/files/documents/cyberframework/cybersecurity-framework-021214.pdf (accessed on 28 February 2019).

Ober, M., S. Katzenbeisser, K. Hamacher. 2013. Structure and Anonymity of the Bitcoin Transaction Graph. *Future Internet* 5: 237–250.

Rameswurlall Basant Roi: Regulatory challenges in a fast-evolving banking system (21 July 2017) Governor of the Bank of Mauritius, at the conference hosted by the Mauritius Commercial Bank Limited for Le Club des Dirigeants de Banques et Etablissements de Credit d'Afrique (Club of Leaders of Banks and Credit Institutions in Africa), Balaclava.

Rangarajan, C. 2014, 18 December. 'Information System Security—Some Concerns' (10th International Conference IDRBT). Hyderabad. Available at http://www.idrbt.ac.in/assets/News/2014/ICISS_RR_Speech_18122014.pdf (accessed on 27 February 2019).

Tolle, M. 2016, 25 July. 'Central Bank Digital Currency: The End of Monetary Policy As We Know It?' *Bank Underground.* Available at https://bankunderground.co.uk/2016/07/25/central-bank-digital-currency-the-end-of-monetary-policy-as-we-know-it/ (accessed on 27 February 2019).

Index

About the Author

Rabi N. Mishra is an Economist by education and a Senior Financial Sector Risk Specialist by profession.

A central banker for more than three decades, he is currently the Executive Director of the Reserve Bank of India (RBI), India's central bank. Previously, he was the Principal Chief General Manager of Risk Monitoring Department of RBI, Mumbai, and head of the Reserve Bank Staff College, training institute of senior central banking professionals of the RBI, Chennai. Dr Mishra was the head of Financial Stability Unit at the RBI and served as head of the RBI in two states: Jharkhand and Uttar Pradesh. He has professional expertise in bank regulation/supervision, financial stability, macrofinancial surveillance and risk mitigating mechanics in banking and central banks.

He completed his MA in Monetary/Financial Economics from Jawaharlal Nehru University (MA) and was a Research scholar at Delhi School of Economics. Dr Mishra earned his PhD from University of Mumbai. He has done post doctorate from the Economics Department of Harvard University. He has written many research papers of topical policy relevance and has spoken in reputed international platforms on areas of monetary economics, banking, financial stability and risk management.

He is an awardee of the Golden Jubilee Scholarship of the RBI and the Diamond Jubilee Fellowship of Indian Institute of Banking and Finance (IIBF). He has authored a book on asset securitization. Dr Mishra can be contacted at rabi60@gmail.com.